THE CAMBRIDGE CO
JOHN F. KEN

C000104248

John F. Kennedy remains central to bo[...] imagination. Featuring essays by leading l[...] scholars, *The Cambridge Companion to Joh*[...] as Kennedy's youth in Boston and his time at Harvard, his foreign policy and his role in reshaping the U.S. welfare state, his relationship to the civil rights and conservative movements, and the ongoing reverberations of his life and death in literature and film. Going beyond historical or biographical studies, these chapters explore the creation and afterlife of an icon, a figure who still embodies – and sparks debate about – what it means to be American.

Andrew Hoberek is Associate Professor of English at the University of Missouri. He is also the author of *The Twilight of the Middle Class: Post–World War II American Fiction and White-Collar Work* and *Considering Watchmen: Poetics, Property, Politics*. Hoberek has published in *Modern Fiction Studies*, *Modern Language Quarterly*, *Studies in American Fiction*, *American Literary History*, and *Contemporary Literature*. He currently serves as the book review editor for *Twentieth-Century Literature*.

AMERICAN STUDIES

This series of Companions to key figures in American history and culture is aimed at students of American studies, history, and literature. Each volume features newly commissioned essays by experts in the field, with a chronology and guide to further reading.

VOLUMES PUBLISHED

THE CAMBRIDGE
COMPANION TO
JOHN F. KENNEDY

EDITED BY

ANDREW HOBEREK
University of Missouri

CAMBRIDGE
UNIVERSITY PRESS

CAMBRIDGE
UNIVERSITY PRESS

32 Avenue of the Americas, New York, NY 10013-2473, USA

Cambridge University Press is part of the University of Cambridge.

It furthers the University's mission by disseminating knowledge in the pursuit of education, learning, and research at the highest international levels of excellence.

www.cambridge.org
Information on this title: www.cambridge.org/9781107663169

First published 2015

Printed in Great Britain by Clays Ltd, St Ives plc

A catalog record for this publication is available from the British Library.

Library of Congress Cataloging in Publication Data
The Cambridge companion to John F. Kennedy / Andrew Hoberek, University of Missouri.
pages cm. – (Cambridge companions to American studies)
Includes bibliographical references and index.
ISBN 978-1-107-04810-2 (hardback) – ISBN 978-1-107-66316-9 (pbk.)
1. Kennedy, John F. (John Fitzgerald), 1917–1963.   2. United States – Politics and government – 1961–1963.   3. Presidents – United States – Biography.
I. Hoberek, Andrew, 1967– editor.
E842.C36   2015
973.922092–dc23   2014043437

ISBN 978-1-107-04810-2 Hardback
ISBN 978-1-107-66316-9 Paperback

CONTENTS

NOTES ON CONTRIBUTORS

SALLY BACHNER is Associate Professor of English at Wesleyan University. She is the author of *The Prestige of Violence: American Fiction, 1962–2002* (University of Georgia Press, 2011) and is currently working on a book about the fictional representation of female embodiment since the age of "women's liberation."

EOIN CANNON is the head speechwriter for Boston's mayor, Martin J. Walsh. He spent six years as a lecturer in history and literature at Harvard University, where his teaching and scholarship focused on urban cultural history. His book, *The Saloon and the Mission* (University of Massachusetts Press, 2013), examines the roots of addiction recovery narrative and its role in American religion, social reform, and literature.

J. D. CONNOR is an assistant professor of the history of art and film history at Yale. His essay on the cinema of the Kennedy era, "Clean Cuts," is forthcoming in *Film and the American Presidency* (ed. Jeff Menne and Christian Long, Routledge, 2015). His book on neoclassical Hollywood, *The Studios after the Studios*, is forthcoming from Stanford. He is currently working on two other books, *Hollywood Math and Aftermath*, about the movie industry during the Great Recession, and *Archives of the Ambient*, a history of tape recording.

DOUGLAS FIELD is a lecturer in twentieth-century American literature at the University of Manchester. His work on American literature and culture has appeared in such publications as *English Literary History, African American Review, Callaloo*, and the *Times Literary Supplement*. He is the author of several books on James Baldwin, the latest of which is *All Those Strangers: The Lives and Art of James Baldwin* (Oxford University Press, 2015). He is the cofounding editor of the *James Baldwin Review*.

PAUL GILES is Challis Chair of English at the University of Sydney, Australia. He is the author of, among other works, *American Catholic Arts and Fictions: Culture, Ideology, Aesthetics* (Cambridge University Press, 1992) and

Transnationalism in Practice: Essays on American Studies, Literature and Religion (Edinburgh University Press, 2010). His most recent book is *Antipodean America: Australasia and the Constitution of U.S. Literature* (Oxford University Press, 2013).

LOREN GLASS is Professor of English at the University of Iowa. He writes on twentieth- and twenty-first-century American literature and culture. His first and second books are *Authors Inc.: Literary Celebrity in the Modern United States* (NYU Press, 2004) and *Counterculture Colophon: Grove Press, the Evergreen Review, and the Incorporation of the Avant-Garde* (Stanford University Press's Post*45 Series, 2013). In addition, he has published work on Presidents Kennedy, Nixon, Clinton, and Bush in *American Imago* and *Postmodern Culture*.

JOHN HELLMANN is Professor of English at the Ohio State University. He is the author of *The Kennedy Obsession: The American Myth of JFK* (Columbia University Press, 1997).

ANDREW HOBEREK is Associate Professor of English at the University of Missouri, where he teaches courses in twentieth- and twenty-first-century literature. The author of *The Twilight of the Middle Class: Post–World War II American Fiction and White-Collar Work* (Princeton University Press, 2005) and *Considering* Watchmen: *Poetics, Property, Politics* (Rutgers University Press, 2014), he is at work on a book-length study of post-1960 U.S. fiction's relationship to the nation's foreign policy.

PETER KNIGHT teaches American studies at the University of Manchester, UK. He is the author of *Conspiracy Culture: From the Kennedy Assassination to* The X-Files (Routledge, 2001) and *The Kennedy Assassination* (University Press of Mississippi, 2007).

LEE KONSTANTINOU is an assistant professor in the English department at the University of Maryland, College Park. He coedited *The Legacy of David Foster Wallace* (with Samuel Cohen; University of Iowa Press, 2012) and wrote the novel *Pop Apocalypse* (Harper Perennial, 2009). He is completing a literary history of countercultural irony called *Cool Characters: Irony, Counterculture, and American Fiction from Hip to Occupy*.

ROBERT MASON is Reader in History at the University of Edinburgh. He is the author of *Richard Nixon and the Quest for a New Majority* (University of North Carolina Press, 2004) and *The Republican Party and American Politics from Hoover to Reagan* (Cambridge University Press, 2012). With Iwan Morgan, he is coeditor of *Seeking a New Majority: The Republican Party and American Politics, 1960–1980* (Vanderbilt University Press, 2013).

SEAN MCCANN is Professor of English at Wesleyan University. He is the author of *Gumshoe America: Hard-Boiled Crime Fiction and the Rise and Fall of New Deal Liberalism* (Duke University Press, 2000) and *A Pinnacle of Feeling: American Literature and Presidential Government* (Princeton University Press, 2008).

AMANDA KAY MCVETY is Associate Professor of History at Miami University. She is the author of *Enlightened Aid: U.S. Development as Foreign Policy in Ethiopia* (Oxford University Press, 2012) and is currently writing a history of rinderpest eradication.

ANDREW PRESTON teaches history at Cambridge University, where he is a Fellow of Clare College and editor of *The Historical Journal*. He is the author or editor of several books, including *The War Council: McGeorge Bundy, the NSC, and Vietnam* (Harvard University Press, 2006) and *Sword of the Spirit, Shield of Faith: Religion in American War and Diplomacy* (Knopf, 2012).

VAUGHN RASBERRY is Assistant Professor of English and an affiliate in the Center for Comparative Studies in Race and Ethnicity at Stanford University. He has published articles in *American Literary History*, *Novel: A Forum on Fiction*, and the collection *James Baldwin: America and Beyond* (ed. Cora Kaplan and Bill Schwarz, University of Michigan Press, 2011) and is currently completing his first book, *Race and the Totalitarian Century: World War and Geopolitics in African American Culture*.

MICHAEL TRASK is the Guy Davenport Professor in English at the University of Kentucky. He is the author of *Cruising Modernism: Class and Sexuality in American Literature and Social Thought* (Cornell University Press, 2003) and *Camp Sites: Sex, Politics, and Academic Style in Postwar America* (Stanford University Press, 2013). He is completing a book on alternative forms of consciousness and ethics in the wake of the 1960s.

MARY ANN WATSON is a Distinguished Professor of Electronic Media and Film Studies at Eastern Michigan University, where her primary research area is media history. She is the author of *The Expanding Vista: American Television in the Kennedy Years* (Duke University Press, 1994) and *Defining Visions: Television and the American Experience in the 20th Century* (Blackwell Press, 2008). Watson has written extensively on postwar broadcasting, including the chapter "Television and the Presidency" in *The Columbia History of American Television*. She has been a consultant to several museum exhibitions and appeared in the documentary *JFK: Breaking the News*, which aired on all PBS stations.

ACKNOWLEDGMENTS

I'm grateful to Lenny Cassuto for suggesting me for this project, and to Ray Ryan for shepherding it from idea to completed product; Ray knew when to send me back to the drawing board in order to make this a better book. This volume would not be anything, of course, without its excellent contributors, whose work speaks for itself. Thanks, finally, to Ramsay Wise, who helped me assemble the Chronology and who put together the Guide to Further Reading and Viewing.

1917   John Fitzgerald Kennedy is born to Joseph Kennedy Sr. and Rose Fitzgerald Kennedy on May 29 in Brookline, Massachusetts. He will become the first U.S. president to be born in the twentieth century.

1920   Kennedy contracts scarlet fever and is hospitalized for more than two months at Boston City Hospital.

1927   The Kennedy family moves to Riverdale, the Bronx, New York, where John attends the Riverdale Country School.

1931–35   Kennedy attends the Choate Boarding School in Connecticut.

1934   Kennedy is hospitalized at Yale–New Haven Hospital, then admitted to the Mayo Clinic, where he is diagnosed with colitis.

1935   Kennedy travels to England with his parents and sister, but he cuts the trip short because of health problems. He enrolls at Princeton but drops out shortly thereafter after becoming ill.

1936   Kennedy transfers to Harvard.

1937   President Franklin Roosevelt names Joseph Kennedy Sr. ambassador to Great Britain.

1938   Kennedy accompanies his father and his elder brother Joseph Kennedy Jr. to England.

1940   Kennedy graduates from Harvard University. He publishes his senior thesis as the book *Why England Slept*. Kennedy attends business school at Stanford.

1941   After health problems prevent him from joining the army, Kennedy enlists in the U.S. Navy.

1942–43   Kennedy serves on a series of torpedo boats in the South Pacific, eventually rising to command several. A Japanese destroyer rams his boat PT-109 in August 1943. Despite suffering injuries that aggravate his chronic lower back condition, Kennedy performs bravely in leading his crew to their eventual rescue. He is awarded the Navy and Marine Corps Medal and the Purple Heart.

1944   Joseph Kennedy Jr. dies on August 12 when his plane explodes during a mission in Europe. The *New Yorker* publishes John Hersey's article "Survival," based on JFK's experience with PT-109, in May; *Reader's Digest* prints a condensed version (at the urging of Joseph Kennedy Sr.) in August.

1945   Kennedy is discharged from the navy and becomes a correspondent for the Hearst newspapers.

1946   Kennedy runs for Congress and is elected representative for Massachusetts' Eleventh Congressional District.

1947   While on a trip to England, Kennedy is diagnosed with Addison's disease, although the public will not learn of his condition until after his election to the presidency.

1948   Kennedy's sister Kathleen dies in a plane crash. JFK is elected to a second term in the House.

1950   Kennedy is elected to a third term in the House.

1952   With his younger brother Robert as his campaign manager, Kennedy defeats the incumbent, Henry Cabot Lodge Jr., to become a Massachusetts senator.

1953   Kennedy marries Jacqueline Bouvier.

1954   Kennedy undergoes spinal surgery to address his chronic back pain.

1956   Kennedy publishes *Profiles in Courage*, written with his speechwriter, Theodore Sorensen. At the Democratic National Convention, Tennessee Senator Estes Kefauver defeats JFK to become Adlai Stevenson's running mate in the upcoming presidential election.

1957   Kennedy is awarded the Pulitzer Prize for *Profiles in Courage*. His daughter, Caroline, is born. He obtains positions on the Senate Foreign Relations Committee and on Harvard University's Board of Overseers. In July, he delivers a speech in Congress supporting Algeria in its struggle for independence from France.

1958   Kennedy is elected to a second term in the Senate.

1960   Kennedy publishes *The Strategy of Peace*. He wins the Democratic nomination for president and chooses Lyndon Johnson as his running mate. During the campaign he participates in the first-ever televised presidential debates with Richard Nixon. He telephones Coretta Scott King when her husband, Martin Luther King Jr., is jailed in Birmingham, Alabama, and Robert Kennedy works behind the scenes to obtain King's release. Kennedy defeats Nixon in a very close election. Shortly thereafter Kennedy's son, John Jr., is born. Kennedy delivers his inaugural address featuring the famous line, "My fellow Americans, ask not what your country can do for you, ask what you can do for your country."

1961   Shortly after being sworn in as president, Kennedy appoints his brother Robert as attorney general and establishes the Peace Corps by executive order. In April, his administration backs an attempted invasion of Cuba that ends in disaster at the Bay of Pigs when the invaders are captured by Fidel Castro's forces. In May, Kennedy sends Lyndon Johnson to meet with President Ngô Đình Diệm of South Vietnam about combating the spread of communism in Southeast Asia. Kennedy and Nikita Khrushchev hold a summit in Vienna in June. Kennedy and Khrushchev clash over the status of divided Berlin, ending when Khrushchev authorizes the construction of the Berlin Wall. The United States and Latin American nations join in the Alliance for Progress, a program designed to forestall future communist revolutions such as Cuba's through development aid.

1962   CBS and NBC simulcast *A Tour of the White House with Mrs. John F. Kennedy* on Valentine's Day, garnering a then-record audience of 56 million viewers. In April, US Steel executives renege on an understanding, reached during negotiations with the United Steelworkers, to not raise prices in exchange for concessions from the union; Kennedy pursues a variety of strategies (including canceling government contracts and having the FBI harass steel executives) to win a reversal. Responding to cosmonaut Yuri Gagarin's 1961 feat of becoming the first man in space, Kennedy proposes a U.S. mission to the moon. In September, Robert Kennedy sends 400 federal marshals to the University of Mississippi to facilitate the enrollment of the black student James Meredith; JFK commits 3,000 U.S. troops when violence erupts. The Cuban Missile Crisis of October 14–28 begins when the United States obtains photos of Soviet nuclear missiles on the island. The tense stalemate between the United States and the Soviet Union ends when the Soviets agree to remove the missiles and the United States promises never to invade Cuba (and secretly agrees to dismantle some of its own missiles in Europe). Kennedy proposes cuts in income and corporate taxes to spur economic growth.

1963   In June, Kennedy gives a speech calling on Congress to enact civil rights legislation. He also during that month establishes the Advisory Council on the Arts, the forerunner of the National Endowment for the Arts, and travels to West Berlin (where he delivers his famous "Ich bin ein Berliner" speech), Ireland, and the Vatican. In August, Kennedy's son Patrick is born and dies after just two days from a lung condition. At the end of August, Martin Luther King Jr., other civil rights leaders, and 100,000 others participate in the March on Washington for Jobs and Freedom. In September the United States, the USSR, and the United Kingdom sign a treaty banning nuclear testing aboveground, in the air, and underwater. A November coup undertaken with U.S. approval deposes Ngô Đình Diệm. Kennedy is assassinated in Dallas, Texas, on November 22, 1963. Lyndon Johnson is sworn in as president on Air Force One, as it sits on Love Field.

ANDREW HOBEREK

Introduction: JFK and/as America

John F. Kennedy was born on May 29, 1917, at the Kennedy family home at
83 Beals Street in the Boston suburb of Brookline, forty-three years before
becoming the first president of the United States born in the twentieth century. Lyndon Johnson (b. 1908), Richard Nixon (b. 1913), Gerald Ford (b.
1913), and Ronald Reagan (b. 1911) would all subsequently assume the
office having been born earlier in the century than Kennedy, in part because
Kennedy was – and remains – the second-youngest person to become president, and the youngest ever elected to the office. (Theodore Roosevelt was
forty-two when he became president in 1901 following the assassination of
William McKinley.) Youth was a major element of Kennedy's persona, both
his own (by presidential standards) and that of the country whose leadership he rose to in large part by constructing a narrative of renewed vigor
and purpose.

Kennedy's brief life and career can be sketched in a relatively short space.
He was sickly as a child, and during long stints in hospitals and in bed at
the family home he developed a taste for reading that set him apart from
his businessman-turned-public-servant father, Joseph, and his more active
older brother, Joseph Jr. He attended the preparatory school Choate and
then, after a brief stint at Princeton that was interrupted by illness, matricu-
lated at Harvard. During his undergraduate years he traveled to the United
Kingdom with his ambassador father and wrote the senior thesis that he
would publish as his first book, *Why England Slept* (1940), an account of
British appeasement policy that his ambitious father promoted (despite its
indirect criticism of Joseph Kennedy's own role in keeping England out of
the war). Following college Kennedy made tentative stabs at a variety of
careers, and then, after being declared unfit for army service because of his
chronic health problems, joined (with the help of family connections) the
navy. In the navy he first served on and then commanded a series of torpedo boats in the South Pacific. In August 1943, the boat he was then com-
manding, PT-109, was sunk by a Japanese destroyer, and Kennedy made

by all accounts creditable efforts to keep his surviving crew together and obtain their rescue. The following year his brother Joseph died in a naval airplane explosion over the English Channel. JFK, after further active duty and a stint in a military hospital, received a number of commendations and became the subject of a magazine article by his friend and onetime romantic rival John Hersey that (again with help from his father) would help launch his political career. He worked briefly as a correspondent for the Hearst newspapers prior to running for, and winning election to, the U.S. House of Representatives as a congressman from Massachusetts. He served three terms in the House, from 1946 to 1952, and then entered the Senate. In 1953, he married the heiress Jacqueline Bouvier, and in 1956 he published his second book (cowritten with his aide Theodore Sorensen), the Pulitzer Prize–winning *Profiles in Courage*. Early in his second Senate term he decided to make a run for the presidency, and after defeating the other candidates for the Democratic nomination and selecting Texas senator Lyndon B. Johnson as his running mate, went on to defeat Vice President Richard Nixon for the office.

Kennedy's presidency got off to a promising start with his early establishment of the Peace Corps, but subsequently received a setback from the disastrous Bay of Pigs affair, when a group of CIA-backed Cuban rebels landed on the island and – after failing to receive air support from the United States – were killed or captured by Fidel Castro's forces. Shortly after the Bay of Pigs, Kennedy had a disappointing series of meetings with Soviet premier Nikita Khrushchev in Vienna, and he clashed with Khrushchev over the divided city of Berlin, a dispute that threatened to escalate until Khrushchev ended it by building the Berlin Wall (thereby tacitly acknowledging the city's political division). In 1962, Kennedy sent troops to Mississippi to deal with violence that erupted when the African American activist James Meredith attempted to enroll at the state university. The year 1962 also brought what many consider the signal event of Kennedy's presidency, the Cuban Missile Crisis of October. During this fraught episode, the United States and the USSR hovered on the brink of nuclear war over the question of Soviet missiles in Cuba. Tensions deescalated when Soviet ships turned back from a U.S. blockade of the island, and the crisis ended when the Soviets agreed to remove the missiles in exchange for a U.S. pledge not to invade the island. (The administration also secretly agreed to remove some of the United States' own missiles from Turkey.) Toward the end of 1962, Kennedy gave an important speech announcing that the United States would seek to put a man on the moon, and in early 1963 he followed it up with another calling on Congress to enact civil rights legislation – two goals that would only be achieved under future administrations. Throughout his presidency Kennedy had dealt with the legacy of the Eisenhower administration's Cold War maneuvers in Southeast Asia, reaching a tentative (and ultimately very fragile) peace agreement in Laos and increasing the number of U.S. advisers in Vietnam. One of the last actions of his administration was to approve the coup that deposed Ngô Đình Diệm, the unpopular president of South Vietnam, an action that was meant to defuse tension but probably only escalated the progress of what would become the Vietnam War. On November 22, 1963, Kennedy was assassinated in Dallas, Texas, in circumstances that remain controversial. Shortly afterward, Johnson was sworn in as his successor.

Kennedy's actions as president were significant but do not alone explain his undeniable impact on both the United States in the early 1960s and all of American culture since then. JFK began his political career in 1946, and his terms in the House and Senate took place against the backdrop of a United States navigating a conspicuous national malaise. Postwar prosperity brought fears that the American middle class had been transformed from self-reliant strivers into soulless corporate drones and bored housewives; on the political front, the stifling of dissent during the anticommunist movement of the early 1950s gave way to the placid consensus symbolized by Dwight D. Eisenhower, an even-tempered but not particularly dynamic leader who, until Ronald Reagan beat him out in 1980, was the oldest man elected to the U.S. presidency.

Kennedy's rise, in this climate, was swift and unexpected but retrospectively unsurprising. Presidential elections were (most today would probably say mercifully) much shorter affairs then, and as W. J. Rorabaugh points out, "At the beginning of 1960, half of Americans had never heard of the senator from Massachusetts."[1] Criticized, as Barack Obama would be nearly a half century later, for his lack of experience, Kennedy turned his relative greenness into a strength at every turn, casting himself as the candidate of new ideas and approaches. When, on the eve of the 1960 Democratic Convention, the last Democratic president, Harry S. Truman, suggested that Kennedy might not be ready for the office, and should stand aside to let a more experienced candidate challenge the Republican nominee, Kennedy called a televised press conference to declare, "I do not believe the American people are willing to impose any such test, for this is still a young country, founded by young men 184 years ago today and it is still young in heart, youthful in spirit, and blessed with new young leaders in both parties, in both houses of Congress, and in governor's chairs throughout the country."[2] Truman also suggested that Kennedy's wealthy father, Joseph P. Kennedy, had played a role in his son's success in the Democratic primaries, and indeed this was not an insignificant factor: Kennedy was able, for instance, to massively outspend his opponents in the primaries. But his reply to Truman demonstrates a perhaps more important consideration, Kennedy's ability to flatter the nation's voters with a renewed sense of historical agency while positioning himself as the right candidate to take the reins of the reawakening nation. In his acceptance speech at the convention, itself held in the perfectly symbolic western outpost of Los Angeles, Kennedy evoked the phrase that would become the unofficial name of his administration, telling the assembled delegates and the national media audience that "we stand today on the edge of a New Frontier."[3] The author Norman Mailer, covering the convention for *Esquire*, recognized what was happening and went so far as to cast Kennedy as an existential superhero: arguing that Kennedy's experiences following the sinking of PT-109 had brought him face-to-face with the "lonely terrain of experience, of loss and gain, of nearness to death, which leaves [the hero] isolated from the mass of others." Mailer declared that Kennedy, in defiance of the "mass man" and his spokesmen who "would brick-in the modern life with hygiene upon sanity, and middle-brow homily over platitude," represented the principle "that violence was locked with creativity, and adventure was the secret of love."[4]

In constructing this outsize, mythological version of Kennedy, Mailer was only catching up with Kennedy himself. This helps to explain why Kennedy is such an appropriate subject for this Cambridge Companions volume, which seeks to assess the thirty-fifth president's relationship to U.S. art and culture as well as politics. There are, of course, numerous biographical and historical accounts of Kennedy and his presidency, beginning with the memoirs written by his advisers like Sorensen and Arthur Schlesinger Jr. after his assassination and continuing to the present day.[5] But as U.S. literary and cultural critics turn their attention to the post-1945 period, it becomes increasingly clear that Kennedy played a crucial role in the nation's culture, as well. Kennedy features as a prominent player, for instance, in both Sean McCann's 2008 study of the relationship between twentieth-century literature and the presidency and Michael Szalay's 2012 account of the transformation of the Democratic Party around the literary and cinematic exploration of cross-cultural hipness.[6] If the early 1960s was, as Rorabaugh notes, "important because it was an in-between time" of tremendous change between the 1950s and the late 1960s (which generally overshadow it in cultural histories of the twentieth-century United States), then "Kennedy put such a stamp upon [the period] that one can scarcely talk about those years without discussing him."[7] This volume devotes itself to addressing the numerous ways that Kennedy was shaped by – and, even more importantly, shaped – the early 1960s and what came after.

Introduction

As John Hellmann argues in his brilliant 1997 study, *The Kennedy Obsession* – a book that belongs on the shelves of anyone interested in post-1945 U.S. culture – Kennedy's great talent was as a shaper of narrative, a role in which he drew on existing cultural narratives to create what was arguably the most influential story of the twentieth-century United States. As a sickly child, Hellmann writes, the young John Kennedy escaped into a heroic world of British history and literature that later provided the ideal of public service he offered to an American public anxious for a renewed sense of historical agency. Kennedy promoted this ideal not only as the author or coauthor of *Why England Slept* and *Profiles in Courage*, but even more importantly as the protagonist of his own heroic narrative, constructed in conjunction with figures like Hersey, his campaign staff, and his presidential advisers. As the nation's chief executive, Kennedy used his narrative skills to shape not only his image but his actions and policies: as Hellmann notes, Kennedy "typically responded to specific problems by shaping them into crisis situations," in the process allowing himself to shape difficult situations "according to his preferred plot and position himself as hero figure." Kennedy's propensity for constructing himself as larger-than-life laid the groundwork, unsurprisingly, for his elevation to mythic status by others – beginning with his wife, Jacqueline – after his assassination.[8]

Kennedy's talent for narrative no doubt underlies his reputation, to which all the contributors to this volume to some degree or another speak, for elevating "style" over "substance." With the possible exception of George Washington, the most celebrated American presidents are the ones who combined practical politics with deep cultural engagements, although the nature of these engagements has, of course, changed over time. Kennedy was not an Enlightenment polymath like Thomas Jefferson, or a brooding moral philosopher like Abraham Lincoln. Rather he was – in ways anticipated by Teddy and Franklin Roosevelt and equaled only by Ronald Reagan – a master of the twentieth-century mass media and their capacity to mirror back to the nation an idealized image of itself. The historian Alan Brinkley, in a piece for the special *Atlantic* issue commemorating the fiftieth anniversary of Kennedy's assassination, links the ongoing mismatch between public appraisals of his presidency and historians' more measured evaluations to Kennedy's status as "a powerful symbol of a lost moment, of a soaring idealism and hopefulness that subsequent generations still try to recover."[9] While Ronald Reagan was able to capture the Kennedy magic despite his many political differences from his predecessor,[10] Barack Obama largely disappointed hopes that he might become a new JFK. This may have as much to do with the new media environment of the early twenty-first century as with Obama himself – a media environment good at mobilizing the so-called netroots for a national election but bad at enabling anyone, even the president, to impose a single coherent narrative onto a host of competing political passions.

This fragmented political environment is apparent in many of the pieces published on the anniversary of the assassination, which deployed Kennedy's legacy in the service of a range of often conflicting political positions. A number of pieces associated Kennedy, unsurprisingly, with the idealism of the 1960s left. Bill Clinton, for instance, contributed a brief piece to the *Atlantic* heralding Kennedy's role as a proponent of civil rights for African Americans,[11] while JFK's nephew Robert F. Kennedy Jr. wrote an article for *Rolling Stone* portraying his uncle as a pacifist who worked with Khrushchev to draw down the Cold War and sought to withdraw Americans from Vietnam.[12] In both cases, there is some evidence for these claims. Kennedy "grew on the job," as Clinton puts it,[13] with reference to civil rights, eventually coming to champion them out of a mixture of opportunism, pragmatism, and principle. And while Kennedy campaigned and governed as a foreign policy hawk, there is general consensus that his experience with the Cuban Missile Crisis convinced him of the necessity to seek peace and led to the 1963 Limited Test Ban Treaty ending U.S., Soviet, and British aboveground nuclear testing.[14] Perhaps less expected than Clinton and RFK Jr.'s encomia, however, were the raft of essays by conservatives claiming Kennedy for the right.[15] While these writers' arguments tended to cherry-pick evidence such as Kennedy's support for a reduction in income tax rates – a move that was in fact recommended by Kennedy's Keynesian advisers and encountered conservative opposition[16] – and are fairly easily rebutted by historians,[17] they demonstrate the way that public memory of the Kennedy administration has floated free of the actual facts and come to express nostalgia for political agency per se. Even a piece like John Dickerson's *Slate* essay on Kennedy's failure to pass Medicare during his presidency (Johnson would eventually sign it into law in 1965[18]) describes this failure in order to provide an implicitly hopeful forerunner of Obama's struggles to uphold the Affordable Care Act: Kennedy fought with Congress and the AMA and was unable to pass Medicare, a fact that "led to the kind of appraisals that President Obama now faces as his approval ratings and personal ratings hit new lows"; eventually, however, Medicare became law and Kennedy achieved his "vigorous reputation and vibrant legacy."[19]

Dickerson's account of Kennedy's efforts to pass Medicare through a combination of public outreach and backroom political maneuvering does, however, get us closer to a fuller picture of his presidency than the frequent tendency to associate him with achievements – such as the 1964 Civil Rights

Act and the 1969 moon landing – that only came about after his assassination. Irving Bernstein's history, *Promises Kept*, similarly focuses on the difficult behind-the-scenes negotiations responsible for not only Kennedy's real presidential accomplishments, such as the Peace Corps, but also the initiatives that were not successful in his lifetime and others that are no longer widely remembered, such as his tax cut. Bernstein's account at times feels more like a description of the Obama presidency than of (our image of) Kennedy's, with members of Congress obstructing legislation or forcing byzantine compromises, and interest groups such as white southerners and (in the case of Medicare) the American Medical Association doing all they could to block the president's initiatives.

What distinguishes the Kennedy era from our own, however, is that Kennedy's opponents, who included Southerners in his own party as well as Republicans, did not believe that their role was to block the operations of government per se. This also marks the fundamental difference between Kennedy's conception of governance and that of Reagan. Insofar as Kennedy posed his new model of American civic agency in opposition to the organization man whose suburban lifestyle and meaningless corporate employment dominated U.S. cultural criticism and literature during the 1950s,[20] Kennedy certainly anticipates the extreme critique of institutions that links both the 1960s Left and the post-Reagan Right. But Kennedy and his acolytes, unlike these later figures, remained committed to the possibilities of working within institutions. Rorabaugh concurs that Kennedy's experiences in the navy played a major role in shaping his subsequent persona, but argues that they provided something more complicated than a romantic model of frontier or existential individualism:

> Kennedy's success was generational. It represented the coming to power of the junior officers of World War II. The war had both enabled and forced that generation to break down stereotypes and class barriers, and its officers had devised ways to promote collective achievement. Exceptionally meritocratic, they measured each other mainly in terms of competence, and yet they (unlike the baby boomers) also respected hierarchy as necessary to provide leadership for large, powerful organizations . . . Their style was aggressive. Attacking the political structure directly, they seized command from below.[21]

Kennedy and his acolytes, unlike the counterculture generation whose rebellion against institutions may well have made them susceptible to Reagan's antigovernment message, remained committed to the possibilities of working within organizations. They distinguished themselves from organization men not on the grounds of total rejection but on the basis of their desire to infuse bureaucracies with forms of charismatic agency capable of reanimating American individualism.

Two fictional naval officers of the 1960s, *Star Trek*'s Captain James T. Kirk and the naval commander/MI-6 spy James Bond (the latter a Kennedy favorite), are classic figures of the Kennedy era in that, as action heroes who work within the chains of command of large organizations, they balance obedience to orders with manly individual initiative. Kennedy's fascination with a certain version of the military capable of harmonizing obedience and initiative is evident in his support of the Green Berets and counterinsurgency more generally,[22] but a similar model of organizational agency also shapes such nonmilitary initiatives as the Peace Corps. As Elizabeth Cobbs Hoffman notes in her history of the group, "The notion of the existential act was implicit in the Peace Corps, from the Kennedy and [Sargent] Shriver emphasis on the act of going ('you will be the personification of a special group of young Americans,' Kennedy told volunteers) to the organizational unwillingness to plan the volunteer assignment in detail lest such plans hamper the moment of epiphany in which individual meaning was realized."[23] What Thomas McCormick identifies as the Green Berets' and Peace Corps' shared status as "youthful elites" is a version of youth culture that we do not generally think of when we think of the 1960s,[24] and indeed the failures of U.S. policy in Vietnam dealt it a significant blow. But in fact it remained a significant component of post-JFK U.S. culture for quite some time.

More than just the thirty-fifth president, then, Kennedy embodied and rewrote American identity at a crucial transitional period. At a time when Americans feared that their traditional individualism was threatened by the increasing size and scale of organizations, Kennedy made it possible to reimagine forms of individualism within such enormous organizations as the government and the military. But although Kennedy shared the Democratic Party's post–New Deal faith in government as an agent of positive change, his investment in style as a medium of individual agency, while directed at the time toward getting things done within institutions, laid the groundwork for more thoroughgoing forms of anti-institutionalism that would later dominate the U.S. Left and, more recently, the U.S. Right.

Of course, while this transformation lies at the center of Kennedy's life and legacy, his place in U.S. culture goes well beyond it. The fact that he came onto the scene at such a charged moment in U.S. culture, and played such an instrumental role in shaping what would come, helps to explain why the keynote in accounts of JFK is so often ambiguity. Born into a politically and socially disadvantaged ethnic and religious group, JFK came to exemplify both the mainstreaming of that group and the transformation of white ethnicity into a source of affirmative pride. A committed Cold Warrior who defended his fellow Irish Catholic Joe McCarthy in the 1950s, he became a hero of the peace-loving counterculture even as its members condemned the war he helped start. A beneficiary on numerous levels of white, male privilege, he helped expand American identity, and in some cases actual American institutions, to include those – young people, people of color – who had previously been excluded. The authors of the chapters that follow take up Kennedy's richly transformative role in accounts that address themes central to his background, his administration, and his legacy. The chapters collectively make a case for Kennedy's interest to literary critics, historians, and general readers alike by highlighting his role as beneficiary, proponent, or both of enormous changes in U.S. society and culture. Many of these changes are associated with the decade of the 1960s that Kennedy early came to embody, and the volume emphasizes Kennedy's relationship to this decade: both the later countercultural period and the early 1960s that have currently became a renewed source of fascination thanks to the popularity of *Mad Men*. But the contributors also relate Kennedy to numerous other changes, not tied to a specific decade, in twentieth-century U.S. culture: changes in racial demographics, changes in Americans' relationship to their government, changes in the public status of intellectuals. Finally, the authors emphasize Kennedy's engagement with, and role in shaping, global events – the Cold War, of course, but also the global anticolonial revolutions that Kennedy, more than any president, helped make central to U.S. foreign policy.

Eoin Cannon's chapter "Kennedy, Boston, and Harvard," begins the volume by placing Kennedy in the context of the early twentieth-century revolution in American ethnicity and class, and the particular forms it took in Boston and Cambridge. Beginning with the local, national, and international influence wielded by Kennedy's maternal grandfather, John Francis Fitzgerald, and his father, Joseph Kennedy, and continuing through Kennedy's own coming-of-age and ascent to the presidency, Cannon tells a dual tale: of the transformation of Irish Americans from powerful but socially excluded others to members of the mainstream white middle class, and of Harvard's reconfiguration, under the presidency of James Bryant Conant, to a new vision of elite American status. Kennedy, who rose to the presidency through a calculated combination of effacing and emphasizing his ethnic background, both benefited from and helped cement these massive changes.

Paul Giles's "Kennedy and the Catholic Church" looks more closely at a major aspect of Kennedy's ethnic background, his Roman Catholic religion. Giles addresses Kennedy's struggle with the perception among many voters that he would do the bidding of the Vatican rather than promote U.S. interests, and the way in which his presidency, by allaying these fears, helped transform Catholicism into a mainstream American religion. Giles also discusses Kennedy's relationship to the Catholic intellectual tradition, illuminating the subtle but important differences between Kennedy's thought and that of the mainstream Protestant tradition central to U.S. thinkers before and since, including Martin Luther King.

In "The Kennedy-Nixon Debates: The Launch of Television's Transformation of U.S. Politics and Popular Culture," Mary Ann Watson takes up the chestnut that Kennedy won the 1960 election because he was a better television debater than Richard Nixon, using it as an entrée point to discuss the transformations in U.S. politics and culture wrought by the new mass medium. Noting that "sometimes folktales carry truth and conventional wisdom is right on the money," Watson addresses Kennedy's commitment not only to style more generally but to a specific kind of style more suited to television broadcasts than to traditional political venues. She also discusses Kennedy's role in shaping the medium through his influential appointment of Newton Minow as chairman of the FCC, and the way in which entertainment as well as news programming responded to the Kennedy presidency.

While these opening chapters consider major transformations in U.S. culture that paved the way for Kennedy's ascent to the presidency, Sean McCann's "'Investing in Persons': The Political Culture of Kennedy Liberalism" turns to the transformations in U.S. government and politics that JFK himself wrought. Using Philip Roth's 1959 novella, *Goodbye Columbus*, specifically its protagonist's desire to escape the constraints of bureaucracy and find a fulfilling career, as a backdrop, McCann discusses how Kennedy reimagined government service as a form of "guerrilla" activity within institutions. In doing so, McCann points out, Kennedy promoted a cult of disinterested national service over – and thereby broke the power of – interest groups like unions. The "desire to rise above the routines of ordinary life and to escape the bargaining of conventional politics," McCann notes, left many of the accomplishments of the New Deal era "without grounding in powerful interest groups, and thus vulnerable to retrenchment when they met conservative opposition." By the late 1960s, he argues – turning to Roth's more cynical take on public service in his 1969 *Portnoy's Complaint* – "the Kennedy era's vision of elite cultural leadership" was fading away, to be replaced by a more sweeping distrust of institutions in general.

The expansion of civil rights for African Americans is often considered one of the major achievements of the Kennedy administration, and in "JFK and the Civil Rights Movement" Douglas Field offers a richly detailed analysis of Kennedy's ambiguous legacy on this front. Focusing this chapter through James Baldwin's understandably suspicious attitude toward the administration, and describing subsequent historiographic debates over whether JFK was a prime mover or a bystander on the civil rights front, Field paints a divided picture. On the one hand, Kennedy did react to rather than drive the struggle for rights; on the other, this showed him to be a leader who could change in response to the political struggles of American citizens. On the one hand, Kennedy's contribution was often more rhetorical than substantive; on the other, style was not in this arena strictly distinguishable from substance, and Kennedy's use of the bully pulpit was in some ways as consequential as his deployments of state power.

JFK is frequently understood to have been more interested in foreign than in domestic policy. While this minimizes his significant accomplishments at home, it is true that he played a major part in reshaping the United States' international role, a subject taken up in three chapters of this volume. Andrew Preston's "Kennedy, the Cold War, and the National Security State" describes Kennedy's prosecution of the Cold War as fraught with ambiguity in ways similar to his approach to civil rights. Kennedy sought to manage "the irony of the Cold War," Preston writes, "by embracing both firmness and flexibility, strength and peace, arms and disarmament." His antibureaucratic rhetoric, however, was belied by his expansion of the national security apparatus, just as his rhetoric of peace was put to the test by his aggressive brinksmanship in places like Berlin and Cuba. For these reasons Kennedy's pursuit of peace following the Cuban Missile Crisis, which was cut short by his assassination, remains a tantalizing historical "What if?"

Amanda Kay McVety's "JFK and Modernization Theory" describes how Kennedy put into practice the theories of economic modernization developed by academics at schools like Harvard and MIT, using these theories to position the United States as a better guide for developing nations than its Soviet rival. Kennedy posed modernization theory, crucially, not only as a strategy for winning the Cold War but also as a way for Americans to renew their sense of historical agency abroad. If, on the one hand, Kennedy presented the United States as a model for the developing world, he also drew on these nations' own rich revolutionary tradition in crafting his image at home and abroad – a topic Vaughn Rasberry takes up in his chapter, "JFK and the Global Anticolonial Movement." As a senator in the 1950s, Kennedy, as Rasberry notes, "distinguished himself as a critic of European colonialism and Eisenhower's foreign policy in the Third World," most explicitly through his support of Algeria in its struggle against the French. As president, Kennedy sought to project such support as a way of distinguishing the United States from the colonial powers of Europe, as well as to thread a difficult path between proponents of civil rights (who could admire his support for the new nations of Africa and other parts of the world) and southern Democrats (who could see him as an effective Cold Warrior). In the end, however, the administration's support for Third World revolution ran aground on pragmatic political considerations, just as modernization theory miscarried in practice.

Kennedy's familiarity with modernization theory exemplifies, none-theless, his very real engagement with the intellectual currents of his day. In "Kennedy and Postwar Intellectual Culture," John Hellmann offers a detailed account of this engagement. Hellmann focuses this account on a close reading of *Profiles in Courage* and its relationship to the thought of the New York Intellectuals, but he also discusses Kennedy's patronage of artists and intellectuals during his campaign and presidency.

Kennedy was, of course, able to take on the patina of intellectual life, which had been a problem for Adlai Stevenson and other U.S. politicians, because he also cultivated a reputation as a man of great style and cha-risma. In "The Camelot Presidency: Kennedy and Postwar Style," Lee Konstantinou discusses the components of this style – Kennedy's refusal to wear hats, his friendship with the Rat Pack and other entertainers, his cultivation of television – and relates them to the myth of Camelot put into place by JFK and, even more, by his wife, Jacqueline, following his assassination. Addressing the question of style head-on, Konstantinou acknowledges that Kennedy paved the way for the contemporary evacua-tion of substance from American politics but also notes the ways in which Kennedy and those around him made style "an instrumental part of effec-tive governing."

Kennedy's profound grasp of the performative aspects of politics, no less than his abrupt and shocking death, all but insured that his legacy would continue to shape American culture in the decades to come. In a pair of chapters, Peter Knight and J. D. Connor trace the profound reverberations of the assassination through the literature and other arts of the past half century. Knight's "The Kennedy Assassination and Postmodern Paranoia" describes the way shifting reactions to the assassination culminated in a distrust of authority and a paranoid suspicion of byzantine plots that – in the work of novelists like Richard Condon and Don DeLillo, and filmmak-ers ranging from Michelangelo Antonioni to Brian DePalma – becomes all but indistinguishable from the period of cultural production we refer to as "postmodern." In "An Eternal Flame: The Kennedy Assassination, National Grief, and National Nostalgia," meanwhile, Connor addresses responses to the assassination in fine art, experimental film, and commemorative archi-tecture, arguing that artists in all these fields try and to some degree fail to reproduce "the Kennedy era's willed unification of national mission and personal style through the immediate application of reflection." For Connor, postmodernism is a result of this failure, a loss of the first two elements in fragmentation and depersonalization and an overemphasis on the last in the form of interminable individual interpretation.

Sally Bachner's "Free the World and Your Ass Will Follow: JFK and Revolutionary Freedom in 1960s Youth Culture," meanwhile, traces the resonance of JFK's personal style on the countercultural movements of the second half of the decade – at least their most well-known, white, male proponents. Beginning with Students for a Democratic Society in the early 1960s and continuing with Timothy Leary and other countercultural figures of the late 1960s, Bachner charts the profound influence of Kennedy's rhetoric and charismatic image even on those who understood themselves to be at odds with his and subsequent administrations. Kennedy's example, Bachner suggests, also paved the way for the transformation of the counterculture into a series of lifestyle choices in the 1970s.

In "The Kennedy Family Romance," Michael Trask describes the role that JFK and the rest of the Kennedy family played in remaking the American conception of the family in the second half of the twentieth century. Beginning with Kennedy's cultivation of the postwar middle-class nuclear family ideal as a counterweight to his aristocratic and in many other ways untraditional American family, Trask segues into JFK's makeover into a figure of Olympian sexual appetites and Jackie's transformation into a queer icon in the decades following the assassination. Ultimately, Trask argues, the possibilities for personal development that JFK found in his family have become – thanks in no small part to the Kennedy myth – a widespread and potentially confining idea of the family as a site of enforced self-expression.

Many of the chapters in this volume explore aspects of Kennedy's well-documented role as an icon of postwar liberalism. Robert Mason's "Kennedy and the Conservatives," by contrast, considers JFK's less-well-known, but quite long-standing, attraction for conservative politicians. While opposition to Kennedy's administration helped drive the conservative renascence in its early years, politicians from Barry Goldwater to – crucially – Ronald Reagan to George W. Bush have attempted, in the years following the assassination, to claim Kennedy for their side. Based in part in decontextualized readings of the historical record (Kennedy's support for tax cuts), in part in fact (Kennedy's very real status as an avid Cold Warrior), these attempts at appropriation drew on Kennedy's legacy as a political idealist and popular constituency builder to make a case for controversial policies, even as they also reinforced the transformation of politics into a form of mass-mediated spectacle.

In his coda, "The Kennedy Legacy: From Hagiography to Exposé and Back Again," Loren Glass briefly outlines the history of writing about Kennedy from his presidency through the recent commemoration of the fiftieth anniversary of his assassination. As Glass notes, Kennedy historiography has gone through cycles, with revelations about his poor health and his sexual appetites tarnishing aspects of his legacy before being reincorporated back into the larger myth. If Kennedy has provided a way of thinking about America itself, Glass concludes, this has been not only the United States that exists but also the United States that might have been had he lived.

Despite the fact that he failed to complete his first term, no post–World War II U.S. president – possibly no president since Lincoln, whose own presidency was similarly cut short – has exerted so great a fascination on the national imagination as John F. Kennedy does. As Knight's and Connor's chapters, along with the "Guide to Further Reading and Viewing" at the back of this book, make clear, Kennedy has been a ubiquitous, at times explicit and at times implicit figure in post-1960 U.S. literature, film, television, and art. Books on various aspects of the Kennedy legacy continue to appear at an undiminished clip, with scholarly studies like Brinkley's 2012 contribution to Times Books' American Presidents Series and Larry Sabato's 2013 *The Kennedy Half-Century* joined by television commentator Chris Matthews's 2011 *Jack Kennedy: An Elusive Hero*; Mimi Alford's 2012 *Once upon an Affair*, about her tryst with the president when she was nineteen; and the still unending stream of books speculating on the as yet unsolved mystery behind Kennedy's assassination. Stephen King's 2011 *11/22/63*, about a schoolteacher who goes back in time and attempts to prevent the assassination, is only the most recent novel to address the profound influence Kennedy's life and death have exerted on the post-1960 United States. And *Profiles in Courage* remains in print alongside various collections of Kennedy's still frequently quoted speeches. In fall 2012, Hyperion released *Listening In*, a set of CDs featuring selections from Kennedy's White House recording system. Some of this recent surfeit can be attributed to the commemorative fervor occasioned by the period between the January 2011 fiftieth anniversary of Kennedy's inauguration and the November 2013 fiftieth anniversary of his assassination. Still: if we factor in all the books that regularly appear about Kennedy and his family, it becomes clear that what Frank Rich has called "Kennedyiana" remains a major pillar of the publishing industry.[25] The chapters in this volume contribute to the already massive bibliography on Kennedy by mediating between the historical facts and the long cultural shadow in an effort to understand his ongoing role in shaping the world in which we live.

NOTES

1 W. J. Rorabaugh, *Kennedy and the Promise of the Sixties* (New York: Cambridge University Press, 2002), 1.

2 Theodore C. Sorensen, ed., *"Let the Word Go Forth": The Speeches, Statements, and Writings of John F. Kennedy* (New York: Delacorte Press, 1988), 93. See also John Hellmann, *The Kennedy Obsession: The American Myth of JFK* (New York: Columbia University Press, 1997), 101–2.

3 Sorensen, *"Let the Word Go Forth,"* 100.

4 Norman Mailer, "Superman Comes to the Supermart," *Esquire* 54, no. 5 (November 1960): 122.

5 Ted Sorensen, *Kennedy* (1965; repr., New York: HarperCollins, 2009); Arthur M. Schlesinger Jr., *A Thousand Days: John F. Kennedy in the White House* (1965; repr., Boston: Houghton Mifflin, 2002).

6 Sean McCann, *A Pinnacle of Feeling: American Literature and Presidential Government* (Princeton, NJ: Princeton University Press, 2008); Michael Szalay, *Hip Figures: A Literary History of the Democratic Party* (Palo Alto, CA: Stanford University Press, 2012).

7 Rorabaugh, *Kennedy*, xix, x.

8 Hellmann, *The Kennedy Obsession*, 99, passim.

9 Alan Brinkley, "The Legacy of John F. Kennedy," *Atlantic*, September 18, 2013, http://www.theatlantic.com/magazine/archive/2013/08/the-legacy-of-john-f-kennedy/309499/, accessed August 30, 2014.

10 See Larry J. Sabato, *The Kennedy Half-Century: The Presidency, Assassination, and Lasting Legacy of John F. Kennedy* (New York: Bloomsbury, 2013), 337–69.

11 Bill Clinton, "Passing the Torch," *Atlantic*, September 18, 2013, http://www.theatlantic.com/magazine/archive/2013/08/passing-the-torch/309513/, accessed August 30, 2014.

12 Robert F. Kennedy Jr., "John F. Kennedy's Vision of Peace," *Rolling Stone*, November 20, 2013, http://www.rollingstone.com/politics/news/john-f-kennedys-vision-of-peace-20131120, accessed August 30, 2014.

13 Ibid.

14 See, for instance, Rorabaugh, *Kennedy*, 59; Sabato, *The Kennedy Half-Century*, 110, 122–27.

15 See, for instance, Ira Stoll, *JFK: Conservative* (New York: Houghton Mifflin Harcourt, 2013); Jeff Jacoby, "Would Democrats Embrace JFK Now?," *Boston Globe*, October 20, 2013, http://www.bostonglobe.com/opinion/2013/10/19/would-jfk-never-liberal-still-find-home-democratic-party/ZrxV7lJYHrvWxOjXItAuZJ/story.html, accessed August 30, 2014; Kyle Smith, "Modern Democrats Would View John F. Kennedy as a Reaganite Extremist," *Forbes*, November 8, 2013, http://www.forbes.com/sites/kylesmith/2013/11/08/modern-democrats-would-view-john-f-kennedy-as-a-reaganite-extremist/, accessed August 30, 2014; George Will, "Kennedy the Conservative," *Washington Post*, November 20, 2013, http://www.washingtonpost.com/opinions/geoege-f-will-john-f-kennedy-the-conservative/2013/11/20/92be8164-513d-11e3-a7fo-b790929232e1_story.html, accessed August 30, 2014.

16 Irving Bernstein, *Promises Kept: John F. Kennedy's New Frontier* (New York: Oxford University Press, 1991), 118–59; Robert Schlesinger, "The Myth of JFK as a Supply Side Tax Cutter," *U.S. News & World Report*,

January 26, 2011, http://www.usnews.com/opinion/articles/2011/01/26/the-myth-of-jfk-as-supply-side-tax-cutter%20, accessed August 30, 2014.

17 Joe Strupp, "Historians: Right-Wing Media Claims of a Conservative JFK are 'Silly' and 'Ludicrous,'" *Media Matters*, November 22, 2013, http://mediamatters.org/blog/2013/11/22/historians-right-wing-media-claims-of-a-conserv/197029, accessed August 30, 2014.

18 See Bernstein, *Promises Kept*, 246–58.

19 John Dickerson, "Kennedycare," *Slate*, November 17, 2013, http://www.slate.com/articles/news_and_politics/history/2013/11/john_f_kennedy_s_health_care_failure_jfk_and_barack_obama_s_tough_fights.single.html, accessed August 30, 2014.

20 Richard H. Pells, *The Liberal Mind in a Conservative Age: American Intellectuals in the 1940s and 1950s* (Middletown, CT: Wesleyan University Press, 1988); Andrew Hoberek, *The Twilight of the Middle Class: Post–World War II American Fiction and White-Collar Work* (Princeton, NJ: Princeton University Press, 2005).

21 Rorabaugh, *Kennedy*, 15.

22 Michael E. Latham, *Modernization as Ideology: American Social Science and "Nation Building" in the Kennedy Era* (Chapel Hill: University of North Carolina Press, 2000), 166.

23 Elizabeth Cobbs Hoffman, *All You Need Is Love: The Peace Corps and the Spirit of the 1960s* (Cambridge, MA: Harvard University Press, 1998), 30.

24 Thomas J. McCormick, *America's Half-Century: United States Foreign Policy in the Cold War and After*, 2nd ed. (1989; repr., Baltimore, MD: Johns Hopkins University Press, 1995), 138.

25 Frank Rich, "What Killed Kennedy?," *New York Magazine*, November 20, 2011, http://nymag.com/news/frank-rich/jfk-2011-11/, accessed August 30, 2014.

I

EOIN CANNON

Kennedy, Boston, and Harvard

John Fitzgerald Kennedy's election to the presidency in 1960 capped a multigenerational American family saga. Beginning with JFK's great-grandparents' immigration to Boston in the middle of the nineteenth century, the Fitzgeralds and the Kennedys vividly enacted the major themes in a quintessential narrative of American identity: flight from privation and oppression; urban hardship, discrimination, and community formation; street-level business and political entrepreneurship; upward mobility, assimilation, and ascendance. Theirs was the "nation of immigrants" story that entered the national creation mythology. "Kennedy's dazzling rise to power," wrote Doris Kearns Goodwin in her biography of the two families, "was a recognition that the great immigrant revolution was finally complete."[1] Overcoming anti-Catholic prejudice in his presidential campaign cemented Kennedy's historical reputation as the catalyst of a new American settlement around identity.

But the Kennedy backstory may have as much to tell us about structural changes taking place in American institutions as it does about immigrant perseverance or the redemption of constitutional democracy from one form of bigotry. Beyond his family, the formative sites of Kennedy's early years were educational, military, and political. At prep school and at college, Kennedy's seemingly minor social victories illuminate the ways America's highest elite was both broadening its membership and consolidating its power at midcentury. Kennedy's heroism in the Pacific, when capitalized by his father's public relations machine, turned the socially unifying effect of World War II into the postwar currencies of celebrity and patriotism. And by combining this war story with the revival of the family's tribal legacy in Boston, the 1946 congressional campaign that launched Kennedy's political career provided an early model for how a liberalized white identity could obscure class and racial conflict in American politics. If Kennedy's great-grandparents worked to "become white," the president himself helped remake American whiteness.[2]

National though these forces were, it was the cultural landscape of Boston that enabled Kennedy's unique influence on the performance and meaning of white ethnicity. Contrasts within the city's political and educational realms turned family ambitions and personal successes into striking new images of identity. From his grandfathers' era through Kennedy's own early life, Boston had the most ethnically conscious Protestant elite and the most politically dominant Irish immigrants of any major city in America. Harvard, meanwhile – which Kennedy was the third generation in his family to attend – was the most WASPish of all universities, yet it advanced the theory and practice of meritocracy that still governs status discourse in American power centers. During John F. Kennedy's formative years, his father rejected Boston in favor of first New York and then London, chafing under the extraordinary parochialism of Boston's elites and the sheer smallness of its global stature. But as the future president came of age, the family returned to Harvard and then to Boston, ultimately attaching JFK's career and identity permanently to the city. The primary pull was a political legacy that was too valuable to ignore. The outcome of this relationship was also cultural: Boston's contrasts provided fields for the future president's ambitions to stand out decisively and become iconic.

The Fitzgeralds and the Kennedys are most closely associated with the role of politics in the rise of the Irish, especially through the image of Boston as a site of intense conflict between Yankee elites and Irish newcomers. The president's grandfathers were John Francis "Honey Fitz" Fitzgerald, a former newsboy from the North End who became a charismatic congressman (1895–1901) and mayor (1906–8, 1910–14), and Patrick Joseph "PJ" Kennedy, a prosperous tavern keeper and influential ward boss and state legislator from East Boston. Both men were leading figures in the Irish political ascendancy in turn-of-the-century Boston – but less because of showdowns with Anglo-nativist "Brahmins" than owing to their skill in backroom intrigues and campaign street battles among their own kind. In their time, while Protestant elites continued to exclude Irish Catholics from positions of influence in finance and culture, the politics of ethnic resentment was a strategic and ritualistic language that arose as a consequence, rather than served as a cause, of Irish electoral dominance.[3]

The field of education, which in Boston more than elsewhere shaped economic and cultural leadership, remained a more daunting territory for the Irish than did politics. Accordingly, schooling became increasingly essential to the Fitzgerald and Kennedy families' stations at the vanguard of immigrant progress. The children of the famine-era arrivals had faced discrimination in Boston's openly Protestant public school system, and they aroused deep suspicion in their subsequent efforts to create an alternative system of Catholic schools. Harvard College, meanwhile, led the elite turn to Anglo-Saxon racial identity in response to mass Irish immigration and later to political nativism in response to subsequent Eastern and Southern European arrivals.[4]

Still, it was Harvard and Boston Latin School, two of Boston's oldest and most venerable institutions, that facilitated the Fitzgeralds' and the Kennedys' rise from neighborhood leaders to citywide, statewide, and ultimately national power players. The different experiences of Fitzgerald and his son-in-law Joseph P. Kennedy at these two schools highlight both the transformative effects of educational access and the frustratingly personal nature of the very short distances they had yet to travel.

After excelling in his public grammar school in the North End, John F. Fitzgerald entered the prestigious Boston Latin as one of those bright children of immigrants for whom the magnet school, long a paragon of intra-Protestant egalitarianism, was becoming a conduit for upward mobility. On the strength of his performance on the school's rigorous final examinations, in 1884 Fitzgerald was accepted without a college degree to Harvard Medical School, where he commenced his studies with the support of his family while living in their North End home. Just before the end of his first year of study, however, his father died, and Fitzgerald withdrew from school so he could go to work to help support his younger siblings. He was a brilliant student and had received technically fair treatment in a meritocratic system, but still his education availed him little by way of a career or a social network to lift him out of potential poverty. Instead he entered politics, apprenticed to the North End ward boss and bolstered by citywide connections he had made as a newsboy and athlete.[5]

By contrast, at the turn of the century Joe Kennedy entered Boston Latin at the behest of his upper-middle-class mother, who was drawn to its prestige. Although a mediocre student, he excelled socially and sought extracurricular leadership, captaining the baseball team and winning the class presidency. When he applied these same talents as a member of Harvard's class of 1912, however, he discovered – despite some success – an impregnable barrier. Although he befriended and impressed the sons of wealthy Protestant families, they would not allow him entrance into their private ranks, and he was blackballed from the most exclusive clubs. This was a fate shared by the majority of Harvard students, who nevertheless were or would become members of a high-ranking and well-networked elite. But for Kennedy, who was very ambitious and placed much stock in the social route to success, it was a scarring and intensely motivating experience. He knew that exclusion from these clubs meant exclusion from affiliated men's clubs, from old-line brokerage houses, and from the highest circles of power.

19

Instead, he went to work for the small neighborhood bank that his father had cofounded, where he applied his business savvy, social charm, and political connections to become the first Catholic appointed as a bank examiner in Massachusetts.[6]

The contrast in educations between the future mayor and the future mogul tells not only of a generation of progress but also of the paradoxically sharpened sense of exclusion that could accompany such advances. Fitzgerald rose through ward politics, where social division was a given and tribal conflict was more an electoral strategy than a personal crisis. Kennedy, by contrast, hitched his future to the burgeoning system by which ambitious members of the middle class could ride the social benefits of educational prestige into higher realms of wealth and power. After discovering the limits of that system, however, for him the resentment was more deeply personal, and it shaped the way he directed his children's education.

Joe Kennedy's experience also differed markedly from that of his future wife, Rose Fitzgerald. The mayor's daughter and future president's mother was an accomplished and charismatic high school student. Perhaps because he had let go of his own educational dream so decisively, Fitzgerald was willing to discard his daughter's, too. Succumbing to religious pressure, he denied his daughter her highest wish – to attend Wellesley College at a time when it was producing national leaders in social reform. He did so in a cruelly drawn-out fashion, moreover, insisting first on a post-high-school year at the Sacred Heart Convent in Boston, and then a year of effective imprisonment at a sister convent in Holland. In Europe Rose came of age by mastering and internalizing a system of pervasive social and religious scrutiny, before completing her studies at that same order's Manhattanville College in New York in 1910.[7]

Rose attributed her transformative year in Holland to the elite fashion of sending children abroad for their final level of schooling; biographers say it is obvious that Fitzgerald wanted to shield his daughter from the explosive corruption trials that were engulfing him in Boston. But it was clearly a matter of gender, too. In Rose's generation, men like Joe Kennedy could choose Harvard over Boston College without much loss of tribal face, and indeed in either college they could be expected to lay the groundwork for a career of high achievements. For Catholic women considering higher education, however, the preservation of the religiously defined family was at stake; in any case, it was a rare set of parents who saw college as anything more than a finishing school for their daughters. Although later in life Rose occasionally bemoaned the exclusion of her family from the highest social circles, the wound that she carried most deeply – losing the chance Wellesley offered her to become not only an exemplary Catholic mother but also a leading woman of her generation – was inflicted by her own kind.

Joseph P. Kennedy and Rose Fitzgerald married in Boston in 1914, soon moving to the near suburb of Brookline, where their second child, John Fitzgerald ("Jack"), was born in 1917. Defying the limits he had perceived at Harvard, Joe Kennedy rose quickly in finance, proving a fierce corporate competitor and then a canny and notoriously unethical speculator, even by the loose standards of the 1920s. But after being blackballed from suburban country clubs in Brookline and Cohasset, Kennedy came to feel that elite anti-Irish exclusion was endemic to Boston and would hold his children back as he felt it had him.[8] In 1927, he abandoned the city, taking Rose and their growing family to suburban New York, adding summer and winter homes in Hyannis Port and Palm Beach, respectively, and sending his sons to school at Choate, a relatively young but fairly elite Episcopalian boarding school in Connecticut. Instead of giving up his belief in the importance of social success at school as a route to power, Kennedy doubled down on this conviction. In this bet he was prescient.

In the first half of the twentieth century, education became increasingly important as a means of achieving, conserving, and enhancing socioeconomic status. Progressive reformers saw access to effective schooling as a right for individuals and a necessity for national welfare. University leaders, in turn, recognized the important social role this elevated function conferred on their institutions. By linking status to ability in its selective credentialing of the upper half, the role of higher education became nothing less than "legitimating the American social order."[9] James B. Conant, Harvard's president from 1933 to 1953 (and a class of 1913 fraternity brother of Joe Kennedy), was the most influential theorist of what became known as "meritocracy" in admissions and financial aid. In essays and speeches authored while John F. Kennedy was an undergraduate at Harvard, Conant argued that in an age of political unrest, educational reform was needed to preserve "the American ideal." Schooling could forge a "Jeffersonian" middle path between capitalist oligarchy and radical leveling, by distributing personal development and social status according to talent and need.[10]

For Conant's Harvard and similarly elite private universities to claim leadership roles in such a system, they had to negotiate deep tensions in their own identities. In an expanded and industrialized nation, their historic role as private institutions of the northeastern social elite diminished both their influence and their meritocratic credibility. At the same time, they relied on the legacy of this role for maintaining and capitalizing the prestige that was essential to retaining influential benefactors and attracting ambitious newcomers. Harvard and others had opened their doors to accomplished second- and third-generation immigrants since the late nineteenth century. But soon afterward, they began instituting policies and practices that allowed them to manage their demographics (primarily to restrict Jewish enrollment) and maintain their definitive relationship with the old guard.

In the 1930s, led by Conant, college administrations brought greater focus to academic qualifications with tools such as standardized tests and nationwide scholarship competitions, while increasing the emphasis on "well-rounded" and "well-adjusted" personality traits that were keyed to the culture of the prep school and its social sphere. In their emphasis on meritocratic measures – despite defining "merit" so as to benefit the upper classes – colleges and then prep schools provided apparent proof that social status reflected innate ability. While after World War II, many white men took advantage of the GI Bill and the expansion of state universities to enter the middle class, elite schools worked on producing what they called a "leadership stratum."[11] At this level, what Conant described as a "continuous process by which power and privilege may be automatically redistributed at the end of each generation" in reality did much to produce results that Pierre Bourdieu (in discussing the French educational system) called "infinitely closer" to "hereditary transfer" than to any re-sorting of status among the populace.[12]

At this upper end of the system, the relatively minor differences of social acceptance that had frustrated Joe Kennedy continued to be important as lifelong passkeys to power. In 1956, the year the fourth and final Kennedy son graduated from Harvard, C. Wright Mills wrote in *The Power Elite*, "The one deep experience that distinguishes the social rich from the merely rich and those below is their schooling, and with it, all the associations, the sense and sensibility, to which this educational routine leads throughout their lives."[13] This process begins in prep school, Mills pointed out, with the result that those who entered Harvard and Yale by other routes never actually crossed the barrier into the highest elite, where access to corporate boardrooms and senate offices was assured. African Americans and others with no plausible claim to whiteness remained, of course, largely excluded from both the technocratic and leadership levels.

"Sense and sensibility" were the terms on which young Jack Kennedy outshone his predecessors and almost all of his classmates at prep school and in college. At Choate from 1931 to 1935, Kennedy struggled with his health and his academic focus, failing to follow in his brother's footsteps as a high-achieving campus leader. But he ultimately proved more adept than either his aggressive father or his straitlaced brother at the subtler social talents required to crack the inner realms of privilege. Although seeming "casual and disorderly" to a degree that infuriated some of his teachers,

Kennedy's louche charm won him acolytes among his peers and, eventually, a tight circle of friends drawn from the sons of the school's wealthiest benefactors.[14] Biographers have interpreted Kennedy's style as a "wry Irishness" that contrasted with his older brother's "heavy" personality and by-the-book newcomer's approach to social acceptance.[15] If we set aside this retrospectively ethnic frame and instead look at his social peers, his privilege, and his bawdy letters to friends, young Jack Kennedy appears as much like the dissolute son of an old Yankee family as he does a charming young Irishman.

By his senior year, Kennedy found fields of action for his winning but quietly anarchic personality. He organized his circle into a rebellious club that showed up the administration, produced a successful yearbook, and hoarded the "superlatives," headed by Kennedy as "Most Likely to Succeed." Headmaster George St. John, solicitous of the wealthy and famous Kennedy parents but rumored to be anti-Irish, saw Kennedy's circle as dangerously cynical and disruptive. St. John denounced them before the assembled school community as "muckers," an old Ivy League term for troublesome working-class locals that had evolved to include young gentlemen who seemed to lack the honorable traits of their class. In defiance, Kennedy led an even more audacious campaign of pranks and insubordinations, and he codified the name: he and his partners in crime had golden shovel pendants made with the inscription CMC for "Choate Muckers Club."[16] More than one biographer has noted the shrewd irony in Kennedy's embrace of a term of abuse that WASPs had developed to describe Irish Americans. While the term might have held a real sting for Joe Kennedy at Harvard, Jack's jovial flaunting of it only proved that his generation lived in no fear of the association and its potential effects on status.

The antics of the Muckers eventually brought a disciplinary crisis for Kennedy, but its outcome was to prove that he could act with the full impunity of a member of his social class. When St. John smoked out a scheme to disrupt an annual spring dance, he nominally expelled all thirteen conspirators. By the time the students' parents arrived on campus for emergency meetings, though, the punishment had been lessened, and in the end there appear to have been no serious repercussions at all. When Joe Kennedy got his son alone, he laughed off the seriousness of the prank, even implicitly approving his son's rebellious spirit.[17] Biographers identify this moment as one in which Joe Kennedy first recognized qualities of independence and leadership in his second son, even as it also exhibited Jack's youthful lack of purpose. But another point may be just as telling: as the headmaster of a gatekeeping institution for the highest elite, St. John ostensibly controlled Kennedy's destiny. And even if he was rumored to harbor that very anti-Irish sentiment that Joe Kennedy feared was his family's glass ceiling, Kennedy's wealth and public standing easily trumped this attitude. Jack Kennedy's personality tested this power dynamic and publicly proved it. For the first time, a Kennedy was not just behaving acceptably at an elite educational institution but was inhabiting fully the role of the dominant class that these institutions existed to serve.

Kennedy's subsequent progress into and through Harvard College was, in this respect, not a matter of an old-guard institution opening its doors more widely to the descendants of immigrants. Instead, it cemented the higher-than-elite social status that was required of future national leaders at such institutions. Harvard's shifting admissions policies in the 1930s were indeed vitally concerned with drawing the top public high school graduates from around the country, to invigorate and nationalize what had been a parochial, academically mediocre undergraduate body. But as Jerome Karabel has shown, these policies were also crafted to reduce the numbers of Jewish students, who were heavily represented among these public school standouts.[18] Kennedy's admission was not affected by this strategy. There was no "Catholic problem" at Harvard, Catholics never having arrived in large numbers and by the 1940s no longer presenting the racial difference attributed to Jews. Kennedy applied as the son of a wealthy alumnus and as a promising but underachieving student from an elite prep school. At first, Kennedy had enrolled at Princeton with his closest friends, rather than at his father's alma mater and the school where his older brother was a junior, as a display of independence. But after illness derailed his freshman year, Kennedy turned to Harvard after all. Harvard had already accepted him based on his June 1935 exams, in which he received honors (but not high honors) grades in two subjects, English and English History. Harvard's communication of these two marks to Princeton was enough for the latter to admit him. To secure his transfer to Harvard the following year, Kennedy had only to write a brief letter to the Admissions Committee explaining that he had been convalescing since being admitted the year before.[19]

Kennedy's entrance to Harvard was thus uncontested. The real question lay in how high he could rise in its social scale. He followed in his older brother's footsteps as a member of the freshman football team, as chairman of the Freshman Smoker Committee (a respected post for the ambitious), as a resident of Winthrop House, and as a member of the Hasty Pudding theatrical club. And where his brother had been elected to the Student Council, John Kennedy served on the editorial board of the *Crimson* newspaper. These distinctions placed him in the top tier of his class, but they did not guarantee access to the highest social realms, the "final" clubs through which elite upperclassmen separated themselves into privately owned residences and established lifelong networks. This was the realm that had eluded Kennedy's father and brother.

What Mills came to call "The Two Harvards" is plainly in evidence in a survey produced by one of Kennedy's classmates and published in the 1940 yearbook.[20] This unflinching (and at the time, controversial) document assembled by Donald Thurber revealed that approximately one-fifth of the class belonged to "social clubs," and that these men drank more than their classmates did. Further divisions focused on family income and type of high school attended. For example, graduates of public high schools said they valued academic enrichment as the greatest gift Harvard had given them, while graduates of private schools placed greater value on the social bonds they had formed in Cambridge. In addition, the majority of the prep schoolers opposed the New Deal and the union movement, while most public school men supported both.[21] Although they would follow their father into Democratic Party politics, and ultimately far outdo him in their concern for the vulnerable, the social group that the Kennedy sons aspired to join was not only Protestant but, by the late 1930s, politically reactionary.

And join them John Kennedy did. The story goes that the clubs' alumni, many from the oldest social circles in Boston, wanted no part of the Fitzgerald or Kennedy names, associated as they were with an Irish political grifter and a stock-swindling parvenu, respectively. But Kennedy's friends thought his personal qualities were worthy of a clubman and so, after excluding another talented Irish Catholic friend from their plans for being too much the "rough diamond," aimed their lobbying efforts at the Spee Club, whose alumni base was by that time more firmly planted in New York than in Boston.[22] Kennedy was accepted and spent his final two years at Harvard living, dining, and studying in the gracious, insular confines of this private club. He concluded his college career by being named a member of the nine-man Permanent Class Committee, guaranteeing him lifelong influence in Harvard's affairs and association with its most powerful graduates. As a senator in 1957 he was elected to the university's Board of Overseers, for which he hosted a meeting in the White House in 1963.[23]

As with the presidency, the "arrival" of Irish Catholics in these most exclusive of Ivy League alumni circles has been attributed to the way Jack Kennedy's personal qualities activated the support of liberal-minded, personally loyal, and well-placed friends. Entrance into the Spee was "his first personal triumph," a prize that his father's wealth and his brother's talents had never been able to buy. But, of course, the family's wealth and power constituted the platform on which he was able to display these qualities. The same week Kennedy was being initiated into the Spee, he revealed to friends that journalists on his father's payroll were leaking premature "news" of the financier's appointment as ambassador to the United Kingdom, thereby forcing the hand of President Roosevelt, who had hoped to make him accept the humbler position of secretary of commerce.[24]

Harvard's institutional and alumni networks may have preferred older, quieter alternatives to this kind of aggressive power grabbing, but as the beneficiaries of unearned privilege they had no basic principles with which they could oppose it. And if the power elite could not hold down Joe Kennedy, neither could its preparatory clubs any longer exclude his son. The Harvard final clubs adapted to this new social and political reality by considering John F. Kennedy's winning personality, a courtesy they had not extended to his father. But the future president's personal charm would have availed him nothing had, for example, he been living at home, as most Catholic Boston boys at Harvard did. When Kennedy was not ensconced at the Spee, his father's ambassadorship allowed him to travel widely in Europe and to research the senior thesis that would later become the book (*Why England Slept*) that attested to his seriousness in foreign policy.

Compare this scope of action with that of the man whose picture sits next to Kennedy's in the class of 1940 yearbook, Richard W. Kelley. Kelley, like Kennedy, was one of the approximately 10 percent of men in the class who were Roman Catholic (about 15 percent were Jewish, by comparison). Kelley was a graduate of nearby Somerville High School. The son of an insurance agent who had no college degree, he lived at home during his time at Harvard. Commuting students found it almost impossible to maintain the rich extracurricular schedules and social lives of their classmates in the houses, and club membership was out of the question. Kelley's only extracurricular claim in his thin yearbook entry was membership in the Caisson Club for undergraduate officers of the ROTC. It is true that, had he not been killed in action in North Africa during World War II, Kelley would have had access to a life of upper-middle-class prosperity surpassing his parents' modest attainments. But he would almost certainly not have had personal influence with his classmate John F. Kennedy, except as a voter. Had he survived to return home to Somerville, just a year later in 1946 he would have become one of his classmate's congressional constituents.[25]

Kennedy too went to war, in service that cemented his coming-of-age and formed the basis of the public identity upon which he would build his political career. A navy lieutenant, Kennedy was in his fourth month as commander of PT-109, one of several dozen torpedo boats based in the Solomon Islands whose mission was to attack Japanese cargo and troop shipments. Cut off from communications with fellow patrol boats one night in August 1943, PT-109 was rammed by a much larger Japanese destroyer, killing two men instantly and leaving the remaining eleven clinging to the floating wreck and suffering various injuries. Under Kennedy's direction, they spent the next day paddling several miles to a nearby island, Kennedy himself shouldering a badly burned crew member for the duration. For the next six days, Kennedy undertook dangerous exploratory swims at night and moved his men from beach to beach, until their rescue by native scouts and an allied coast watcher. Many accounts have exaggerated Kennedy's role in the final rescue. But the twenty-six-year-old's crew swore to his courage and leadership during the harrowing crisis, and their testimony has never been plausibly contested.[26]

The tale of PT-109 is a good example of the socially cohesive effect of World War II – and an even better one of the storytelling that accentuated and gave shape to that effect.[27] Prominent newspaper coverage emphasized Kennedy's heroism and his status as the son of the recent ambassador to the UK. But PT-109 was not transformed into a legend until John Hersey, who was writing on events in the Pacific for the *New Yorker*, met Kennedy in the Solomons. Kennedy agreed to give an interview, on the condition that the writer talk to crew members first. Hersey met three of them stateside and proceeded to write a piece called "Survival," which appeared in the June 17, 1944, issue of the *New Yorker*. Hersey later said he was struck by Kennedy's desire to ensure that the story was true to the memories of his crew. Personally impressed, Hersey framed his piece with an implicit statement of the social significance of this source base, which drew "Lieutenant John F. Kennedy, the ex-Ambassador's son" together with "three enlisted men named Johnston, McMahon, and McGuire" (evoking the way an officer would have addressed them, Hersey never gives their first names).[28] The piece reveals Kennedy occasionally stumbling in his judgment and authority when dealing with fellow officers, but accepting wholly the obligations of leadership in regard to his crew. That August, Joe Kennedy convinced *Reader's Digest* to publish a condensed version of the essay that circulated more widely and became, in John Hellmann's words, "the true beginning of the production of John F. Kennedy as a popular hero."[29] The PT-109 story paved the way for Kennedy's entry into politics.

In his first congressional campaign in 1946, Kennedy made strategic use of not only his war story, but also the family's legacy in Boston's Irish-dominated political culture. The Eleventh Congressional District, covering parts of Cambridge, Somerville, and Boston, was largely blue collar and heavily Irish. Kennedy was a stranger in this land, and everyone, most of all his opponents, knew it. As young adults, Kennedy and most of his siblings evinced little interest in being Irish or Catholic. Ethnic identity in the 1930s, when they came of age, had become a mode of working-class consciousness encouraged by Marxist writers but alien to the Kennedys and their upwardly mobile approach to power. The family's primary transatlantic social bond was with, ironically, the English aristocracy. At twenty-nine, Kennedy remained unfamiliar with the lived experience of Irish-descended Bostonians and disdainful of their self-conscious political identity.[30]

Joe Kennedy, however, funded and directed his son's successful campaign using two main assets: a nearly inexhaustible bank account and a still-formidable political influence that was rooted in the family's prominence among Massachusetts's Irish Democrats. Using this influence required not simply wielding power behind closed doors but publicly presenting young Jack Kennedy as the legitimate heir to the family's legacy. In order to play his part, JFK had to overcome not only chronic illness but also an aversion to self-promotion, poor public speaking skills, and almost no experience socializing with people outside his own elite (and largely Protestant) social sphere.

Joe Kennedy's overwhelming influence notwithstanding, the lasting imagery of the campaign is that of Jack Kennedy going door to door and function hall to function hall in working-class neighborhoods like Charlestown, winning voters over singly and in small groups with his earnest manner, his war veteran's credibility, and his genuine empathy with their concerns. In stories by advisers like David Powers, and in photographs from the campaign trail, Kennedy appears out of place but game and receptive, as if studiously absorbing the heritage onto which his father was grafting his campaign behind the scenes. The campaign's slogan, "The New Generation Offers a Leader," quietly asserted the family's parochial legacy while gesturing beyond it to the universal, youthful promise of Kennedy's glamorous image. Rose Kennedy, meanwhile, helped to consolidate the women's vote in formal teas that appealed to the postwar social aspirations of working- and middle-class families.[31]

There was thus an intentional quality to the creation of Kennedy's "Boston Irish" identity that illuminates the sometimes hidden politics of post–World War II white racial identity. JFK's reattachment to his family's immigrant legacy in 1946 – invoked even more openly in his 1952 campaign for the Senate – was a political strategy devised in order to overcome class difference and class consciousness among whites.[32] Its success had deeply personal and broadly social implications. It sparked Kennedy's own interest in his ancestry, while launching the career that led him to become the first Catholic occupant of the White House. It made him a spokesman for the last generation in the famine-era immigration narrative. And, ultimately, Kennedy's "Boston" persona helped to initiate and consolidate an ascendant new mode of American whiteness.

Kennedy's election as president marked not just the completion of the Irish mobility saga but also the beginning of a new kind of mainstream but hyphenated American identity, one that did not hide this history of struggle but instead asserted it with pride. Kennedy experienced this change personally. Beginning in 1947, he undertook a series of visits to Ireland in which he explored his family's roots, eventually identifying an "emerald thread" that bound the Irish diaspora together at a nearly spiritual level, through a shared legacy of suffering.[33] This pattern culminated in President Kennedy's state visit to Ireland in 1963, where his articulation of an enduring bond with the ancestral homeland was a formative moment in the "white ethnic revival" of the 1960s and beyond.[34]

JFK's supposed self-invention as "the first Irish [Boston] Brahmin," may have liberated many of his co-ancestral contemporaries from feelings of inferiority.[35] But his embrace of an Irish identity at the moment of his American ascendancy also, ultimately, helped liberate many white Americans from feelings of responsibility for a racial advantage that was now untrammeled. With an aggression more like Joe Kennedy's backroom horse-trading than Jack Kennedy's earnest speechifying, the white ethnic movement muted both class conflict and racial dominance. It claimed authenticity and denied privilege in ways that became ideologically useful to everyone from Tom Hayden to Ronald Reagan. And it has helped Boston, in which deep economic inequality has replaced ethnic rivalry as the governing contrast, to appear in popular culture as a blue-collar, Irish American city.[36]

NOTES

1 Doris Kearns Goodwin, *The Fitzgeralds and the Kennedys: An American Saga* (New York: Simon & Schuster, 1987), 810.
2 Noel Ignatiev, *How the Irish Became White* (New York: Routledge, 1995).
3 James J. Connolly, *The Triumph of Ethnic Progressivism: Urban Political Culture in Boston, 1900–1925* (Cambridge, MA: Harvard University Press, 1998), 15–16.
4 Barbara Miller Solomon, *Ancestors and Immigrants, A Changing New England Tradition* (Boston: Northeastern University Press, 1956), 59ff., 104–5.
5 Goodwin, *The Fitzgeralds and the Kennedys*, 61–70.
6 Ibid., 124, 208–41.
7 Ibid., 130–44.
8 Ibid., 365–68.
9 Jerome Karabel, *The Chosen: The Hidden History of Admission and Exclusion at Harvard, Yale, and Princeton* (Boston: Houghton Mifflin, 2005), 542.
10 James B. Conant, "The Mission of American Universities," *Harvard Alumni Bulletin*, February 25, 1938, 597; "The Future of Our Higher Education," *Harper's Magazine*, May 1938, 561–70.
11 Karabel, *The Chosen*, 410, 485.

12 James B. Conant, "Education for a Classless Society: The Jeffersonian Tradition," *Atlantic Monthly*, May 1940, 593–602; Pierre Bourdieu, *The State Nobility: Elite Schools in the Field of Power* (Palo Alto, CA: Stanford University Press, 1998), 5, 288.
13 C. Wright Mills, *The Power Elite* (New York: Oxford University Press, 1956), 63.
14 Nigel Hamilton, *JFK: Reckless Youth* (New York: Random House, 1992), 134.
15 Chris Matthews, *Jack Kennedy: Elusive Hero* (New York: Simon & Schuster, 2011), 15.
16 Hamilton, *JFK*, 123.
17 Ibid., 121–27.
18 Karabel, *The Chosen*, 175–77.
19 Hamilton, *JFK*, 144, 165.
20 Mills, *The Power Elite*, 67.
21 Donald M. D. Thurber, "The Truth about '40." *Harvard College Class Album, Class of 1940*, 44–53, 248–58. Harvard University Archives.
22 Hamilton, *JFK*, 207.
23 "Overseers Will Meet in Washington," *Harvard Crimson*, March 14, 1963.
24 Hamilton, *JFK*, 209–12.
25 *Class Album*, 204; *Class of 1940 Sexennial Report*, 1946, 22–23. Harvard University Archives.
26 Michael O'Brien, *Rethinking Kennedy: An Interpretive Biography* (Chicago: Ivan R. Dee, 2009), 42–49.
27 Richard Slotkin, "Unit Pride: Ethnic Platoons and the Myths of American Nationality," *American Literary History* 13, no. 3 (2001): 469–98.
28 John Hersey, "Survival," *New Yorker*, June 17, 1944, 31.
29 John Hellmann, *The Kennedy Obsession: The American Myth of JFK* (New York: Columbia University Press, 1997), 38.
30 Arthur M. Schlesinger, Jr. *A Thousand Days: John F. Kennedy in the White House* (Boston: Houghton Mifflin, 2002), 89–91.
31 Robert Dallek, *An Unfinished Life: John F. Kennedy, 1917–1963* (Boston: Little, Brown, 2003), 122–31.
32 O'Brien, *Rethinking Kennedy*, 70–71.
33 John F. Kennedy, "Remarks of Senator John F. Kennedy before the Irish Fellowship Club of Chicago," March 17, 1956. John F. Kennedy Presidential Library and Museum, online collection.
34 Matthew Frye Jacobsen, *Roots Too: White Ethnic Revival in Post-Civil-Rights America* (Cambridge, MA: Harvard University Press, 2009), 11–16; Ignatiev, *How the Irish Became White*, 2–3.
35 Goodwin, *The Fitzgeralds and the Kennedys*, 810–11; David M. Shribman, "His Life Fulfilled the Irish Dream. His Death Shattered It," *Boston Globe*, November 23, 2013; Thomas Maier, *The Kennedys: America's Emerald Kings* (New York: Basic Books, 2003), 246.
36 Tom Hayden, *Irish on the Inside: In Search of the Soul of Irish America* (New York: Verso, 2001); Ronald Reagan, "Remarks to the Citizens of Ballyporeen, Ireland," June 3, 1984. *American Presidency Project* (online), ed. Gerhard Peters and John T. Woolley.

2

PAUL GILES

Kennedy and the Catholic Church

The relationship between U.S. politics and institutional forms of religion has always been problematic, since the United States itself has one of the highest rates of church attendance of any Western country, but the First Amendment of its Constitution insists that "Congress shall make no law respecting an establishment of religion." This Constitution, framed controversially as it was during an era of Enlightenment skepticism, was viewed askance by many church leaders in the early republic, but various American presidents, from George Washington to Kennedy's immediate predecessor, Dwight D. Eisenhower, have attempted to reconcile this apparent anomaly by bringing to office an air of vague piety without exercising themselves unduly about any specific sectarian end.[1] The majority of American presidents have been nominally Episcopalian or Presbyterian in their denominational affiliation, with Methodists, Baptists, and Unitarians also well represented. To this day, John F. Kennedy has been the only serving American president who was also a practicing Catholic, and this fact in itself says something about the often tense and fractious relationship between U.S. culture and the Roman Catholic religion.

When the governor of New York, Al Smith, became the Democratic Party's nominee for president in 1928, he was readily stereotyped by the country's more conservative rural interests as someone not to be trusted since he was uncomfortably close to both a sinister urban world of gambling, prostitution, and liquor and a Catholic faith antipathetic to free Protestant instincts. Commenting upon Smith's candidacy, Kansas newspaper editor William Allan White proclaimed that Protestants "cannot look with unconcern upon the seating of the representative of an alien culture, of a medieval Latin mentality, of an undemocratic hierarchy, and of a foreign potentate in the great office of the President of the United States."[2]

Smith subsequently blamed his loss to Herbert Hoover on this vehemently anti-Catholic rhetoric, although JFK's father, Joseph P. Kennedy, the grandson of immigrants to Boston during the Irish famine of the 1840s, defied such religious logic by voting for Hoover rather than Smith. Joseph Kennedy was subsequently looked upon with favor by Franklin D. Roosevelt as one of the few successful businessmen willing to support his New Deal politics in the 1930s, and Kennedy was rewarded by appointments first as chairman of the U.S. Securities and Exchange Commission and then, in December 1937, as ambassador to Britain. Kennedy, who sympathized with Prime Minister Neville Chamberlain's attempted appeasement of Nazi Germany and around whom accusations of anti-Semitism long hovered, subsequently became notorious as what one British government minister later called "the most unhelpful representative that the United States had ever sent us."[3] With Joseph Kennedy's memory still vivid, British prime minister Harold Macmillan wrote anxiously to his foreign secretary when the prospect of JFK's election became imminent of how he had "for some time been think-ing how we would handle the new American President if it should be a Kennedy." Macmillan's concerns were subsequently borne out by the way that, during his state visit to Ireland in 1963, JFK attended a memorial ser-vice for leaders of the Easter 1916 uprising against British rule, indirectly lending his support to the cause of Irish independence by commending how "Irish volunteers played so predominant a role in the American Army dur-ing the War of Independence."[4]

A major part of Joseph Kennedy's drive for social success for himself and his family involved putting behind them the social slights that he imagined himself to have faced at Harvard and elsewhere on account of his Irish Catholic background. Yet JFK's Catholic heritage was an integral component of his upbringing. Indeed, during Joseph Kennedy's ambas-sadorial tenure, Roosevelt had asked him to attend the 1939 coronation of Pope Pius XII, the first time the United States had been represented at such a papal ceremony since 1846, and all of the ambassador's immediate family, including the twenty-two-year-old JFK, were present at this cere-mony. JFK had earlier spent one year at the Catholic Canterbury School in New Milford, Connecticut, before transferring to Choate. Yet, despite the elder Kennedy's attachment to grander aspects of his religious heritage, JFK was able to turn this Catholic provenance to his political advantage. Though JFK came from a wealthy and privileged background, he could also play upon his Irish American ethnicity to appeal to broader political constituencies. During his first campaign for public office, when he was running (successfully) for Congress in 1946, he took care to endear him-self to the blue-collar Irish and Italian voters in Boston's Eleventh District, and he subsequently preserved a chameleonic capacity to mutate between Irish Catholic and WASP establishment personae, according to the politi-cal demands of the day. In the period after World War II, Catholics began to move decisively beyond the embattled minority position in which they had still been locked in the days of Al Smith: the total Catholic population in the United States increased by some 90 percent between 1945 and 1965, from 23.9 million to 45.6 million, with the number of Catholic clergy also up 52 percent, and enrollments in Catholic colleges and universities expanding from 92,000 to 385,000.[5] Kennedy took care to position himself as the political voice of this emerging new generation's self-confidence. He published his pamphlet *A Nation of Immigrants* in 1958 and in the same year supported the application to the Social Science Research Council of Lawrence H. Fuchs, a Jewish American scholar, to study the impact of various aspects of ethnicity on U.S. politics. Fuchs subsequently wrote speeches for Kennedy (and later helped shape immigration reform as an adviser to President Carter).[6]

At the same time, Kennedy was always aware of the tenuous and shifting nature of these ethnic identifications. Cognizant that now comfortably assimilated Irish and Italian Americans had generally been regarded as a "savage mob" only a couple of generations ago, Kennedy always retained that sense of not quite belonging as part of his political style.[7] These tensions were in many ways exacerbated rather than ameliorated by the rapid growth of an American Catholic middle-class presence in the 1950s, with the Catholic Church, once marginal and ghettoized, becoming increasingly recognized as a pressing threat to traditional U.S. values. Eleanor Roosevelt, the widow of the thirty-fourth president, loudly opposed Kennedy both for his support of parochial school funding as a Massachusetts congressman in the 1940s and for being in 1954 the only Senate Democrat not to vote to censure Joseph McCarthy for his anticommunist inquisitions. McCarthy, a graduate of Marquette University and a practicing Catholic himself, was very popular among Massachusetts's working-class Irish Catholics, but JFK also admired him personally, praising McCarthy as late as February 1952, at a Harvard Spee Club dinner, as "a great American patriot."[8] The papacy in the early 1950s was staunchly anticommunist – Pope Pius XII went so far in 1949 as to excommunicate any Catholic propagating "materialistic" doctrines – and both McCarthy and Kennedy were implicitly following the church line in the intensity of their zeal against the atheist regimes behind the Iron Curtain.

Nonetheless, as the Catholic vote became more significant, politicians of all stripes took care to address this important new constituency. President Eisenhower spoke at the University of Notre Dame graduation ceremony in 1959, and he also made a point of appointing a Catholic, William Brennan, as a Supreme Court judge. There was talk in 1956 of nominating JFK as vice presidential candidate, partly in response to concerns among Democratic

Party leaders about the general lack of enthusiasm among Catholic voters for the urbane liberal intellectual Adlai Stevenson. Peter Viereck, in a telling aside of 1953, described Catholic baiting as "the anti-Semitism of the liberals." The enthusiastic endorsement of censorship campaigns among mainstream Catholic communities made them appear out of step with the more avant-garde intellectual aspects of the Beat generation, and David Halberstam noted a particular "uneasiness" about the prospect of a Catholic president within "the *New Republic* crowd, the intellectuals and the liberals."[9]

Against this backdrop, part of Kennedy's broad appeal involved his skill in evading easy categorizations of every kind. Though he gave off a progressive and intellectual air, he also declared as a senator in 1953 that he was "not a liberal at all" but "a realist."[10] Indeed, it was in part JFK's antipathy to the high-toned liberal politics of Stevenson and others that made him not only popular among Catholic blue-collar voters but also trusted by Republicans for whom the Soviet Union was the greatest existential threat. In this, Kennedy was adhering to the model promoted by Eisenhower, whereby a formal adherence to religious convention became associated with the established U.S. way of life. Sociologist Will Herberg published in 1955 his treatise *Protestant-Catholic-Jew*, which sharply critiqued the ways in which "the religiousness characteristic of America today is very often a religiousness without religion, a religiousness with almost any kind of content"; however, for both Eisenhower and Kennedy, such evasiveness on substantive theological questions in favor of a vague "piety on the Potomac," in Herberg's dismissive phrase, was integral to the symbolic nature of their office.[11] During his tenure, Eisenhower legally added "under God" to the Pledge of Allegiance, and he also instituted the practice of opening cabinet meetings with prayers, thereby manifesting the outward adherence to Christian tenets that was considered de rigueur for all American politicians at this time.[12] Similarly Kennedy, though actually quite knowledgeable about doctrinal affairs, always tended to be publicly evasive on these matters, once avoiding the issue by saying, "It's hard for a Harvard man to answer questions in theology."[13] Despite security fears, Kennedy continued consistently to attend church on Sundays during the term of his presidency, but he had to work hard to avoid the image that had dogged Al Smith in 1928 of being beholden to and ensnared within the corrupt world of Catholic machine politics. Both before and during the three years of his administration, JFK went out of his way to avoid any suspicion of granting special favors to Catholic interests. He was by this time consistently opposing parochial school funding and refusing to countenance the idea of U.S. diplomatic representation at the Vatican, and he only endorsed the nomination of Robert McNamara as secretary for defense after exhaustive inquiries proved that, despite his name, McNamara did not in fact have any Irish Catholic connections.[14]

This charge that he would be in thrall to the dictates of Rome, thereby rendering the office liable to undue influence from a foreign power, was one of the most substantial hurdles faced by Kennedy as a Catholic candidate for president. This fear of Roman Catholicism as both manipulative and tyrannical struck a deep chord in the American psyche, one going back to the days of the Pilgrim Fathers who had fled across the Atlantic in search of freedom of conscience. An anti-Catholic pressure group, Protestants and other Americans United for the Separation of Church and State (POAU), was established in 1948, and the following year Paul Blanshard published *American Freedom and Catholic Power*, which described "the Catholic people of the United States" as "not citizens but *subjects* in their own religious commonwealth," a disenfranchised group which had "no representatives of their own choosing in their own local hierarchy or in the Roman high command."[15] Blanshard's book was not just a marginal or extreme event, being praised by no less a figure than John Dewey for its "exemplary scholarship, great judgment, and tact," while receiving endorsements from Eleanor Roosevelt, philosopher Bertrand Russell, and eminent Protestant theologian Reinhold Niebuhr. It also achieved widespread public recognition, going through eleven printings in a year and remaining on the *New York Times* best-seller list for seven months. Dr. Nelson Bell, the editor of *Christianity Today* and father-in-law of Billy Graham, heightened the controversy by declaring, in the midst of the Cold War, that "Rome was little better than Moscow."[16]

In response to these consistent accusations, Kennedy decided during his presidential campaign to take the bull by the horns and to address a meeting of the Greater Houston Ministerial Association, where, on September 12, 1960, he assured Protestant ministers that he believed "in an America where the separation of church and state is absolute." Kennedy went on to stress how he was "not the Catholic candidate for President," but rather "the Democratic Party's candidate for President who happens also to be a Catholic."[17] He also made it clear that he was committed to the dissociation of church and state "as a matter of personal deep conviction": whereas historically "many of the countries in Europe have a close union between church and state," observed Kennedy, the United States was "unique" in not wanting "an official state church." He added that "if ninety-nine percent of the population were Catholics, I would still be opposed to it," since he objected as a matter of principle to the idea of "civil power combined with religious power."[18]

Hence the notion, still prevalent among more traditional Catholic apologists, that Kennedy had been "forced by some anti-Catholic opponents to continually reaffirm his commitment to fortify the boundary between church and state" betrays a fundamental misunderstanding of how Kennedy chose to position himself in relation to the Catholic Church.[19] Although the Vatican newspaper *L'Osservatore Romano* continued in 1960 to publicly defend the church's right to assert binding doctrine on certain public issues, many of the more progressive Catholic theologians of this era, particularly in the United States, were coming to regard the political wisdom of the Vatican as inherently fallible because susceptible to historical change. Robert D. Cross, a professor at Swarthmore College, published in 1958 *The Emergence of Liberal Catholicism in America*, in which he argued that the church should follow what Pope Pius XII called "the providential path of history and circumstances" and thus avoid trying to defend as universal truths applications that might be suitable only in certain times and places. Cross cited the general condemnation of usury and the defense of a heliocentric theory of the universe as policies that had once been propagated by papal bulls but that were now, by the mid-twentieth century, no longer valid or relevant. There is only a fleeting reference to Kennedy in Cross's book – he comments on how "in the spring and summer of 1956, Democratic politicians seriously considered nominating a Catholic for vice-president" – and this suggests how the emergence of what Cross calls "liberal Catholicism" in the United States during the late 1950s was part of a much broader social phenomenon, with Kennedy himself being part of this phenomenon rather than its source.[20]

The leading Jesuit intellectual who was exploring this conceptual territory at the time was John Courtney Murray, a scholar based at Woodstock College in New York, whose erudite attempts to move beyond traditional neoscholastic models of organic society by acknowledging the historical nature of the church, and thus the categorically differential aspects of its spiritual and temporal arms, caused him to achieve a certain prominence, if not notoriety, in American Catholic intellectual circles. Murray castigated as old-fashioned the tendency of Paul Blanshard to reduce church and state to a single monistic entity, and he suggested instead that the double framework of the American Constitution, in which public and private realms were constitutionally separated, offered a unique opportunity to guarantee both "the freedom of the citizen" and "the freedom of the Church."[21] Murray was forbidden by the Vatican in 1954 to publish anything more on church-state relations, but Kennedy's speechwriter, Theodore Sorensen, asked Murray to vet Kennedy's address on these issues to the Greater Houston Ministerial Association in September 1960. On December 12, 1960, Murray himself appeared on the cover of *Time* magazine, where, in an article remarkable by today's standards for both its historical and theological complexity, he was described as exemplifying the new era of "post-modern man" and heralded as "the intellectual bellwether of this new Catholic and American frontier."[22]

This process of American Catholic modernization was crucially helped by the accession to the papacy in 1958 of John XXIII, who inaugurated a policy of *aggiornamento*, bringing the church up-to-date. The church council charged with considering institutional change was originally established in January 1959, and it subsequently morphed into the Second Vatican Council (1962–65), which introduced Sunday mass in languages other than Latin and emphasized the need for what Catholic historian Patrick W. Carey called "legitimate diversity within the unity of the faith."[23] These Vatican reforms ran alongside the Kennedy presidency, with the early 1960s widely recognized among American Catholics as the era of "the two Johns"; indeed, John XXIII also achieved wider recognition, with the pontiff being nominated as *Time* magazine's "Man of the Year" for 1962. In a 1963 address at Boston College, Kennedy specifically acknowledged his debt to John XXIII's *Pacem in Terris*, an encyclical encouraging the causes of justice and peace while opposing the stockpiling of nuclear weapons, saying, "As a Catholic I am proud of it and as an American I have learned from it."[24] Murray, though initially excluded from the deliberations of this Second Vatican Council because of his potentially heretical views, subsequently participated as a special adviser to Cardinal Spellman (formerly the archbishop of New York), and indeed Murray helped to write the council's final declaration on religious liberty.

Kennedy himself had a reputation for being what Presbyterian theologian Robert McAfee Brown in 1959 called "a rather irregular Christian," and on a personal level this may well have been true: JFK's wife, Jacqueline, said that by comparison with his brother Robert Kennedy, who "never misses mass and prays all the time," the president was "a poor Catholic."[25] Nevertheless, the systematic dissociation of spiritual from secular that so much perturbed Brown was not just an individual idiosyncrasy on Kennedy's part. It was also part of progressive Catholic thought at this time. The kind of philosophical compartmentalization between sacred and secular spheres outlined in Murray's theological essays found its counterpart in Kennedy's deliberate dissociation of worldly politics from metaphysical truth. A Catholic cleric, angered by Kennedy's apparently nonchalant response at a Catholic girls' school in the 1950s that "recognition of Red China was not a moral issue," asked him, "Senator Kennedy, do you not believe that all law comes from God?" JFK replied, "I'm a Catholic so of course I believe it – but that has nothing to do with international law."[26] By accident or design, Kennedy's

37

instinctive worldliness on questions of politics found its correlative in the categorical division between spiritual and temporal that Murray's "post-modern" theology was beginning to explore. Though William F. Buckley and other conservative Catholics of this era accused Kennedy of making religion seem a matter of indifference, the president was effectively part of a much broader movement to modernize the basis of Catholic thought and culture by circumscribing its parameters more precisely.[27]

So far as the 1960 election itself went, Nixon complained afterward, with some justification, that he "was getting it from both ends: Republican Catholics were being urged to vote for Kennedy because he was of their religion; and Republican Protestants were being urged to vote for him to prove that they were not biased against Catholics." Evangelist Billy Graham advised Nixon to turn the election into a straightforward referendum on the Protestant-Catholic divide, arguing that Kennedy "will capture the Catholic vote – no matter what concessions you make to the Catholic Church" but that he would surely be defeated by an en bloc Protestant vote for the Republicans.[28] However, Nixon was reluctant to go down this path, less as a matter of ethics than of political strategy: Eisenhower as Republican candidate had garnered 53 percent of the Catholic vote in the 1952 election, and Nixon was himself popular among the Catholic community for his doggedly anticommunist stance, with the University of Notre Dame awarding him its title "Patriot of the Year" in February 1960. But even though Nixon had specifically ordered that no one in his campaign was to speak about religion, the Kennedys were skilful in turning anti-Catholic rhetoric to their own political purposes. One GOP leader in New York was reported in *Time* magazine of October 1960 as saying that "every time one of those blankety-blank Southerners opens his mouth about the Catholic Church, we lose twenty votes for Nixon up here." By September 1960, former president Harry Truman – who in September 1959 had privately opposed Kennedy's nomination by arguing that no Catholic president would be able to separate church and state – was actively campaigning for his party's nominee and charging Nixon with the tolerance of anti-Catholic prejudice.[29]

The American Catholic Church avoided any official endorsement of either Kennedy or Nixon, and in the event the election was decided by a complicated smorgasbord of many different factors. Kennedy ended up attracting about 70 percent of the Catholic vote, along with a similar proportion of the African American electorate, plus about 80 percent of the (much smaller) Jewish vote, helped by Harvard professor J. K. Galbraith's success in actively imploring New York's Jewish American liberals to overcome their traditional religious antagonisms and support Kennedy. The fact that these Catholic voters tended to be congregated in key electoral swing states such as New York, Michigan, and California helped Kennedy's campaign, though he became nervous in October 1960, just a month before the election, when two Catholic bishops in Puerto Rico issued a pastoral letter instructing their parishioners not to vote for the regime of Governor Luis Muñoz-Marín. This threatened to undermine Kennedy's principled stance on the dissociation of church and state, and, as he acknowledged to Sorensen, "if enough voters realize that this is American soil, this election is lost." Boston archbishop Cardinal Cushing, a keen supporter of Kennedy, tried to help JFK's cause by putting out a statement saying he was "confident the Roman Catholic hierarchy in the United States would never take political action similar to that of the Puerto Rican bishops."[30] Ultimately, Kennedy confronted the issue of Catholicism in 1960 much as Barack Obama handled the issue of race in 2008: while using his own ethnic background to attract a core of sympathetic voters, he also exploited a detached WASP demeanor to give the impression of rising above such fractious divisions, thereby projecting himself as someone able to offer leadership to all Americans. Kennedy was the first man elected American president who did not receive a majority of the Protestant vote, but he was able to present this less as a breakthrough for a member of a minority than a symptom of the progressive temper of a naturally tolerant, increasingly multicultural society.

After his election, Kennedy promoted minority ethnic interests in only a cautious, gradualist manner. He appointed for the first time ever two Jewish cabinet members – Arthur Goldberg as secretary of labor and Abraham Ribicoff as secretary of health, education, and welfare – and he chose to remain conspicuously neutral when the Supreme Court banned prayer in public schools. He also angered religious leaders by vetoing a bill providing for the censorship of obscene publications on the grounds that it had, in his view, serious constitutional defects. Although the JFK era saw mass celebrated at the White House for the first time in history, after his first year in office the liberal Protestant *Christian Century* applauded Kennedy for having a "better record on the issue of separation of Church and State than any other President we have had in the past 30 years."[31] Kennedy did undertake official visits to Ireland and the Vatican, where he met in 1963 with John XXIII's newly installed successor, Pope Paul VI, but most of his time as president was occupied with the business of the Cold War, particularly in relation to rising tensions with the Soviet Union over Cuba. In a Gallup poll taken in April 1962, 63 percent of Americans thought the issue of war and peace to be the most important problem facing the country, with only 6 percent nominating racial problems and segregation, and the internationalist focus in Kennedy's abbreviated term of office reflected this kind of balance.[32]

The question of domestic race relations was also subtly shaded by religion. There were always radical differences of perspective between the Kennedys and Martin Luther King, with part of this divergence attributable to their allegiance to branches of Christianity that had historically been antagonistic. Martin Luther King's very name, of course, troped on that of the German Protestant Reformation leader, and indeed during the 1960 election hard-line fundamentalist groups circulated buttons with the words "Stand Up and Be Counted" and the numerals "1517," as a reminder to Protestants to follow Martin Luther's stand in nailing his 95 Theses to the door of Wittenberg Castle Church in 1517 in defiant rejection of Roman Catholic corruption. King's approach to political life through a framework of biblical prophecy was philosophically deeply at odds with Kennedy's more cold-eyed, legalistic approach to civil rights issues, and indeed in 1965 Garry Wills, another Catholic intellectual who was coming to prominence in this period, wrote in the *National Catholic Reporter* a highly critical review of King's "Letter from Birmingham Jail," faulting both its scholarship and its logic: "King is so convinced that all right and justice and truth are attuned to the civil rights movement," complained Wills, "that he reaches out toward anything that calls up noble emotions . . . and appropriates it without further thought."[33] Conversely, King made it clear in 1962 that he found Kennedy wanting in addressing the ethical dimensions of racial segregation, stating publicly that he felt the president "could do more in the area of moral persuasion by occasionally speaking out against segregation and counselling the nation on the moral aspects of the problem."[34] Both temperamentally and ideologically, Kennedy tended to resist the Manichaean dialectic of light against darkness that was characteristic of a Protestant Evangelicalism: "we must remember there are no permanent enemies," JFK characteristically observed during his address to the Irish parliament in June 1963.[35] It was this willingness to entertain contraries that led leaders such as King to suggest the Kennedy clan chose always to elevate pragmatism above principles, as in the standoff over the admission of a black student to the University of Mississippi, where Robert Kennedy as attorney general expressed sympathy for the political dilemma in which Ross Barnett as the governor of that state found himself. But by 1963, for all of his discomfort with both African American radicalism and the establishment liberalism endorsing it – Eugene Rostow, dean of the Yale Law School, was a particular thorn in his flesh – Kennedy was coming round increasingly to the view that civil rights reform needed to be presented to the nation as a biblical imperative. On June 11, 1963, Kennedy gave a television address announcing his decision to ask Congress for a civil rights law, saying: "We are confronted primarily with a moral issue. It is as old as the scriptures and is as clear as the American Constitution. The heart of the question is whether all Americans are to be afforded equal rights and equal opportunities."[36]

Such rhetoric did not come naturally to Kennedy because, as Michael Novak observed, his "distinctly Catholic, even Irish Catholic, sensibility" was always at odds with the kind of "civil religion" derived from "the dominant Protestant type" that has been much more common in American political life.[37] As William V. Shannon argued in *The American Irish*, "more than he may realize . . . Kennedy has an approach to the fundamentals of politics identical with Catholic teaching," particularly in his concern for pragmatic solutions rather than more typological schemes of redemption, his preference for "prudence" over any visionary city on a hill, and his general skepticism about the social prospects of "heavenly perfection," which in the "theology of liberalism" was associated more with "a Protestant vision."[38] Shannon's book was published while Kennedy was still alive, and it exemplifies a marked academic interest during the early 1960s in how American social norms were being recalibrated through modes of ethnic and religious difference. Kennedy was thus not only "a symbol of success" for aspiring middle-class Catholics, as Jay P. Dolan noted, but also more generally the emblem of a challenge to Protestant hegemony, and of the prospects of opening up U.S. society to alternative theoretical perspectives of many different kinds.[39] In this sense, the religious debates of the early 1960s can be seen as an important precursor to the more vituperative debates around race and gender that gathered pace later in the decade.

For some observers Kennedy's assassination was a grim indication of the fatal consequences of the U.S. presidency soiling its hands with the murky world of Catholic machine politics. The assassination served to annex Kennedy to an "ethos of suffering and pain" that Robert A. Orsi has identified as endemic to American Catholic culture of the early twentieth century, when martyrdom was seen as a royal road to the most consummate achievement.[40] In a more worldly sense, however, Kennedy's conviction that politics was (as he said in 1956) "the fine art of conciliating, balancing, and interpreting the forces and factions of public opinion" – itself a rejection of millennial doctrines – expressed itself rhetorically in a political language based not on prophecy or revelation but around paradox, parallelism, and analogical reversal.[41] Unlike Abraham Lincoln's biblical cadences that sought to imbue the terrestrial world with a transcendental spirit, Kennedy's oratorical style characteristically involved turning established categories on their head, as in his inauguration address: "ask not what your country can do for you; ask what you can do for your country." The construction here is quite different in tone from George W. Bush's apocalyptic jeremiads, or Bill Clinton's sentimental intonation of his belief in "a town called Hope," or Jimmy Carter's attempt in 1979 to invoke "a rebirth of the American spirit." Unlike these rhetorical attempts typologically to transpose corrupt matter into pure spirit, Kennedy's style involved a method of reversal, whereby he would take received ideas and approach them deliberately from a heterodox perspective. "Let us never negotiate out of fear," he proclaimed in the inauguration speech that he drafted himself. "But let us never fear to negotiate." It is this paradoxical flourish, the twisting of one category into its opposite, that is especially redolent of the Kennedy manner.

In his work *The Analogical Imagination*, Catholic theologian David Tracy contrasts the sacramental language of analogy that he sees as characteristic of Catholicism with a Protestant dialectical language that emphasizes instead the estrangement or distance between antithetical positions. Whereas Catholic analogy stresses "unity-in-difference," argues Tracy, Protestant dialectics emphasize a "purging fire" of negation that tends to keep polar opposites distinct.[42] It was Kennedy's particular genius to fabricate a political persona where many apparent polarities – worldliness and spirituality, political maneuvering and patriotic freedom, the shadow of corruption and the altruism of sacrifice – appeared to enter productively into conversation with one another, to be mutually enhancing rather than contradictory. One of the reasons many observers were wary of Kennedy, then as now, was because he seemed relaxed about where the boundaries between light and darkness might lie, and indeed willing to entertain the prospect of the two being relatively loosely intertwined with each other. The Puritan mind-set has never been comfortable with such purgatorial conceptions of mixed morality, and in this sense a subliminal anti-Catholicism, the translation of explicit religious prejudice into its more amorphous secular equivalents, has arguably been a more significant and enduring aspect of Kennedy's cultural legacy than the more overt hostility of Blanshard and other Protestant leaders in his own lifetime. To some extent, religious differences have now become less of an issue in American politics: few today would take the trouble theologically to scrutinize the Catholic principles of John Kerry or Joe Biden, Obama's secretary of state and vice president, respectively, and discussion of Mitt Romney's Mormonism was conspicuously absent from all but the fringes during the 2012 election. But the Catholic provenance of Kennedy's public emergence was a flamboyant affair, not only because of the spectacular visibility of his own large family but because he served as president during an era when the relationship between ancestral Protestantism and a more demotic Catholicism was coming to seem crucial to the future definition of the American republic.

NOTES

1 Isaac Kramnick and R. Laurence Moore, *The Godless Constitution: The Case against Religious Correctness* (New York: Norton, 1996).
2 Lawrence H. Fuchs, *John F. Kennedy and American Catholicism* (New York: Meredith Press, 1967), 67.
3 Lord Longford, *Kennedy* (London: Weidenfeld and Nicolson, 1976), 12.
4 Ibid., 80, 153.
5 Patrick W. Carey, *Catholics in America: A History* (Westport, CT: Praeger, 2004), 93.
6 Fuchs, *John F. Kennedy*, vii.
7 See Matthew Frye Jacobson, *Whiteness of a Different Color: European Immigrants and the Alchemy of Race* (Cambridge, MA: Harvard University Press, 1998), 55.
8 Robert Dallek, *John F. Kennedy: An Unfinished Life* (London: Allen Lane, 2003), 162.
9 Peter Viereck, *Shame and Glory of the Intellectuals: Babbitt Jr. vs. the Rediscovery of Values* (Boston: Beacon Press, 1953), 45; Thomas Carty, "The Catholic Question: The 1960 Democratic Presidential Nomination," *Historian* 63, no. 3 (2001): 582.
10 Dallek, *John F. Kennedy*, 178.
11 Will Herberg, *Protestant-Catholic-Jew: An Essay in American Religious Sociology*, rev. ed. (New York: Anchor-Doubleday, 1960), 260.
12 Jerry Bergman, "Religion and the Presidency of Dwight D. Eisenhower," in *Religion and the American Presidency: George Washington to George W. Bush, with Commentary and Primary Sources*, ed. Gaston Espinosa (New York: Columbia University Press, 2009), 267, 262.
13 James S. Wolfe, "The Religion of and about John F. Kennedy," in *John F. Kennedy: The Promise Revived*, ed. Paul Harper and Joann P. Krieg (New York: Greenwood Press, 1988), 288.
14 Thomas J. Carty, "Religion and the Presidency of John F. Kennedy," in *Religion and the American Presidency: George Washington to George W. Bush, with Commentary and Primary Sources*, ed. Gaston Espinosa (New York: Columbia University Press, 2009), 300.
15 Paul Blanshard, *American Freedom and Catholic Power* (Boston: Beacon Press, 1949), 5–6.
16 Mark S. Massa, SJ, *Anti-Catholicism in America: The Last Acceptable Prejudice* (New York: Crossroad, 2003), 69, 59, 77.
17 Carty, "Religion and the Presidency of John F. Kennedy," 314, 316.
18 Fuchs, *John F. Kennedy*, 185.
19 Thomas A. Tweed, *America's Church: The National Shrine and Catholic Presence in the Nation's Capital* (New York: Oxford University Press, 2011), 188–89.
20 Robert D. Cross, *The Emergence of Liberal Catholicism in America* (Cambridge, MA: Harvard University Press, 1958), 221, 207.
21 John Courtney Murray, SJ, "Contemporary Orientations of Catholic Thought on Church and State in the Light of History," *Theological Studies* 10 (June 1949): 210, 223.

22 "City of God and Man," *Time*, December 12, 1960, 64, 70. In preparing his presentation to the Greater Houston Ministerial Association, Kennedy was also assisted by John Cogley, former editor of the Catholic magazine *Commonweal*. See Dallek, *John F. Kennedy*, 283.

23 Carey, *Catholics in America*, 113.

24 William L. Vance, *America's Rome: Volume 2, Catholic and Contemporary Rome* (New Haven, CT: Yale University Press, 1989), 57; Wolfe, "The Religion of and about John F. Kennedy," 291.

25 Robert McAfee Brown, "Senator Kennedy's Statement," *Christianity and Crisis* 9 (March 1959): 25; Carty, "The Catholic Question," 583.

26 Fuchs, *John F. Kennedy*, 208.

27 Thomas J. Carty, *A Catholic in the White House?: Religion, Politics, and John F. Kennedy's Presidential Campaign* (New York: Palgrave Macmillan, 2004), 1, 150; Carty, "The Catholic Question," 592–93.

28 Carty, "Religion and the Presidency of John F. Kennedy," 294.

29 Patrick Allitt, *Catholic Intellectuals and Conservative Politics in America, 1950–1985* (Ithaca, NY: Cornell University Press, 1993), 88.

30 Theodore C. Sorensen, *Kennedy* (New York: Harper and Row, 1965), 236; Fuchs, *John F. Kennedy*, 184.

31 Carty, *A Catholic in the White House?*, 159.

32 Dallek, *John F. Kennedy*, 492.

33 Garry Wills, "Dr. King's Logic," *National Catholic Reporter*, August 4, 1965, 8.

34 Dallek, *John F. Kennedy*, 512.

35 Fuchs, *John F. Kennedy*, 250.

36 Dallek, *John F. Kennedy*, 604.

37 Michael Novak, *Choosing Our King: Powerful Symbols in Presidential Politics* (New York: Macmillan, 1974), 141, 71.

38 William V. Shannon, *The American Irish* (New York: Macmillan, 1963), 402–3.

39 Jay P. Dolan, *The American Catholic Experience: A History from Colonial Times to the Present* (Garden City, NY: Doubleday, 1985), 422.

40 Robert O. Orsi, "Mildred, Is It Fun to Be a Cripple?: The Culture of Suffering in Mid-Twentieth-Century American Catholicism," *South Atlantic Quarterly* 93, no. 3 (Summer 1994): 575.

41 Dallek, *John F. Kennedy*, 178.

42 David Tracy, *The Analogical Imagination: Christian Theology and the Culture of Pluralism* (New York: Crossroad, 1981), 414, 417.

3

MARY ANN WATSON

The Kennedy-Nixon Debates: The Launch of Television's Transformation of U.S. Politics and Popular Culture

Although Senator John F. Kennedy lost his bid to be the vice presidential nominee on the Democratic ticket in 1956, his consolation prize was far more valuable. He delivered the convention speech nominating Adlai Stevenson as the presidential candidate. Kennedy, the winsome war hero, quickly learned the value of prominent TV exposure. The young senator from Massachusetts was soon the most sought-after speaker in the Democratic Party and clearly a strong contender for the top spot in 1960. Kennedy's reelection to the Senate in 1958 was a romp. The 1957 Pulitzer Prize for his book *Profiles in Courage* raised Kennedy's stature as an intellectual and made him an extremely attractive guest on network public affairs programs. He understood that the medium was his ally.

No one else on the national political scene was more aware of the benefits in catering to the needs of TV or the danger in underestimating the magnitude of its impact. Kennedy expressed this sophisticated thinking in an article he wrote for the November 14, 1959, issue of *TV Guide*, "A Force That Has Changed the Political Scene." Kennedy's understanding of American history also allowed him to contemplate with astonishing accuracy the future of politics in the Television Age – especially key issues in the presidential campaign of the following year. Television image, he argued, in not simply a counterfeit measure of a candidate's capacity to govern and lead. Rather, it is a substantive factor. "Honesty, vigor, compassion, intelligence – the presence or lack of these and other qualities make up what is called the candidate's 'image,'" he wrote. "My own conviction is that these images or impressions are likely to be uncannily correct."[1]

As the 1960 primary season unfolded, Kennedy's Catholicism held the promise of trouble. Against the advice of many seasoned politicians, the candidate decided to confront religious prejudice straightaway, instead of sidestepping it. For almost two weeks before the West Virginia primary election, Kennedy boldly referred to his faith in personal appearances. "Nobody asked me if I was Catholic when I joined the United States Navy," he said.

"And nobody asked my brother if he was Catholic or Protestant before he climbed into an American bomber plane to fly his last mission."[2] The Sunday before the voting, the Kennedy campaign purchased thirty minutes of television time to feature a discussion program with Franklin Roosevelt Jr. asking the questions. Within the first few minutes of the program, as planned, Roosevelt raised the question of religion. Kennedy did not direct his answer to Roosevelt. He looked directly into the lens of the camera – into the eyes of the voters – as he delivered an impassioned statement of principle on the separation of church and state.

Kennedy's polished use of television in West Virginia was enhanced by his opponent's naïveté. The night before the primary election Humphrey participated in an ill-advised telethon. Failing to understand the importance of controlling all the factors of a telecast over which one has control, the Humphrey campaign devised a program of true spontaneity, not one that simply gave the illusion of spontaneity. The Humphrey broadcast was a fiasco. The Minnesota senator sat at a desk with a telephone and answered unscreened questions coming in over two phone lines. Viewers insulted him, asked long questions, taking circuitous routes to get to their points, and during one call the operator broke in demanding that the line be cleared for a medical emergency. The Kennedy forces were already too sophisticated about television to make such an elementary mistake. Kennedy later joked that had he known about the acceptance of unscreened calls he would have had his brother Bobby phone in a question or two for Humphrey. The presidential campaign trail in 1960 was no place for someone who had not yet learned to manage television to his advantage.

John Kennedy accepted his first-ballot nomination as the Democratic presidential candidate in front of 60,000 people in the Los Angeles Coliseum. Box seats around the podium sold for ten dollars each. Shortly before Kennedy was scheduled to speak, campaign manager Robert Kennedy was disturbed that many of the reserved seats were unoccupied. "He had them opened up to the public," Walter Cronkite reported during CBS's convention coverage, "so those stands would be filled and the television picture would be a little more impressive."[3] The more important audience was the 35 million viewers at home. In his *TV Guide* article, Kennedy had pointed out that the persuasive reach of television could reduce the need for the kind of "hard travel" that exhausted Woodrow Wilson in his cross-country tour to plead the cause of the League of Nations.[4] As a presidential candidate during the general election, Kennedy concentrated personal appearances in swing states. His team was fully aware of the dividends of local and national TV coverage. His Republican opponent, Richard Nixon, on the other hand, was an old-fashioned campaigner who pledged to visit all fifty states.

As a candidate, and later as president, Kennedy shunned silly hats and kissing babies. Looking presidential mattered. He also jettisoned conventional wisdom about the rhetoric of campaign stumping. Kennedy didn't make homespun references to the town he was in or pretend to be interested in the winning season of a local sports team. He greeted audiences with hand waves that were tentative, rarely above shoulder height. Kennedy held back; he didn't give himself to a crowd. He maintained control even when passionate. On television, a medium that magnifies personalities and mannerisms, Kennedy's reserve translated into a dignified, statesmanlike persona. Conversely, Nixon was always well briefed on local color, particularly football scores, and used this information to structure applause points into his speeches. Nixon's movements were broad; his hand waves were vigorous and exaggerated. His facial expressions verged on mugging. Nixon's style was geared to live audiences and intended to rouse a crowd, but on television, the candidate looked almost cartoonish compared with Kennedy's composure.

Throughout the 1960 presidential campaign, Kennedy displayed far greater astuteness about the process of television production than his opponent did. The most critical example of his attention to detail emerged in the first of the four televised Great Debates. What transpired in the studio of WBBM, Chicago's CBS affiliate station, on the evening of September 26, 1960, has entered American folklore. Conventional wisdom holds that Kennedy's more attractive image was the turning point in his razor-thin margin of victory over Richard Nixon. Sometimes folktales carry truth and conventional wisdom is right on the money.

President Eisenhower, as did other Republicans, advised his vice president not to participate in the prime-time joint appearances with the young senator. Many believed the telecasts would elevate Kennedy's limited experience in leadership by conveying the image of two equally qualified candidates, despite Nixon's fuller résumé. But Nixon had prided himself on being a champion debater at Whittier College. The prospect of looking as if he were chickening out of a fair fight was unacceptable. "Had I refused the challenge," he wrote in his first memoir, *Six Crises*, "I would have opened myself to the charge that I was afraid to defend the Administration's and my own record."[5]

In reality, the format of the broadcasts had little resemblance to classic debate. In precise terms, they weren't debates at all; they were closer to side-by-side news conferences or panel show appearances. Nevertheless, the coverage was focused on the idea that there would be a winner and a loser. Nixon planned on winning the old-fashioned way – by being in command of the facts and figures. Kennedy was equally prepared on substance, but he planned on winning the modern way – by being in command of his television image.

The director of the telecast, CBS News producer Don Hewitt, recalled that in the days before the debate both candidates were invited to meet with him to discuss the set design and shooting patterns, to familiarize themselves with the venue. "Kennedy was very curious," he said. "He wanted to know, 'Where do I stand?' 'How long do I have to answer?' 'Will I get a warning when I've gone too far?' He really wanted to know the nuts and bolts of what we were going to do." The opponent declined the same opportunity for a technical briefing. "I never saw Nixon before they arrived in the studio that night," Hewitt remembered. "They just didn't think it was that important," the director concluded about the Republican candidate's inner circle.[6]

A number of unfortunate factors converged for Richard Nixon that night. He had not completely recovered from a staph infection that required a lengthy hospitalization and large doses of antibiotics. His media adviser, Ted Rogers, explained: "No TV camera, no makeup man can hide bone-weariness, physical fatigue. He was actually sick. He had a fever." He had also lost weight, which caused his shirt collar to sag. He chose a bland light-gray suit that blended into the gray backdrop. Kennedy, on the other hand, looked crisp and sharp in a dark suit against the neutral backdrop. Both candidates were offered professional makeup services by the network. Kennedy needed no complexion enhancement and declined. Nixon did, but he was concerned about possible reports that he used makeup and Kennedy didn't. So, he too declined and was touched up questionably by a member of his staff. Moments before air, Robert Kennedy was looking at the image of the candidates on the monitor. He was surprised at Nixon's peaked appearance. When Nixon spotted him checking the screen, he asked what the younger Kennedy thought. "Dick," he said, "you look great."[7] As the debate commenced, Hewitt exercised his prerogative to cut to reaction shots of the nonspeaking candidate whenever he chose. Nixon's visible perspiration and occasional wiping of his brow moved Ted Rogers to ask, unsuccessfully, for no reaction shots at all. Rogers later accused Hewitt of maliciously selecting shots to make Nixon look bad, as if he were sweating out how he might reply. Kennedy had been coached to remain impassive when not speaking, to look as though Nixon's remarks were of no concern because they could be easily rebutted.

Whether or not Nixon and Kennedy were substantively peers that evening hardly mattered. In the image horserace, the Democrat outdistanced the Republican by furlongs. In the jargon of pollsters, Kennedy created a "victory psychology" and Nixon precipitated a decline in his "enthusiasm quotient."

The majority of national news coverage in the days following focused on the impact of the appearance and technique of the candidates rather than a flowchart of issues. The black press, however, did look beyond stylistics and pointed out the irrationality of having a debate focused on domestic affairs that ignored civil rights. The *Pittsburgh Courier* noted: "Both candidates are apparently riding 'high and dry' over issues most important to the Negro voter. All discussions on the rights of minorities were conspicuously omitted from the 'great debate.' "[8]

The image gulf between the two men was not as wide in the following three debates. More sleep, more calories, and more carefully applied makeup softened the vice president's appearance. But he still showed little interest in the mechanics of the medium. ABC News produced the final two debates and offered each candidate full use of studio facilities for rehearsal in the day and a half before the programs. Kennedy rehearsed more than seven hours before each of the final broadcasts. The Kennedy team also engaged the services of Fred Coe, the renowned theater and television producer, to supervise the ABC rehearsals. Nixon declined the network's offer, arriving at the TV studio twenty-four minutes before the third debate and nine minutes before airtime for the fourth.

The significance of television in the outcome of the election became the subject of widespread speculation in the mass media and in academic inquiries. One senior citizen told an interviewer conducting research on the election for the University of Michigan that she didn't vote for Nixon because "I didn't like the look in his eyes – especially the left one."[9] In September 1961, the *New York Times* reported results of a survey conducted by Professor Elihu Katz of the University of Chicago and Jacob J. Feldman of the National Opinion Research Center. The men analyzed twenty-two research studies on the subject and presented their findings at the annual meeting of the American Sociological Association. They concluded, as did Kennedy himself, that television was indeed the edge in his narrow margin of victory and that the first debate was the most critical TV appearance.[10] An alliance had been formed, a symbiotic bond between the future thirty-fifth president of the United States and the evolving medium. The resulting transformation of American governance began immediately. Five days after he took the oath of office, Kennedy conducted the first live televised press conference. The idea was presented to the president-elect by his press secretary, Pierre Salinger. "Why don't you open up your press conferences to live television?" he recalled asking. "I don't think there's any doubt you can handle it. You proved that against Nixon in the debates."[11]

Kennedy considered the disadvantages of the forum before agreeing. He knew that overexposure on the airwaves could result in diminished citizen interest. He also understood that vexing print journalists – the Gutenberg Boys, as they were called – by appearing to favor television could lead to problems. Kennedy did not, however, accept the arguments made by sincere critics, some on his own staff, who believed that off-the-cuff government was hazardous. The thinking was that a slip of the presidential tongue could easily embarrass the United States or its allies. "The stakes are too high," believed David Lawrence, chief editor of *U.S. News and World Report*.[12] But Kennedy was sure enough of his own rhetorical and intellectual capabilities to take the uncushioned chance. A New York TV consultant, Bill Wilson, was brought in by the White House to work on the staging at the spacious State Department auditorium, where the sessions would take place. More than four hundred reporters attended JFK's press conference debut. One of them, CBS correspondent Robert Pierpoint, recalled, "The President stood on stage, which gave him a psychological advantage, much like a judge seated above the rest of the courtroom."[13]

The thirty-fifth chief executive knew he could mobilize public opinion by speaking one-on-one to American citizens. CBS correspondent George Herman recalled how skillfully Kennedy accomplished this in the press conference of March 23, 1961. Before the questions, the president delivered a prepared statement on the advance of communist-backed rebels in Laos. "He didn't look at any reporter in the auditorium," Herman said. "He was not trying to give the appearance of a news conference; he wasn't looking around the room. He looked right over our heads, right into the camera with the red tally light on it, the one he knew was on. It was clear to me at the time that this was a man who was extraordinarily professional and that this was something carefully planned. This was to go directly to the people."[14] Kennedy's spontaneous humor, his grace under pressure, and his capacity to retain information were undeniably impressive. So too was his willingness to forgo a politician's instinct to elaborate, sometimes answering a question with a single word: "no."

The president was able to review the first few conferences because a local station in Washington carried them on a delayed basis. Press Secretary Pierre Salinger remembered that Kennedy was concerned about his appearance and the lighting. "That's why we brought Schaffner down. To take a look at our setup."[15] Salinger was referring to famed TV and film director Franklin Schaffner, who had worked on many prestigious television series, such as *Studio One* and *Playhouse 90*.

Live press conferences altered one of the primary functions of newspaper reporters, which was to offer a summary of what transpired in the questioning of the president. Kennedy likened the process of preparing for his press conferences to cramming for a final exam every two weeks, but he wanted to keep open the channel that allowed his message to be delivered unadulterated. Because of his frequent press conferences, the president was cautiously selective about other television appearances. He understood the mystique of leadership could not survive unsparing entry. He asked the networks for airtime only when he believed it was critical. The president spoke to the country after his 1961 summit with first secretary of the Communist Party of the Soviet Union, Nikita Khrushchev, in Vienna, during the Cuban Missile Crisis in October 1962, and to offer his civil rights "manifesto" in June 1963.

The Kennedy administration courted television with a perceptible favoritism. Robert Pierpoint wrote: "Pierre Salinger started deferring to the networks. He was quicker to answer television correspondents' calls, more accessible to us in his private office, and began a relationship of daily phone conversations and periodic meetings with network Washington bureau chiefs."[16] Some print journalists complained to Salinger that television had been given a higher priority and they had become "little more than props." "Television is here to stay," he responded. "The people are getting a closer view of their president and the presidency than they've ever had – and that's just what we wanted."[17]

Yet, the president kept the upper hand in the relationship by playing hard to get. He was available for TV interviews only when he needed or wanted to reach the public. Otherwise, the numerous requests were turned down. But, in December 1962, Kennedy thought the time might be perfect for the TV interview the networks were clamoring for. His mettle had been tested and proven superior during the Cuban Missile Crisis. The president was at the top of his game and ready to talk about it. Each network had individually requested a televised discussion with the commander in chief at year's end. Pierre Salinger surprised the news divisions when he called them to Washington on December 11 to propose a joint interview. He offered the president for a sixty-minute program, with one newsman from each network asking questions. It would be less formal than a press conference. But absolutely mandatory to the plan was this provision: ninety minutes would be taped and thirty minutes would be edited out of the conversation. This way, Salinger explained, slow sections or less interesting comments could be deleted and a better program would result. The editing decisions would be made by a committee composed of one representative of each of the three networks. The White House would not interfere. The interview took place in the Oval Office on December 16 with correspondents Bill Lawrence of ABC, George Herman of CBS, and Sander Vanocur of NBC. The president sat in his rocking chair, and the three men sat just a few feet away in a cozy cluster. After about fifty minutes, Kennedy suggested they all take a coffee break. Then they continued to talk for another half hour. The program was officially titled *After Two Years: A Conversation with the President*, but the press dubbed it "The Rocking Chair Chat." It aired on all three networks the day after it was recorded.

Every broadcast in which he participated enhanced the image of John Kennedy. But reporter Mary McGrory believed this telecast was the "most effective appearance of his entire presidency . . . It was perfectly delightful."[18] Kennedy displayed a range of admirable qualities. He was clever and funny. He was contemplative and charming. He would occasionally interrupt himself and change course in midsentence. He was, viewers had to conclude, the genuine article. The president's graceful command of the English language was the most impressive of traits as he looked back at the first half of his term. In referring to the Bay of Pigs, or as he called it "the Cuber of 1961," he said, "Success has a hundred fathers and defeat is an orphan." In a candid stroke of self-assessment, he claimed, "Appearances contribute to reality."

What viewers couldn't see was the amount of control Kennedy exercised over the situation. George Herman recalled one of the questions he asked that was deleted from the broadcast. He reminded Kennedy that presidential scholar Richard Neustadt had written, "Any president who hopes to be considered great by future historians must be widely accused of subverting the Constitution in his own time." "If that's true," Herman posed, "what have you been subverting lately?" It was a tough, witty question. "Well, he gave me," the newsman remembered, "I think, the coldest stare I'd had from anybody. He really sort of looked at me from my head down to my feet and back up again with a look that sort of put icicles on me. And I thought to myself, 'What did I say? What did I do?' And then he said, 'No, I don't believe that's true.' And then he changed the subject completely." Only after George Herman was out of the circumstance could he fully understand the president's strategy and the insistence of the White House that more material be taped than used. Herman realized, "Every time we asked an unfriendly question, he gave the most magnificently dull answer that I have ever heard in my life with the certain knowledge that we were going to have to cut out one-third of the material . . . All his dull answers to these unfriendly questions were almost certain to be dropped. It was a fascinating performance of skill."[19]

In the Kennedy years, gaining as much control as possible over image and message became a presidential imperative. The staffs of previous presidents engaged in news management, but the ante was raised dramatically in the 1960s as the American public came to rely on television as its primary news source. The medium, with bounding technical advancements, altered the conduct of the presidency stylistically as well as structurally. By the time Lyndon Johnson took the oath of office as the thirty-sixth president of the United States, the forcefulness of television in the formation of public opinion had become the foundation of all presidential communication strategies.

During the 1950s, the broadcast industry had grown comfortable in the expectation of nothing more than moderate regulation from the federal government. The Federal Communications Commission grappled with technical issues but was little involved with programming responsibilities. John Kennedy's appointment of Newton Minow to be chairman of the FCC was disappointing to broadcast executives who believed TV had been good to JFK in the 1960 campaign and, perhaps, a reward was in order. Instead, Minow, a young activist, believed that the FCC had a role in encouraging better programs and was determined to do something about it.

In his first address to the National Association of Broadcasters on May 9, 1961, Chairman Minow invited those in his audience to watch their own TV stations for one full day. "I will assure you," he warned, "that you will observe a vast wasteland." Minow's promise of stiffening enforcement of license renewal procedures and increased scrutiny of network operations "left his broadcaster audience stunned and indignant," according to *Broadcasting*, the major trade journal of the industry.[20] The raised eyebrow of government was becoming the flexed muscle.

The chairman's image as the protector of the public interest aggravated those he regulated, but he was a supremely popular New Frontiersman. By the end of his first year on the job, he made more appearances on radio and TV than any other member of the Kennedy administration did, except the president himself. Minow was a media darling long before the term was used. Those he regulated did not love him, but his demands could not be ignored. So, at the same time industry leaders were attempting to show the FCC's new ardor concerning program content was wrong – in fact, unconstitutional – television programmers adjusted content to meet new expectations. Attempts at appeasement to ward off government regulation were conspicuous. During Minow's tenure there was a lessening of prime-time violence. Action-adventure series were being replaced with character dramas, which, particularly in the 1963–64 season, evolved into a forum for the examination of issues of social justice. Prime-time series featured lawyers, doctors, teachers, and social workers who seemed to be asking, "What can *I* do for my country?" There was also a marked improvement in the quality of children's programming and the number of blue-ribbon news and documentary programs spiked.

The special TV event that served as a barometer of the public's fascination with its young, beautiful first lady was broadcast on Valentine's Day 1962.

A Tour of the White House with Mrs. John F. Kennedy – or "The Jackie Show" as it was called – was seen by three out of every four Americans.

Mrs. Kennedy's one-year project to make the White House a living symbol reflecting the presidency of the United States was drawing to a close and she was justifiably proud of what she had accomplished. In *The Powers That Be*, author David Halberstam writes that the idea of the TV tour originated with the president himself and he "easily talked CBS into doing a show with Jackie at the White House."[21] Public anticipation about the event was great. It was not the story of the president's house that compelled viewers, of course. It was the possibility that his regally inward wife would reveal something more about herself during the hour in which she willingly took her place on America's center stage. The cover of *TV Guide* the week of the broadcast featured a close-up shot of Jacqueline Kennedy with slightly tousled hair and direct gaze. The casually posed photo suggested the TV tour would be a more candid affair, however, than it turned out to be.

Viewers saw an inhibited Jacqueline Kennedy and a somewhat fawning correspondent, Charles Collingwood of CBS, walk through a panoply of treasured historical artifacts. To any objective observer, the first lady's awkwardness was palpable. The 1962 audience overlooked the program's shortcomings, however. Most viewers were just as smitten as the *Chicago Daily News* critic who wrote with hyperbole, "Here was an example of television at its best."[22] The day after the broadcast, Newton Minow received a highly unusual personal call from President Kennedy. "I want to know what the rating was on that program. Can you find out?" Minow dutifully called Frank Stanton, the president of CBS, and asked uncomfortably for the ratings on *A Tour of the White House with Mrs. John F. Kennedy*. "Who wants to know? Stanton wondered, "The ratings aren't in yet – it was only yesterday." "Let's not get into that," the FCC chairman said. "When will you get it?" Stanton promised to get him the information as soon as it was available, a few days at least. When the numbers arrived, Minow forwarded the favorable figures to the Oval Office and made a follow-up call to the president. "It's on its way over there," he said. "You'll be interested to know it's higher than your press conference."[23] The TV tour was an international event, as well. The first lady recorded a brief introduction to the program in French and Spanish for foreign distribution. The overseas reviews were as glowing as those domestic.

Not everyone was enchanted with the first lady's performance, though. The July 1962 issue of *Esquire* carried a piece by Norman Mailer entitled "An Evening with Jackie Kennedy." He was not afflicted with the generous blind spots of other critics. Rather, he displayed a savage insight that Mrs. Kennedy would find hard to forgive. "Do you remember the girl with the magnificent sweater who used to give weather reports on television in that swarmy [*sic*] singsong tone?" Mailer asked his readers in describing the first lady's "public voice." He had heard better voices "selling gadgets to the grim" in Macy's at Christmastime than "the manufactured voice Jackie Kennedy chose to arrive at." She walked through the tour, according to Mailer, "like a starlet who is utterly without talent . . . She moved like a wooden horse." With paradoxical compassion, the author concluded that Jacqueline Kennedy was a "royal phony." "She was trying, I suppose, to be a proper first lady and it was her mistake."[24]

Mailer's critique might have been the most accurate of all, but, nonetheless, "The Jackie Show" permeated popular culture. For example, in a November 1962 episode of the prime-time series *The Donna Reed Show*, the lead character runs for city council. Her husband, a prominent pediatrician, has a nightmare about where her political ambitions might lead. When she becomes the first female president, he, of course, gives a televised tour of the White House explaining his attempts to "preserve the historical charm." The feature film produced the following year, *Kisses for My President*, uses the same gag when the first male "first lady" also gives a similar stroll through the executive mansion.

The biggest takeoff on the TV Tour was on the phenomenally successful comedy phonograph record *The First Family*, starring Kennedy impersonator Vaughn Meader. The collection of sketches sold more than one million copies in the first two weeks of release and the troupe of performers made prominent TV appearances. The longest cut on the album is a seven-minute parody entitled "The Tour." In it, a stiff-sounding newsman walks with a breathy, apparently not-too-bright first lady. When asked to point out the various paintings on the walls, she says, "There's this one and this one, and that great big one over there and this little teeny one down here." No changes were made in the Blue Room, she mews, because "we decided to leave it just the way President Blue had it originally." The satire hit on one of the program's most vulnerable points, the somewhat unsubtle way in which Mrs. Kennedy plugged the donors of several pieces. For instance, in the real broadcast, the audience was informed that a painting of Benjamin Franklin was a "gift of Mr. and Mrs. Walter Annenberg of Philadelphia" and a portrait of Alexander Hamilton was a "gift of Mr. and Mrs. Henry Ford of Grosse Pointe, Michigan." On the album, the newsman notices a good deal of dust on the furniture in the Grant Drawing Room. "Yes." The first lady sighs. "And that dust was a gift from Mrs. B. P. Landon of Wilkes-Barre, Pennsylvania." The studio audience is convulsed with laughter. Mrs. Kennedy's personal secretary, Mary Barelli Gallagher, recalled, "It infuriated her to hear or even see the Vaughn Meader record ... There are very few things that got Jackie as excited as the subject of Vaughn Meader."[25]

The president, though, understood the advantage in being a good sport. At his press conference of December 12, 1962, he was asked about the "heavy barrage of teasing and fun-poking" and whether it produced "annoyment [sic] or enjoyment?" "Annoyment? No," Kennedy responded. And then, going for the laugh himself, the president said, "Actually, I've listened to Mr. Meader's record, but I thought it sounded more like Teddy than it did me – so now he's annoyed."[26]

There was no escaping the Kennedy influence on popular culture – rocking chairs, fifty-mile hikes, touch football, pillbox hats, and Boston accents were all the rage. The mass marketing of Kennedy-inspired amusements such as coloring books, paper dolls, and photo albums were inevitable. No matter how dyspeptic the regulatory policies of the New Frontier might have left network executives, they didn't shy away from indulging the American public's obvious enjoyment of the president and his myriad relatives.

Prime-time series were replete with references to the first family. In an episode of *Car 54, Where Are You?* titled "Hail to the Chief," officers Gunther Toody and Francis Muldoon are chosen to be President Kennedy's drivers during a brief presidential visit to New York. Muldoon is so overcome by the responsibility that he faints every time he hears the president's name. The tranquilizers he's given to steady his nerves put him to sleep, and the stimulants taken to counteract the tranquilizers make him giddy. Of course, the assignment gets bungled. The Secret Service man in charge of the motorcade ends up a nervous wreck. He's told he'll be put on light duty while he recuperates – "Like watching Caroline's pony for a few weeks." Elsewhere on the dial, the housekeeper lead character of *Hazel* tells her boss that Abraham Lincoln was "way ahead of his time." The sixteenth president, she says, "had a rockin' chair in the White House a hundred years ago." Standing in front of 1600 Pennsylvania Avenue while on a vacation in the nation's capital, the Mitchell family of *Dennis the Menace* contemplates how similar they are to the occupants of the mansion, in particular Dennis to Caroline. And on *Leave It to Beaver*, when Beaver Cleaver plans on going away to boarding school, father Ward likens his feelings to "the way Joe Kennedy must have felt when he sent his first son to Washington."

On variety programs, meanwhile, political nepotism became a well-worn gag prompted by Robert Kennedy's appointment as attorney general and Edward Kennedy's entrance into the race for the U.S. Senate in 1962. Comedian Red Skelton, for example, recalled on his show the days when politicians promised a chicken in every pot, but the new slogan from the White House was "A Kennedy in every office." Continuing in the same vein,

Skelton told of the president's conference with his father, Joe, the former ambassador to Great Britain, to complain about his kid brothers – "Teddy and Bobby are playing with my country!"

Despite the quantity of Kennedy material, the parodies and jokes were not stinging but rather the humor of endearment. The climate was beginning to change, though, as the entertainment value of politics was becoming a larger part of the mix. In November 1963, NBC aired a special preview of a show that was scheduled to debut in January 1964. The series *That Was the Week That Was*, based on a British program, took potshots at people with power. The series only lasted until 1965, but it was an incubator for more cynical topical musings on TV and the barbed satire that all of Kennedy's successors would endure.

The New Frontier is a time set apart in our national memory. Television as a bond of common culture reached its acme of cohesion during the early 1960s. The news and entertainment of the three networks permeated public perceptions and defined the popular American identity. The Kennedy years were bookended with TV milestones. In the years between the Great Debates and the TV coverage of the president's assassination and funeral, the medium had become central to life in the United States. John F. Kennedy's campaign for the presidency, his administration, and his death constitute a discrete chapter of modern history – one in which American politics and society had been transformed.

NOTES

1 John F. Kennedy, "A Force That Has Changed the Political Scene," *TV Guide* 7, no. 46 (November 1959): 6–7.
2 Robert V. Friedenberg, *Notable Speeches in Contemporary Presidential Campaigns* (Westport, CT: Praeger Publishers, 2002), 49.
3 Walter Cronkite commentary during CBS News coverage of John F. Kennedy acceptance speech, July 15, 1960, Democratic National Convention, Los Angeles Coliseum, viewed at the John F. Kennedy Presidential Library and Museum.
4 Kennedy, "A Force That Has Changed the Political Scene," 7.
5 Richard M. Nixon, *Six Crises* (New York: Touchstone, 1990), 323.
6 Don Hewitt, quoted in Jeff Kisseloff, *The Box: An Oral History of Television, 1920–1961* (New York: Viking, 1995), 239.
7 David Halberstam, *The Unfinished Odyssey of Robert Kennedy* (New York: Bantam Books, 1969), 183–84.
8 Alice A. Dunnigan, "Washington Inside Out" *(Pittsburgh) Courier*, October, 8, 1960, 6.
9 Angus Campbell, "Has Television Reshaped Politics?" *Columbia Journalism Review*, vol. 1, no. 3 (Fall 1962): 12.
10 Donald Janson, "Kennedy Determined Debates' Winner," *New York Times*, September 3, 1961, 40.

11 Pierre Salinger, quoted in Harry Sharp Jr., "Live from Washington: The Telecasting of President Kennedy's News Conferences," *Journal of Broadcasting* 13, no. 1 (Winter 1968–69): 24.

12 David Lawrence quoted in "The President on TV," *Television Magazine*, May 1961, 48.

13 Robert Pierpoint Papers, notes from his book *At the White House: Assignment to Six Presidents* (New York: Putnam, 1981), box 5, folder 4, State Historical Society of Wisconsin.

14 George Herman, "Press Panel Oral History Interview with White House Correspondents: George Herman, Peter Lisagor, and Mary McGrory JFK #1 8/4/1964," 53. John F. Kennedy Oral History Collection, JFKOH-PRP-01, John F. Kennedy Library and Museum.

15 Pierre Salinger interview with author in Toronto, October 16, 1988.

16 Pierpoint, *At the White House*, 156.

17 "Plucky," *Newsweek* 57, no. 18 (May 1, 1961): 63.

18 Mary McGrory, "Press Panel Oral History Interview with White House Correspondents: George Herman, Peter Lisagor, and Mary McGrory JFK #1 8/4/1964," 63. John F. Kennedy Oral History Collection, JFKOH-PRP-01, John F. Kennedy Library and Museum.

19 Herman, "Press Panel Oral History," 65.

20 "Black Tuesday at the NAB Convention," *Broadcasting*, May 15, 1961.

21 David Halberstam, *The Powers That Be* (New York: Knopf, 1975), 387.

22 Mary Ann Watson, "A Tour of the White House: Mystique and Tradition," *Presidential Studies Quarterly* 18, no. 1 (Winter 1988): 95.

23 Newton N. Minow interview with author in Chicago, March 6, 1986.

24 Norman Mailer, "An Evening with Jackie Kennedy: Being an Essay in Three Acts," *Esquire* 58, no. 1 (July 1962): 57.

25 Mary Barelli Gallagher, *My Life with Jacqueline Kennedy* (New York: Paperback Library, 1969), 177.

26 "546 – The President's News Conference," December 12, 1962, American Presidency Project, http://www.presidency.ucsb.edu/ws/index.php?pid=9054& st=meader&st1=, accessed December 7, 2014.

4

SEAN MCCANN

"Investing in Persons": The Political Culture of Kennedy Liberalism

When Neil Klugman, the protagonist of Philip Roth's *Goodbye, Columbus*, travels in pursuit of Brenda Patimkin up from working-class Newark to the village of Short Hills, New Jersey, his journey dramatizes some of the core premises of the culture of postwar liberalism. Passing beyond "the packed-in tangle of railroad crossings, switchmen shacks, lumber yards, Dairy Queens, and used-car lots"[1] that surround Newark, Neil leaves behind the industrial city and arrives in a world of miraculous abundance, where "fruit grew in . . . [the] refrigerator and sporting goods dropped from the trees."[2] At once lustfully "acquisitive" and ironically self-aware, young Neil can't help thinking himself "closer to heaven."[3]

But, of course, that impression is not to last. Roth's protagonist soon realizes the impermanence of suburban wealth. His true satisfactions, the novella suggests, will not be found in the "pursuit and clutching" that Brenda embodies, but in the duty represented by his work as a librarian serving the African American youth of Newark and his effort, in fulfilling the mission, to contest the conservatism of his bureaucratic superiors.[4] This is the particular combination that makes Neil a paradigmatic figure of the postwar liberal imagination: the keen awareness of quotidian abundance, the civic-minded disdain for mere consumerism, the struggle against restrictive bureaucracy, and the mission to bring his talents to a disenfranchised public. An ambitious young man with a college education, Neil encounters a world where even the children of working-class Jews can expect to enter a thriving middle class. But it is crucial to his self-realization that this world elicits in him a desire for values that seem deeper than "money and comfort" and that such values will be realized in a career that combines appreciation for elite cultural expression with a self-conscious mission of service to the nation's most marginalized population.[5] Roth's novella ends with Neil staring at his reflection in Harvard's Widener Library and dreaming of throwing a rock through the window – as if to free both himself and the wisdom trapped inside the library walls

59

for greater purposes. Neil Klugman is on his way to becoming a Kennedy liberal.

Indeed, in some respects, Neil appears quite similar to the contemporary man described by Arthur Schlesinger Jr. as "the archetypal new frontiersman." Looking back on the Kennedy years from the vantage of the mid-1960s, Schlesinger thought the true spirit of the Kennedy administration was best displayed by Richard Goodwin, the assistant special counsel to the president, who had first joined the Kennedy campaign as a junior speechwriter.[6] Like Roth's protagonist, Goodwin was a second-generation heir to aspiring Jewish immigrants. Just two years older than Roth, Goodwin, too, had grown up in a working-class family during the Depression and had found a path to success through his accomplishments in school. Having graduated from Tufts University summa cum laude, Goodwin attended Harvard Law on scholarship, graduating first in his class and going on to clerk for Felix Frankfurter at the Supreme Court. (Goodwin later described Harvard as "one of the great agents of upward mobility in this country."[7]) His accomplishments brought the young man to the attention of then senator John F. Kennedy, who a few years later would recruit Goodwin to his presidential campaign and then to his administration. There Goodwin would play a role in shaping Kennedy's Latin American policy and his developing ideas about federal support for the arts. Following Kennedy's assassination, Goodwin would go on to join Lyndon Johnson's White House as chief speechwriter, where he would play a part in influencing Johnson's commitment to civil rights and his declaration of a War on Poverty. It was Goodwin who coined Johnson's phrase "Great Society" and who helped lead Johnson's investment in "community action," the most celebrated and ultimately most controversial aspect of the War on Poverty.

For Schlesinger, Goodwin's very ability to leap from one arena to the next in the effort to craft programs that would serve the public good was the quality that most defined him as an exemplary figure of Kennedy liberalism. "A man of uncommon intelligence," Goodwin was, in Schlesinger's account, one of the elite few who conducted "the currents of vitality [that] radiated out of the White House . . . and created a vast sense of possibility" throughout the nation.[8] In particular, Schlesinger emphasized, Goodwin was not a party politician or a bureaucrat. He was rather a "supreme generalist" whose rare intellectual gifts enabled him to "resist specialization."[9]

Goodwin agreed. Indeed, by his account, the struggle against the deadening grip of bureaucracy was the key theme of JFK's presidency. Praising what he invoked as "New Frontier heroics," Goodwin declared that he and his peers in the Kennedy administration were members of a "democratic nobility" who had been inspired by Kennedy's determination to bring leadership and vision to a stolid federal government and an otherwise complacent American society.[10] It was "the role of the president," Goodwin later recalled, "to lead, morally and in action . . . to revive a flagging America and draw the nation to new heights of grandeur."[11]

That vision was widely shared by liberal intellectuals during the latter 1950s and early 1960s. Kennedy himself had long nurtured a fascination with aristocratic leadership. In the best-selling books he published before gaining the presidency – *Why England Slept* (1940), *Profiles in Courage* (1956), and *The Strategy of Peace* (1960) – he had suggested that an elite class of tribunes was needed to counter the factionalism and stasis that bedeviled democratic governments. Indeed, JFK's most renowned phrase – his call for Americans to "ask not what the country will do for you" but rather "what you can do for your country" – was adapted from a slogan of his prep school, Choate.[12] As president, Kennedy effectively cast himself as prep school master to the nation, inviting his countrymen to aspire to Choate's vision of aristocratic national service.

That language of elite service helped make a fascination with charismatic leadership common among liberal intellectuals during the Kennedy years. Indeed, JFK and his supporters cast his presidency as something of a referendum on competing theories of executive power and on the broader assumptions about social organization they reflected. Kennedy's predecessor, Dwight D. Eisenhower, had presented a carefully honed image of presidential restraint. Reacting against the legacy of executive expansion that had emerged from the New Deal and World War II, Eisenhower had portrayed himself as a manager who brought regularity, thrift, and caution to a sprawling federal government. Although decades later even some former Kennedy liberals would come to admire what they now viewed as the subtlety of Eisenhower's "hidden hand presidency," liberal intellectuals during the 1950s saw only weakness and timidity in the Eisenhower style. Over the course of the decade, they voiced increasing complaints about an absence of energy and intelligence in the White House, and they often suggested that Eisenhower's lack of charisma had leached out across the whole of a somnolent American society. As John Kenneth Galbraith famously quipped, in a remark echoed by JFK himself, the Eisenhower presidency seemed to the era's liberals a case of the "bland lead[ing] the bland."[13]

Kennedy campaigned for the White House on the promise that he would reverse these conditions and bring direction to both foreign and domestic policy. In JFK's vision, the chief executive would be a "vigorous proponent of the national interest" rather than a "passive broker for conflicting private interests." Promising to take charge of an unresponsive federal bureaucracy and to incite a dormant nation to meet "the challenging, revolutionary sixties," Kennedy encouraged his administration, and ultimately his political constituency, to think of themselves as a redemptive insurgency battling to awaken and direct a slumbering behemoth.[14] In the view of the New Frontiersmen, the president's allies amounted to an elite, irregular force whose rare talents would enable them to outwit the routines of bureaucrats and managers. In the words of Daniel Moynihan, the Kennedy men aspired to be "guerillas" who "liv[ed] off the administrative countryside, invisible to the bureaucratic enemy but known to one another."[15] Richard Goodwin was more direct. He described himself as American liberalism's Che Guevara.[16]

That vision of insurgent leadership – of the struggle of the rebel visionary against the complacent bureaucrat – resounded widely through American culture during the early 1960s. Indeed, the Kennedy administration was surrounded by a cohort of intellectuals who echoed Schlesinger in urgently pressing "the moral need for strong leadership."[17] Along with Schlesinger and Galbraith, the historian James McGregor Burns, the political scientist Richard Neustadt, the journalist Theodore White, and a host of like-minded thinkers warned that the United States needed visionary leadership to overcome the rigidity and parochialism of the political system and to challenge "a vacancy in the soul of America."[18] But even beyond the immediate circles surrounding the Kennedy White House, the theme gained purchase. More radical political thinkers like the sociologist C. Wright Mills and the political theorist Sheldon Wolin warned that the values of democracy and citizenship could be squelched by what Wolin's aptly titled *Politics and Vision* called the "megastate." Norman Mailer famously urged Kennedy to assume the mantle of existential hero to a smugly consumerist nation – to be the Superman who challenged the Supermarket and thus reunited the banal "life of politics" and the spiritually grand "life of myth."[19] The youthful political insurgencies that emerged alongside Kennedy liberalism in the early 1960s – the rising New Right associated with the Young Americans for Freedom and the effervescent New Left of the Students for a Democratic Society – spoke a quite similar language. Each attacked an ossified political system that they viewed as "a Leviathan . . . out of touch with the people, and out of their control," as the leader of the New Right, Barry Goldwater, put it his best-selling 1960 book, *The Conscience of a Conservative*.[20] Each assumed, along with the Kennedy administration, that an increasingly bureaucratic government failed to meet "the real concerns and real needs of the people." All called for a politics of "national salvation" against it.[21]

Similar attitudes echoed throughout the United States at the time. Literature and popular culture were rife with stories – Ken Kesey's *One Flew over the Cuckoo's Nest* (1962), Madeleine L'Engle's *A Wrinkle in Time* (1962), Sylvia Plath's *The Bell Jar* (1963)[22] – that painted ominous portraits of incipiently totalitarian bureaucracies breaking the spirits of the youthful and gifted. These dystopian fantasies were complemented meanwhile by the sudden appearance throughout the arts of visionary young innovators who threw off the formal restraints and tonal moderation that had been prominent in the aesthetic canons of the 1950s. The impulse was apparent in the post-Bop explorations of Ornette Coleman and Sonny Rollins, who pressed jazz beyond what their admirer Martin Williams decried as "the harmonic maze." "Someone had to break through the walls . . . and restore melody," Williams wrote.[23] It was apparent as well in the sudden popularity of folk music, whose emerging hero, Bob Dylan, urged his peers to "step out" of the restraints of both commercial pop culture and faux authenticity.[24] It was still more evident in the flourishing movement of Beat writers who sought, in Michael McLure's words, to pursue "vision" against "the chill, militaristic silence" of conventional society.[25] Not least, it was central to the work of the ludic novelists – including Joseph Heller, Thomas Pynchon, and Bruce Jay Friedman – grouped together by critics under the label "black humor." In darkly comic works like *Catch-22* and *V.*, those writers boldly jumbled and reassembled the conventions of mimetic fiction to render, and rise above, life in a bureaucratic world.

So, too, did a youthful generation of visual artists brush aside the restraint and earnest sobriety that had characterized the high art of the 1950s. The photographs in Robert Frank's incendiary collection *The Americans* (1959) elicited a wave of popular revulsion, and a smaller burst of coterie enthusiasm, not only for the grim scenes of misery and aimlessness they revealed but for their seemingly unrefined form and structure. "The pictures took us by ambush," John Szarkowski remembered, because they ignored "the rules and formulations . . . [of] good photography."[26] Similar responses greeted the post-abstract expressionist painting of Robert Rauschenberg and Jasper Johns, the pop art of Warhol and Lichtenstein, and the "happenings" of Allan Kaprow. All rudely challenged boundaries between high and low, good taste and bad taste, art and life that had been core assumptions of serious expression in the decade or so after the war. Everyone in the early 1960s art world seemed to agree with Neil Klugman on the need to smash the glass window of academic formalism.

Indeed, more often than not, the young artists of the day agreed with Kennedy in viewing the contemporary landscape as a place, in McClure's account, of bureaucratic regimentation and "spiritual drabness," and they urged a heroic response that often sounded quite similar to the project of national renovation that Kennedy liberals like Goodwin demanded. In his "Independence Day Manifesto" (1959), Allen Ginsberg lamented the fact of a "soulless America" controlled by "abstract bureaucracies" and called for an inspired "illuminati" to lead a return to a "wild and beautiful America."²⁷ Similarly, in "The Death of Emmett Till" (1962), the work sometimes said to be his breakthrough to serious songwriting, Bob Dylan addressed his contemporaries and warned those who could not speak out against racial injustice, "your mind is filled with dust / Your arms and legs they must be in shackles and chains." Against that image of spiritual bondage, Dylan invoked an uplifting alternative of national purpose to be created by dedicated leadership: "If all of us folks that thinks alike, if we gave all we could give / We could make this great land of ours a greater place to live."

James Baldwin made the theme most explicit in his novel *Another Country* (1962). At one moment in Baldwin's narrative of bohemian misery, the unhappy housewife, Cass thinks of the failure of her husband – an imitative artist who doesn't have "passion" or "any real work to do" – and comes to see him as typical of a vacuous nation. "This isn't a country at all," she laments. "It's a collection of football players and Eagle Scouts. Cowards. We think we're happy. We're not. We're doomed."²⁸ Cass's lament is implicitly answered, however, by the musings of the genuine writer, Vivaldo. Vivaldo and his friends are Baldwin's version of the kind of cultural insurgency that Kennedy liberals envisioned – a small cohort of elite rebels, alienated from a larger debased society, and bearing in themselves, as the novel's title hints, the potential to re-create a sense of national mission. To drive this point home, Vivaldo at one moment unwittingly invokes the Kennedy language of the New Frontier, along with the signal Kennedy policy of space exploration. Staring into the night sky, he muses: "The sky looked, now, like a vast and friendly ocean . . . To what country did this ocean lead? for oceans always led to some great good place: hence sailors, missionaries, saints, and Americans."²⁹

Why were such visions so prominent in the late 1950s and early 1960s? The rhetoric of elite leadership and national salvation that writers like Ginsberg and Baldwin shared with political figures like Goodwin and Schlesinger prospered during the Kennedy years in part because of the way it spoke to the expectations of a rising class of professional workers who had been educated in the new meritocratic institutions of postwar higher education. During the 1950s, the proportion of Americans between the ages of eighteen and twenty-four seeking college degrees grew by 1.3 million, from 14 to 22 percent of that segment of the national population.³⁰ The expansion of colleges and universities in which these students were educated had been justified to the public on the idea that it would create a talented new leadership class capable of advancing America's global power. (As one observer, quoting Edmund Burke, approvingly noted, the assumption was that "a great empire and little minds go ill together."³¹) The young people who flourished in the new world of mass higher education came equipped therefore with more than training that encouraged them to value sophistication and innovation. As Nicholas Lemann points out, they were also nurtured in the "original principal of the American meritocracy" – that people would be chosen for "positions of authority" not for "their suitability for specific roles but for their general worth."[32]

The postwar expansion of higher education, in other words, created a cohort of young people who had been primed to think of themselves, in the manner of Richard Goodwin, as a "democratic nobility." JFK's rhetoric, which claimed to speak on behalf of "a new generation of Americans," fit neatly with that self-understanding. Much of the cultural expression and the political energy of the day hinged, as well, on the concerns that seemed most pressing to America's rising meritocrats – whether their gifts would be acknowledged, whether their intelligence would be rewarded with power, whether, unlike Cass's husband, they would find "real work to do." Indeed, for the liberal intellectuals who surrounded the Kennedy White House, the thrill of JFK's presidency came from the conviction, in Schlesinger's words, "that intelligence was at last being applied to public affairs."[33] Even those who found JFK disappointingly conservative tended to frame the issues of the day in these terms. Recalling his own dawning radicalism in the early 1960s, the former New Left leader Todd Gitlin remembered his growing frustration with the Kennedy administration's unwillingness to hear the voices of young reformers: "Where were the signs that knowledge meant power?"[34]

Such attitudes seemed especially plausible during the Kennedy years because of the seemingly new and transformed nature of the American political economy. Since the end of World War II, the United States had experienced a remarkably extended period of robust economic growth. Over the course of the 1950s alone, the American economy had expanded by 37 percent and median family income had grown, in adjusted dollars, by 30 percent. This growth in turn sparked a boom in suburban housing and in consumer culture that was especially rewarding to the growing class of college graduates and white-collar workers.[35] In addition to fueling a widely noted sense of national promise, growth also inspired the common belief that the American economy had changed in fundamental ways, apparently leaving behind the problems of conflict, inequality, and insecurity that had previously seemed integral to capitalism.

A wide range of commentators made this argument during the 1950s, but it was most influentially framed by Kennedy adviser John Kenneth Galbraith, whose best-selling book of the same title identified the postwar United States as an "Affluent Society." In Galbraith's view, the economic boom of the postwar years indicated that the United States had entered a new stage of capitalism – one whose vast productive capacities created a world of abundance and obviated the classical economic focus on scarcity. The issues of hunger, inequality, and insecurity no longer mattered, except as relics of the unnecessary but still potent orthodoxy that Galbraith memorably dubbed "the conventional wisdom."[36] Instead, a new set of problems confronted contemporary Americans. Inspired by a need for constant growth in productivity, and no longer urged on by want, businessmen responded by inventing new consumer desires, which were "synthesized, elaborated, and nurtured by advertising and salesmanship."[37] Americans thus allowed their new wealth to be diverted into a bounty of unnecessary and ugly consumer products, even as the "public goods" of education, health, and common safety were allowed to degrade. The contemporary United States, Galbraith famously declared, had become a land of "private opulence and public squalor."[38]

In response, Galbraith called for a return to "social balance." Rather than seeking out ever more tawdry private satisfactions, he argued, Americans should invest in education, health, public safety, and public support for the arts. Expanding such public goods, he contended, would do far more to address the real problems of contemporary life – lingering poverty amid affluence, urban blight in a suburbanizing country, the rising urban crime that contemporaries described as "juvenile delinquency" – than would the conventional emphasis on economic equality and security. Galbraith's friend Schlesinger made much the same point, arguing that postwar affluence meant that a new "qualitative liberalism," concerned with improving the kinds of lives people led, would supplant the older "quantitative liberalism" of the New Deal. Both expected that the movement for such qualitative liberalism would be led by a "New Class" of white-collar workers whose dependence on education and the non-pecuniary reward of "prestige" made them especially aware of the value of immaterial, as opposed to material, goods. Indeed, the "rapid expansion of this class," Galbraith explained, should be "*the* major goal of the society."[39]

As if to answer Galbraith and Schlesinger's call for a new qualitative liberalism, the Kennedy years witnessed a sudden renaissance of social criticism. The trend began in the late 1950s with complaints against middle-class conformity like William Whyte's *The Organization Man* (1956).[40] It deepened in the early 1960s in a host of brilliant works that ultimately redefined the liberal agenda by drawing attention to the evils and injustices that persisted amid consumer affluence: Paul Goodman's *Growing Up Absurd* (1960), Jane Jacobs's *The Death and Life of Great American Cities* (1961), Michael Harrington's *The Other America* (1962), Rachel Carson's *Silent Spring*

(1962), Martin Luther King Jr.'s "Letter from a Birmingham Jail" (1963), Betty Friedan's *The Feminine Mystique* (1963), and Baldwin's *The Fire Next Time* (1963).[41]

The writers of such works were typically bolder than most members of the Kennedy administration. Indeed, even Galbraith and Schlesinger's advocacy of investment in public goods was far from the dominant view inside the Kennedy administration. The "qualitative liberalism" Galbraith and Schlesinger espoused competed with and was largely overshadowed by an alternative approach to domestic policy represented most potently by Walter Heller, the chairman of the Council of Economic Advisers, who pushed an agenda of "growth liberalism." Despite the remarkable prosperity of the postwar decades, the American economy had entered a severe recession in late 1957. (GDP plunged 3.7 percent in the first half of 1958.) Campaigning on the slogan of "getting America moving again," Kennedy had promised voters that his administration would deliver a 5 percent rise in GDP per year. Heller, who had been charged with making good on that promise, pushed for a program of major tax cuts and a generous rise in the depreciation allowance for business investment to stimulate demand. With the support of JFK, Heller's position easily preempted Galbraith's call for investment in public goods. Indeed, with the significant exceptions of the Space Program and the defense budget, where the administration achieved steep growth in spending, JFK proposed little in the way of public investment while in office. Until the growing civil rights movement forced him to take a moral stand against segregation in 1963, moreover, Kennedy paid far less attention to domestic issues than to the grand drama of the Cold War. Compared to events like the Bay of Pigs, JFK commented privately to Richard Nixon, "Who gives a shit if the minimum wage is $1.15 or $1.25?"[42]

And, yet, despite its apparent marginality, the qualitative liberalism advocated by Galbraith and Schlesinger turned out to complement rather than to compete with the growth liberalism pursued by the Kennedy administration – and to comport nicely as well with JFK's philosophy of governance. For one thing, during most of Kennedy's time in office, conservative opposition in Congress prevented the administration from realizing its plans to stimulate economic growth. As an alternative, Kennedy sought to use the tools of presidential power honed by presidents before him – executive orders, presidential commissions and special counselors, and collaboration with nonprofit organizations (such as the Carnegie, Ford, and Rockefeller Foundations) – to spur policy innovation outside the routines of legislation and the executive bureaucracy. These approaches, which worked especially well for policy issues without established stakeholders, were suited to placing new issues on the domestic policy agenda. Among other initiatives, the administration established a President's Committee on Youth Crime and Juvenile Delinquency whose members, in collaboration with experts supported by the Ford Foundation, would lay the groundwork for the War on Poverty. It created a President's Panel on Mental Retardation, which would eventually lead to legislation for spending on mental health and disabilities, and an Advisory Committee to the Surgeon General on the health dangers of smoking, which would produce a transformative public report responsible for changing the national perception of the dangers of tobacco. In addition, the Kennedy White House established a Commission on the Status of Women that would eventually foster the creation of the National Organization of Women and an Advisory Council on the Arts whose reports would culminate in the Johnson administration's creation of the NEA and the NEH.

But the complementarity of the growth liberalism and the qualitative liberalism of Kennedy liberals was more than fortuitous. The Kennedy administration's approach to domestic policy perfectly joined a view of the nation's political economy with a charismatic philosophy of governance. By their very nature, public goods appeared to exceed the narrow agendas of the various interests groups that ordinarily worked through the mechanisms of representative government. As Galbraith and Schlesinger contended, without a new elite able to rise above the routines of conventional politics, qualitative liberalism would seem impossible.

Most crucially, the Kennedy administration's domestic policy thinkers assumed that organized labor would play a role of little importance in the future of liberalism. In the view of Galbraith, for instance, the issues that had been crucial to the labor movement simply were no longer central to an affluent society. "The increase in the security and incomes of Americans at the lower income levels" meant that a once paramount goal of organized labor – the redistribution of wealth and power – no longer mattered.[43] "Few things are more evident in modern social history," Galbraith wrote, "than the decline of interest in inequality."[44]

And, in fact, Galbraith's perspective met little disagreement. The defining domestic issue of the day, virtually all observers eventually came to recognize, was the enormity of the Jim Crow system of racial oppression. JFK was notoriously reluctant to embrace the civil rights movement. But when, compelled by the moral grandeur of the movement and by the brute oppression practiced by southern racists, Kennedy finally took a stand and called for the legislation that would eventually become the landmark Civil Rights Act of 1964, he did so in the language of elevated national purpose that was central to his presidency. Civil rights, Kennedy told the country, was not "a partisan issue . . . not even a legal or legislative issue alone." It was "a moral issue . . . as old as the Scriptures and . . . as clear as the American Constitution." "This nation," he added, "will not be fully free until all its citizens are free."[45]

The issue of racial justice, in other words, was comparable to the problem of public goods stressed by Galbraith because it appeared to exceed the ordinary structures of interest group politics and thus to demand a program of elite leadership and reformed national community. By comparison, the interests of the labor movement seemed to many observers neither profound nor especially progressive. Liberal intellectuals like Galbraith assumed that organized labor had become an interest group rewarded with affluence and effectively enmeshed in the bureaucratic negotiations of the modern state. The era's leading radical, C. Wright Mills, similarly argued that the left's traditional investment in "the working class" was merely "a legacy" of "Victorian Marxism" and its misplaced "labor metaphysic."[46] The real hope for radicalism, Mills argued, lay in "the young intelligentsia."[47] Mills' followers within the emerging New Left agreed. Seeking "a movement among persons whose economic role in the society is marginal or insecure," they dismissed organized labor for its ties to "the Democratic Party and private enterprise" and sought to envision an alliance of students with "the Negro movement and . . . the unorganized poor."[48] Such an alliance, the young radicals argued, would bring cultural power to the poor while "improving our quality of work."[49]

None of these thinkers foresaw that organized labor in the United States, then at a historical peak but already significantly weakened by antiunion legislation, would soon suffer a precipitous decline in power. Nor did they anticipate that, following the economic stagnation of the 1970s, the New Right would push forward a profound political and economic transformation that would make economic inequality once again a fundamental fact of American life. Indeed, the assumption that the United States would remain an affluent society increasingly governed by a rising new class of professional workers shaped postwar intellectuals' most basic perceptions. Even when such thinkers addressed seemingly economic questions about wealth or opportunity or labor, they tended to see these matters as "qualitative" issues of education and cultural orthodoxy. Thus, when Galbraith addressed "the new position of poverty," he imagined that it was an unnecessary legacy of an older world.[50] It could be explained by some individuals' "inability to adapt to the discipline of modern economic life" or by the fact that some portions of the population were confined to a culturally impoverished "environment" – "an 'island' of poverty" amid a sea of affluence.[51] The way to address such people's exclusion from affluence was not to get them more income, but rather to provide their cultural backwaters with the very public goods valued by members of the "new class": "high-quality schools, strong health services, special provision for nutrition and recreation."[52] Poverty, in short, was not an issue of economic distribution but a problem of "human investment."[53]

As the Kennedy administration and the United States more broadly began to turn to the issue of poverty toward the end of JFK's presidency, they did so primarily in the terms that Galbraith and other qualitative liberals provided. Nothing was more common in the public discourse of the era than to refer to the nation's "islands" or "pockets" of poverty – the favored locations typically being the ghettos of the inner city or the hills of Appalachia. Michael Harrington's *The Other America* – the landmark work that put the problem of poverty on the national agenda – opened by citing Galbraith and went on to describe the impoverished as marginal figures who were being left behind by a modernizing economy, "the first minority poor in history."[54] Drawing on the idea of a "culture of poverty" that the anthropologist Oscar Lewis had recently made prominent, Harrington expanded on the implications of Galbraith's suggestion that poverty was mainly a problem of poor education and thus of public investment. "Their entire environment, their life, their values, do not prepare them to take advantage" of the opportunities of an affluent economy, Harrington wrote. They've "proved immune to progress."[55]

Such a perspective, as Harrington himself came to recognize, cast issues of wealth and poverty in a manner that fit well with the political temper of the New Frontier. In stressing education and investment, this perspective appeared to avoid the emphasis on economic redistribution that Galbraith and Schlesinger and other Kennedy liberals associated with an outworn past. By the same token, it envisioned the poor not as political stakeholders with interests that could be served by representative government. Rather, it cast the impoverished in something quite similar to the role that African Americans, artists, and intellectuals all played in the political imagination of Kennedy liberals – people who, living outside a bureaucratic political system, presented a moral challenge calling for charismatic leadership and a reformed national community. As Harrington pithily noted in 1964, "The poor are not a social and political class in the sense that organized workers are."[56]

Such is the perspective taken by both Neil Klugman and Richard Goodwin. When Neil forges a friendship with a poor black boy on the basis of their shared appreciation for the paintings of Gauguin and their common indifference toward the legalistic rules of the library, he achieves something close to what Goodwin imagined would be achieved by community action in the

War on Poverty. By the same token, Klugman's accomplishment resembles what Galbraith hoped would occur when improved education came to the nation's islands of poverty and what the young radicals of the New Left hoped would be achieved by an alliance of students and the poor. Stepping away from the comforts of consumer wealth and outside the restrictions of public bureaucracy, Neil envisions a cultural alliance of outsiders – one that points toward a reformed national community, while making his own professional work newly valuable.

Neil's example suggests with equal precision some of the key strengths and weaknesses of the liberal politics of the 1960s. John F. Kennedy encouraged his constituency to view themselves as an elite who saw beyond the parochial interests that bound others to the political system and whose gifts could create a more fully realized nation. That vision would help inspire many activists and intellectuals in the 1960s to make good on Arthur Schlesinger's prophecy of a new qualitative liberalism, in the process fundamentally transforming the contours of American life. But the very desire to rise above the routines of ordinary life and to escape the bargaining of conventional politics would leave many of these achievements without grounding in powerful interest groups, and thus vulnerable to retrenchment when they met conservative opposition. Likewise, when the political winds began to change in the later 1960s, the Kennedy vision of charismatic leadership would leave a once brash elite ripe for disappointment. Having entered political life with a sense of himself as one of a handful destined to remake America, Richard Goodwin by the early 1970s had "come to the rejection of politics as a vehicle for social change in America." "Washington," Goodwin complained, "is a steering wheel that's not connected to the engine."[57]

Similarly, Roth, having portrayed in Klugman a young man poised to realize a life of public mission, ruthlessly mocked that vision by the end of the 1960s. In Alexander Portnoy, the hero of his landmark work *Portnoy's Complaint* (1969), Roth created a perfect satire of the Kennedy liberal. The assistant commissioner for the City of New York Commission on Human Opportunity, Portnoy epitomizes both the agenda of qualitative liberalism and the way that its aspirations have been co-opted by the bureaucratic routines it once hoped to transcend. In the extended first-person monologue that comprises Roth's novel, Portnoy reveals himself to be a man whose intellectual gifts and avowed civic purposes are belied by his desperate yearning for prestige and by his poisonous sexual and racial resentments. At one key point in the novel, Portnoy recites Yeats' poem "Leda and the Swan" to a beautiful but undereducated lover from impoverished Appalachia who has just performed fellatio upon him. The moment highlights not the lovers' shared understanding, but rather the unbridgeable "chasm" that divides the cultural elite from the less educated, and the distrust and resentment that inevitably fills it.[58] As Roth could not have said more clearly, by the end of the 1960s, the Kennedy era's vision of elite cultural leadership was dying.

NOTES

1   Philip Roth, *Goodbye, Columbus* (New York: Vintage, 1959), 8.
2   Ibid., 43.
3   Ibid., 8.
4   Ibid., 135.
5   Ibid., 96.
6   Arthur M. Schlesinger Jr., *A Thousand Days: John F. Kennedy in the White House* (1965; repr., New York: Mariner Books, 2002), 213.
7   Jon Bradshaw, "Richard Goodwin: The Good, the Bad, and the Ugly," *New York Magazine*, August 18, 1975, 35.
8   Schlesinger Jr., *A Thousand Days*, 210–11.
9   Ibid., 213.
10 Richard N. Goodwin, *Remembering America: A Voice from the Sixties* (New York: Harper and Row, 1988), 3, 185.
11 Ibid., 73.
12 Alan Brinkley, *John F. Kennedy* (New York: Henry Holt and Co., 2012), 59.
13 John Kenneth Galbraith, *The Affluent Society* (Boston: Houghton Mifflin, 1958), 16.
14 Theodore C. Sorensen, ed., *Let the Word Go Forth: The Speeches, Statements, and Writings of John F. Kennedy* (New York: Delacorte Press, 1988), 18.
15 Daniel Patrick Moynihan, *Maximum Feasible Misunderstanding: Community Action in the War on Poverty* (New York: Free Press, 1969), 75.
16 Goodwin, *Remembering America*, 494, 530.
17 Arthur M. Schlesinger Jr., *The Politics of Hope* (Boston: Houghton Mifflin, 1962), 26.
18 Goodwin, *Remembering America*, 105.
19 Norman Mailer, "Superman Comes to the Supermarket," *The Presidential Papers* (New York: G. P. Putnam's Sons, 1963), 41.
20 Barry Goldwater, *The Conscience of a Conservative* (New York: Hillman Books, 1960), 20.
21 Ibid., v, iv.
22 Ken Kesey, *One Flew Over the Cuckoo's Nest* (New York: Viking Press, 1962); Madeleine L'Engle, *A Wrinkle in Time* (New York: Farrar, Strauss & Giroux, 1962); Victoria Lucas (Sylvia Plath), *The Bell Jar* (London: Heinemann, 1963).
23 Martin T. Williams, *Jazz in Its Time* (New York: Oxford University Press, 1989), 213.
24 Quoted in David Hadju, *Positively 4th Street: The Lives and Times of Bob Dylan, Joan Baez, Mimi Baez Fariña, and Richard Fariña* (New York: Farrar, Strauss, and Giroux, 2001), 134.
25 Michael McClure, *Scratching the Beat Surface: Essays on New Vision from Blake to Kerouac* (New York: Penguin, 1982), 13.

26 Quoted in Jonathan Day, *Robert Frank's* The Americans: *The Art of Documentary Photography* (Chicago: University of Chicago Press, 2011), 135, 37.
27 Allen Ginsberg, *Deliberate Prose: Selected Essays, 1952–1995* (New York: HarperCollins, 2000), 5, 4.
28 James Baldwin, *Another Country* (1962; repr., New York: Vintage, 1993), 406.
29 Ibid., 309.
30 James T. Patterson, *Grand Expectations: The United States, 1945–1974* (New York: Oxford University Press, 1996), 313.
31 Don K. Price, "Administrative Leadership," *Daedalus* 90, no. 4 (1961): 751.
32 Nicholas Lemann, *The Big Test: The Secret History of the American Meritocracy* (New York: Farrar, Strauss, and Giroux, 1999), 347.
33 Schlesinger Jr., *A Thousand Days*, 214.
34 Todd Gitlin, *The Sixties: Years of Hope, Days of Rage* (New York: Bantam, 1987), 95.
35 Patterson, *Grand Expectations*, 312–13.
36 Ibid., 17.
37 Ibid., 14.
38 Ibid., 203.
39 Ibid., 267.
40 William H. Whyte, Jr., *The Organization Man* (New York: Simon and Schuster, 1957).
41 Paul Goodman, *Growing Up Absurd: Problems of Youth in the Organized Society* (New York: Random House, 1960); Jane Jacobs, *The Death and Life of Great American Cities* (New York: Random House, 1961); Michael Harrington, *The Other America: Poverty in the United States* (New York: Macmillan, 1962); Rachel Carson, *Silent Spring* (New York: Houghton Mifflin, 1962); Martin Luther King, Jr., "Letter from a Birmingham Jail," in *Why We Can't Wait* (New York: Harper & Row, 1963); Betty Friedan, *The Feminine Mystique* (New York: W. W. Norton, 1963); *The Fire Next Time* (New York: Random House, 1963).
42 Quoted in Robert Dallek, *Nixon and Kissinger: Partners in Power* (New York: HarperCollins, 2007), 21.
43 Galbraith, *The Affluent Society*, 77.
44 Ibid., 72.
45 Sorensen, *Let the Word Go Forth*, 193–94.
46 C. Wright Mills, "Letter to the New Left," in *The Politics of Truth: Selected Writings of C. Wright Mills*, ed. John H. Summers (New York: Oxford University Press, 2008), 263.
47 Ibid., 266.
48 Tom Hayden and Carl Wittman, "An Interracial Movement of the Poor?" SDS pamphlet, 1963, 17, 18, 19.
49 Ibid., 22.
50 Galbraith, *The Affluent Society*, 250.
51 Ibid., 252, 253.
52 Ibid., 256.
53 Ibid., 257.
54 Michael Harrington, *The Other America: Poverty in the United States* (New York: Touchstone, 1962), 9.

55 Ibid., 9.
56 Quoted in Maurice Isserman, *The Other American: The Life of Michael Harrington* (New York: Public Affairs, 2000), 216.
57 Quoted in Bradshaw, "Richard Goodwin," 41, 35.
58 Philip Roth, *Portnoy's Complaint* (New York: Vintage, 1969), 192.

5

DOUGLAS FIELD

JFK and the Civil Rights Movement

On May 17, 1963, a painting of the African American writer James Baldwin appeared on the front cover of *Time* magazine. The accompanying article claimed that "in the U.S. today there is not another writer – white or black – who expresses with such poignancy and abrasiveness the dark realties of the racial ferment in North and South."[1] The *Time* article caught the prevailing tensions in the civil rights movement, which would result in 1,340 demonstrations in more than two hundred cities in thirty-six states between May and August of that year.[2] By the end of May 1963, Martin Luther King Jr. "warned the White House of an impending national calamity" brought on because of the "snail like pace of desegregation," a view forcefully echoed by the Reverend James Bevel, a colleague of King's in the Southern Christian Leadership Conference: "Some punk who calls himself the President has the audacity to tell people to go slow. I'm not prepared to be humiliated by white trash the rest of my life, including Mr. Kennedy."[3]

Baldwin's appearance on the cover of *Time* serves as a useful starting point to evaluate the Kennedy administration's record during the civil rights movement. In a speech two years before he appeared in *Time* magazine, Baldwin had pondered Robert F. Kennedy's pronouncement that one day, a black American could become president of the United States. "What really exercises my mind," Baldwin said, "is not this hypothetical day on which some other 'first' will become the first President. What I am really curious about is just what kind of country he'll be President of."[4] Baldwin's publications in the early 1960s suggested that the writer was not convinced by Robert Kennedy's optimistic pronouncement; his essays of that period rather shine a torch onto the murky and troubled racial landscape that JFK would preside over. In 1962, the *New Yorker* published a 20,000-word essay by the writer, "Letter from a Region in My Mind," a searing indictment on the racial iniquities of the United States during the Kennedy era. Published a hundred years after Emancipation, Baldwin's widely read essay made it clear that black Americans in the north and south were growing impatient with the lumbering pace of desegregation. "It is entirely unaccept-able that I should have no voice in the political affairs of my own country," Baldwin wrote in a clear parting shot to the president, "for I am not a ward of America; I am one of the first Americans to arrive on these shores."[5] Not surprisingly, as Arthur Schlesinger recalls, Baldwin was on Robert Kennedy's radar after his inflammatory and eloquent *New Yorker* article, which was expanded in 1963 as *The Fire Next Time*, a book that became a manifesto of the civil rights movement.[6]

Baldwin's role in the story of JFK and the civil rights movement extended beyond his influential writing about the racial politics of the 1950s and 1960s. A week after he was featured on the cover of *Time* magazine, Robert Kennedy, the attorney general, held a meeting with Baldwin and others in his New York apartment. At this meeting, on May 24, 1963, RFK met Baldwin and a diverse cohort of artists and activists, including the politi-cally engaged actor Harry Belafonte, the playwright Lorraine Hansberry, the psychologist Dr. Kenneth Clark, Martin Luther King's lawyer, Clarence Jones, and Jerome Smith, who had "probably spent more months in jail and been beaten more often than any other CORE [Congress of Racial Equality] member."[7] According to Layhmond Robinson in the *New York Times*, the meeting "was seen as evidence of growing concern over criticism voiced by Negroes across the country on its handling of the civil rights issue."[8] Baldwin, who would later describe "the laughter and bitterness and scorn" that greeted RFK's insistence that a black American could become presi-dent within forty years, was unequivocal in his assessment of JFK's civil rights record.[9] Robinson observed that Baldwin had "been sharply critical of President Kennedy for not moving more forcefully in civil rights crises in the South. He has charged that the President has 'not used the great prestige of his office as the moral forum it can be,'" adding that Baldwin urged the attorney general to "use his influence to get the President to make a series of talks to the nation on the civil rights issue."[10]

Baldwin and his comrades pointed to JFK's shortcomings on civil rights issues in no uncertain terms, highlighting a prevailing view that the president was slow to implement effective policies on racial inequality. Scholars such as Garth E. Pauley have argued that the president "did not comprehend the significance of race as the dominant factor in African Americans' troubled lives," adding that "overall, race was often just another political issue to Kennedy; in fact, he usually saw civil rights issues as a peripheral issue and wanted to keep it that way."[11] As I explore later in this chapter, historians have debated why it took the Kennedy administration nearly three years to take a strong moral stance on federal civil rights issues: campaigners would have to wait until February 23, 1963, for JFK to finally submit a legislative program on civil rights. Baldwin's accusation that the president had "not used the great prestige of his office as the *moral* forum it can be" was a barbed but prescient critique of JFK's detached approach to civil rights.[12] During the first three years of his presidency, historians, friends, and aides frequently describe JFK as "cool, sceptical and pragmatic."[13] It was not until Kennedy's famous address to the nation concerning civil rights legislation on June 11, 1963, just weeks after Baldwin's meeting with the attorney general, that JFK finally discussed racial inequality as a "moral" issue in what has been described as "the first sustained moral argument by an American president on civil rights."[14]

The Baldwin–Robert Kennedy meeting undoubtedly shaped the direction of the weeks leading up to JFK's address to the nation. While it is hard to gauge the extent that RFK "use[d] his influence to get the President to make a series of talks to the nation on the civil rights issues," the meeting clearly shook the attorney general, who was also the president's closest aide and adviser on civil rights matters. According to Philip A. Goduti Jr., the "Baldwin meeting was a turning point for [Robert] Kennedy in many ways" although it was a fractious and heated encounter.[15] Recounting the horrors of his experience in the South as he protested with CORE, Jerome Smith made it clear that he was on the point of renouncing nonviolence. "When *I* pull the trigger," he warned, "kiss it goodbye."[16] Smith further incensed Kennedy by stating that he would refuse to fight for his country, a remark that enraged the deeply patriotic attorney general, who was shouted down when he tried to suggest that he too had been discriminated against because of his Irish heritage.[17] Baldwin told RFK that he did not "understand our urgency," and the meeting ended, as Clark recalled, with the attorney general becoming "silent and tense . . . He no longer continued to defend himself. He just sat and you could see the tension and pressure building in him."[18]

The confrontational meeting clearly gave RFK an insight into the depth of African American anger and frustration at the lack of clear strategy on civil rights issues. The meeting, Tom Adam Davies observes, "left [Robert] Kennedy in little doubt that the clock was ticking for the nonviolent and gradualist approach of the civil rights establishment."[19] Arthur Schlesinger, a Kennedy aide, recalled that days after talking to Baldwin and his cohort, the attorney general began "to grasp as from the inside the nature of black anguish," telling his press secretary, Edwin Guthman, that if he were African American, he would share the views of those with whom he had clashed with at the meeting.[20] In James Hilty's estimation, this episode was something of an epiphany for RFK, who "gained insight into the larger meaning of the civil rights movement" that he would later share with his brother, using his position as adviser and family member to influence JKF's piecemeal approach to civil rights.[21] Within weeks of the Baldwin–Robert Kennedy meeting, JFK gave a largely extemporized address to the nation on June 11, 1963, a speech that marked what Peniel E. Joseph claims "might have been the single most important day in civil rights history." In fact, for Joseph, "without the moral forcefulness of the June 11th speech, the bill [the 1964 civil rights act signed by Lyndon Johnson] might never have gone anywhere."[22] So how did JFK, who "had been routinely criticized by black leaders for being timid on civil rights," become in Garth E. Pauley's words, "a champion of civil rights?"[23]

Any attempts to map out JFK's record on the civil rights movement needs to take account of the wider historiography of these turbulent years. In "Freedom Then, Freedom Now: The Historiography of the Civil Rights Movement," Steven Lawson argues that early accounts from the 1960s and 1970s "focused on leaders and events of national significance," while in the 1980s historians emphasized the roles that grassroots organizations and local communities played in the movement. Lawson contends that the continuing interest in the civil rights movement is inextricably bound to "cycles of nostalgia that prompt Americans to recall the historical era of their youth. Memories dredged up turbulent and unsettling times, yet they also harked back to inspirational moments when ordinary people exhibited extraordinary courage."[24]

JFK's assassination in November 1963, shortly after the August 27 March on Washington, has undoubtedly clouded critical opinion on the political achievements and shortcomings of the thirty-fifth president of the United States. In the wake of JFK's assassination, memoirs by the former president's aids and friends proffered largely favorable accounts of his time in office, and in particular his record on civil rights. His former aide Theodore Sorensen, for example, though conceding that JFK acted "more as a matter of course than of deep concern," maintains that the late president was deeply aware of racial inequalities from the start of his political career.[25] Sorensen, like early allies including Harris Wofford (JFK's main adviser on civil rights issues) and Arthur Schlesinger, claims that both Kennedys' views on civil rights were deeply shaped by their Irish heritage, arguing that their early speeches "invoked comparisons to the discrimination suffered by their Irish grandparents."[26] Early accounts of JFK and the civil rights movement, such as Carl Brauer's *John F. Kennedy and the Second Reconstruction* (1977), painted a picture of the president at the forefront of policy changes at a national level, claiming that he was the first chief executive "who genuinely committed his administration to broad action taken specifically to improve the position of the Negro."[27] By 1980, the historiography of the civil rights movement started to shift away from accounts of prominent politicians to focus instead on civil rights organizations and their leaders. As Malcolm Smith concluded, "By exploiting a heart-rending problem for his political gain, and by failing then to honor the promise, the President betrayed the Negroes."[28] For James Hilty, the Kennedys were "splendid opportunists" whose "soaring eloquence raised expectations and promised greatness for their country and themselves," although "In both life and death the Kennedys often got credit for more than they achieved."[29]

More recent notable accounts of JFK's record on civil rights include Nick Bryant's acclaimed book, *The Bystander: John F. Kennedy and the Struggle for Black Equality* (2006), which, according to Sheldon M. Stern, is the first to "examine, systematically and comprehensively, John F. Kennedy's leadership (or lack of it) on race and civil rights, not only in the thousand days of his presidency but also during his six years in the House of Representatives and his eight years in the Senate."[30] As Stern observes, JKF emerges in Bryant's account as a complex figure who demonstrated "a willingness to make important symbolic gestures about race and civil rights, coupled with a reluctance to take political risks."[31]

In 1946 when Kennedy won his first election, "five black Georgians were murdered merely for attempting to vote."[32] From his early days in office, JFK was careful and pragmatic about his stance on racial politics; his "strongest impulse was to empower blacks rather than dethrone Jim Crow."[33] As Bryant observes, "Even the friendliest biographers have suggested that civil rights failed to interest Kennedy in the early stages of his political career and touched only the fringes of his consciousness." Even close aides, such as Sorensen, recalled that the future president "simply did not give much thought" to the civil rights movement, adding that he had "no background or association of activity."[34] In his early political years, Kennedy had little experience of the Deep South, which he did not visit until the mid-1950s, and he had little contact with African Americans aside from his trusted valet, George Taylor; as Bryant writes, "No blacks managed to penetrate his close circle of friends."[35]

While Bryant concludes that racial inequality "seemed to trouble him [JFK] intellectually rather than arouse him emotionally," he nonetheless provides a complex picture of the future president.[36] On the one hand, JFK's cool pragmatism and intellectualism enabled him to think strategically about his future ambitions, which necessarily involved courting the southern vote. According to Garth E. Pauley, by the late 1950s JFK "transformed himself from a symbol of southern opposition into an adopted southerner." As a result of Kennedy's 1957 tour of the region during his campaign to win the 1960 Democratic Party presidential nomination, "the South had accepted JFK as one of their own and came to know him as 'Dixie's favorite

Yankee.' "[37] JFK's political maneuvering as he courted the South meant that he would only indicate his support for the 1954 *Brown* ruling if pressed to do so. And yet his well-crafted public persona belied his record on civil rights legislation. As Bryant has demonstrated, "From the very outset of his [JFK's] career, he voted unfailingly for civil rights and signaled his intentions early on by lending enthusiastic support to a series of bills calling for the abolition of the poll tax."[38] In fact, in JFK's early political years, "He boasted a voting record that matched, if not surpassed those of most northern colleagues."[39]

During the presidential campaign of 1960, it became clear to the Kennedys that they could not avoid questions about civil rights. In response they adopted a rhetoric that they hoped would appeal to traditional segregationists as well as advocates of social change. During the closely fought campaign for the presidency, which JFK would win by less than 120,000 votes, several factors emerged as key: the state of the economy, foreign relations with the Soviet Union, JFK's Catholicism, and the burgeoning struggle for civil rights. While it is often noted that there had never been a Catholic president, it is also the case that no other presidential campaign had made African American civil rights a central issue. According to Taylor Branch, "Race played a large role in the campaign, less because of the civil rights movement than because polls were showing the Negro vote to be divided and volatile."[40] The Kennedys could not afford to lose the southern vote, which they would do if they vociferously opposed segregation; yet in so doing, they risked losing the African American vote. JFK's political predicament and maneuvering did not go unnoticed. "Senator Kennedy has been equivocating on civil rights so long," the African American journalist Chuck Stone wrote, "he wouldn't know a forthright statement on racial equality if he were dragged across his breakfast table." More specifically, Stone seemed to catch JFK out in his attempts simultaneously to vote for civil rights legislation and ingratiate himself with the South: "Has he ever condemned the South's barbaric attitude?" the journalist asked, "Has he ever shown deep concern about the second-class citizenship?"[41] This was not the only time that JFK's maneuvering nearly cost him dearly. After JKF voted against Eisenhower's Civil Rights Act of 1957, he emerged "looking opportunistic and unprincipled" in what was widely viewed as a blatant attempt to gain southern allies while underestimating African American support.[42] Later, CORE founder Bayard Rustin would describe JFK as "the smartest politician we have had in a long time," adding that the president pledges to support African Africans but then "turns and bows to Dixiecrats," echoing one Student Nonviolent Coordinating Committee (SNCC) member's description of Kennedy's "quick-talking and double-dealing."[43]

During the 1960 presidential campaign, neither Nixon nor Kennedy "embraced a strong, vigilant civil rights platform."[44] In fact, both candidates put their faith in the power of the southern vote, which complicated their reliance on the support of the unpredictable African American vote. Nixon and JFK were both keen to seek endorsements, not only from civil rights leaders but also from high-profile African American entertainers and sportsmen. The influential former baseball player and activist Jackie Robinson had been vocal in his distrust of Kennedy, going so far as to pledge his support for Nixon: "As long as he [JFK] continues to play politics at the expense of 18,000,000 Negro Americans, then I repeat: Sen. Kennedy is not fit to be President of the U.S."[45] Despite concerted attempts to convert Robinson to the Kennedy camp, the former baseball player remained deeply distrustful of Kennedy's allegiance with the South. In May 1960, JFK held a meeting with Harry Belafonte to discuss, among other issues, the possibility of "organizing Negro stars" to support the Kennedy campaign. Belafonte's advice was a pivotal turning point in the presidential campaign: "Forget me – forget Jackie Robinson . . . If you can join the cause of King, and be counseled by him, then you'll have an alliance. That will make a difference."[46]

King would need persuading that Kennedy was the right Democratic presidential candidate to support. As David Garrow records, King was only too aware how JFK had voted on the 1957 Civil Rights Act and he viewed the Massachusetts senator with some suspicion, believing that he "was so concerned about being President of the United States that he would compromise basic principles to become President."[47] After a private meeting on June 23, 1960, King changed his mind, noting that the presidential candidate "lacked 'a depthed understanding' of civil rights" but he conceded that he " was very impressed by the forthright manner in which he discussed the civil rights question."[48] Nonetheless, after a second meeting in mid-September King refused to endorse either Nixon or JFK, warning the latter that "something dramatic must be done to convince the Negroes that you are committed on civil rights."[49]

Within a month of their second meeting, Kennedy did just that, interceding when King was arrested and convicted for a probation violation after participating in an Atlanta sit-in. In a well-documented gesture, JFK called Coretta Scott King to offer his support. This act concerned RFK, who was worried that the campaign workers "had managed to align his brother publicly with a national symbol of black activism."[50] Louis Martin, Kennedy's sole black adviser, turned this problem around by alerting African American news organizations to the Kennedy–Coretta Scott King telephone call. By contacting black – but not white – journalists, Martin was able to increase Kennedy's stature in the black community without running the risk of alienating white southern voters. The tactic worked: the *Pittsburgh Courier* reported that with the help of the Kennedys, King was "the biggest Negro in the United States," while the story barely made it into *Time*.[51] This incident displayed JFK's frequently noted adroitness at symbolic actions, a quality that has led some critics to charge that his policies were vague in terms of strategy and light on substance.

Historians such as James H. Meriwether have noted that the October 1960 telephone call to Coretta Scott King "has become the campaign's iconic event and a storied explanation for the outcome of the election," an event understood as having "endeared Kennedy to a skeptical black America and provided the critical boost for his ultimate victory."[52] Meriwether rightly observes how the story of the telephone calls has become "canonized" in influential works such as Taylor Branch's *Parting the Waters: America in the King Years, 1954–63* (1988), noting that this mythologization has obscured other tactics employed by Kennedy to obtain the important black vote.[53] In particular, Meriwether calls attention to JFK's interest in and engagement with the dozen or so African nations that gained independence during the presidential campaign. JFK mentioned Africa during his presidential campaign more frequently than civil rights, a strategy that enabled him to engage with black politics, but from an international, rather than a domestic, perspective. The continent of Africa represented for Kennedy "the newest frontier, one where he could burnish his Cold War credentials by enrolling newly independent states on the side of the West while making himself known as a candidate sympathetic to black Americans."[54]

In fact both 1960 presidential candidates were more preoccupied with international affairs than domestic concerns, with Nixon in particular "convinced that the continent [of Africa] was a Cold War battlefield that needed more American attention," as illustrated by a steady increase in the number of African students studying in the Soviet Union.[55] As race increasingly became an international issue from the late 1950s onward, both Nixon and Kennedy were only too aware that negative images of domestic civil rights would hinder the United States' foreign policy agendas. This awareness was illustrated by a key event in the presidential campaign. In 1960, Jackie Robinson, on behalf of the African American Students Foundation (ASAF), asked Nixon to help fund the airlift of 250 East African students (including President Obama's father) who had won scholarships to U.S. and Canadian universities. Robinson appealed to Nixon's interest in foreign policy by pointing out that the Soviet Union was planning to open a "University of Friendship of People" in Moscow that would offer "free education for four thousand African, Asian and Latin American Students."[56] Nixon wanted

Robinson's support but was unable to find a way of securing the necessary funds to airlift the African students. JFK was quick off the mark and secured the money through the Joseph P. Kennedy Foundation, a charitable organization set up to honor the senator's older brother who was killed during the war. News of the donation spread quickly; the Republican Hugh Scott spoke up against "the long arm" of the Kennedy family, accusing them of trying to "take over the function of the Government in advance of an election."[57] Both presidential candidates were aware that Kennedy's donation would endear him to the black American voter, despite mutterings that the Democratic senator had bought, rather than earned, that crucial African American support. With this move, Kennedy had managed to outmaneuver Nixon, who at that point had a much stronger civil rights record, while also adroitly maintaining the support of the important bloc of (anticommunist) white southern voters.

The first major civil rights crisis that the Kennedy administration faced occurred during the Congress of Racial Equality (CORE) Freedom Rides during 1961, when integrated groups rode buses into the segregated South after the December 1960 Supreme Court decision outlawing segregation in bus and train terminals involved in interstate travel. On May 14 in Anniston, Alabama, white mobs smashed the windows of one of the buses, which was later firebombed by another group of rioters as the riders left church.[58] A second bus, carrying the CORE leader James Peck, was attacked and several riders were badly beaten, with one Ku Klux Klan member shouting, "Just tell Bobby [Kennedy] and we'll do him in too."[59] Robert Kennedy was furious about the incident, claiming he had not been aware of the Freedom Rides, which came at an inopportune time politically: JFK was scheduled to meet the Soviet leader in a few weeks' time, and Khrushchev, who "rarely missed an opportunity to point out America's racial injustice," would now "have an opportunity to humiliate the president on the world stage."[60] Despite the mounting violence, however, the Kennedys were reluctant to employ federal troops, maintaining that these were state, not federal incidents. RFK's mantra was clear: the national government would only intervene when "there was a specific and clear 'federal responsibility.' "[61] After one of RFK's closest aides, John Seigenthaler, was badly beaten in Montgomery, Alabama, the attorney general "refused still to publicly condemn the violence or issue any press statements on the crisis."[62] The situation escalated when Martin Luther King, along with a group of Freedom Riders and sympathizers, was trapped in a Baptist church by a mob of several thousand whites until they were rescued by several hundred marshals. For critics of the Kennedys, the lack of federal intervention in this case underscored JFK's cautious approach to the civil rights movement and his belief in gradual rather than radical change – something that would come under greater scrutiny the following year.

In 1962 speculation was rife about how the Kennedy administration would commemorate the hundredth anniversary of the Emancipation Proclamation. Owing to a scheduling mix-up, Kennedy would not appear at the September commemorations, instead spending time at the America's Cup yachting races. In his absence, Kennedy recorded a brief taped message that "was vague and numbingly banal."[63] The timing was unfortunate, not least because of mounting unrest in Mississippi. This came on the back of a difficult campaign which tried, but failed, to end all segregation in the city of Albany, Georgia. Then on October 1, 1962, James Meredith became the first black student to enroll at the University of Mississippi after the Fifth Judicial Circuit concluded that the university was unlawfully maintaining a segregated admissions policy. State officials and a number of students opposed the decision, which escalated into riots as federal marshals escorted Meredith to the university in what RFK called "the mightiest internal struggle of our time."[64]

The Battle of Ole Miss was a turning point in the history of the civil rights movement. Ostensibly the Kennedy administration showed the world, through the use of federal troops, that it was committed to ending racial injustice. Black leaders, however, remained less convinced: King and Baldwin bemoaned the president's "lack of moral conviction," with the former convinced that U.S. civil rights "no longer commanded the conscience of the nation."[65] Determined to make progress in the South, King launched a new campaign in Birmingham, Alabama, in April 1963. This campaign resulted in numerous clashes with Bull Connor, the commissioner for public safety, who would deploy dogs and hoses against peaceful protesters of segregation. By May 1963, weeks before RFK's meeting with James Baldwin, the Birmingham campaign was resolved, but Kennedy's detractors were increasingly disillusioned with the administration's handling of the bloody events in Alabama and the South more generally. Harris Wofford recalls that the president had a tendency to react hurriedly to issues involving racial equality, noting that he frequently took action "at the last minute, in response to Southern political pressures without careful consideration of an overall strategy."[66] King observed that JFK "has got the political skill . . . but the moral passion is missing," a point the Baptist minister would underscore, bemoaning his own inability to "force the President . . . to speak out in moral terms."[67] In the wake of Alabama governor George Wallace's declaration to bar all African American students from enrolling at the University of Alabama, Robert Kennedy realized that it was time for his brother to act swiftly.

On June 11, 1963, JFK addressed the nation on live television, referring to recent events in Birmingham and Alabama. Midway through his speech, Kennedy put down his script and extemporized. As he called on every American to "stop and examine his conscience about this and other related incidents," JFK framed the struggle for racial equality in explicitly moral terms, something that his detractors had found lacking in his earlier pronouncements.[68] The president made it clear that this was a national, not a regional problem, stating, "Difficulties over segregation and discrimination exist in every city, in every State of the Union, producing in many cities a rising tide of discontent that threatens the public safety." He declared, "We are confronted primarily with a moral issue. It is as old as the scriptures and is as clear as the American Constitution." In echoes of James Baldwin's conclusion to *The Fire Next Time*, which warned of "a cosmic vengeance" in Old Testament rhetoric, JFK described how "the fires of frustration and discord are burning in every city, North and South."[69]

The June 11 address undoubtedly shaped JFK's legacy, although he would soon be tested with further tragedies. On the night of the presidential address, Medgar Evers, the field secretary of the Mississippi State National Association for the Advancement of Colored People, was murdered by Byron De La Beckwith, a Ku Klux Klan member. During the August 28 March on Washington the president kept a low profile, and he maintained a "reserved reaction" after the death of four schoolgirls in the September 15 bombing of the 16th Street Baptist Church in Birmingham, Alabama. This suggests, in Bryant's words, "that he had not yet fully evolved his thinking about America's racial crisis."[70]

Had Kennedy lived, it is likely that he would have secured passage of the 1964 Civil Rights Act. At the time of his assassination, however, JFK's record was not strong on civil rights issues. Martin Luther King, for example, "estimated that if integration continued at the current pace, it would take until 2054 for southern schools to be completely desegregated."[71] For historians such as Bryant, Kennedy's civil rights achievements are not always quantifiable, and Bryant notes that JFK's "symbolic approach to the race problem meant that many of the changes he ushered in were largely cosmetic."[72] For Jill Abramson, JFK "remains all but impossible to pin down," despite the fact there are some 40,000 books on the late president.[73] The record offers a complex picture of JFK's commitment to civil rights. While his June 11 speech galvanized the nation and almost certainly had a direct impact in the shaping of American race relations, it is also the case that JFK was the victim of his own inertia during his first two years in office. Kennedy's legacy on this issue is by no means secure. It will no doubt remain the subject of contention between critics who point to his civil rights achievements and those who claim that JFK was a bystander.

NOTES

1 "Nation: 'The Root of the Negro Problem," *Time*, May 17, 1963, vol. 81, no. 20: 26.
2 Nick Bryant, *The Bystander: John F. Kennedy and the Struggle for Black Equality* (New York: Basic Books, 2006), 1.
3 Ibid., 2.
4 James Baldwin, "From Nationalism, Colonialism, and the United States: One Minute to Twelve – A Forum," in *The Cross of Redemption: Uncollected Essays*, ed. Randall Kenan (New York: Pantheon Books, 2010), 9.
5 James Baldwin, "The Fire Next Time," in *Collected Essays*, ed. Toni Morrison (New York: Library of America, 1998), 342.
6 See Tom Adam Davies, "Black Power in Action: The Bedford-Stuyvesant Restoration Corporation, Robert F. Kennedy, and the Politics of the Urban Crisis," *Journal of American History* 100, no. 3(2013): 742, n15.
7 Arthur M. Schlesinger Jr., *Robert Kennedy and His Times* (New York: Ballantine Books, 1978), 331.
8 Layhmond Robinson, "Robert Kennedy Consults Negroes Here about North," *New York Times*, May 25, 1963, 1.
9 James Baldwin, "An American Dream and American Dream," *Collected Essays*, ed. Toni Morrison (New York: Library of America, 1998), 718.
10 Robinson, "Robert Kennedy Consults Negroes Here about North," 1.
11 Garth E. Pauley, *The Modern Presidency and Civil Rights: Rhetoric on Race from Roosevelt to Nixon* (College Station: Texas A&M University Press, 2001), 110, 111.
12 Robinson, "Robert Kennedy Consults Negroes Here about North," 1; emphasis mine.
13 Pauley, *The Modern Presidency and Civil Rights*, 108.
14 Ibid.
15 Philip A. Goduti Jr., *Robert F. Kennedy and the Shaping of Civil Rights, 1960–1964* (Jefferson, NC: McFarland and Company, 2013), 192.
16 Davies, "Black Power in Action," 742.
17 Goduti Jr., *Robert F. Kennedy and the Shaping of Civil Rights*, 191.
18 Ibid., 192.
19 Davies, "Black Power in Action," 742.
20 Goduti Jr., *Robert F. Kennedy and the Shaping of Civil Rights*, 192.
21 James Hilty, *Robert Kennedy: Brother Protector* (Philadelphia: Temple University Press, 1997), 357.
22 Peniel E. Joseph, "Kennedy's Finest Hour," *New York Times*, June 10, 2013, http://www.nytimes.com/2013/06/11/opinion/kennedys-civil-rights-triumph.html?_r=0. Accessed May 17, 2014.
23 Ibid.; Pauley, *The Modern Presidency and Civil Rights*, 106.
24 Steven F. Lawson, "Freedom Then, Freedom Now: The Historiography of the Civil Rights Movement," *American Historical Review* 96, no. 2 (1991): 456.
25 Theodore Sorensen, *Kennedy* (New York: Harper and Row, 1965), 471.

26 Theodore Sorensen, *The Kennedy Legacy* (New York: MacMillan, 1969), 217–18.
27 Carl Brauer, *John F. Kennedy and the Second Reconstruction* (New York: Columbia University Press, 1977), 316.
28 Malcolm E. Smith, *John F. Kennedy's 13 Great Mistakes in the White House* (New York: Suffolk House, 1980), 166–67.
29 Hilty, *Robert Kennedy*, 3.
30 Sheldon M. Stern, "John F. Kennedy and the Politics of Race and Civil Rights," *Reviews in American History* 35, no. 1 (March 2007): 118.
31 Ibid., 118–19.
32 Bryant, *The Bystander*, 20.
33 Ibid.
34 Ibid., 25.
35 Ibid., 24.
36 Ibid., 30.
37 Pauley, *The Modern Presidency and Civil Rights*, 105.
38 Bryant, *The Bystander*, 26
39 Ibid., 29.
40 Cited by Goduti Jr., *Robert F. Kennedy and the Shaping of Civil Rights*, 27.
41 Smith, *John F. Kennedy's 13 Great Mistakes*, 160.
42 Bryant, *The Bystander*, 79.
43 Schlesinger Jr., *Robert Kennedy and His Times*, 315.
44 Goduti Jr., *Robert F. Kennedy and the Shaping of Civil Rights*, 27.
45 Mary Kay Linge, *Jackie Robinson: A Biography* (Westport, CT: Greenwood Publishing House, 2007), 125.
46 Goduti Jr., *Robert F. Kennedy and the Shaping of Civil Rights*, 28.
47 David J. Garrow, *Bearing the Cross: Martin Luther King Jr. and the Southern Christian Leadership Conference* (London: Vintage, 1993), 139.
48 Ibid., 139; Goduti Jr., *Robert F. Kennedy and the Shaping of Civil Rights*, 28.
49 Garrow, *Bearing the Cross*, 142.
50 Ibid., 147.
51 Bryant, *The Bystander*, 185.
52 James M. Meriwether, "'Worth a Lot of Negro Votes': Black Voters, Africa, and the 1960 Presidential Campaign," *Journal of American History* 95, no. 3 (2008): 737–38. See also Philip E. Muehlenbeck, *Betting on the Africans: John F. Kennedy's Courting of African Nationalist Leaders* (New York: Oxford University Press, 2012).
53 Meriwether, "Worth a Lot of Negro Votes," 738.
54 Ibid., 739.
55 Ibid., 743, 749.
56 Ibid., 752.
57 Ibid., 737.
58 Goduti Jr., *Robert F. Kennedy and the Shaping of Civil Rights*, 64.
59 Ibid., 64
60 Bryant, *The Bystander*, 264.
61 Schlesinger Jr., *Robert Kennedy and His Times*, 304.
62 Bryant, *The Bystander*, 269.
63 Ibid., 329, 330.

64 Schlesinger Jr., *Robert Kennedy and His Times*, 325.
65 Ibid., 327.
66 Harris Wofford, *Of Kennedys and Kings: Making Sense of the Sixties* (New York: Farrar, Straus, and Giroux, 1980), 124.
67 Ibid., 129, 157.
68 John F. Kennedy, "Address on Civil Rights, June 11, 1963," http://millercenter.org/president/speeches/detail/3375. Accessed January 22, 2014.
69 Baldwin, "The Fire Next Time," 346.
70 Bryant, *The Bystander*, 442.
71 Ibid., 463.
72 Ibid., 464.
73 Jill Abramson, "The Elusive President," *New York Times*, October 27, 2013, http://www.nytimes.com/2013/10/27/books/review/the-elusive-president.html. Accessed March 18, 2014.

6

ANDREW PRESTON

Kennedy, the Cold War, and the National Security State

Few presidents have left office on a pessimistic note, and one might not assume the genially patriotic Dwight D. Eisenhower to be among them. But in January 1961, after eight years in the White House, Eisenhower performed one of his last official acts as president, delivering his farewell address, on an unusually somber note. After a decade of prosperity, and with no foreign conflicts since Korea, a war he had inherited and quickly ended, Eisenhower could have permitted himself a valedictory of self-congratulation. Instead, he sounded two notes of alarm.

The first was familiar to all Americans during the Cold War: communist expansionism. Eisenhower described communism in classically bipolar terms as "a hostile ideology" that was "global in scope, atheistic in character, ruthless in purpose, and insidious in method." Perhaps most worryingly, the communist threat "promise[d] to be of indefinite duration." To meet this threat, the federal government needed to maintain an unprecedentedly large standing military and pursue the containment of communism globally, while at home American citizens had to remain on a permanent war footing. Vigilance was the price of liberty.

Yet here lay the origin of Eisenhower's second warning, for vigilance in the Cold War was double-edged: it kept communism at bay overseas, but it also threatened to undermine the essence and purpose of American freedom at home. The expansion of the state, beginning with the New Deal and growing exponentially in World War II and the Cold War, was necessary to meet the crises of modernism and industrialism that had caused the Depression and spurred the rise of fascism, Nazism, and communism. But by 1961, Eisenhower worried that the state's domineering role in the private economy, both industrial and agricultural, had itself become a danger that was eroding "the very structure of our society." At the apex of this internal threat was a new relationship between private industry and government expenditures. Americans, Eisenhower concluded, "must guard against the acquisition of unwarranted influence, whether sought or unsought, by

89

the military-industrial complex. The potential for the disastrous rise of misplaced power exists and will persist. We must never let the weight of this combination endanger our liberties or democratic processes."[1]

When John F. Kennedy delivered his inaugural address three days after Eisenhower bid farewell, he not only recognized the irony of the Cold War, but sought to reconcile it by embracing both firmness and flexibility, strength and peace, arms and disarmament. To the communist powers, Kennedy offered "not a pledge but a request: that both sides begin anew the quest for peace, before the dark powers of destruction unleashed by science engulf all humanity in planned or accidental self-destruction." Kennedy had, however, learned the lessons of the 1930s – and of his father's support for appeasement as ambassador to Great Britain – well, and his speech was as much a rejection of appeasement as it was a peace offering.[2] "We dare not tempt them with weakness," he warned of America's communist enemies. "For only when our arms are sufficient beyond doubt can we be certain beyond doubt that they will never be employed. So let us begin anew – remembering on both sides that civility is not a sign of weakness, and sincerity is always subject to proof. Let us never negotiate out of fear. But let us never fear to negotiate."[3]

Stirring though it was, Kennedy's inaugural vision remained trapped between the imperatives of security and the ambitions of idealism. The new president wanted peace without the appearance of weakness and firmness without provoking war. In trying to navigate these clashing objectives, Kennedy's foreign policy oscillated from one extreme to another. Only days after his ominous warning about the military-industrial complex, Eisenhower met with the soon-to-be-president Kennedy and urged him to intervene, militarily if necessary, in the tiny, impoverished, strategically insignificant country of Laos.[4] Eisenhower could not escape the irony of the Cold War; nor could JFK.

Eisenhower did not use the term, but what he feared was the national security state, a government that operated under something close to permanent wartime conditions, tolerated high military spending, and facilitated intimate cooperation between public and private interests in the pursuit of national security. The national security state may have been unwanted, but Eisenhower could see no other alternative. Nor, despite his different approach to the Cold War, could Kennedy. Instead, JFK merely entrenched the national security state even deeper in America's public life and political economy. In Berlin, Cuba, and Indochina, Kennedy's foreign policy whipsawed between the extremes of confrontation and reconciliation. In forward strategic planning, particularly regarding nuclear weapons, he oscillated between alarmism and negotiation. In military spending, he sought savings but wound up with the same expenditures and a much more lethal military. In overseas development and foreign aid, he promised much but ultimately delivered little. Kennedy began his foreign policy career by founding the Peace Corps, and he ended it at American University with one of the most eloquent peace addresses in history. In between, however, the inconsistencies of his approach twice brought the superpowers to the brink of war and augmented the power of the military-industrial complex his predecessor had warned about.

Kennedy did transform the national security state in one regard, by radically concentrating its bureaucratic procedures. Before Kennedy, the position of "national security adviser" did not exist. The special assistant for national security affairs, as the position had been known, was established with the creation of the National Security Council (NSC) in 1947. The special assistant was supposed to be a clerical position, an administrator who would process paperwork and coordinate decisions for the NSC. The role of policy making would still remain with cabinet officials, such as the secretaries of state and defense and their subordinates. But Kennedy distrusted the national security bureaucracy, and he wanted to act as his own secretary of state. To facilitate this, he appointed McGeorge Bundy, then serving as the dean of Harvard College, to be his special assistant for national security affairs. With Kennedy's approval, Bundy – who had not left Harvard to become a White House clerk – transformed his post from a powerless administrator to a decision maker with nearly the same level of influence and authority as Secretary of State Dean Rusk and Secretary of Defense Robert McNamara. Based in the White House, Bundy's small staff of desk officers had direct access to the president. They also, thanks to Bundy, had direct access to all classified national security communications. Bundy's "foreign office in microcosm," as Undersecretary of State George Ball called the NSC staff, was able to use its presidential access and institutional dexterity to shape foreign policy. This system was obviously prone to abuse, and although Bundy used his power judiciously he laid the groundwork for subsequent national security advisers, such as Henry Kissinger and Zbigniew Brzezinski, who wielded immense institutional authority over U.S. foreign policy.[5]

As the reform of the NSC showed, Kennedy thought of himself as a modernizer. According to Kennedy aide and chronicler Arthur M. Schlesinger Jr., Kennedy practiced "the politics of modernity" in order to "dissolve the myths which had masked the emerging realities in both domestic and foreign affairs. His hope was to lead the nation beyond the obsessive issues of the past and to call forth the new perceptions required for the contemporary world." The 1960s, JFK promised, would break the shackles of the 1930s and 1940s, because the old way of thinking no longer applied to an increasingly modernizing world.[6] "Today our concern must be with the future," he declared upon accepting the Democratic nomination for president in June 1960. "For the world is changing. The old era is ending. The old ways will not do. Abroad, the balance of power is shifting," and not in America's favor. "We stand today on the edge of a New Frontier – the frontier of the 1960s – a frontier of unknown opportunities and perils – a frontier of unfulfilled hopes and threats."[7]

As usual with Kennedy, soaring rhetoric masked a much more complicated reality. Kennedy's pragmatic and fiscally cautious liberalism had more in common with that of his predecessors Franklin Roosevelt and Harry Truman – or even with Eisenhower's moderate conservatism – than it did with the more ambitious reformism of his successor Lyndon Johnson. Wary of deficits and committed to a policy of "sound money," as well as fettered by the constraints of the Bretton Woods system, Kennedy sought economic growth and liberal reform within established parameters. He displayed similar caution, even reluctance, when it came to pressing domestic issues such as civil rights.[8] Foreign policy, however, allows presidents more freedom of maneuver, and on these matters Kennedy showed a boldness lacking in his domestic agenda. He laid out an ambitious plan to recapture the momentum he feared the United States had lost to the communist world, one reliant on expansive conceptions of economic power, national security, and American ideology. But even in the realm of foreign affairs, Kennedy left behind an ambivalent legacy.

In part this was because Kennedy's approach to crises was often aggressive, sometimes reckless, and occasionally driven by panic. Immediately upon becoming president, he was beset by crises overseas. The period between 1958 and 1963, bracketed by periods of relative superpower calm, were "the crisis years" that brought the United States and the Soviet Union closer to a direct conflict than at any other time in the Cold War.[9] As a result, Kennedy found himself on the defensive in several parts of the world, most notably Berlin, Cuba, Laos, and Vietnam. Lawrence Freedman has dubbed these four conflicts "Kennedy's wars," describing them as hostilities epitomizing his ambivalent approach to the world.[10]

If Kennedy had noticed Eisenhower's warning about the military-industrial complex, he did not act on it. To be sure, defense spending did not significantly increase in the Kennedy era. In fiscal year (FY) 1961, Kennedy inherited a budget of $49.6 billion; by FY 1964, this had risen to $54.8 billion, hardly a dramatic increase when inflation is accounted for. When economic growth is also considered, the increase is even less significant. For example, over the same three-year period, America's gross domestic product

(GDP) rose by an annual average of 4 percent, meaning that as a share of GDP defense spending actually declined under JFK from 9.4 percent to 8.5 percent.[11]

What did increase under Kennedy was the striking force of the U.S. military. Under Secretary of Defense Robert S. McNamara – whom Kennedy had poached from the Ford Motor Company and tasked with cutting spiraling costs and waste at the Pentagon – the U.S. military spent more on deployable and sophisticated weapons systems while holding overall spending steady. As Kennedy's secretary of defense, McNamara applied the systems analysis techniques he had employed as one of the "Whiz Kids" who had rescued Ford from insolvency in the years after World War II, saving the Pentagon billions in new efficiencies. So if the quantity of military spending remained fairly constant under Kennedy and McNamara, it saw tremendous qualitative changes, particularly in the realm of the nuclear weapons that allowed the United States to maintain its overwhelming strategic dominance over the Soviet Union.[12]

This enhancement of defense capabilities was an integral part of "flexible response," as the Kennedy administration's overall strategy was known. Flexible response was intended to replace Eisenhower's New Look, which had sought to curtail defense spending through a reliance on cheaper nuclear weapons and a reduction in the deployment of much more expensive conventional forces. Eisenhower, it seemed, had entered office much as he left it, alarmed by deficits, wary of the military-industrial complex, and fearful that higher defense spending would usher in a "garrison state" thanks to higher taxes and a more interventionist government.[13] But critics, including Kennedy and many who would fill the ranks of his administration, said that Eisenhower's foreign policy was static and passive, and they charged that he had ceded the global initiative to more dynamic communist and nationalist movements. In *The Uncertain Trumpet*, a landmark book published in time for the 1960 election campaign, Maxwell D. Taylor, a recently retired army general and fierce critic of the New Look, warned that the United States would be unable to counter revolutionary movements and wars of national liberation in the Third World. Unlike the Soviet Union or the People's Republic of China, which had fixed industrial and metropolitan targets and thus could be deterred with nuclear weapons, decolonization and nationalist movements relied on rudimentary military technology and had few if any industrial targets. Against such adversaries, which the Soviets were adeptly cultivating with their pledge to aid the oppressed, nuclear arms were useless. The answer, Taylor argued, was for Washington to augment its conventional forces, particularly in counterinsurgency, so it could meet new threats on their own terms.[14]

After Kennedy's election, Taylor's views were adopted throughout the Kennedy administration, and Taylor himself served JFK first as a White House military adviser, then as chairman of the Joint Chiefs, and finally as ambassador to South Vietnam.[15] Under the premises of flexible response, the Kennedy administration would have been expected to increase its conventional forces – and it did. Yet the tenets of flexible response should also have led the Kennedy administration to decrease America's reliance on its nuclear arsenal – and this it did not. Despite flexible response's promised turn from the Eisenhower administration's provocatively named doctrines of "brinkmanship" and "massive retaliation," very little actually changed. In fact, according to John Lewis Gaddis, Kennedy oversaw "an increase of 150 percent in the number of nuclear weapons available, a 200 percent boost in deliverable megatonnage, the construction of ten additional Polaris submarines (for a total of 29) and of 400 Minuteman missiles (for a total of 800) above what the previous administration had scheduled."[16]

Moreover, Kennedy did nothing to alter the strategic premises based on the Pentagon's Single Integrated Operational Plan (SIOP). In the event of the outbreak of war with the Soviet Union, the SIOP made provisions for an automatic overwhelming nuclear strike of total annihilation – the Pentagon's estimate was that 2,500 missile launches would kill 350 million people.[17] Kennedy and many of his officials were critical of indiscriminate slaughter on this scale – Bundy, for instance, believed "there was really no logic whatever to 'nuclear policy,' " and most civilian officials in the administration shared his view – yet the SIOP remained unaltered until well into the Nixon presidency more than a decade later. In other words, while his rhetoric was more careful, Kennedy relied just as much on "massive retaliation" as Eisenhower had.[18]

The 1961 Berlin Crisis provides a good example. West Berlin had little military or strategic significance, but it had long been a source of political, economic, and cultural vulnerability for the Soviet Union. The thousands of refugees from communism who poured across the boundary from East to West Berlin were an embarrassment to communist internationalism. And in a global conflict in which political appearances mattered as much as military realities, West Berlin constituted a unique strategic asset for the United States and its allies. By the summer of 1961, after three years of bluster, Khrushchev had had enough. While neither side wanted Berlin to spark a war, the Soviets could not allow West Berlin to continue acting as a haven for people fleeing communism. Tensions increased to the point where war seemed a real possibility. Kennedy's dilemma was not as acute as Khrushchev's, but it was real enough. On one hand, he felt he could not appear weak and passive in the face of communist aggression. At a summit in Vienna in June, in a humiliating experience that was widely reported in the press, Khrushchev had openly bullied the young and inexperienced president. On the other hand, however, Kennedy did not want to lose control of events and oversee the start of World War III.[19]

His response, in a televised address to the nation on July 25, threaded the needle between war and peace, even as its frank acknowledgment that nuclear war was a realistic possibility worried many.[20] In the end, Kennedy's dilemma was solved for him. To stem the tide of refugees without triggering war, Khrushchev authorized the construction of the Berlin Wall in August 1961. Relieved, the Kennedy administration remained silent and did not protest the violation of Berliners' freedom of movement. Nor did Kennedy condemn the fact that the escape route for millions of Eastern Europeans had been shut off. Kennedy took a great deal of criticism on both counts in Europe and at home. But he was willing to bear that burden if it meant avoiding war and settling the issue of Berlin.

The overwhelming nuclear superiority that underlined massive retaliation also came into play during the most dangerous crisis of Kennedy's presidency, over Cuba. Fidel Castro had been in power in Havana for a year when Kennedy entered office, though he not yet completed his conversion from revolutionary nationalism to doctrinaire communism. Nonetheless, the Eisenhower administration had begun to isolate Cuba diplomatically and economically, and the CIA had begun to plan for the United States to arm, train, and transport more than a thousand anticommunist Cuban exiles to invade Cuba and remove Castro from power. Kennedy inherited this covert plan, and after some initial misgivings approved it for action in April 1961. The result was the biggest failure of his presidency, the Bay of Pigs invasion, which fell apart when Kennedy decided not to support the overmatched exiles with U.S. air power or ground troops.[21]

The invasion attempt prompted Castro to seek the protection of the Soviet Union, thereby pushing him sharply leftward and firmly into the communist camp. But while picking a fight with Cuba now meant picking a fight with the Soviet Union, Kennedy went on the offensive. He authorized Operation Mongoose, an indefinite campaign of economic warfare and political sabotage that also included several assassination attempts against Castro himself. Mongoose in turn prompted Castro to request further assistance from Moscow. Seeing an opportunity to not only cement an alliance with Cuba but also to redress the nuclear imbalance with the United States, Khrushchev deployed nuclear missiles to the island. He did so in secret, hoping to present Kennedy with a fait accompli. When U-2 spy planes uncovered evidence of the deployment, Kennedy convened a series of top secret crisis meetings that have gained legendary status as ExComm. After ruling out capitulation and invasion, Kennedy opted for a middle path of blockading the island and offering Khrushchev a face-saving way out: in exchange for the removal of the missiles, the United States would publicly vow not to invade Cuba and privately promise to remove U.S. nuclear missiles from Turkey.[22]

Kennedy was hailed, at the time and often since, for his peaceful solution to the crisis. There is some truth to this verdict – most of ExComm's members advocated an air strike against the missile installations and many pushed for an all-out invasion – but it ignores the facts that it was JFK who chose to escalate the situation into a crisis in the first place, and that he did so for largely political and symbolic reasons. As Kennedy himself (along with McNamara) admitted, Soviet missiles in Cuba did nothing to change the superpowers' nuclear imbalance: the Soviet Union would be just as strategically inferior with them as it was without. Kennedy remarked in one of the first ExComm meetings that "it doesn't make any difference if you get blown up by an ICBM [intercontinental ballistic missile] flying from the Soviet Union or one that was 90 miles away. Geography doesn't mean that much."[23] But the Republicans, particularly Senator Kenneth Keating from New York, had spent the months before the crisis attacking Kennedy's record on Cuba; Keating had even accused the Soviets, accurately as it turned out, of secretly placing nuclear weapons on the island, a charge the Kennedy administration initially denied. Thus the world came perilously close to nuclear Armageddon thanks to Kennedy's need to not only address an imagined strategic weakness but also shore up his domestic political credentials before the 1962 midterms.

Kennedy's categorical victory in the crisis – "We were eyeball to eyeball," Rusk is reported to have said when news of Khrushchev's capitulation reached Washington, "and I think the other fellow just blinked"[24] – was possible only because of the overwhelming strategic advantage the Pentagon's nuclear arsenal gave the president. Once Kennedy decided to impose a blockade against Cuba, Khrushchev had little choice but to withdraw. But what Kennedy did next was unexpected. He did not boast or press home his advantage. Instead, he conceded an effective parity with the USSR, known as mutual assured destruction (designated by the fitting acronym of MAD). Despite America's strategic superiority, the missile crisis made it clear that both sides would lose a nuclear war, even if one side could "win" by incurring fewer casualties. Herman Kahn and Kissinger had theorized that the United States could wage "limited" nuclear wars, but nobody before had actually faced the realistic – indeed, imminent – prospect of a nuclear exchange. The reality terrified Kennedy, along with McNamara and most other members of his administration. Nuclear superiority was pointless; instead, Kennedy now settled for sufficiency, a suitable amount of firepower to deter a Soviet attack and an assurance that U.S. forces could launch a retaliatory attack against the Soviet Union after absorbing a Soviet first strike. The logic of MAD was perverse, but it helped maintain peace.[25]

After the Cuban Missile Crisis, moreover, Kennedy's new top priority became cementing the new relationship of peace. In June 1963, in the commencement speech at American University, Kennedy acknowledged that Americans and Soviets were human beings with different political systems but the same basic interests and the same desire for a peaceful world. Nuclear weapons had made their ideological disputes too dangerous to continue unregulated, and he promised to seek new ways of managing superpower tensions. It may seem simple now, but this was the first time a U.S. president had acknowledged moral equivalency with the Soviet Union since World War II. If there was a key turning point in the short-lived Kennedy presidency, one that carried with it real potential for a genuinely new era, it was this.[26]

Another crucial aspect of flexible response was the widespread use of unconventional military but nonnuclear force, and here Kennedy's difference from his predecessor was more pronounced. While the Eisenhower administration had readily resorted to covert operations – for example, using clandestine operatives and psychological warfare to topple the governments of Iran in 1953 and Guatemala in 1954 – Kennedy imagined a much wider, more integrated, and more aggressive system of covert operations and counterinsurgency.[27] Under Kennedy, both the CIA and the Pentagon expanded their counterrevolutionary operations. Kennedy himself was fascinated by espionage and intelligence, though much of his knowledge was derived from Ian Fleming's James Bond novels rather than from briefings.[28] He was also fascinated with the advent and spread of guerrilla warfare, and terrified that the Soviets were taking advantage of it. When Soviet premier Nikita Khrushchev vowed to assist "wars of national liberation" around the world, Kennedy disseminated a copy of the speech throughout his administration. "Read, mark, learn and inwardly digest," he instructed his aides. "Our actions, our steps should be tailored to meet these kinds of problems."[29] With presidential support, the CIA expanded its operations and planned for coups and assassinations against the leaders of Cuba, Congo, and even the United States' ally South Vietnam. Prodded by Kennedy, the Pentagon established the Green Berets and other counterinsurgency operations and augmented the School of the Americas, an anticommunist training center for right-wing Latin American military officials based at Fort Benning, Georgia.[30] As Stephen Rabe has shown, the "Kennedy Doctrine" pledged there would be "no more Cubas."[31] In these ways Kennedy promised, in contrast to the supposed passivity of

Eisenhower and his useless nuclear arsenal, a suitably dynamic response to a world in the throes of revolution.

In practice, this meant an excessive reliance on military solutions and counterinsurgency operations by the CIA and the Department of Defense. But Kennedy officials recognized that many of the problems facing the United States were political, ideological, and especially economic in nature, and so they also offered a suitably nonmilitary solution in response: modernization.[32] It is no surprise that many of the Kennedy administration's most important foreign policy initiatives aimed to put modernization theory into practice. The Peace Corps, for instance, was Kennedy's attempt to harness the era's burgeoning and highly idealistic youth culture to the aims of U.S. foreign policy. Peace Corps volunteers would live in the developing world and assist in the modernization process, both by participating in local microeconomic development projects and by simply carrying with them the optimistic values of American democratic capitalism.[33] Another instance of modernization in action was the Alliance for Progress, which pledged billions of development aid to nations south of the border in order to stave off the communist advance. In the words of Schlesinger, the Alliance "by its very existence warned Fidel Castro that he could no longer count on the Latin American states falling into Marxist revolution of their own weight."[34] The goal was to build a middle class who would then create durable liberal democracies throughout Latin America. Unfortunately, this lofty goal was never funded sufficiently and ultimately was sacrificed in exchange for the certainties of military repression and counterinsurgency.[35]

But it was in Indochina where modernization, counterinsurgency, and other nonnuclear components of flexible response were applied most extensively. Nowhere were the paradoxes of the Kennedy presidency sharper than in Vietnam. After reaching a 1962 settlement on the neutralization of Laos, where a communist insurgency battled a U.S.-backed conservative regime, Kennedy shored up the anticommunist position in neighboring South Vietnam. Despite the peaceful promise of the American University speech's offer of détente, the summer of 1963 also saw the deterioration of South Vietnamese security and the beginning of America's descent into the Vietnam War. Kennedy inherited from Eisenhower a firm but limited commitment to South Vietnam that consisted of fewer than 1,000 U.S. military personnel; that commitment had grown to more than 9,000 by the end of 1962 and 16,300 by November 1963, plus a significantly larger amount of military hardware that Kennedy had authorized in 1962's "Project Beefup."[36] Through the Strategic Hamlet program, which aimed to separate peasants from insurgents by placing them in fortified modern villages, South Vietnam became a laboratory for techniques in modernization and counterinsurgency – less modernization and more counterinsurgency as time went on.[37]

In backing the regime of President Ngô Đình Diệm, however, the United States had sided firmly with Catholic authoritarianism in an overwhelmingly Buddhist country. When Buddhist monks led demonstrations against the Diệm regime in the spring and summer of 1963, Saigon's security services cracked down hard. This only led to further protests, punctuated most famously by the self-immolation of several Buddhist monks. Kennedy oscillated between reaffirming America's commitment and warning that his patience with Diệm was not inexhaustible, an uncertainty that continued right up to the day of Kennedy's assassination. Speculating about what he might have done in Vietnam had Lee Harvey Oswald missed has become a cottage industry among historians, driven by the fact that he left clues leading to several different conclusions.[38] What we do know is that he deepened the U.S. commitment at a time when South Vietnam was increasingly unable to defend itself. Lyndon Johnson was thus confronted with a situation Kennedy never had to face: if the United States withdrew, South Vietnam would quickly collapse, leading to a reunified Vietnam under communist rule. Whether JFK would have handled that decision more adeptly is a mostly academic question, for the war that did unfold was as much Kennedy's making as it was Eisenhower's or Johnson's.

Ultimately, the foreign policy of John F. Kennedy was marked by a profound ambivalence, and an uncertainty over which direction the United States should take. This ambivalence is reflected in the historiography. Most presidents divide historical opinion, but few have drawn sharper distinctions than Kennedy. JFK has been presented as everything from heroic to villainous. In truth, he was neither, but the division of opinion says a great deal about the widespread sense that his presidency was a lost opportunity. The longing for what might have been is especially acute when it comes to foreign policy, for Kennedy was a president who began his term as an embattled warrior flailing helplessly on the beaches of Cuba, only to end it as an eloquent spokesman for world peace. Perhaps the greatest tragedy of Kennedy's presidency is that he was killed in Dallas just as he was coming to terms with his ambivalence and working his way toward a possible solution.

NOTES

1 Dwight D. Eisenhower, "Farewell Radio and Television Address to the American People, January 17, 1961," in *Public Papers of the Presidents of the United States: Dwight D. Eisenhower, 1960–1961* (Washington, DC: Government Printing Office, 1961), 1037–38 (hereafter *PPP*).

2 See David Nasaw, *The Patriarch: The Remarkable Life and Turbulent Times of Joseph P. Kennedy* (New York: Penguin Press, 2012), 283–486, 505–522; and Robert Dallek, *An Unfinished Life: John F. Kennedy, 1917–1963* (Boston: Little, Brown, 2003), 61–67.

3 "Inaugural Address, January 20, 1961," in *PPP: John F. Kennedy, 1961* (Washington, DC: Government Printing Office, 1962), 2.

4 See the memos for the record of conversations between Eisenhower and Kennedy and their respective advisers, January 17 and January 19, 1961, *Foreign Relations of the United States, 1961–1963*, vol. 24, *Laos Crisis* (Washington, DC: Government Printing Office, 1994), 12–25.

5 George W. Ball, *The Past Has another Pattern: Memoirs* (New York: W. W. Norton, 1982), 172. On the changes under Kennedy, see Andrew Preston, "The Little State Department: McGeorge Bundy and the National Security Council Staff, 1961–1965," *Presidential Studies Quarterly* 31 (December 2001): 635–59. On the evolution of the NSC system and its subsequent abuses, see John Prados, *Keepers of the Keys: A History of the National Security Council from Truman to Bush* (New York: William Morrow, 1991); Ivo H. Daalder and I. M. Destler, *In the Shadow of the Oval Office: Profiles of the National Security Advisers and the Presidents They Served – from JFK to George W. Bush* (New York: Simon & Schuster, 2009); and Andrew Preston, "A Fine Balance: The Evolution of the National Security Adviser," in *Rethinking Leadership and "Whole of Government" National Security Reform: Problems, Progress, And Prospects*, ed. Joseph R. Cerami and Jeffrey A. Engel (Carlisle, PA: Strategic Studies Institute/U.S. Army War College, 2010), 127–48.

6 Arthur M. Schlesinger Jr., *A Thousand Days: John F. Kennedy in the White House* (Boston: Houghton Mifflin, 1965), 739.

7 Quoted in Dallek, *An Unfinished Life*, 275–76.

8 See Nick Bryant, *The Bystander: John F. Kennedy and the Struggle for Black Equality* (New York: Basic Books, 2006).

9 Michael R. Beschloss, *The Crisis Years: Kennedy and Khrushchev, 1960–1963* (New York: HarperCollins, 1991).

10 Lawrence Freedman, *Kennedy's Wars: Berlin, Cuba, Laos, and Vietnam* (New York: Oxford University Press, 2000).

11 John Lewis Gaddis, *Strategies of Containment: A Critical Appraisal of American National Security Policy During the Cold War*, rev. ed. (New York: Oxford University Press, 2005), 225. See also Aaron L. Friedberg, *In the Shadow of the Garrison State: America's Anti-Statism and Its Cold War Grand Strategy* (Princeton, NJ: Princeton University Press, 2000), 140–48.

12 On McNamara's background and work in systems analysis, see Deborah Shapley, *Promise and Power: The Life and Times of Robert McNamara* (New York: Simon & Schuster, 1993). On the imbalance between American and Soviet forces in the period between 1950 and 1965, one that afforded the United States tremendous strategic dominance, see Gareth Porter, *Perils of Dominance: Imbalance of Power and the Road to War in Vietnam* (Berkeley: University of California Press, 2005).

13 On the New Look, see Robert R. Bowie and Richard H. Immerman, *Waging Peace: How Eisenhower Shaped an Enduring Cold War Strategy* (New York: Oxford University Press, 1997); and Gaddis, *Strategies of*

Containment, 125–96. On Eisenhower and the garrison state, see Friedberg, *In the Shadow of the Garrison State*.

14 Maxwell D. Taylor, *The Uncertain Trumpet* (New York: Harper, 1960).

15 On Taylor's ideas and influence, see Freedman, *Kennedy's Wars*, 18–20.

16 Gaddis, *Strategies of Containment*, 217.

17 Freedman, *Kennedy's Wars*, 47.

18 Francis J. Gavin, "The Myth of Flexible Response: United States Strategy in Europe during the 1960s," *International History Review* 23 (December 2001): 850–54, 873; Bundy quoted in Andrew Preston, *The War Council: McGeorge Bundy, the NSC, and Vietnam* (Cambridge, MA: Harvard University Press, 2006), 56.

19 For the most comprehensive account of the Berlin Crisis, see Marc Trachtenberg, *A Constructed Peace: The Making of the European Settlement, 1945–1963* (Princeton, NJ: Princeton University Press, 1999), 251–351.

20 "Radio and Television Report to the American People on the Berlin Crisis, July 25, 1961," *PPP: JFK, 1961*, 533–40.

21 The Bay of Pigs is thoroughly examined in a wide variety of sources, but the best succinct account is Howard Jones, *The Bay of Pigs* (New York: Oxford University Press, 2008).

22 The literature on the missile crisis is enormous, but the best one-volume account, which also considers the Bay of Pigs and Operation Mongoose, remains the thoroughly comprehensive Aleksandr Fursenko and Timothy Naftali, *"One Hell of a Gamble": Khrushchev, Castro, and Kennedy, 1958–1964* (New York: W. W. Norton, 1997). For a more focused, recent account, see Michael Dobbs, *One Minute to Midnight: Kennedy, Khrushchev, and Castro on the Brink of Nuclear War* (New York: Alfred A. Knopf, 2008).

23 Transcript of meeting, October 16, 1962, in Ernest R. May and Philip D. Zelikow, eds., *The Kennedy Tapes: Inside the White House during the Cuban Missile Crisis* (Cambridge, MA: Harvard University Press, 2009), 90–91.

24 Quoted in Dino A. Brugioni, *Eyeball to Eyeball: The Inside Story of the Cuban Missile Crisis* (New York: Random House, 1991), 483.

25 On the shift from superiority to sufficiency that resulted in the embrace of MAD, see Freedman, *Kennedy's Wars*, 92–111, 281–84; and Lawrence Freedman, *The Evolution of Nuclear Strategy*, 3rd ed. (New York: Palgrave Macmillan, 2003), 213–42.

26 "Commencement Address at American University in Washington," *PPP: JFK, 1963* (Washington, DC: Government Printing Office, 1964), 459–64. Some historians have argued that for this reason, 1963 marked the crucial turning point in the Cold War – perhaps even ending the Cold War itself. See, for example, Vladislav Zubok and Constantine Pleshakov, *Inside the Kremlin's Cold War: From Stalin to Khrushchev* (Cambridge, MA: Harvard University Press, 1996), 236–37; John Lewis Gaddis, *We Now Know: Rethinking Cold War History* (New York: Oxford University Press, 1997), 291–92; Trachtenberg, *A Constructed Peace*, 352, 379–82, 398–402; James G. Hershberg, "The Crisis Years, 1958–1963," in *Reviewing the Cold War: Approaches, Interpretations, Theory*, ed. Odd Arne Westad (London: Frank Cass, 2000), 319–20; Jennifer W. See, "An Uneasy Truce: John F. Kennedy and Soviet-American Détente, 1963," *Cold War History* 2 (January 2002): 161–94; Preston, *War Council*, 54–74; and Anders Stephanson, "Cold War Degree Zero," in *Uncertain*

Empire: American History and the Idea of the Cold War, ed. Joel Isaac and Duncan Bell (New York: Oxford University Press, 2012), 19–49.

27 Michael McClintock, *Instruments of Statecraft: U.S. Guerrilla Warfare, Counter-Insurgency, Counter-Terrorism, 1940–1990* (New York: Pantheon, 1992), 161–298.

28 Christopher Moran, "Ian Fleming and the Public Profile of the CIA," *Journal of Cold War Studies* 15 (Winter 2013): 139–44.

29 Quoted in Richard Reeves, *President Kennedy: Profile of Power* (New York: Simon & Schuster, 1993), 41.

30 Jan Knippers Black, *Sentinels of Empire: The United States and Latin American Militarism* (New York: Greenwood Press, 1986), 36–37; Stephen G. Rabe, *The Most Dangerous Area in the World: John F. Kennedy Confronts Communist Revolution in Latin America* (Chapel Hill: University of North Carolina Press, 1999), esp. 125–47. More broadly, see Greg Grandin, *Empire's Workshop: Latin America, the United States, and the Rise of the New Imperialism* (New York: Metropolitan Books, 2006), 46–49. The history of the SOA is surprisingly understudied, but for a compelling anthropological account, see Lesley Gill, *The School of the Americas: Military Training and Political Violence in the Americas* (Durham, NC: Duke University Press, 2004).

31 The phrases are Rabe's. See, respectively, Rabe, *Most Dangerous Area in the World*, 79–98; and Stephen G. Rabe, *The Killing Zone: The United States Wages Cold War in Latin America* (New York: Oxford University Press, 2011), 85–96.

32 See Amanda Kay McVety's chapter in this volume.

33 Michael E. Latham, *Modernization as Ideology: American Social Science and "Nation Building" in the Kennedy Era* (Chapel Hill: University of North Carolina Press, 2000), 109–49.

34 Schlesinger Jr., *A Thousand Days*, 759.

35 Latham, *Modernization as Ideology*, 69–108.

36 George C. Herring, *America's Longest War: The United States and Vietnam, 1950–1975*, 4th ed. (New York: McGraw-Hill, 2002), 103–9, 139.

37 Latham, *Modernization as Ideology*, 151–207; James M. Carter, *Inventing Vietnam: The United States and State Building, 1954–1968* (New York: Cambridge University Press, 2008), 117–29.

38 The best overview of the Kennedy counterfactual is still Fredrik Logevall, "Vietnam and the Question of What Might Have Been," in *Kennedy: The New Frontier Revisited*, ed. Mark J. White (New York: New York University Press, 1998): 19–62.

7

AMANDA KAY MCVETY

JFK and Modernization Theory

In his 1961 State of the Union Address, John F. Kennedy announced that he intended "to ask the Congress for authority to establish a new and more effective program for assisting the economic, educational and social development of other countries and continents." The request was not unexpected, coming on the heels of a promise made ten days earlier during Kennedy's inaugural address: "To those peoples in the huts and villages across the globe struggling to break the bonds of mass misery, we pledge our best efforts to help them help themselves, for whatever period is required."¹ He added a special promise for Latin America. "To our sister republics to the south, we have pledged a new alliance for progress," Kennedy continued in his State of the Union. "Our goal is a free and prosperous Latin America, realizing for all its states and all its citizens a degree of economic and social progress that matches their historic contributions of culture, intellect and liberty." Promises by American presidents to assist other countries' development were not new. Harry Truman had begun the practice in his own inaugural address back in 1949. But listeners were greeted with a new concept in Kennedy's speeches: development was as much about society as it was about economics.

In his address, Truman had told the American people, "We must embark on a bold new program for making the benefits of our scientific advances and industrial progress available for the improvement and growth of underdeveloped areas." Point Four, the name of the aid program that came out of the speech, emphasized the importance of sharing technical knowledge and encouraging capital investment. It maintained a strong material focus, centered on helping to provide the tangible objects that most Americans believed made their lives easier and better. "Our aim," Truman explained, "should be to help the free peoples of the world, through their own efforts, to produce more food, more clothing, more materials for housing, and more mechanical power to lighten their burdens."² Point Four, a 1949 policy paper explained, "is broadly economic. It seeks the advancement of peoples of underdeveloped areas through a continuing and balanced expansion of their production and distribution of goods and services essential to meeting their needs." Point Four proposed primarily economic and technical solutions to what was perceived to be primarily an economic and technical problem: underdevelopment. It aimed "to help attain the 'nonmaterial ends' of peace and freedom through 'material means,' i.e., through improved living conditions."[3]

Point Four the idea became Point Four the program in 1950, with the creation of the Technical Cooperation Administration (TCA) within the State Department. The program soon began the work of using material means to secure nonmaterial ends on the very modest budget of $35 million. Kennedy, then in the House of Representatives, voted against the program, thinking it wasteful. A 1951 extended trip around Asia and the Middle East, however, changed his mind. The following summer, he argued in the House for the importance of maintaining aid to the region. "To cut technical assistance when the Communists are concentrating their efforts in this vital area seems to me a costly and great mistake," he insisted.[4] In July of 1953, the Eisenhower administration turned the TCA into the Foreign Operations Administration and then, in 1955, into the International Cooperation Administration (ICA). The name changed, but the essence of the program did not, a fact that some observers – including the now senator from Massachusetts who had an eye toward the White House – viewed as a serious problem. Underdevelopment, they began arguing, was a nonmaterial problem that required nonmaterial solutions and more aggressive action on the part of the United States. Introducing a resolution to extend greater aid to India in 1958, Kennedy insisted that the United States needed to extend "programs of real economic development" that would allow "Asian and African nations . . . [to] find the political balance and social stability which provide the true defense against Communist penetration."[5] The United States not only needed to offer more aid; it needed to offer better aid.

Eugene Burdick and William Lederer's 1958 novel *The Ugly American* became an instant best seller by giving literary expression to this discontent. An account of development efforts in a fictional Asian nation, the novel, as Robert D. Dean has argued, "portrayed arrogant overseas American diplomats and foreign aid bureaucrats as soft, lazy men, ignorant of the local languages, huddling in their enclaves enjoying a comfortable lifestyle of colonial privilege, vulnerable to the seductions of the orient."[6] Meanwhile, the communists are out in the fields, doing the hard work of actually winning the hearts and the minds of the locals. The book's heroes are two American men who attempt to redeem both their own manhood and their nation's aid efforts through hard, dirty work performed side by side with the locals.

Kennedy loved the book and its call for smarter and stronger aid policies. He sent a copy to every member of the Senate and used it to help frame some of his attacks on the Eisenhower administration (which did begin reforming its foreign aid programs in 1958) during the 1960 election.[7]

Kennedy's frustration with the ICA clearly stemmed from his sense that the country was not acting aggressively enough in the field – that it was losing ground to the communists as a result of both complacency and misguided policies. This sense was reinforced by a December 1960 report by Kennedy's Task Force on Economic Policy, which lamented that the current aid program "has been designed primarily as an instrument *against* Communism, rather than *for* constructive economic and social advancement. It is heavily *oriented* toward supporting military and short-run political objectives rather than toward the longer-run political problems of national development." The ICA is not, the report insisted, "suited to the decade of the Sixties." Soviet aid efforts were "impressive"; America's needed to be more so.[8]

Kennedy promptly asked two consultants to that task force – the economists and political thinkers John Kenneth Galbraith and Walt W. Rostow – for ideas about how to reform it. Galbraith sent his report to McGeorge Bundy, special assistant to the president, on February 1. Many nations, "including some heavily aided ones," have made no "appreciable advance" in the last twelve years, Galbraith wrote, primarily because "economic aid does not deal with decisive barriers to development – these being illiteracy, lack of an educated elite, inimical social institutions, no system of public administration, a lack of any sense of purpose." Economic aid is not enough, he concluded, and the Soviets know it, because their approach to development addresses larger factors. If it was to compete with its Soviet counterpart, American development policy needed to do so, as well.[9] Rostow, the administration's new deputy special assistant for national security affairs, sent Kennedy his memo on reform later that month, writing that the ICA was hindered by its "short-run perspective," its emphasis on specific projects instead of on entire nations, and its personnel of "technical assistance types." "The goal is to help other countries learn how to grow," Rostow insisted, and this requires a "new look," instead of a "defensive effort to shore-up weak economies." He told Kennedy that the United States required a program that would actually be able to move nations into self-sustained growth. Such a program needed to be bigger and bolder than anything that had come before.[10] This, it turned out, was exactly what Kennedy wanted to hear.

Kennedy had not, of course, selected Galbraith and Rostow at random. The president-elect came to them because he was already familiar with their ideas about development. In their academic positions at Harvard (Galbraith) and MIT (Rostow), the two were participants (albeit Galbraith on the periphery) in a conversation surrounding a new field of thought known as "modernization theory." This field promised a solution to the problem of underdevelopment that moved beyond the Point Four model in both action and aim. Modernization theory officially entered U.S. politics with the men Kennedy brought with him to Washington, the so-called action intellectuals.[11] "I was, simply, an early member of what was to become in 1959–1960 a large group of academics interested in public policy who were purposefully recruited by Kennedy," Rostow later recalled. "We were about the same age. Our outlook on affairs was similar."[12] Arthur Schlesinger Jr. called these men "the Charles River group" in reference to their academic homes in Boston.[13] Their outlook encompassed both fear that the Soviets were gaining ground from the United States in the developing world and confidence that Washington had the ability to stop them. That confidence came from a certainty in the universal value and universal attainability of American-style development. Modernization theorists did not dispute Point Four's goal of encouraging development. They did, however, dispute that it was possible to achieve development through economic growth alone. Development, they insisted, "required the modernization of entire social structures and ways of thought and life."[14]

This bold claim had deep roots in Western thought, but most scholars trace modernization theory's midcentury manifestation to a single book: Harvard sociologist Talcott Parsons's *The Structure of Social Action*.[15] Published in 1937, the book insisted that the self was not nearly as independent as scholars – particularly economists – had previously argued, but was, in fact, dominated by society. Humans make choices that reflect the cultural and social values that surround them, Parsons contended, which means that they cannot be studied simply as so-called rational economic actors. The "nonrational" actions determined by people's culture, social structures, and institutions played just as critical a role. In collaboration with his fellow theoretical sociologist Edward Shils, Parsons went on to categorize the noneconomic motivations that guided decision making in various societies. Parsons and Shils laid out a not-so-subtle dichotomy of "traditionalism" versus "rationalism" thereby opening the door to conversations about the distinction between "traditional" and "modern" societies.[16] "At this point," Nils Gilman has shown, "Parsons's theory began to appeal to the sociologists and political scientists trying to grasp what was going on in postcolonial regions. Even though economic improvement was the agreed sine qua non of development, social scientists in fields outside economics insisted that understanding the noneconomic implications and causes of economic growth was crucial for achieving that end."[17] It suddenly seemed clear that it was "the *structure* of society that mattered, rather than capital or training."[18]

Parsons's work was part of a larger shift taking place during the period. Daniel Rodgers has argued that "strong readings of society" were "one of the major intellectual projects of the middle decades of the twentieth century." "Structuralist interpretations of society and culture ran hard through the big books" of the period, drawing increased attention to social science disciplines beyond economics.[19] This was particularly true in the field of development. Economists had done an excellent job creating the framework of postwar European recovery, but they had failed to achieve the same results in the underdeveloped world. Modernization theorists argued that they could never hope to do so alone and needed the help of sociologists, political scientists, and psychologists "for a stipulation of the context of development."[20] Yet despite their respect for particularity, most modernization theorists looked to the past of a small number of nations for guidance, believing that the history of "modern" nations provided a clear guide for the future of "traditional" ones. They were thus ironically certain of the universal applicability and usefulness of their ideas.

Rostow, who lamented his fellow economists' general lack of a historical sense, was modernization theory's loudest proponent. His popular 1960 book *The Stages of Economic Growth* sold ideas he had been working on throughout the 1950s. Rostow saw the evolution of "society" as the key to development. He placed all societies (all over the globe, throughout all history) within five universal stages: "the traditional society, the preconditions for take-off, the take-off, the drive to maturity, and the age of high mass-consumption." Passage through these stages equaled "development." There were clear economic factors involved in that passage: "maturity," Rostow explained, required a redistribution of capital out of the hands of landed aristocrats and into the hands of capitalists, for one. But economic factors alone were not enough. "Maturity" also required a rejection of large family traditions "and, above all, the concept . . . that man need not regard his physical environment as virtually a factor given by nature and providence, but as an ordered world which, if rationally understood, can be manipulated in ways which yield productive change and, in one dimension at least, progress."[21] Culture had to change. Society had to change. "Development" was no longer an economic exercise, but a social passage.

Modernization theory began as a series of academic conversations about human agency and the relationship between the self and society. It developed a following outside of academia because it promised solutions to the widely perceived problem of underdevelopment – but not just any solutions. Modernization theory offered solutions that bolstered already existing beliefs about the United States within the United States: its society, culture, political systems, and place in the world. "Modernization became powerful in Cold War America," Michael Latham has persuasively shown, "because it crystallized a much deeper set of assumptions that were already held in common by a wide range of policymakers, scholars, journalists, and opinion leaders. In contrast to the more defensive phrasing of 'containment,' it emphasized the far more ambitious, liberal internationalist goal of transforming the structural environment itself."[22] Kennedy loved its possibilities – not only for the developing world but also for the United States.

Andrew Hoberek has argued that Kennedy "saw past modernization theory's sometimes dry formulations to its vision of foreign policy as a terrain on which Americans might reanimate their sense of historical mission and thereby reclaim their command of history's leading edge."[23] Kennedy believed that revitalizing U.S. foreign policy toward the underdeveloped world could revitalize the United States as a whole. "If we are to regain the initiative in world affairs, if we are to arouse the decent emotions of Americans, it is time again that we seek projects with the power of stirring and rallying our hopes and energies," he announced when introducing his 1958 bill for assistance to India. "Once again our national interest and creative magnanimity can merge in the service of freedom."[24] Kennedy wanted bold policies: they had to be big in order to make the kind of impact he desired, both at home and abroad. Modernization theory fit the bill. It gave new purpose to U.S. foreign policy, addressing the many struggles – of war, peace, prejudice, science, poverty, and beyond – that awaited the United States in the "New Frontier" of the 1960s.[25] Kennedy and his action intellectuals became New Frontiersmen, ready to fight battles abroad through reimagined aid programs.[26] Development, as Nick Cullather has argued, "spoke our dreams: a transparent, modernizing world mastering man and the environment with American technology."[27] Modernization was an adventure.

In March of 1961, rolling with the momentum created by his inaugural address, Kennedy told Congress, "no objective supporter of foreign aid can be satisfied with the existing program – actually a multiplicity of programs" whose administrative and procedural weaknesses "have begun to undermine confidence in our efforts both here and abroad." Although U.S. foreign aid had helped recipient countries, the president acknowledged, "it is a fact that many of the nations we are helping are not much nearer sustained economic growth than they were when our aid operations began." Aid needed to change. "This Congress at this session must make possible a dramatic turning point in the troubled history of foreign aid to the under-developed world," Kennedy insisted.[28] He requested a five-year commitment for a new "program of social and economic development." We will launch, he insisted, "a decade of development on which will depend, substantially, the kind of world in which we and our children shall live."[29]

Senator J. William Fulbright introduced the bill for the new program on behalf of the administration that May. The new program promised to achieve its goals through "well-conceived plans" directed toward "the social as well as the economic aspects of economic development." It would "emphasize long-range development assistance as the primary instrument of such growth."[30] At the heart of the bill was a request to secure approval in 1961 to make large-scale loans through 1966. In the attached letter, Kennedy insisted that this approval was crucial, because "real progress in economic development cannot be achieved by annual, short-term dispensations of aid and uncertainty as to future intentions." This method, he went on, represents "a departure from previous patterns in economic aid programs" that is "essential" to the effectiveness of the United States' new approach because it allows for long-term planning and long-term commitments.[31] Congress denied the request for five-year lending approval, wanting to keep a firm hand on the aid budget, but passed the act in September, creating the United States Agency for International Development (USAID). Even with the revisions, large-scale loans and large-scale planning would become early hallmarks of the new organization, which promised to provide Washington greater flexibility in its international relations, particularly with the nonaligned world. Modernization theory made neutralism acceptable, labeling it a manifestation of particular stages of development, a temporary stage that modernization itself would ultimately conquer. In this way, modernization both reinforced and granted new flexibility to the policy of containment.[32]

This was particularly obvious in the Alliance for Progress. Kennedy's program for aid to Latin America was a blatant attempt to halt the spread of Cuban-style communism through development. The initiative called for a ten-year commitment by the United State to provide aid to nations that promised to institute egalitarian political and legal reforms.[33] The alliance's 1961 charter further committed it to "accelerating the economic and social development of the participating countries."[34] The Kennedy administration did not think the task would be particularly challenging. "We believed that most of the region, especially the larger countries of South America and Mexico, were on the threshold of a Rostovian take-off," Task Force for Latin America member (and Harvard economist) Lincoln Gordon later explained. They just needed a helpful push forward from the United States.[35] These pushes would resemble those undertaken by USAID around the world, largely because USAID administered the Alliance for Progress. In the end, most Latin American countries ended up working around the alliance altogether, instead taking their requests directly to USAID, which subverted the idealistic goals of partnership ensconced in the charter.[36] Instead of heralding a new era of cooperation, the alliance ended up reinforcing long-standing concerns about northern imperialism.[37] Unfortunately, it gradually became clear that expanded aid did not necessarily mean "better" aid – from anyone's perspective. But what became obvious by 1965 was still not apparent, at least to most observers, in 1961.

In the optimism of that year, the Kennedy administration seized upon the idea of aid for modernization, and not just for economic development, as a way of confronting the manifold complexities facing the United States in the New Frontier. This greatly expanded the scale of U.S. development aid. USAID moved aid far from the grassroots, technical focus that had dominated previous programs.[38] Now, "experts" – as opposed to the "technical assistance types" Rostow disparaged – would use large sums of money to enact large-scale plans that would reshape landscapes, societies, cultures, and, eventually, economies. This confidence in the power of expertise and macroeconomic planning exemplified what David Harvey and James C. Scott have called "high modernism," which contrasted with the "low modernism" that had animated Point Four. High modernists embraced "a particularly sweeping vision of how the benefits of technical and scientific progress might be applied – usually through the state – in every field of human activity." In contrast, low modernists argued that development could come through small-scale grassroots projects that targeted individual need. Both high and low modernists wanted development, but they pursued it through very different means.[39]

Modernization theory, with its commitment to universals and ambitious scale, determined the original shape of both USAID and the Alliance for Progress. But these were not the only aid initiatives that came out of the White House in 1961. The history of the other one challenges the idea that modernization theory lay behind all of Kennedy's foreign aid programs. As Daniel Immerwahr has shown, the roots of the Peace Corps lay in community development, not modernization theory. Yet despite this difference the Peace Corps ultimately served similar goals, and was subject to some of the same problems, as other administration initiatives.

The idea of the Peace Corps did not originate with Kennedy; he inherited it from Hubert Humphrey and Henry Reuss, who had initially dubbed it the "Point Four Youth Corps." Reuss had come up with the idea after visiting private community development aid programs in Asia. The men working within them were engaged in exactly the kind of efforts that the authors of *The Ugly American* celebrated: "little things" and "tiny battles."[40] After Kennedy's election, there was a moment when it seemed likely that the Peace

Corps would move away from its low modernist origins. Kennedy asked Max Millikan, a prominent modernization theorist, to come up with a plan for the agency. Millikan did, and it looked just like what one would expect a modernization theorist to create. But it was never implemented. Instead, Kennedy handed the Peace Corps over to his brother-in-law, Sargent Shriver, who largely rejected Millikan's ideas. The Corps' volunteers, Shriver insisted, would go abroad not to serve the grand ambitions of the State Department, but "to teach, or to build, or to work in the communities into which they are sent. They will serve local institutions, living with the people they are helping."[41] The Corps' leadership, Elizabeth Cobbs Hoffman has argued, "tended to place more faith in the idealism of its volunteers than in the content of specific projects," which differed significantly from the procedure at USAID.[42] Both programs, however, were testaments to American hubris. Both were also decidedly Cold War tools. The ultimate goal was a world developed out of the communists' reach.

Nowhere was this truer than in South Vietnam. In 1956, Kennedy told attendees of the Conference on Vietnam Luncheon that what "we must offer [the Vietnamese] is a revolution – a political, economic and social revolution far superior to anything the Communists can offer." Behind this declaration lay a decidedly Rostow-esque vision. "We must," Kennedy continued,

> supply capital to replace that drained by the centuries of colonial exploitation; technicians to train those handicapped by deliberate policies of illiteracy; guidance to assist a nation taking those first feeble steps toward the complexities of a republican form of government. All this and more we can offer Free Vietnam, as it passes through the present period of transition on its way to a new era – an era of pride and independence, and an era of democratic and economic growth – an era which, when contrasted with the long years of colonial oppression, will truly represent a political, social and economic revolution.[43]

This was easier said than done, as Kennedy would quickly discover as president.

Kennedy wanted to develop South Vietnam economically and socially, in the process making it an example to show the developing world what U.S. nation-building efforts could accomplish. As Edward Miller has shown, Ngô Đình Diệm, Kennedy's South Vietnamese counterpart, wanted development, as well, but he did not always want to structure that development along the lines the Americans tried to sell him. In order to keep moving forward, nation-building activities in South Vietnam demanded compromises from both sides – a reality that highlighted one of the key limitations of modernization theory: it worked far better in theory than in practice, because it required negotiation with real people, not idealized ones. Ngô Đình Nhu, who worked closely with the Americans on development projects, "explicitly rejected Rostow's portrayal of modernization" and was "particularly suspicious of high modernist plans for development," forcing the Americans to rely more heavily on low modernist ones. The Ngô brothers wanted modernization on their own terms. "Like other Third World nativist leaders during the 1950s and 1960s, Nhu thought of economic development not as a choice among competing Western models but as a process that ought to fit with Vietnamese priorities and Vietnamese cultural needs."[44] This put Nhu into direct conflict with an administration that insisted that nation-building plans for underdeveloped countries needed to demonstrate "a clear understanding of the desired pace and direction of modernization, *based on our objectives* and on the limits and possibilities set by the particular country's stage of political, social and economic development."[45]

South Vietnam was far from the only country where the modernization objectives of the United States failed to perfectly correspond with the development objectives of national leaders.[46] Instead of changing its theoretical model in response, however, the Kennedy administration began looking for ways to alter its implementation. As it quickly became clear that it was not going to be as easy as modernization theorists had imagined to plug nations into the formula they had created, they began calling for alliances with the key group within nations that could enforce American objectives: the military. During the early 1950s, American academics had tended to criticize military-led regimes as backward and repressive. But they had already altered that assessment by the late 1950s. In a series of reports between 1959 and 1960, several key modernization theorists and Washington policy makers argued in favor of using military forces to administer economic and social development programs in underdeveloped countries.[47] The idea gained early traction in the Kennedy administration. "Beginning in 1961," Bradley Simpson wrote, citing one prime example, "the State Department recommended supplementing traditional military training for Indonesian officers with . . . training in 'legal [affairs], public safety, public health, welfare, finance, and education, economics, property control, supply, management, [and] public communications."[48] A 1962 State Department report insisted that military forces in Latin America should be "directly involved in bringing the benefits of the Alliance to the people, especially in rural areas."[49] In 1963, under Rostow's direction, the State Department Policy Planning Staff produced a study calling for the widespread use of the armed services in undeveloped nations as "a powerful potential group of 'modernizers' and a conduit [for] contemporary Western thought and values."[50] The Kennedy administration willfully decided to delay democracy in favor of pursuing stability. There were, predictably, consequences.[51] In the aftermath of the shift, as Daniel Immerwahr explained, "modernization projects became simultaneously more violent and less tethered to local conditions. From the perspective of any number of emerging perspectives – including human rights, environmentalism, participatory democracy, pacifism, and peasant movements – modernization projects became harder and harder to justify."[52] They also became harder to sell both at home and abroad.

The outcome of modernization theory in action made it increasingly unpopular, but it was not just the politics of modernization that were called into question. So, too, were its fundamental premises. Voices of criticism grew louder inside and outside of the United States, with violent domestic discontent ironically helping to make untenable claims that the country was *the* model of development. By the early 1970s, modernization theory had been thoroughly discredited within academia, within Washington, and within the developing world.[53] The New Frontiersmen's adventure collapsed under the weight of expansive disappointment and disillusionment.

Kennedy brought modernization theory into the White House because he liked what it promised to do with foreign aid, and because it fit so well with his existing vision of history and of America's place within it. Modernization theory offered a progressive foreign policy option in an otherwise conservative moment. Kennedy badly wanted to deploy American "expertise" and American "liberalism" abroad; modernization theory gave him a justification for doing so.[54] He had the will and had found a way. Under Kennedy, John McClure wrote, "once again . . . the non-Western world [was] to be the site of Western adventures, the battlefield on which Westerners tired of domestic routines [could] find urgency, adventure, and glory."[55] But the glory never materialized.

The 1960s did not live up to Kennedy's promise of being the "development decade." There were many reasons for the failure of that promise, reasons that went far beyond Kennedy's forced early exit from the scene. It is too easy to simply blame the inherent weaknesses within modernization theory itself, although these weaknesses did exist and led academics to turn away from it during the late 1960s. But in fact the policies inspired by modernization theory were always distorted by Cold War imperatives. In Kennedy's White House, Michael Hunt has argued, "the third world was still a collection of trouble spots where freedom was a mixed good and sometimes even downright dangerous." The administration "clutched at 'modernization theory' as an enlightened way of managing these trouble spots."[56] Despite the administration's rhetoric, the "managing" was always the most important part. Kennedy definitely wanted to spread development, but global security concerns limited his vision of what that development could look like. And this, in turn, limited what development could achieve.

Reflecting on Kennedy's "third world policy" in 1965, Schlesinger wrote, "The Charles River approach represented a very American effort to persuade the developing countries to base their revolutions on Locke rather than Marx. Perhaps this was a dream," he conceded, but it "represented an immense improvement over the philosophy of the country store" – Eisenhower's hodgepodge of aid programs. "It gave our economic policy toward the third world a rational design and a coherent purpose," Schlesinger insisted. "Its spirit was generous and humane. It may have fallen short of the ferocities of the situation. But, given the nature of our institutions and values, it was probably the best we could do."[57] Schlesinger's was too generous an interpretation even for 1965. Kennedy was aware of the limitations of the "Charles River approach" from the beginning, though he seemed often to forget them, or to proceed as if he had forgotten them. "We must face the fact," he had stated in the fall of 1961, "that the United States is neither omnipotent nor omniscient – that we are only 6 percent of the world's population – that we cannot impose our will on the other 94 percent of mankind – that we cannot right every wrong or reverse every adversary – and that therefore there cannot be an American solution to every problem."[58] The Charles River approach, which built policies out of modernization theory, was a decidedly American solution to the problem of underdevelopment. It suffered for its hubris, but far less than the millions of people who found themselves on the receiving end of its policies – victims of the effort to master the New Frontier.

NOTES

1 "Text of Kennedy's Inaugural Outlining Policies on World Peace and Freedom," *New York Times*, January 21, 1961, 8.

2 Truman's Inaugural Address, January 20, 1949, http://www.trumanlibrary.org/calendar/viewpapers.php?pid=1030, accessed December 8, 2014.

3 "Objectives and Nature of the Point IV Program," enclosed in memorandum from Dean Acheson to Harry Truman (March 14, 1949), in *Foreign Relations of the United States, 1949* (Washington, DC: United States Government Printing Office, 1976), 1:776–77.

4 W. W. Rostow, *Eisenhower, Kennedy, and Foreign Aid* (Austin: University of Texas Press, 1985), 58–60.

5 Kennedy quoted in Jeffrey F. Taffet, *Foreign Aid as Foreign Policy* (New York: Routledge, 2007), 26.

6 Robert D. Dean, "Masculinity as Ideology: John F. Kennedy and the Domestic Politics of Foreign Policy," *Diplomatic History* 22, no. 1 (Winter 1998): 38–39.

7 Ibid., 36–43. On reforms under Eisenhower, see Arthur M. Schlesinger Jr., *A Thousand Days: John F. Kennedy in the White House* (Boston: Houghton Mifflin, 1965), 589–91.

8 The Task Force on Foreign Economic Policy, "Report to the Honorable John F. Kennedy" (December 31, 1960); Task Force Report 12/31/60, Foreign Economic Policy, box 297, National Security Files, Kennedy Presidential Library.

9 John Kenneth Galbraith, "A Positive Approach to Economic Aid" (February 1, 1961); Foreign Aid 12/60–2/61, box 297, National Security Files, Kennedy Presidential Library.

10 Rostow to Kennedy, Memorandum (February 28, 1961), *Foreign Relations of the United States, 1961–1963*, ed. Glenn W. LaFantasie et al. (Washington, DC: U.S. Government Printing Office, 1995), 9:204–09.

11 Theodore H. White, "The Action Intellectuals," *Life*, June 9, 1967, 43–76.

12 Rostow quoted in Michael Latham, *Modernization as Ideology: American Social Science and "Nation Building" in the Kennedy Era* (Chapel Hill: University of North Carolina Press, 2000), 58.

13 Schlesinger Jr., *A Thousand Days*, 587.

14 Ibid., 586–87.

15 Nils Gilman, *Mandarins of the Future* (Baltimore, MD: Johns Hopkins University Press, 2003), 24–76; Talcott Parsons, *The Structure of Social Action: A Study in Social Theory with Special Reference to a Group of Recent European Writers* (New York: McGraw-Hill Book Company, Inc., 1937).

16 Ibid., 74–87; Latham, *Modernization as Ideology*, 30–36.

17 Gilman, *Mandarins of the Future*, 82.

18 Odd Arne Westad, *The Global Cold War* (Cambridge: Cambridge University Press, 2007), 31.

19 Daniel T. Rodgers, *Age of Fracture* (Cambridge, MA: Harvard University Press, 2011), 4.

20 James Smoot Coleman, *Nationalism and Development in Africa: Selected Essays*, ed. Richard L. Sklar (Berkeley: University of California Press, 1994), 162.

21 W. W. Rostow, *The Stages of Economic Growth*, 3rd ed. (Cambridge: Cambridge University Press, 1990), 4, 18–19.

22 Michael Latham, *The Right Kind of Revolution* (Ithaca, NY: Cornell University Press, 2011), 58.

23 Andrew Hoberek, "The New Frontier: *Dune*, the Middle Class, and Post-1960 U.S. Foreign Policy," in *American Literature and Culture in an Age of Cold War*, ed. Daniel Grausam and Steven Belletto (Iowa City: University of Iowa Press, 2012), 86.

24 Quoted in Rostow, *Eisenhower, Kennedy, and Foreign Aid*, 8.

25 Kimber Charles Pearce, *Rostow, Kennedy, and the Rhetoric of Foreign Aid* (East Lansing: Michigan State University Press, 2001), 21.

26 John A. McClure, *Late Imperial Romance* (London: Verso, 1994), 40–49.

27 Nick Cullather, "Development? It's History," *Diplomatic History* 24, no. 4 (Fall 2000): 652.

28 "Text of Kennedy's Message to Congress Proposing a New Foreign Aid Program," *New York Times*, March 23, 1961, 14.

29 Ibid.

30 *Hearings on S. 1983 before the Committee on Foreign Affairs, United States Senate (May–June 1961), Eighty-Seventh Congress, First Session* (Washington, DC: U.S. Government Printing Office, 1961), 1–25.

31 Ibid., 25–26.

32 David Webster, "Regimes in Motion: The Kennedy Administration and Indonesia's New Frontier, 1960–1962," *Diplomatic History* 33, no. 1 (January 2009): 100–101. See also Robert B. Rakove, *Kennedy, Johnson, and the Nonaligned World* (Cambridge: Cambridge University Press, 2013), 174–90.

33 Taffet, *Foreign Aid as Foreign Policy*, 5.

34 Latham, *Modernization as Ideology*, 82.

35 Quoted in ibid., 80.

36 Taffet, *Foreign Aid as Foreign Policy*, 39.

37 Walter LaFeber, *Inevitable Revolutions*, 2nd ed. (New York: W. W. Norton, 1993), 150–96.

38 Amanda Kay McVety, "Pursuing Progress: Point Four in Ethiopia," *Diplomatic History* 32, no. 3 (June 2008): 371–403.

39 James C. Scott, *Seeing Like a State* (New Haven, CT: Yale University Press, 1998), 90; David Harvey, *The Condition of Post-Modernity* (Oxford: Basil Blackwell, 1989); Jess Gilbert, "Low Modernism and the Agrarian New Deal," in *Fighting for the Farm*, ed. Jane Adams (Philadelphia: University of Pennsylvania Press, 2003), 129–46.

40 Daniel Immerwahr, "Quests for Community" (PhD diss., University of California–Berkeley, 2011), iv, 124; Elizabeth Cobbs Hoffman, *All You Need Is Love* (Cambridge, MA: Harvard University Press, 1998), 41–42.

41 Immerwahr, "Quests for Community," 123.

42 Hoffman, *All You Need Is Love*, 61.

43 Remarks of Senator John F. Kennedy at the Conference on Vietnam Luncheon in the Hotel Willard, Washington, DC (June 1, 1956), available at http://www.jfklibrary.org, accessed December 8, 2014.

44 Edward Miller, *Misalliance* (Cambridge, MA: Harvard University Press, 2013), 235–36.

45 Basic National Security Policy for 1962, quoted in Bradley R. Simpson, *Economists with Guns* (Stanford, CA: Stanford University Press, 2008), 8; emphasis mine.

46 Larry Grubs, *Secular Missionaries* (Amherst: University of Massachusetts Press, 2009); Nick Cullather, *The Hungry World* (Cambridge, MA: Harvard University Press, 2010), 159–231; Dennis Merrell, *Bread and the Ballot* (Chapel Hill: University of North Carolina Press, 1990), 169–203; Amanda Kay McVety, *Enlightened Aid* (New York: Oxford University Press, 2012), 161–94.

47 Simpson, Economists with Guns, 67–69.

48 Ibid., 70.

49 Latham, *The Right Kind of Revolution*, 131–32.

50 Simpson, *Economists with Guns*, 72.

51 In addition to Simpson, *Economists with Guns*, see Stephen M. Streeter, "Nation-Building in the Land of Eternal Counter-Insurgency: Guatemala and the Contradictions of the Alliance for Progress," *Third World Quarterly* 27, no. 1 (2006): 57–68; and Jeremy Kuzmarov, "Modernizing Repression: Policy Training, Political Violence, and Nation-Building in the 'American Century,'" *Diplomatic History* 33, no. 2 (April 2009): 191–221.

52 Daniel Immerwahr, "Modernization and Development in U.S. Foreign Relations," *Passport* 43:2 (September 2012): 23.

53 David Ekbladh, *The Great American Mission: Modernization and the Construction of an American World Order* (Princeton, NJ: Princeton University Press, 2010): 226–56; Gilman, *Mandarins of the Future*, 203–56; Latham, *The Right Kind of Revolution*, 157–82.

54 Leerom Medovoi, "Cold War American Culture as the Age of Three Worlds," *Minnesota Review* 55, no. 57 (2002): 167–69; Andrew Hoberek, "Postmodernism and Modernization," *Twentieth-Century Literature* 57, nos. 3–4 (Fall–Winter 2011): 341–53.

55 McClure, *Late Imperial Romance*, 45.

56 Michael H. Hunt, *The American Ascendancy* (Chapel Hill: University of North Carolina Press, 2007), 208.

57 Schlesinger Jr., *A Thousand Days*, 589.

58 Kennedy quoted in Robert A. Packenham, *Liberal America and the Third World* (Princeton, NJ: Princeton University Press, 1973), 84.

8

VAUGHN RASBERRY

JFK and the Global Anticolonial Movement

In 1961, John F. Kennedy confronted a seemingly peripheral but highly symbolic foreign policy dilemma: whether to finance Ghana's Volta River Project (VRP), a massive dam construction designed to generate electricity, promote modernization, and diversify Ghana's economy – a project similar in scope to the 1933 Tennessee Valley Authority, which proponents lauded as a success story that could be replicated in the non-Western world.

In 1960, Eisenhower had pledged $30 million toward construction of the VRP but soon reneged on the offer when the assassination of Kwame Nkrumah's Congolese protégé Patrice Lumumba – whose elimination the CIA plotted if not executed – soured relations between Washington and Accra. Recent history indicated what consequences might ensue from this decision. A few years prior, on July 19, 1956, the Eisenhower administration withdrew funding for Gamal Abdel Nasser's Aswan Dam project, which the Egyptian leader likewise envisioned as a massive modernizing project necessary for his country's future. Many observers viewed the withdrawal of financing as a provocation against Nasser and a catalyst for the Suez Crisis, inaugurated when Nasser – in an act of defiance celebrated across the Third World – nationalized the British- and French-controlled Suez Canal Company on July 26, 1956. Swiftly, Britain, France, and Israel collaborated in an ill-fated invasion of Egypt that summoned superpower involvement and nearly precipitated world war.

As a Massachusetts senator in the late 1950s, JFK distinguished himself as a critic of European colonialism and Eisenhower's foreign policy in the Third World. Whereas Eisenhower reneged on a critical foreign aid project in Africa, supposedly to disastrous effect, Kennedy expanded development projects in Africa while cultivating relationships with the continent's leadership. Exemplary of the confluence of diplomacy and development, projects like the VRP tested Kennedy's anticolonial mettle as much as they frustrated leaders like Nkrumah. Consider, for example, Richard Wright's admonition to Nkrumah in his conclusion to *Black Power* (1954): "Beware of a Volta

Project built by foreign money. Build your own Volta, and build it out of the sheer lives and bodies of your people!"[1] Yet many African leaders, including Nkrumah, found such counsel difficult to put into practice.

While fielding divergent views from his cabinet, public opinion, and other politicians, Kennedy also – idiosyncratically – sought the counsel of numerous African heads of state on the VRP. Why, historian Philip E. Muehlenbeck asks, did Kennedy ultimately decide to finance the VRP?[2] Few inside or outside of Kennedy's cabinet supported aid for a project initiated by Nkrumah, whom officials perceived, at best, as a mercurial practitioner of nonalignment and, at worst, as an anti-Western radical with Soviet inclinations. At the same time, Kennedy was aware that Nkrumah represented one of the most prominent voices on the continent. In private conversations with JFK, pro-Western African leaders were critical of Ghana's prime minister, whom they saw as a megalomaniacal aspirant to pan-African leadership. Nonetheless, most Africans advised the president to support the VRP. If he did not, their argument went, the continent would lose faith in Kennedy's commitment to African development and Nkrumah would be forced to seek out Soviet assistance. Kennedy's deliberations on the VRP, emblematic of his approach to foreign policy in the Third World and the global anticolonial movement, illuminates the ways in which his strategy intersected, and conflicted, with other domestic and foreign policy priorities: anticommunism, desegregation, and modernization.[3]

Scholars of Kennedy's stance on decolonization and foreign policy in the Third World differ markedly on the substance and novelty of his approach. Whether negative or positive, however, assessments of Kennedy's relation to decolonization usually proceed with scant reference to the intellectual history of the global anticolonial movement itself. Yet since this debate hinges in large measure on the complex meanings of decolonization, this intellectual history is crucial to gauging Kennedy's postcolonial legacy. Toward this end, this chapter aims to construct a dialogue between JFK's intellectuals and anticolonial thought: one constellated around dilemmas flowing from the rise of decolonization, on the one hand, and the apex of Cold War tensions, on the other.

Critics of JFK's record on decolonization contend that his commitments were largely rhetorical and continuous with Eisenhower's policies; these critics rightly cite his dedication to anticommunism and covert adventures like the Bay of Pigs debacle, proxy wars in Vietnam and Laos, and the CIA's involvement in the assassination of Lumumba and attempts on the life of Fidel Castro. Some highlight JFK's inaction on apartheid South Africa. Still other critics suggest that his endorsement of African independence was calculated to secure African American voter support without actually undertaking civil rights reform, which would have alienated an indispensible southern Democratic constituency. For some commentators, modernization theory represents a serious effort, in the volatile context of decolonization, to promote change that would make the Third World look like "us" – a synecdoche for postwar liberalism – and not like "them," the Soviets or Chinese. For others, modernization theory rebranded Manifest Destiny and imperialism while disavowing its intellectual heritage in Enlightenment philosophies of history that subordinated non-Western peoples to advanced Western societies.[4]

Scholars like Muehlenbeck have defended Kennedy's African policies, arguing that the president – at considerable political risk – combined powerful rhetoric and diplomacy with substantive development measures in an unmatched attempt to court African leaders, constrain colonial aggression by European allies like France and Portugal, and advance economic and nation building projects in Africa, Asia, and Latin America. For example, Kennedy pressured Portugal to relinquish its colonial occupation of Mozambique and Angola, despite counsel from military officials and other cabinet members who worried that antagonizing Lisbon would result in the United States losing its strategic military base in the Azores, a cluster of islands controlled by Portugal. When newspapers quoted (or misquoted) G. Mennen Williams, assistant secretary of state for African affairs, as proclaiming, "Africa is for the Africans," Kennedy qualified but did not retreat from Williams' controversial remark. When queried at a press conference, Kennedy gamely replied: "The statement 'Africa is for the Africans' does not seem to me to be a very unreasonable statement. He made it clear that he was talking about all those who felt that they were Africans, whatever their color might be, whatever their race might be. I do not know who else Africa should be for."[5] No doubt Kennedy expanded his conception of African identity (to include European settler communities in Africa) after facing a backlash from Portuguese, South African, and French colonialists, but he also envisioned indigenous Africans – at least those who seemed winnable to the liberal Democratic sphere – as the agents of the continent's future.

Though JFK's rhetorical support for decolonization did not always translate into equally robust policy, perhaps his forceful language constitutes his most enduring legacy in the postcolonial arena. What one scholar wrote in regard to Eisenhower's foreign policy in Africa also applies to Kennedy's: "While scholars may bemoan the confusion of style and substance, oratory and action, it is often difficult to distinguish between them."[6] Indeed, that difficulty is amplified in the case of JFK, the nation's most literary president. But it is inaccurate to suggest that Kennedy differed little – either in style or substance – from his predecessors.

On first glance, previous presidents established precedents for Kennedy's own anticolonial posture. In the 1920s, Woodrow Wilson electrified anticolonial nationalists in Egypt, Vietnam, and India with his pronouncements of national self-determination as a universal principle supported by the U.S. government.[7] In 1941, Churchill and Roosevelt advanced the Atlantic Charter, which proclaims: "They respect the rights of all peoples to choose the form of government under which they will live; and they wish to see sovereign rights and self-government restored to those who have been forcibly deprived of them."[8] But in the same way that Wilson's Fourteen Points applied to European nations reeling from the belligerence and destruction of the First World War, the Atlantic Charter addressed primarily European nations threatened by Nazism and Fascist aggression – *not* non-Western nations under the yoke of colonialism. Subsequent statements by Truman and Eisenhower betrayed a similar tendency. In the decade after World War II, these presidents struggled to reconcile competing demands that would later vex Kennedy: Western, anti-Soviet unity and postwar reconstruction in Europe, on the one hand, and the increasingly untenable colonial status quo, on the other. Under these constraints, the Truman and Eisenhower administrations muted their opposition to colonialism in order to preserve Cold War and NATO solidarity.[9]

Kennedy's rhetoric far exceeded the equivocal language of his predecessors. As a young senator in July of 1957, Kennedy delivered a speech to the Senate, "The Challenge of Imperialism: Algeria," that repudiated the French colonial war in Algeria and electrified the Afro-Arab world. "The most powerful single force in the world today," the speech begins, "is neither communism nor capitalism, neither the H-bomb nor the guided missile – it is man's eternal desire to be free and independent." Freedom is under threat by both Soviet *and* Western imperialism, and among global infringements on national freedom, Algeria stands out "above all the rest." Consequently Algeria has become a matter for U.S., not only French, foreign policy. Kennedy ridiculed the notion that the Eisenhower administration offended neither side in the conflict with its "head-in-the-sands policy – when, in truth, we have earned the suspicion of all."[10] Given the Eisenhower administration's provision of weapons to France through NATO, its tacit acceptance of colonial rule (despite vague and occasional references to national independence for all nations), and its unwillingness to promote French-Algerian mediation via the UN or other diplomatic channels, the United States, as Kennedy understood, was hardly agnostic in the conflict – especially from the Third World vantage point. Failure to shift this policy portended ill for the Cold War, as communists wasted no opportunity to capitalize on Western depredations in Asia, Africa, and

Latin America. Kennedy's speech frames the conflict as a hindrance to the successful operation of NATO, and for this reason a properly global concern. Yet Kennedy also draws deftly on the revolutionary histories of France and America to legitimate Algerian struggles for liberation, imbuing the conflict with what his Western audience would recognize as a "universal" dimension.

Domestically, Republicans censured Kennedy's speech and reaffirmed their support for France, America's oldest ally. Secretary of State Dulles replied that if Senator Kennedy wanted to arraign colonialism, "he ought to concentrate on the Communist variety rather than the French."[11] Even Adlai Stevenson, the racial liberal, denounced the senator's speech on Algeria. In France, the speech elicited sharp criticism, and in Algeria a bomb detonated outside the American consulate.

In France, the Algerian War was a crucible for intellectuals, shaping the postwar discourse on the interwoven themes of revolutionary violence, decolonization, and identity politics. According to James Le Sueur, as intellectuals on the left and right "intervened in the public debate over decolonization . . . they were frequently targeted by the state, military, police, other intellectuals, vigilante groups, and even the fascistic terrorism of the OAS (Organisation de l'Armée Secrete) for their real or perceived roles *as* intellectuals."[12] Famously, Frantz Fanon resigned from his post as a psychiatrist in Algeria's Blida-Joinville hospital, where he had analyzed the effects of Algerian mental disorders in the context of French colonial war. Renouncing his French identity, Fanon adopted the Algerian struggle as his own, joining the resistance as a military theorist – and employing, as Tunisian intellectual Albert Memmi noted, the first-person plural pronoun *we* (as in *We Algerians*) to signify his identification with the resistance. JFK's celebrated emphasis on courage (defined as "grace under pressure," which he is said to have adapted from Hemingway) stands in recto verso relation to the heroic subjectivities of figures such as Fanon. Outside the precincts of power but far from powerless, many anticolonial intellectuals were free to experiment with various forms of solidarity politics, often beyond the boundaries of the nation-state or liberal democratic norms. If the constraints of elected office required distance between official support for Third World independence and actual liberation movements, Kennedy relied on diplomacy, powerful rhetorical pronouncements, pressure on European colonial allies, and foreign aid and modernization schemes as means to circumvent the war and violence that Fanon (and communism) imagined as intrinsic to decolonization.

But when conciliatory methods failed, Kennedy's administration advocated covert military operations in geographies deemed irreversibly interwoven with communism. Kennedy proved as ardent an anticommunist as his predecessors, but unlike Truman and Eisenhower he was better able to distinguish between communist radicalism and Third World – especially African – nationalism, and to recognize the latter movements' legitimate aspirations. He grasped that leaders like Nkrumah, Nasser, Ben Bella, Sekou Toure, and Julius Nyerere were suspicious of communism but keen to manipulate the Soviet Union and the United States to their advantage: one of the geopolitical innovations of nonalignment. But there were limits, of course, to Kennedy's indulgence of anticolonial leaders who veered too closely to the Soviet sphere or otherwise disrupted the calibrations of U.S. foreign policy. Vietnam, Laos, and Cuba stand out as the exemplary cases of this clash between anticolonial agency and anticommunist imperatives.

In Latin America, a region where the administration suspected the Cold War would not be won but could well be lost, Cuba "was an immediate priority for John Kennedy." At a press conference on April 12, 1961, amid suspicions of U.S. hostility to the Cuban Revolution, Kennedy announced to the world that the United States did not intend to invade Cuba: "there will not be, under any conditions, any intervention in Cuba by United States armed forces, and this government will do everything it possibly can . . . to make sure that there are no Americans involved in any actions inside." [13] But days after this announcement, the Bay of Pigs invasion not only embarrassed Kennedy and vitiated his anticolonial clout but also redounded to Soviet power in the region.

Contrast Kennedy's public image after this debacle with Khrushchev's speech on January 6, 1961, when he outlined an ambitious new foreign policy, welcoming "Fidel Castro as a legitimate member of the Soviet bloc. And in deference to both Castro and Mao Zedong," Aleksandr Fursenko and Timothy Naftali write, "who considered themselves more revolutionary than the peasant bureaucrat in the Kremlin, Khrushchev added that for the first time the Kremlin viewed national liberation struggles as 'sacred wars' that merited assistance and would probably require violence to succeed. As examples of this kind of war, he offered the struggles in Algeria and Vietnam." [14] No doubt the Soviet language of sacred war resonated with Fanonism and its various progeny, such as the Black Panther movement. Yet for many liberal African American activists working within democratic institutional processes, anticolonial struggle involved not a turn to violence or to transnational militancy but rather patient, methodical, and relentless mastery of the institutions that maintained power.

As Carol Anderson argues, in many instances "black liberals were like stealth fighters who imbibed the strategy pronounced by the first

African-American leader of the NAACP, James Weldon Johnson. Johnson noted that 'the black man fights passively . . . He bears the fury of the storm as does the willow tree.' That stealth resistance, to bend like the willow instead of taking the blows and snapping like an oak, has made it difficult to discern what role black liberals played at all in decolonization." These African American liberals were the older urbane intellectuals with whom the Kennedy administration felt it could communicate – not the younger generation of writers like James Baldwin and Lorraine Hansberry, who in May of 1963 met in Robert Kennedy's Manhattan apartment, warning him of the "explosive situation" of racial discrimination in the northern cities.[15]

This older generation included figures like Ralph Bunche, the diplomat and secretary of the United Nations who at that time was embroiled in the Congo conflict. In early June of 1960, in the midst of the presidential campaign, JFK sent Robert Kennedy to proposition Bunche about the prospect of assisting his campaign as an adviser on international affairs. Robert Kennedy, according to Bunche's UN colleague and biographer, Brian Urquhart, "said that his brother recognized that foreign affairs would be the most important challenge facing the new president and needed sound advice by someone who was 'practicing' rather than theorizing in the field."[16] Devoted to the United Nations, an institution he helped to build, Bunche declined this request.

But Kennedy's intuition about Bunche – who was nothing if not a "practicing" diplomat – was astute, and it provides some terms with which to gauge the future president's own relation to decolonization. In 1936, Bunche published his searing Marxist-inflected treatise, *A World View of Race*, about which he later wrote that it was earning him the label "Red." But over time he toned down his radical proclivities, if not his dedication to African independence, and labored for decades within the U.S. foreign policy establishment in some of the world's most volatile conflicts. Like Kennedy, Bunche advocated Third World independence but was also an anticommunist who sought to mediate decolonization through international institutions like the UN. During the 1940s, Bunche developed the system of "trusteeship," which facilitated a gradualist approach to independence.

Kennedy understood that the gradualist approach had, in the early 1960s, become untenable, and like Bunche he too increasingly found his ideals diluted by practical considerations. As one commentator notes, three and a half years after his controversial speech on the French war in Algeria, Kennedy "viewed the Algerian situation through a presidential political lens. He now confronted the same dilemma that had plagued his predecessor: How to advance the principle of anti-colonialism without jeopardizing U.S. security interests? . . . Would the cause of containment best be served by aligning with the political 'wave of the future' in the Third World, or by backing the colonial policies of important NATO allies?"[17] Vis-à-vis anticolonialism, Kennedy's own premium on courage could not withstand the pressure of presidential realpolitik. As Miloud Barkaoui notes, JFK had repeatedly urged the Eisenhower administration to intervene in the conflict via NATO or UN negotiations. "As president, however, he became much more concerned about the threat which international communism was believed to be posing not only to Algeria but also to the entire region, at a time when the Cold War rivalry was becoming more endemic."[18] Amid these pressures, Kennedy reverted to the Eisenhower approach to Algeria – containment, anticommunism, accommodation to France and American Europeanists – during his tenure in office.

Aware that the NATO and Soviet spheres were competing for their allegiance, Africans questioned the sincerity of Kennedy's commitment to African independence. If the nation subjugated its own black population, what did JFK's outreach to Africa mean? Was it merely a Cold War ploy? As commentators have claimed, much of Kennedy's outreach to the Third World functioned as a proxy for addressing domestic civil rights concerns. "The global decolonization movement," Renee Romano writes, "contributed to a growing concern about the problem of domestic discrimination, particularly in an administration that was more interested in foreign than domestic policy."[19] The domestic situation enabled anticolonial leaders like Mao, in 1963, to articulate his support of the Afro-American struggle in the following terms: "The Kennedy administration is insidiously using dual tactics," Mao asserted. "On the one hand, it continues to connive and take part in discrimination against Negroes and their persecution, and it even sends troops to suppress them. On the other hand; in the attempt to numb the fighting will of the black people and deceive the masses of the country the Kennedy administration is parading as an advocate of 'the defense of human rights' and 'the protection of the civil rights of Negroes,' calling upon the black people to exercise 'restraint' and proposing the 'civil rights legislation' to Congress. But more and more Afro-Americans are seeing through the tactics of the Kennedy administration."[20]

Like his anticolonial support for Algeria and Angola, JFK's courtship of African and other Third World leaders was meant to appeal to African Americans – but Kennedy, aware of the need to placate southern segregationists, could characterize anticolonialism as a Cold War imperative rather than an explicitly racial issue.

This strategy conscripted the Kennedy administration into the civil rights maelstrom in a manner it might have preferred to avoid, or at least postpone.

Though Kennedy prioritized foreign policy over desegregation, intensifying racial conflict and militancy among black Americans forced his administration to confront racial equality domestically. Historians trace the president's increased attention to civil rights to the spring of 1963, when Kennedy began to deliver speeches couching racial equality as a "moral issue" and the State Department's Dean Rusk appeared before the Senate Commerce Committee in July to promote civil rights legislation. The early years of the Cold War compelled every U.S. presidential administration to undertake some measure of global public diplomacy that projected racial progress and countered Communist propaganda. But Rusk, unexpectedly, asserted that the imperative of civil rights reform transcended Cold War public relations. "We must try to eliminate discrimination due to race, color, religion, not to make others think better of us but because it is incompatible with the great ideals to which our democratic society is dedicated."[21] Under the sway of Robert Kennedy, who was influenced by Pedro Sanjuan, a member of the subcabinet committee on civil rights also charged with rectifying discrimination against visiting African diplomats, John Kennedy began to focus on legislation that would form the basis of the Civil Rights Act of 1964.

But Kennedy's energetic commitment to foreign policy and decolonization superseded his investment in desegregation. In a 1960 address to the National Council of Women, Kennedy spoke on the topic "The New Nations of Africa." He begins with the observation that "the course of European empire had moved southward – along the coast of Africa, and around the Cape of Good Hope to the east. With the discovery of America, the kings, the generals, and the traders turned westward, leaving Africa to become the neglected and undeveloped province of a few European nations." But today, "more than four centuries later, the work of Columbus is being reversed," and the "nations of the West once more look toward Africa." Paternalistic in tone ("we have done almost nothing to educate the African people"), his language reveals a recurrent ambiguity: the image of the West looking toward Africa suggests, on the one hand, that the continent now represents an agential, perhaps avant-garde force in history; on the other hand, the language of "neglect" implies that the continent remains in a client or tutelary relation to America and the West.[22]

Where the United States was concerned, Kennedy's rhetorical aim was to naturalize this relation, with respect to the demands of noblesse oblige among rich countries and to America's self-image as the "first" anticolonial nation. What better qualified nation than the United States, so the argument went, to guide the aspirations of newly independent African and Asian nations – to fan, in Harold Macmillan's phrase of 1960, the "wind of change" sweeping throughout Africa?[23]

"We want an Africa," Kennedy insisted, "which is not a pawn in the Cold War – or a battleground between East and West." Then he added: "And this, too, is what the African people want."[24] And yet it is difficult to deny that Kennedy viewed Africa and Asia precisely as Cold War battlegrounds. In a 1958 speech to the Senate on Indian nationalism, Kennedy argued: "India stands as the only effective competitor to China for the faith and following of the millions of uncommitted and restless peoples. Should India fall prey to internal disorder or disillusionment among either its masses or [its] leaders and become absorbed in the Communist system, the free world would suffer an incalculable blow." The key phrase in this and other speeches on the nonaligned world is "uncommitted nations": he saw nonaligned or "uncommitted" nations not as a threat but as an opportunity for Western recruitment; and he invoked America's own history of "noninvolvement in the great international controversies of the nineteenth century" as a way to appeal to both Cold War opponents of nonalignment and Third World nationalists.[25]

In Kennedy's helicopter ride around Washington, DC, with Leopold Senghor – the president of Senegal and poet who held an *agrégé* degree (the French equivalent of the doctorate), and with whom Kennedy shared an intellectual sympathy – the U.S. president elicited the Senegalese leader's advice on Nkrumah's VRP. In "spite of this man's [Nkrumah's] instability," Senghor replied, "in spite of his radical politics with most of which I disagree, Mr. President, you have no alternative but to go along with the project, particularly if it's economically feasible. Otherwise the Africans will accuse you of violating your own policies in regard to neutrality and nonalignment."[26] Even the conservative, pro-Western Félix Houphouët-Boigny, who believed that Nkrumah possessed a "messianic complex," expressed a similar view in a conversation with Robert Kennedy. "Despite his feelings about the leader," writes Muehlenbeck, "Houphouët-Boigny believed that the United States should finance the dam, but only after forcing Nkrumah to make a clear-cut choice about aligning with either the West or the East."[27] Doubting that Nkrumah would capitulate to such a condition, Robert Kennedy countenanced a withholding of U.S. aid for the VRP.

For Fanon, this Cold War courtship of continental leaders like Senghor and Houphouët-Boigny was ripe for parody. "These men at the head of empty countries," Fanon writes, "who talk too loud, are most irritating. You'd like to shut them up. But, on the contrary, they are in great demand. They are given bouquets; they are invited to dinner. In fact, we quarrel over who shall have them . . . African and Asian officials may in the same month follow a course on socialist planning in Moscow and one on the advantages of the liberal economy in London or Columbia

University." For Fanon, the truly modern subjects and genuine "political animals" are the "native and underdeveloped men" hunched over their transistor radios, absorbing the geopolitical backdrop to the fates of figures like "Phouma and Phoumi, Lumumba and Tshombe, Ahidjo and Moumie, Kenyatta, and the men who are pushed forward regularly to replace him." Fanon's natives "live in the atmosphere of doomsday, and they consider that nothing ought to be let pass unnoticed. That is why they understand these [Third World] figures very well" and "can unmask the forces working behind them."[28]

One of the central "forces" behind these new North-South relationships involved Kennedy's commitment to global modernization, a massive undertaking in which "benevolent intentions and self-serving economic interests are hopelessly intertwined."[29] Through the lens of modernization theory, Kennedy's administration articulated a version of what commentators now refer to as the "global South."[30] As Kennedy declared, sounding a note not all that different from the proponents of decolonization themselves, "The great battleground for the defense and expansion of freedom today, is the whole southern half of the globe – Asia, Latin America, Africa, and the Middle East – the lands of the rising peoples. Their revolution is the greatest in human history. They seek an end to injustice, tyranny and exploitation. More than an end, they seek a beginning."[31] Modernization theory sought, we might argue, to incorporate the revolutionary energies of decolonization movements into the United States' Cold War narrative. Like a deus ex machina, modernization theorists descended on those developing nations, especially in Latin America, that they envisaged as situated in a "transitional" phase between tradition and modernity, with the goal of foreclosing social revolution or communist subversion. Kennedy initiatives like the Alliance for Progress and the Peace Corps constituted the means to facilitate this transition to the modern democratic capitalist order.

More than a development initiative, Alianza para el Progreso formed part of an ambitious plan to "complete the revolution of the Americas, to build a hemisphere where all men can hope for a suitable standard of living and all can live out their lives in dignity and freedom," as Kennedy characterized the Alliance in a commemoration speech. "Like Truman before him," writes María Saldaña-Portillo, "John F. Kennedy responded to revolutionary movements in the Third World with a dual strategy of military intervention and development aid."[32] Yet what is surprising, she argues, is how the rhetoric of development imbued, and served mutually to constitute, both the modernization discourses pioneered by the Kennedy administration and revolutionary appeals in the Americas by the Zapatistas in Mexico or figures like Che Guevara and Malcolm X. For Kennedy and Rostow as much as for Guevara and Castro, modernization was revolutionary, but this process required the "peasant" and other classes to undergo regimes of discipline and transformations in consciousness before reaping the benefits of modernity.

Modernization, then, entailed more than large-scale industrialization and development projects. In order for developing nations to become modern, non-Western peoples must replace their "traditional" values with "modern" values. Modernization theorists, according to Michael Latham, associated traditional values with fatalism, superstition, emotionalism, stagnancy, romanticism, inertia, and apathy; they identified modern values as industriousness, rationalism, cleanliness, self-discipline, orderliness, and efficiency. Moreover, modernization theorists hoped that the distinctively "American" traits of empathy, altruism, entrepreneurialism, idealism, and ingenuity would demonstrate the superiority and benevolence of U.S. foreign policy and thus rub off on the developing world.

On this theory, modern infrastructural and industrialization efforts could only succeed if accompanied by the cultivation of modern habits, values, and modes of conduct. In her posthumously produced play written in 1960, *Les Blancs*, Lorraine Hansberry portrays a fictitious African country, Zatembe, in the throes of revolution. A rebuttal to Genet's *Les Noirs*, the play reverses the ethnographic gaze of colonialism, diagnosing the subjectivity of *les blancs*: the coterie of European doctors, missionaries, and military officials who labor in a ramshackle hospital and, despite intensifying "terrorist" attacks by local insurrectionaries, try to maintain order and security in their colonial outpost. As one character, Dr. Dekoven, explains to Charlie Morris, an American journalist: "Mr. Morris, there is a hospital for Europeans only seventy-five miles from here. Entirely modern. Here things are lashed together with vines from the jungle. Surely you must have wondered why." Charlie says, "Well, I assumed I knew why – that it was obvious . . ." Dr. Dekoven replies: "Is it? Electric lines between here and Zatembe could be laid within weeks, a road in six months. The money exists. All over the world people donate to Missions like this. It is not obvious, not obvious at all."[33] After generations of secular and religious missionary work, wonders Dr. Dekoven, why does the starkly unequal distribution of modernity continue to exist in places like Zatembe?

Like the development experts in Kennedy's cabinet, the white characters in *Les Blancs*, if obviously paternalistic and missionary in their attitudes, are not unsympathetic. The problem is less that modern resources and development aid are channeled only to white colonists at the expense of blacks; the problem, in Hansberry's estimation, is that both the European civilizing mission as well as the ideology promoted by Kennedy's "New Frontier" – with its undercurrent of Manifest Destiny and Enlightenment racialization – disfigures the noble dream of universal modernization itself. In the affectively charged milieu of decolonization, it engenders a violent social fragmentation, irrespective of the intentions of ordinary blacks and whites who have managed to get along in colonial society. "Mr. Morris," Dr. Dekoven explains, "the struggle here has not been to push the African into the Twentieth Century – but at all costs to keep him *away* from it! We do not look down on the black because we really think he is lazy, we look down on him because he is wise enough to resent working for us."[34]

Influenced by Kennedy's modernization theorist contemporaries as well as their progenitors in the Chicago School of Sociology, the African American writer Richard Wright also adopted the idiom of "traditional" and "modern" societies to describe the gulf between the South and North. However, Wright drew sharply different conclusions about how modernization would unfold in postcolonial nations. In his 1957 lecture "Tradition and Industrialization: The Historic Meaning of the Plight of the Tragic Elite in Asia and Africa," Wright asserts his qualification to speak on this topic by virtue of his sense that as "a Negro living in a white Western Christian society, I've never been allowed to blend, in a natural and healthy manner, with the culture and civilization of the West." This condition "creates a psychological distance . . . between me and my environment. I'm self-conscious."[35] As a roving observer of the global decolonization movement, Wright's intuition was that this psychological distance, an internalized (dis-)location inside and outside the West, likewise afflicted his Asian and African contemporaries. Wright insisted that the Third World must hasten modernization in order both to defend itself from Western encroachments and to interrupt the master-client relationship of the development paradigm. But he also intuited that this massive social transition to modernity – a process the postcolonial world must accomplish within decades, versus the course of development transpiring over centuries in the West – presaged intense emotional, religious, and psychological fractures in Asia and Africa: what recent commentators have chosen to identify as the cultural source of a current "clash of civilizations."

"The West must trust that part of itself," Wright continues, "that it has thrust, however blunderingly, into Asia and Africa. Nkrumah, Nasser, Sukarno, and Nehru, and the Western educated heads of these newly created national states, must be given *carte blanche* to modernize their lands without overlordship of the West, and we must understand the methods that they will feel compelled to use."[36] Wright does not elaborate on what methods Third World modernization will entail (and he faced criticism for endorsing militarist measures toward this end), but he was convinced that postcolonial modernity must proceed along an autonomous path lest it transmogrify into neocolonial farce.

With the advantages of hindsight, a growing body of literature has diagnosed the dilemmas of foreign aid and development – and proposed why such initiatives were likely doomed from the start. Yet if the short tenure of Kennedy's presidency could not envisage the autonomous path for Third World development that Wright had in mind, it had little inkling of the impending failures of modernization theory or the intractable tensions between anticommunist imperatives and anticolonial support. It is left to the practitioners of counterfactual history to imagine what shape another 1,000 or 3,000 days of JFK's leadership might have meant for U.S. foreign policy and the postcolonial world.

NOTES

1   Richard Wright, *Black Power: Three Books from Exile: Black Power; The Color Curtain; and White Man Listen!* (New York: HarperCollins, 2008), 418.
2   Philip E. Muehlenbeck, *Betting on the Africans: John F. Kennedy's Courting of African Nationalist Leaders* (Oxford: Oxford University Press, 2012), 85.
3   See Douglas Field, Andrew Preston, and Amanda Kay McVety's chapters in this volume.
4   Nils Gilman, *Mandarins of the Future: Modernization Theory in Cold War America* (Baltimore, MD: Johns Hopkins University Press, 2007); and Michael E. Latham, *Modernization as Ideology: American Social Science and "Nation Building" in the Kennedy Era* (Chapel Hill: University of North Carolina Press, 2000); and Michael E. Latham, *The Right Kind of Revolution: Modernization, Development, and U.S. Foreign Policy from the Cold War to the Present* (Ithaca, NY: Cornell University Press, 2010).
5   John F. Kennedy, "President's News Conference, Washington, DC, March 1, 1961," in *"Let the Word Go Forth": The Speeches, Statements, and Writings of John F. Kennedy, 1947 to 1963*, ed. Theodore C. Sorensen (New York: Delacorte Press, 1988), 369.
6   Thomas J. Noer, *Cold War and Black Liberation: The United States and White Rule in Africa, 1948–1968* (Columbia: University of Missouri Press, 1985), 34.
7   See Erez Manela, *The Wilsonian Moment: Self-Determination and the International Origins of Anticolonial Nationalism* (Oxford: Oxford University Press, 2009).
8   "'The Atlantic Charter': Declaration of Principles Issued by the President of the United States and the Prime Minister of the United Kingdom, August 14, 1941," http://www.nato.int/cps/en/natolive/official_texts_16912.htm. Accessed December 13, 2014.
9   On the precedent set by Wilson for a liberal, international order, the continuation of this program by Roosevelt, Truman, and Eisenhower, and its subsequent interface with modernization theory and decolonization, see Latham, *The Right Kind of Revolution*, 22–32.

10 John F. Kennedy, "The Challenge of Imperialism: Algeria," in Sorensen, *Let the Word Go Forth,"* 334. On Eisenhower's foreign policy in the Third World, see Robert J. McMahon, "Eisenhower and Third World Nationalism: A Critique of the Revisionists," *Political Science Quarterly* 101, no. 3 (1986): 453–73.

11 Russell Baker, "Kennedy Urges U.S. Back Independence for Algeria," *New York Times,* July 3, 1957.

12 James D. Le Sueur, *Uncivil War: Intellectuals and Identity Politics during the Decolonization of Algeria* (Lincoln: University of Nebraska Press, 2001), 4–5.

13 Aleksandr Fursenko and Timothy Naftali, *"One Hell of a Gamble": The Secret History of the Cuban Missile Crisis* (New York: W. W. Norton, 1998), 81–91.

14 Ibid., 73.

15 Layhmond Robinson, "Robert Kennedy Consults Negroes Here about North," *New York Times,* May 25, 1963.

16 Brian Urquhart, *Ralph Bunche: An American Odyssey* (New York: W. W. Norton, 1993), 303.

17 Jeffrey A. Lefebvre, "Kennedy's Algerian Dilemma: Containment, Alliance Politics and the 'Rebel Dialogue,'" *Middle Eastern Studies* 35, no. 2 (April 1999): 62.

18 Miloud Barkaoui, "Kennedy and the Cold War Imbroglio: The Case of Algeria's Independence," *Arab Studies Quarterly* 21, no. 2 (Spring 1999): 40.

19 Renee Romano, "No Diplomatic Immunity: African Diplomats, the State Department, and Civil Rights, 1961–1964," *Journal of American History* 87, no. 2 (September 2000): 549.

20 Mao Zedong, "Statement Supporting the Afro-American in Their Just Struggle against Racial Discrimination by U.S. Imperialism, August 8, 1963," in *Afro Asia: Revolutionary Political and Cultural Connections between African Americans and Asian Americans,* ed. Fred Ho and Bill V. Mullen (Durham, NC: Duke University Press, 2008), 93.

21 Romano, "No Diplomatic Immunity," 546.

22 Kennedy, "The New Nations of Africa," in Sorensen, *"Let the Word Go Forth,"* 367.

23 See Latham, *Modernization as Ideology,* 64–65.

24 Kennedy, "The New Nations of Africa," 366.

25 John F. Kennedy, "The New Nationalism: India," in Sorensen, *"Let the Word Go Forth,"* 339.

26 Philip M. Kaiser, *Journeying Far and Wide: A Political and Diplomatic Memoir* (New York: Scribner, 1993), 192.

27 Muehlenbeck, *Betting on the Africans,* 146.

28 Frantz Fanon, *The Wretched of the Earth* (New York: Grove Press, 1963), 81.

29 María Josefina Saldaña-Portillo, *The Revolutionary Imagination in the Americas and the Age of Decolonization* (Durham, NC: Duke University Press, 2003), 19.

30 For a critical analysis of NATO in the formation – and pauperization – of the "global South," see Vijay Prashad, *The Poorer Nations: A Possible History of the Global South* (London: Verso Books, 2013).

31 "President Kennedy's Special Message to the Congress on Urgent National Needs, May 25, 1961," *John F. Kennedy Presidential Library and Museum,* http://www.jfklibrary.org/Research/Research-Aids/JFK-Speeches/United-States-Congress-Special-Message_19610525.aspx, accessed December 20, 2014.

32 Saldaña-Portillo, *The Revolutionary Imagination*, 25.
33 Lorraine Hansberry, *Les Blancs: The Collected Last Plays* (New York: Vintage Books, 1972), 113.
34 Ibid.
35 Richard Wright, *Black Power: Three Books from Exile*, 705.
36 Ibid., 725.

9

JOHN HELLMANN

Kennedy and Postwar Intellectual Culture

A war hero and the scion of a powerful businessman, John F. Kennedy distanced himself from liberals while serving in Congress in the early postwar period. But once elevated to the Senate in 1952, he hired the "militant liberal" Theodore Sorensen as his assistant, and together they directed what one biographer has called "a literary campaign" for the presidency.[1] This campaign consisted of a steady production of articles under Kennedy's byline for journals and magazines. In his memoir Sorenson describes the intent of creating "an image of intensive progressive thought, nationally disseminating his personal philosophy and helping balance the flood of superficial articles about his good looks and his romance with Jackie."[2] Kennedy and Sorenson's collaboration on *Profiles in Courage* (1956) took this "literary campaign" to another level. Enjoying a positive critical reception, the book became a best seller and was awarded a Pulitzer Prize for biography. Rather than a treatise on policy, it was a work of middlebrow literature that combined narrative verve with a meditative voice to elicit an emotional adherence to a series of politicians who, at crucial moments in American history, had defied their constituents. That voice concluded by posing the ultimate question, to be decided outside the text, of whether the book's author, John F. Kennedy, and his reader were similarly capable of defying social, political, and institutional pressures in the higher interests of the nation: "The stories of past courage can define that ingredient – they can teach, they can offer hope, they can provide inspiration. But they cannot supply courage itself. For this each man must look into his own soul."[3]

A number of recent studies have focused on ways in which *Profiles in Courage* reflects mainstream thinking of the postwar era about the American past. One scholar, for instance, points out that "Kennedy's representation of Reconstruction was in keeping with the prevailing historiography," and that "he had only a fragmentary understanding of American history as regards the indignities of slavery and the brutal realities of its legacy throughout the South."[4] Such observations, while significant, overlook the elements of *Profiles in Courage* that made the book seem a unique, perhaps even a risky, project for a future presidential aspirant.

Those same elements can be found in the writings of a community of postwar radicals who became known as the New York intellectuals. In the account of historian Allen J. Matusow, Kennedy only set out to win liberal intellectuals in 1959, when he "began making occasional trips to Boston to meet with Cambridge academics, soliciting their advice, sometimes even taking it."[5] But Kennedy had already modeled his self-presentation in *Profiles in Courage* upon the premises of the New York intellectuals. These writers and thinkers were increasingly influential in the late 1940s and 1950s, and the Harvard academic and liberal political activist who was Kennedy's most important contact with liberals, Arthur Schlesinger Jr., was their strong ally. One scholar has argued that the Irish Catholic Kennedy's main purpose in writing *Profiles in Courage* was "to identify him with the heroic mythology of a nation that still identified its mainstream as white, Anglo-Saxon, and Protestant."[6] But the community whose ideas drive Kennedy's book, while not all Jewish (Mary McCarthy was a Catholic from the West Coast and a graduate of Vassar), has been characterized as having a "particularly Jewish ethos."[7] The courage they advocated, rather than a simplistic national legend, was a variation upon the solitary self-making that they found in the European existentialism of Jean-Paul Sartre. And, while they were influenced by the tragic and ironic Christian vision of Reinhold Niebuhr, they were secular in orientation, former or present anti-Stalinist Marxists, who looked to cultural modernism, Freud, and Tocqueville to warn of the potential dangers of the irrational and the totalitarian lurking in the moral passions of American democracy.

In several identifiable respects, *Profiles in Courage* hews to the existentialist, tragic, and complex vision of the New York intellectuals. Throughout the book, Kennedy asks the question of whether and when a politician, or any citizen, should leap into the abyss of separation from one's society for the higher interests of that society. He starkly urges a reader to consider the costs, not the rewards, of pursuing the lonely course of alienating one's "constituents, friends, a board of directors or our union, whenever we stand against the flow of opinion on strongly contested issues."[8] He implies that the Democratic majority should always be questioned and, if the stakes are sufficiently great, resolutely defied. *Profiles in Courage* is a lonely, a cautionary, book in its vision of a succession of heroes who were marginalized and isolated, who in some cases failed to achieve the aims for which they sacrificed their career, and who, the narrator considers, in some cases may even have been wrong.

Tracing the sources of *Profiles in Courage* to postwar ideas flowing from the New York intellectuals can bring into focus neglected aspects of the significance of Kennedy's image, both as a presidential candidate and, more than half a century later, as an enduring icon in American culture. By focusing upon the distinctive preoccupations of *Profiles in Courage*, and locating how they parallel the critique of American society offered by the New York intellectuals, we can bring into focus the forward-thinking aspect of Kennedy's book and of the unfolding cultural narrative that constructed Kennedy's compelling public image.

During the postwar era the New York intellectuals, many of them former Trotskyite and independent radicals who were veterans of battles with Stalinists and fellow travelers during the 1930s and 1940s, modified New Deal liberal thinking to valorize the individual over the collective. They argued that intellectuals needed to show toughness and courage in their thought and in their public stands, confronting the utopian collectivist creeds on the left and right that had culminated in the Soviet brutalities and the Nazi death camps. Anti-utopian though not conservative, the New York intellectuals emphasized tensions, uncertainties, and anxieties as inevitable conditions of human existence. They saw conflict, fallibility, and frustration rather than a malleable creature that could be perfected. Instead of adherence to an ideology, they valued independent determination and creativity. The worldview of the New York intellectuals thus combined Marxism with literary and artistic modernism. While they wrote for other journals, as well, extending their influence into numerous literary and cultural communities, *Partisan Review* was their home, and they attracted many like-minded writers well beyond their immediate circle to its pages. Richard Pells describes the highly influential role of *Partisan Review* in the late 1940s and 1950s, when it appeared (with the exception of a brief period as a bimonthly) on a monthly basis:

> Though its circulation hovered around 10,000, the journal was required reading for intellectuals, not least because at one time or another it printed the work of almost every major American writer. In any issue one might find an essay, story, or poem by Edmund Wilson, Saul Bellow, Paul Goodman, Meyer Shapiro, Alfred Kazin, Leslie Fiedler, Daniel Bell, C. Wright Mills, Arthur Schlesinger, Diana Trilling, Pauline Kael, James Agee, Irving Howe, Harold Rosenberg, Richard Chase, Ralph Ellison, James Baldwin, Norman Mailer, Bernard Malamud, Robert Brustein, Mary McCarthy.[9]

As they gained prominence, the New York intellectuals, formerly ignored and marginalized, increasingly disseminated their ideas into the wider culture of educated readers through the pages of such magazines as the *New Yorker, Esquire,* and *McCall's.*

The premises of the New York intellectuals pulse through the pages of Kennedy's *Profiles in Courage*. This should not be surprising, considering Kennedy's omnivorous reading, especially of nonfiction; his wife Jacqueline's love of literature and the arts; and his assistant Sorensen's grounding in liberal activism. The ideas of the New York intellectuals were as available as the magazines, book clubs, and shelves of paperbacks that in the postwar era accompanied the expansion of higher education and of a professional middle class. Editors and writers took their cues from such prominent New York intellectuals as Lionel Trilling, Alfred Kazin, and Dwight Macdonald, as well as from close affiliates of their community like David Riesman and Arthur Schlesinger.

The central theme of *Profiles in Courage* echoes the emphasis of the New York intellectuals upon the necessarily tense, lonely, and sacrificial relation of the heroically independent thinker to society. Kennedy's profiles of heroic senators resemble the New York intellectuals' profiles of their own position. *Partisan Review* founder and editor, Philip Rahv, asserted that the modernist movement in literature and the arts was, as an avant-garde, dedicated to "resisting the bourgeois incentives to accommodation, and perforce making a virtue of its separateness from society."[10] As Hugh Wilford observes of the New York intellectuals' interest in modern literature, "There were, it seemed to them, startling correspondences between the suffering and loneliness of the alienated modern artist and their own experience of marginalization."[11] Articles in *Partisan Review* argued that modern authors, both artists and intellectuals, must suffer a "terrible loneliness" if they were to maintain independence from the pressures and lures of society.[12] Irving Howe, one of the core New York intellectuals, recalled that vision: "We felt that we were always on the rim of heroism, that the mockery we might suffer at the moment would turn to vindication in the future, that our loyalty to principle would be rewarded by the grateful masses of tomorrow."[13] If the New York intellectuals adopted for themselves the same heroic ideal that they found in the suffering, isolated modern artist, *Profiles in Courage* extends that heroic ideal to courageous politicians who accept the price of being ahead of society. Kennedy's profiles celebrate politicians who on great issues are willing to suffer precisely that "terrible loneliness." In *Profiles in Courage*, Kennedy repeatedly emphasizes that his heroic politicians find vindication only later in their lifetimes or in posterity.

Kennedy's characterizations and historical narration also demonstrate the influence of the New York intellectuals' modernist assertion of complexity. Lionel Trilling, one of the most prominent of the New York intellectuals, had been widely touting the importance of modern literature to contemporary politics in essays on culture and politics that first appeared in the late

1940s in journals such as *Partisan Review*, *Kenyon Review*, and *American Quarterly*, influential magazines of culture and politics such as the *New Leader* and the *Nation*, and the middlebrow *New York Times Book Review*. Trilling compiled these articles for *The Liberal Imagination: Essays on Literature and Society* (1950), which sold 100,000 copies as one of the first "serious" books issued in paperback, making its author a public figure.[14] Trilling had succeeded Edmund Wilson as the nation's most eminent literary critic, and he recognized that the striving postwar generation of upwardly mobile, optimistic professionals, as their intellectual interests expanded at an energetic pace, welcomed his guidance on cultural matters; during the 1950s he even wrote "monthly reports to subscribers of book clubs."[15]

Beyond its role in literary criticism, *The Liberal Imagination* was regarded as a major statement of the outlook of postwar liberal intellectualism. In the preface, Trilling emphasized that "just as sentiments become ideas, ideas eventually establish themselves as sentiments." He therefore argued that "the connection between literature and politics will be seen as a very immediate one."[16] Dismissing protest and propagandistic literature, such as the proletarian novels favored in the 1930s, Trilling instead "stressed the political relevance of those artists (particularly Proust, Joyce, Lawrence, Eliot, Yeats, Kafka, and Gide) who most accurately portrayed the 'variousness, possibility, complexity, and difficulty' of human life."[17]

In *Profiles in Courage*, Kennedy produced a work that avoids advocating a specific political cause or even his own Democratic Party's point of view, focusing instead on establishing a tragic sentiment similar to the modernist vision of life as full of the variety, possibility, complexity, and difficulty that Trilling was urging liberals to adopt. In his opening chapter, for instance, Kennedy focuses on the myriad pressures and conflicting interests facing senators in order to show that it is never an easy task for a sincere idealist to decide what is right or precisely when the stakes are sufficiently important that one should defy one's constituents. Enhancing the complexity of *Profiles in Courage*, Kennedy characterizes his heroes as compounds of strengths and weaknesses; addressing John Quincy Adams's chronic dissatisfaction with himself and Daniel Webster's readiness to accept monetary gifts, Kennedy arguably portrays these heroes as neurotic (a trait the New York intellectuals idealized as accompanying creative thinking) or, in some regard, self-deceiving. In this way Kennedy's book exemplifies Trilling's "moral realism." Trilling believed that the political Left, which he judged excessively rational and thus naive in its outlook, should turn to the insights of modernist artists because "an appreciation of their work could give liberals a modesty and toughness they presently lacked."[18] *Profiles in Courage* elicits precisely such a sentiment.

If *Profiles in Courage* appears to bear the influence of Trilling's "liberal imagination," it seems even more strongly to follow the lead of Arthur Schlesinger Jr.'s postwar call for a "vital center." The Harvard historian Schlesinger wrote in his memoir that he was not a New York intellectual, but that he enjoyed "friendly relations with them through Mary McCarthy, Dwight Macdonald and Lionel and Diana Trilling." He also expressed admiration for the editors of *Partisan Review*, William Phillips and Philip Rahv, who "were putting out the most stimulating magazine of the day."[19] Alexander Bloom observes: "Schlesinger moved into the New York Intellectual orbit, although he was never assimilated into the heart of the community. He came to this place in the late 1940s by roads very different from those taken by the other New Yorkers."[20] Neil Jumonville describes the alliance:

> When the politics of the *Partisan* circle had cooled into liberalism after World War II, Schlesinger shared their liberal anticommunism, wrote *The Vital Center* (1949) in defense of that outlook, contributed to some of their publications, attended an occasional conference, and joined their American Committee for Cultural Freedom.[21]

The educational background, war service, and politics of this close associate and ally of the New York intellectuals made him a congenial resource and valuable liberal contact for the author of *Profiles in Courage*. As undergraduates only one year apart at Harvard, Kennedy and Schlesinger had both expanded their senior honors theses into published books.[22] Both had subsequently served overseas in the war. In London, while a member of the Office of Strategic Services (OSS), Schlesinger learned of Kennedy's heroism after the sinking of PT-109 in the South Pacific when he "read an article in the June 17, 1944, *New Yorker* by John Hersey about a young fellow he distantly remembered from Harvard named John F. Kennedy, class of 1940."[23] As returned veterans, Schlesinger and Kennedy found themselves placed together on the Jaycees' 1946 list of "Ten Outstanding Young Men of the Year."[24] In 1952, Schlesinger, by then an associate professor of history at Harvard, was also a significant figure in liberal activism. When Kennedy ran for the Senate that year against Republican Henry Cabot Lodge, his father, Joe, "delegated James Landis, who was on good terms with Massachusetts liberals, to get in touch with Arthur Schlesinger, Jr., a founder of Americans for Democratic Action (ADA), and arrange for Jack to appear before the executive committee."[25]

In the preface of *Profiles in Courage*, Kennedy credits Schlesinger's criticisms for having "greatly improved" chapters 2 through 10.[26] Schlesinger had responded positively to Kennedy's letter asking if the historian would consider reading and providing feedback on his manuscript. Kennedy was likely motivated to involve Schlesinger in his book for more than his expertise in American history. The move represented an opportunity to strengthen his contact with a leading liberal intellectual who had served on the campaign staff of the Democratic nominee for president, Adlai Stevenson, in 1952 and would do so again in 1956. In his letter to Schlesinger of June 23, 1955, Kennedy wrote, "I hope that you will be ruthlessly frank . . . not only on the historical accuracy of these chapters, but also on the general themes, style, and overall contribution." After receiving a detailed critique from Schlesinger, Kennedy included in his response a gesture of his interest in further contact: "I hope that you will be pleased with the final product – and that we may have a chance to get together in the near future."²⁷

Kennedy had good reason to believe Schlesinger might regard his manuscript favorably, for *Profiles in Courage* reads like a narrative illustration of Schlesinger's major political treatise of the postwar period. Highly influential, with sections first published in *Partisan Review*, the *Nation*, *Life*, and the *New York Times Sunday Magazine*, Schlesinger's *The Vital Center: The Politics of Freedom* (1949) popularized the major themes and sensibility of the New York intellectuals. In its fundamental premises, Kennedy's *Profiles in Courage* follows Schlesinger's *The Vital Center* in reproducing the New York intellectuals' worldview.

Profiles in Courage also follows *The Vital Center* in stressing the relevance of modernist literature to contemporary politics. Schlesinger takes his epigraph for *The Vital Center* from modern poet W. B. Yeats's "The Second Coming" (1920), which describes the turbulent atmosphere after World War I. The poem famously laments:

> The best lack all conviction, while the worst
> Are full of passionate intensity.

Since that situation only led to World War II, Schlesinger calls for liberal centrists this time around to match the tenacity of utopian-minded extremists. Kennedy similarly opens his book by invoking Ernest Hemingway's definition of courage as "grace under pressure." He uses the Nobel Prize–winning modern novelist's tense figurative phrase to frame his own historical analysis of politicians who, in critical moments of American history, stood up to constituents possessed by zealous fervor. Both Schlesinger and Kennedy begin their books by fulfilling the New York intellectuals' call to look to the great modern artists to help assert the relevance of a tough-minded liberal approach to politics.

Profiles in Courage also shares *The Vital Center*'s positive view of American democracy, a view it holds even while acknowledging American society's frustrations and imperfections. Both books reproduce the New York intellectuals' celebration of the broad success of democracy in the United States, a decisive shift from New Deal liberals' fascination during the 1930s and 1940s with the utopian project in the Soviet Union. Rather than abolitionists and Radical Republicans, or secessionists and sectionalists, Kennedy extols those – northern or southern, Democrat or Republican – who worked to preserve the democratic system responsible for conversation and contention, and to prevent any particular faction from achieving totalitarian control. Consistently privileging Schlesinger's "vital center," Kennedy celebrates senators such as Daniel Webster, who, amid the passions over slavery and secession in the years leading up to the Civil War, sought compromise with the North; Sam Houston, who refused to vote for secession in the South; Edmund Ross, a Radical Republican who in the Civil War's aftermath voted against President Andrew Johnson's impeachment; and Lucius Lamar of Mississippi, who voted against the sectional interests of the South on the issue of "free silver."[28] In the twentieth century, Kennedy admires Nebraska Republican George Norris for his filibuster against the Armed Ship Bill that Norris believed was designed to push the United States into World War I, and he praises Ohio Republican Robert Taft for his principled stand after World War II against an ex post facto law to punish Nazi and Japanese leaders for "waging an aggressive war."[29]

A third discernible parallel between Kennedy's *Profiles in Courage* and Schlesinger's *The Vital Center* is their shared investment in the New York intellectuals' vision of complexity and ambiguity. The New York intellectuals were strongly influenced by Reinhold Niebuhr's emphasis on original sin and the "irony of history," and in his book Schlesinger refers to Niebuhr's theological insights as valuable metaphors for human limitation. *The Vital Center* asserts that the utopian visions of both the right and the left have lost credibility in the aftermath of Hitler and Stalin: "Indeed we have no assurance that any solution is possible. The twentieth century has at least relieved us of the illusion that progress is inevitable."[30] *Profiles in Courage* expresses a similar lesson about the dangers of self-righteousness or ideological purity drawn from Kennedy's own political experience: "And nine years in Congress have taught me the wisdom of Lincoln's words: 'There are few things wholly evil or wholly good. Almost everything, especially of Government policy, is an inseparable compound of the two, so that our best judgment of the preponderance between them is continually demanded.'"[31] In *The Vital Center*, Schlesinger laments: "Utopians believed man to be perfectible; and that radiant belief permitted some of them to slide over into the inevitable next step – that is, to believe that they, at least, were already perfect."[32] In *Profiles in Courage*, Kennedy goes to considerable lengths to

emphasize the imperfections of his heroes. No one, reading Kennedy's portraits, would wittingly turn over absolute power to any of them. Kennedy's
concluding chapter, "The Meaning of Courage," includes an ironic dig at
conventional hagiography:

> Some of them may have been pure and generous and kind and noble through-
> out their careers, in the best traditions of the American hero; but most of them
> were not. Norris, the unyielding bitter-ender; Adams, the irritating upstart;
> Webster, the businessmen's beneficiary; Benton, the bombastic bully – of such
> stuff are our real-life political heroes made.[33]

Kennedy's book reflects the vision of human fallibility that Schlesinger and
the New York intellectuals found in the theology of Niebuhr and the literature of the high modernists, mobilizing this vision to offset the easy utopian
certainties that, in the postwar mind, had led to both Hitler and Stalin.

Kennedy, finally, also follows Schlesinger in the belief that knowledge of
human fallibility and of the grim prospects for success are no excuses for
inaction. Rather than apathy or despair, Schlesinger argues that the loss of
faith in utopianism can be replaced by a courageous embrace of postwar
uncertainty: "There is no more exciting time in which to live – no time more
crucial or more tragic." Schlesinger looks with the New York intellectuals to
Jean-Paul Sartre's existentialism for his vision of the free individual engaged
in heroic self-making: "By making choices, man makes himself: creates or
destroys his own moral personality. This is a brave and bleak expression
of our dilemma."[34] In *Profiles in Courage*, Kennedy vividly illustrates this
"brave and bleak expression" with accounts of politicians who refused to
flee from their freedom to act. In his last chapter, dismissing conventional
platitudes concerning heroic selflessness, he echoes Schlesinger's and the
New York intellectuals' celebrations of existential self-making:

> On the contrary, it was precisely because they did *love themselves* – because
> each one's need to maintain his own respect for himself was more important
> to him than his popularity with others – because his desire to win or maintain
> a reputation for integrity and courage was stronger than his desire to maintain
> his office – because his conscience, his personal standard of ethics, his integrity
> or morality, call it what you will – was stronger than the pressures of public
> disapproval – because his faith that *his* course was the best one, and would
> ultimately be vindicated, outweighed his fear of public reprisal.[35]

One scholar of the New Deal liberalism of the 1930s has pointed out its
philosophical emphasis upon security: "In its 'ideal' form, social security
had as much to do with modernist alienation as it did with financial insecurity; it was the New Deal's answer not simply to unemployment and other
economic exigencies, but far more broadly, to the displacing conditions of

modern life in a rapidly evolving capitalist society."[36] In *The Vital Center*, Schlesinger distinguishes postwar liberalism from its 1930s version by stating the need to recognize "that security is a foolish dream of old men, that crisis will always be with us."[37] In *Profiles in Courage* Kennedy in turn illustrates Schlesinger's dismissal of the desire for security by constructing a historical memory consisting of successive crises, each of which was met by an individual who gave up security in an act of heroic defiance.

In the opening chapter of *Profiles in Courage*, Kennedy expresses his concern about a particularly strong postwar source of standardization and uniformity of opinion, observing that "our everyday life is becoming so saturated with the tremendous power of mass communications that any unpopular or unorthodox course arouses a storm of protests such as John Quincy Adams – under attack in 1807 – could never have envisioned."[38] Kennedy is touching upon one of the major themes of the New York intellectuals during the 1950s, their fear of mass culture, which they alternatively called popular culture or kitsch, and their greater fear of middlebrow culture, which they found even more insidious for its pretense of seriousness and originality. Deploring the spread of mass-produced ideas and art for excluding anything not conforming to popular norms, for creating and satisfying artificial fake desires, and for turning culture into a manipulative commodity, they regarded the combination of middlebrow and mass culture as a variety of benign totalitarianism, preferable to the Soviet kind, but nevertheless to be resisted as antithetical to intellectual values.[39] In a 1952 symposium in *Partisan Review* on "Our Country and Our Culture," Lionel Trilling, David Riesman, C. Wright Mills, Arthur Schlesinger, and Norman Mailer presented their views on this threat. Mailer expressed his disdain for any suggestions that artists should give up the stance of isolation "and decide whether we can work with the movies."[40]

Coming of age in the late 1940s and 1950s, Mailer was a "third-generation" New York intellectual who had won early fame with his war novel, *The Naked and the Dead* (1946). Five years after the *Partisan Review* symposium, Mailer once again addressed the fear of standardization and uniformity, this time in a controversial essay celebrating marginalized and self-marginalized communities and individuals who in the postwar United States were resisting the forces of repression. In "The White Negro: Superficial Reflections on the Hipster," originally published in a 1957 issue of *Dissent*, Mailer developed his theory of the hope to be found in such rebellion. Pells succinctly summarizes the argument:

> In Mailer's eyes, the hipster, the blacks, the hoodlums, the Beats, and the juvenile delinquents were linked by their "emphasis upon courage at the moment of crisis." Ultimately, he submitted, the "isolated courage of isolated people"

might provide a "glimpse of the necessity of life to become more than it has been," thereby "widening the arena of the possible" for everyone.[41]

In language, however removed in context from Kennedy's, that echoes the heroic existential preoccupations of *Profiles in Courage*, Mailer writes in "The White Negro" that "the heart of Hip is its emphasis upon courage at the moment of crisis."[42]

In the 1960 presidential campaign Mailer would find his hipster in the author of *Profiles in Courage* himself. Michael Szalay has observed: "No liberal politician could run on Mailer's vision. But Mailer thought that John F. Kennedy came close to doing so, by way of Hemingway."[43] Assigned by *Esquire* to cover the party conventions, Mailer was granted an interview with the presidential candidate at the Kennedy family compound in Hyannis Port, where he was greeted by campaign aides including Schlesinger, now a Kennedy speechwriter. Mailer produced an article that would be widely noted for its application of rich description and metaphor to politics and that now stands as "a foundation stone of the New Journalism" of the 1960s.[44] In "Superman Comes to the Supermarket," Mailer interprets Kennedy's relation to the public in terms that echo the "terrible loneliness" that the *Partisan Review* editors had felt to be the necessary stance of modern artists and intellectuals in relation to the mass: "Kennedy's most characteristic quality is the remote and private air of a man who has traversed some lonely terrain of experience, of loss and gain, of nearness to death, which leaves him isolated from the mass of others."[45] In Mailer's profile of Kennedy, the presidential candidate now appeared strikingly like one of the heroes of *Profiles in Courage*.

Mailer speculates that, if they put Kennedy in the White House, Americans could break free of dull postwar conformity by identifying with a heroic presidential image that would encourage them to pursue their suppressed fantasies: "America's politics would now be also America's favorite movie, America's first soap opera, America's best-seller."[46] Mailer here departs from his fellow New York intellectuals' hopelessness before the specter of mass-produced commodities or art. The strident participant in the *Partisan Review* symposium of 1952 who had contemptuously dismissed the idea of the artist's attempting to "work with the movies" now sees the possibility of change in the unexpected form of a politician. Kennedy's mass-produced image as "hero," Mailer writes, "can capture the secret imagination of a people," and "so allows each private mind the liberty to consider its fantasy and find a way to grow."[47]

From the elevated platform of the White House, President Kennedy and his wife, Jacqueline, promoted the life of the mind and the status of intellectuals.

They began by inviting writers and artists to the inaugural festivities. Robert Frost read the first inaugural poem. Robert Lowell wrote Elizabeth Bishop after the event, "With a lot of reservations, I feel like a patriot for the first time in my life."[48] During the administration the president and First Lady repeatedly expressed the importance they placed on the role of intellectuals and artists in American society.[49] In 1962 they held a state dinner for Nobel Prize winners to which they invited many eminent creative figures. Lionel and Diana Trilling were among the small group invited upstairs to the East Room afterward for a more intimate gathering.[50]

Other New York intellectuals found themselves invited upon occasion to dine at the White House. Alfred Kazin lunched with the president but resisted his overtures, and Kazin was surely not alone in his skepticism. Schlesinger, serving in the administration as special assistant to the president, later recalled of Kazin: "A few months later he came to dinner and announced that the New York intellectuals considered Kennedy slick, cool and empty, devoid of vision, an expert and a calculating pragmatist." Schlesinger added, "Yet, most of the radicals, even at their most critical, felt a sense of reluctant kinship with the President."[51] And in fact many of the most prominent would later testify to the elevation in status and increased connection with their government that they felt with Kennedy in office.[52]

At the time, Kennedy understood their ambivalence. In 1963, at a memorial service for Robert Frost, the president echoed the view of the modern artist that the New York intellectuals had adopted as their own, calling Frost "the last champion of the individual mind and sensibility against an intrusive society and an officious state."[53] Nevertheless, he was determined to strengthen that state's role in the arts. On June 12, 1963, Kennedy announced the establishment of the Advisory Council on the Arts, the forerunner of the National Endowment for the Arts, asserting, "The concept of the public welfare should reflect cultural as well as physical values, aesthetic as well as economic considerations."[54] And Kennedy looked to intellectuals when he considered future policy. After Kennedy read Dwight Macdonald's 13,000-word, fifty-page essay-review in the *New Yorker* on books about poverty in the United States, he became intent upon launching a campaign after the 1964 election to break poverty's cycle.[55] Schlesinger had persuaded Kennedy to invite novelist William Styron to the White House. Learning that Styron was working on a novel about Nat Turner, who had led a nineteenth-century slave uprising in Virginia, Kennedy questioned the author intently about slavery. At a subsequent social event in New York, shortly before his assassination, Kennedy asked Styron if he could help him reach out to black men of letters: "Did I know any Negro writers? Could I suggest some Negro names for a meeting at the White House?"[56] During the 1960s the New York intellectuals, as their status ascended, quietly dropped their opposition to middlebrow and mass culture. Perhaps they recognized that with *Profiles in Courage*, and the resulting inflection of its author's mass-produced image, Kennedy had employed the apparatus of middlebrow and mass culture to vividly impress upon the public precisely the worldview he had adopted from them.

NOTES

1 Ted Sorensen, *Counselor: A Life at the Edge of History* (New York: Harper, 2008), 85; Herbert S. Parmet, *Jack: The Struggles of John F. Kennedy* (New York: Dial, 1980), 480.
2 Sorensen, *Counselor*, 144–45.
3 John F. Kennedy, *Profiles in Courage* (1956; repr., New York: Harper, 2003), 225.
4 Nick Bryant, *The Bystander: John F. Kennedy and the Struggle for Black Equality* (New York: Basic, 2006), 49, 50.
5 Allen J. Matusow, "John F. Kennedy and the Intellectuals," *Wilson Quarterly* 7 (Autumn 1983): 149.
6 John Michael, "*Profiles in Courage*, JFK's Book for Boys," *American Literary History* 24 (Fall 2012): 432.
7 Joseph Dorman, *Arguing the World: The New York Intellectuals in Their Own Words* (New York: Free Press, 2000), 9.
8 Kennedy, *Profiles in Courage*, 224.
9 Richard H. Pells, *The Liberal Mind in a Conservative Age: American Intellectuals in the 1940s and 1950s* (New York: Harper and Row, 1985), 72–73.
10 Philip Rahv, "Our Country and Our Culture," *Partisan Review* 19 (1952): 309–10.
11 Hugh Wilford, *The New York Intellectuals: From Vanguard to Institution* (Manchester: Manchester University Press, 1995), 3.
12 Ibid., 74.
13 Quoted in Neil Jumonville, *Critical Crossings: The New York Intellectuals in Postwar America* (Berkeley: University of California Press, 1991), 74.
14 Thomas Bender, "Lionel Trilling and American Culture," *American Quarterly* 42 (June 1990): 324.
15 Ibid., 341.
16 Lionel Trilling, *The Liberal Imagination: Essays on Literature and Society* (New York: Viking, 1950), xi.
17 Pells, *The Liberal Mind in a Conservative Age*, 136–37.
18 Ibid., 137.
19 Arthur M. Schlesinger Jr., *A Life in the Twentieth Century: Innocent Beginnings, 1917–1950* (Boston: Houghton Mifflin, 2000), 432.
20 Alexander Bloom, *Prodigal Sons: The New York Intellectuals and Their World* (New York: Oxford University Press, 1986), 179.
21 Jumonville, *Critical Crossings*, 60.
22 Schlesinger's book *Orestes A. Brownson: A Pilgrim's Progress* (Boston: Little, Brown and Company, 1939) chronicled the development of the nineteenth-century

New England intellectual and activist; Kennedy's *Why England Slept* (1940) was a study of Great Britain's failed appeasement policy in the 1930s.

23 Andrew Schlesinger and Stephen Schlesinger, eds., *The Letters of Arthur Schlesinger, Jr.* (New York: Random, 2013), xxx.

24 Michael Wreszin, "Arthur Schlesinger, Jr., Scholar-Activist in Cold War America: 1946–1956," *Salmagundi* 63–64 (Spring–Summer 1984): 261.

25 David Nasaw, *The Patriarch: The Remarkable Life and Turbulent Times of Joseph P. Kennedy* (2012; repr., New York: Penguin, 2013), 666.

26 Kennedy, *Profiles in Courage*, xxii.

27 Schlesinger and Schlesinger, *Letters*, 108, 118.

28 Kennedy, *Profiles in Courage*, 157.

29 Ibid., 197–98.

30 Arthur M. Schlesinger Jr., *The Vital Center: The Politics of Freedom* (1949; repr., Boston: Houghton Mifflin, 1962), 10.

31 Kennedy, *Profiles in Courage*, 222.

32 Schlesinger, *The Vital Center*, 161.

33 Kennedy, *Profiles in Courage*, 221.

34 Schlesinger, *The Vital Center*, 52.

35 Kennedy, *Profiles in Courage*, 218–19.

36 Michael Szalay, *New Deal Modernism: American Literature and the Invention of the Welfare State* (Durham, NC: Duke University Press, 2000), 9.

37 Schlesinger, *The Vital Center*, 10.

38 Kennedy, *Profiles in Courage*, 17.

39 See Jumonville, *Critical Crossings*, 151, 164–65.

40 Edith Kurzweil, ed., *A Partisan Century: Political Writings from Partisan Review* (New York: Columbia University Press, 1996), 120.

41 Pells, *The Liberal Mind in a Conservative Age*, 209.

42 Norman Mailer, *Advertisements for Myself* (1959; repr., Cambridge, MA: Harvard University Press, 1992), 355.

43 Michael Szalay, *Hip Figures: A Literary History of the Democratic Party* (Stanford, CA: Stanford University Press, 2012), 106.

44 J. Michael Lennon, *Norman Mailer: A Double Life* (New York: Simon & Schuster, 2013), 271.

45 Norman Mailer, "Superman Comes to the Supermarket," *The Presidential Papers* (1963; repr., New York: Berkley, 1970), 48.

46 Ibid., 44.

47 Ibid., 42.

48 David Laskin, *Partisans: Marriage, Politics, and Betrayal among the New York Intellectuals* (New York: Simon & Schuster, 2000), 233.

49 See Norman Mailer, "1958–1967: Rounding Camelot," in *The History of the National Institute of Arts and Letters and the American Academy of Arts and Letters as Told, Decade by Decade, by Eleven Members*, ed. John Updike (New York: Columbia University Press, 1998), 173–82.

50 William Styron, *Havanas in Camelot: Personal Essays* (New York: Random, 2008), 9.

51 Arthur M. Schlesinger Jr., *A Thousand Days: John F. Kennedy in the White House* (Boston: Houghton Mifflin, 1965), 744, 749.

52 Bloom, *Prodigal Sons*, 324–25.

53 Quoted in Lawrence Thompson and R. H. Winnick, *Robert Frost: A Biography*, ed. Edward Latham (New York: Holt, Rinehart, and Winston, 1981), 515.

54 Szalay, *Hip Figures*, 202.

55 Robert Dallek, *An Unfinished Life: John F. Kennedy 1917–1963* (2003; repr., New York: Little, Brown, 2004), 640.

56 Styron, *Havanas in Camelot*, 15–17.

10

LEE KONSTANTINOU

The Camelot Presidency: Kennedy and Postwar Style

In the 2002 foreword to *A Thousand Days* (1965), his Pulitzer Prize–winning account of the Kennedy presidency, Arthur M. Schlesinger Jr. expressed his desire to "disentangle [the] myth and reality" of John F. Kennedy's short time in office.[1] To banish pernicious "myth," to secure "reality," Schlesinger felt the need first to "dispose of Camelot," a "myth that time turned into a cliché."[2] The idea that Kennedy's Washington resembled Arthur's Camelot originated, as Schlesinger notes, in an interview Jacqueline Kennedy gave to the journalist Theodore H. White for *Life* magazine a week after the president's assassination in 1963. The president had loved the popular Broadway musical *Camelot* – his Harvard and Choate classmate Alan Jay Lerner wrote the show's book, based on T. H. White's *The Once and Future King* – and he would often play the cast recording before going to bed. "I'm so ashamed of myself," a grieving Jackie told White, "all I keep thinking of is this line from a musical comedy."[3] The line she was thinking of comes from the show's title song: "Don't let it be forgot, that once there was a spot, for one brief shining moment that was known as Camelot." Unabashed, White repeats the refrain at the very end of his *Life* article, in his own voice, in effect endorsing the view that Jackie was proposing: that Kennedy's time in office was a singularity, a magically optimistic moment in American political history, now lost forever.

It is understandably tempting to dismiss the Camelot figure as a cloying retrospective myth, popularized by Kennedy hagiographers; as a revisionist whitewashing of the president's limited domestic accomplishments and controversial foreign policy choices; or as a contemporary "organizing framework for collective memory" meant to justify political cynicism in the present by imagining a heroic but conveniently past age of American optimism.[4] Indeed, Roger Hilsman, an undersecretary of state under Kennedy, once claimed that "if Jack Kennedy heard this stuff about Camelot, he would have vomited."[5] In the years following the publication of his *Life* article, White backed away from the lavish metaphor.[6] Jackie, too, came to

149

qualify her comparison.[7] After all, as Schlesinger observed, "King Arthur's Camelot was hardly noted for marital constancy, and concluded in betrayal and death."[8] More than fifty years after the assassination, the Camelot comparison is widely considered either to be "overdone" or to be a pernicious obfuscation of the "dark side" of Kennedy's questionable legacy.[9] Against such easy dismissals, this chapter takes Camelot seriously and argues that the figure names a major midcentury transformation in the relationship between culture and politics in the United States. Camelot responded to, facilitated, and crystallized a new phase of American presidential power.

From its origin, the American presidency has been freighted with myth, legend, and symbolic power. It has always had a performative dimension. In the early nineteenth century, the so-called cult of Washington elevated George Washington to superhuman stature, using his historical memory for a range of political purposes and flooding the market with Washington memorabilia, including miniatures and other visual reproductions.[10] In time, the cult of the presidency became an important symbolic counterpart to a radical expansion of executive power. As Sean McCann notes, many Americans transformed their imaginative relationship to the executive branch at the end of the nineteenth century. For those sick of partisan competition, the presidency – and the figure of the president – seemed capable of transcending party affiliations and local interests. Advocates of a strong executive worked "toward the creation of a new political system in which American voters would abandon their party affiliations to embrace a personal relationship with the president," seeing the chief executive as a "national redeemer who could restore the sovereignty of the people and return America to its democratic mission."[11] Many presidents aspired to become another Lincoln, to make themselves a metonym for the American people, a centralized avatar for the Union, someone whose election would stage a second American Revolution. In his inaugural claim that "the torch has been passed to a new generation of Americans," and in his description of a "peaceful revolution of hope," Kennedy aptly employed this executive rhetoric, reminding Americans "that we are the heirs of that first revolution."[12] But Kennedy did much more than continue the tradition of the strong executive that McCann documents. He brought this tradition into an age of electronic media, integrating the presidency fully into the culture industry, making the symbolic figure of the president – as we will see – the natural counterpart to technocratic governance.

Kennedy saw his power not only in terms of practical politics but also as a function of his capacity to manage his public image, which he did with great care and great success. That Kennedy carefully exploited image culture is, of course, a historiographical commonplace.[13] Kennedy and his associates were, as Robert Dallek writes, "extraordinarily skillful at creating positive images that continue to shape public impressions."[14] Kennedy's friend Charles Spalding recalls, "Jack was very much concerned about image . . . It wasn't even called 'image' then . . . So even though he was terribly self-conscious about it, he was always interested in seeing whether he had it – the magnetism – or didn't have it. We spent hours talking about it."[15] In her comments to White, Jackie thus did not betray her husband's conception of presidential power but rather consolidated it. This becomes clear in White's memoir, *In Search of History: A Personal Adventure* (1978). When she called him to Hyannis Port, White recalls, Jackie hoped to ensure that "Jack was not forgotten in history."[16] Jackie did not fear that history might *forget* Jack, but rather that he might become *merely* historical. She felt angry toward journalists who were "assessing the President, just dead, by his achievements. She wanted to rescue Jack from all these 'bitter people' who were going to write about him in history. She did not want Jack left to the historians."[17] Over the course of the conversation, Jackie makes several similar remarks about history. "History! . . . History . . . it's what those bitter old men write," she said, "or just: 'History . . .'"[18] Jackie was referring specifically to articles written by Arthur Krock and Merriman Smith, but a broader argument emerges from her lament. There are two kinds of history for Jackie: on the one hand, "bitter" histories that assess presidents on the basis of their achievements, and, on the other hand, what Jackie describes as her husband's own idea of history, not bitter but "idealistic" and "full of heroes."[19] Camelot is an apt name for this heroic model of history and presidential power.

Jack and Jackie Kennedy were able to popularize Camelot not only because they were politically canny but also because they arrived on the American political scene during a revolutionary transformation in the mass media. In an analysis that used the Kennedy-Nixon debate as a major point of reference, the historian and media critic Daniel J. Boorstin described this revolution in terms of what he called "pseudo-events." By Boorstin's classic account, which anticipated better-known analyses of image culture by Guy Debord and Jean Baudrillard, the pseudo-event is "planned, planted, or incited" for the benefit of "reporting or reproducing media," and is therefore a "self-fulfilling prophecy" whose "underlying reality . . . is ambiguous."[20] Though Boorstin wished to preserve some authentic reality apart from the image, his analysis constantly confronts the impossibility of restoring the old order of events. The pseudo-event threatens to crowd out an older sort of "spontaneous" event from the public sphere. Viewed this way, Camelot is not only a myth that has organized the historical memory of Kennedy's time in office but is also a metaphor that had (and has) a special power within the interlocking institutions and emerging cultures of postmodern media. Because of these transformations, metaphor making arguably gained a new political efficacy. Camelot is therefore a good name for what Diane Rubenstein and other critics have called the "postmodern presidency," the president as pure media image.[21] Though we might argue that every president after Kennedy is postmodern in this sense, Kennedy and his associates self-consciously used midcentury image culture to specific political ends.

First, Kennedy made the image of the American presidency less formal in its verbal and visual rhetoric. This informality had a different character than, to take an obvious point of comparison, the informality of FDR's fireside chats. After all, Kennedy wasn't only a political leader but also a sartorial trendsetter, a visual presence in the living room of almost every American, a sex symbol, and a lifestyle model – who, as Caitlin Flanagan notes in a recent essay in the *Atlantic*, might also be viewed as a template for a certain kind of "singular masculinity."[22] Kennedy was a bridge figure who helped push American ideals of manhood from an era of gray-flannel-suited conformity to what George Frazier in 1968 dubbed the Peacock Revolution.[23] Kennedy was frequently noted for his failure to don formal attire, for wearing two-button suits (which he wore because of his back brace), for not wearing button-down collars.[24] Kennedy's wardrobe has been described as providing the "building blocks of Don Draper's wardrobe: narrow lapels, narrow ties, white shirts with small-proportioned point collars" as well as the foundations of "classic American sportswear: button-down shirts, polos, crew-neck sweaters, khakis, sneakers, Ray-Bans."[25] The president is, of course, credited with – or blamed for – nothing less than killing the American hat, partly because he did not wear one during his inaugural address.[26] Kennedy's famous aversion to hats was a point of frustration with Alex Rose, president of the United Hatters, Cap, and Millinery Workers International Union, who strongly supported Kennedy's nomination. Rose "present[ed] [Kennedy] with hats at every opportunity," hoping that the presidency might stimulate hat consumption.[27] Kennedy reportedly hated hats "because they hid his hair," which he regarded as one of his best features.[28] As the journalist Neil Steinberg writes, "In a hat he looked far older and almost unrecognizably ugly. And he knew it."[29] Kennedy was tremendously vain about his appearance, spending the week before his inauguration obsessed with reducing his weight and with tanning (so that he would look good on black-and-white televisions). Before his inauguration, he flew from Palm Beach to New York City to have his teeth whitened.

"Before marrying Jackie," the journalist and historian Thurston Clarke writes, "Kennedy had been a sloppy dresser who favored baggy suits, clashing shirts and ties, and ratty tennis shoes."[30] Under Jackie's tutelage, he "became conscious of not only his appearance but that of those around him."[31] As John L. Steele wrote in *Life* in 1961, the new president "does not hesitate to make his views known" to those around him, offering withering sartorial critiques of members of his administration, paying "close attention not only to his own attire but also to what is being worn by the people around him, men and women alike."[32] Steele describes Kennedy as "almost certainly the most clothes-conscious occupant of the White House since Martin Van Buren, who showed up in church wearing a velvet collar, lace-tipped cravat and yellow kid gloves."[33] This is not to say that Kennedy confused fashion-consciousness with formality. As Steele reports, "At formal affairs he often manages to avoid being completely formal," understanding that "it is sometimes possible to be *too* correct, and therefore not correct at all."[34] The president's "business suits fail to conform to current Ivy League fashion."[35] As the president's tailor, Samuel Harris, explained, "We don't follow Ivy League or beatniks. We make gentlemen's clothes."[36] Harris's comment recalls Norman Mailer's invocation of the two worlds – the square and the hip – that Kennedy's election would supposedly bridge. For all his flaws as a political analyst, Mailer pegged Kennedy's style.

Kennedy's informality was in evidence not only in his sartorial choices but also in the imaginative relationship that he invited the American people to have with his household. The increasingly porous boundary between public and private presidential space was apparent in Jackie Kennedy's intimate White House tour, which was originally broadcast by CBS and NBC on February 14, 1962, and then rebroadcast four days later on ABC. At the end of the tour, Collingwood interviews the president himself. In his comments, Kennedy offers a telling account of the importance of the White House restoration, implicitly answering Collingwood's previous question to Jackie about the relationship of art and state power. By Kennedy's account, Jackie's restoration efforts "bring us much more intimately in contact with all the men who lived here" and "make these men much more alive."[37] Kennedy suggest that the "White House is becoming more and more important to the American people. Over 1,300,000 people passed through our [here Kennedy hesitates and laughs] home." If those who pass through the White House "in a sense touch the people who've been here then . . . they'll become better Americans." These improved Americans will learn that former presidents are "people who are legendary but who actually were alive and were in these rooms." Of course, these comments tacitly refer not only to those who have or will physically tour the White House but also to the television audience. Indeed, the tour was at that time the most watched documentary of all time, with a live audience estimated at 46 million people.[38] One cannot avoid the conclusion that the tour was meant in fact to bring the American viewer "more intimately in contact" with the Kennedys, to render them "much more alive," to affirm that they themselves are both "legendary" and "alive." By getting within range to "touch" the Kennedys, viewers are told they will "become better Americans." This project of cultivating televisual intimacy had an international dimension. As Carol B. Schwalbe notes, the White House tour was broadcast and shown, via the USIA, to "an audience estimated in the hundreds of millions" worldwide.[39] Jackie also appeared in two USIA propaganda films organized by George S. Stevens Jr., which documented her goodwill tours of India and Pakistan. The goal of these tours was, as Schwalbe notes, to build "international support for the Kennedy administration during the Cold War."[40]

In Jackie's huge propaganda value – her capacity to command international attention – we also catch a glimpse of the second major dimension of Kennedy's media image. For at the same time that the American public became more intimate with the First Family, Kennedy sought to make the presidency a repository of glamour, cultivating relationships with advertisers, actors, artists, writers, musicians, and intellectuals – as well as members of the Rat Pack. The journalist Christian Chensvold notes, "Kennedy had something no American leader had ever had before: cool."[41] Mailer famously agreed, calling Kennedy "the hipster as Presidential candidate," though he described Jackie as the "Public Man's Eighteenth-Century Wife."[42] The journalist and editor of the satirical *Monocle*, C. D. B. Bryan, described Kennedy as of "our generation, hip, with it, funny, so satire was a way of laughing with him, we felt he got the joke."[43] Kennedy invited a new sort of attention to the male body – and the body of the president – not to mention to the body of the president's wife, whom Mailer thought might be "the most beautiful First Lady in our history."[44] The president moved away from an older ideal of masculine style toward an ideal of cool, self-assurance, and irony.[45] This new masculinity was of a piece with a range of other developments at the start of the 1960s. Steve Watts writes:

> The ideal of the team-oriented business executive, the family man in the gray flannel suit moved to the sidelines before a new idea of the vibrant, vigorously heterosexual male who was bold, irreverent, hip, and successful. The new type popped up everywhere – in fictional figures such as James Bond, in politicians such as John F. Kennedy, and in entertainers such as Sinatra and the Rat Pack. In the public imagination, Hugh Hefner joined this group as he personified the *Playboy* lifestyle.[46]

Kennedy, of course, loved Fleming's Bond series, listing *From Russia with Love* as his ninth-favorite book.[47]

Under Kennedy, the American president and his family became global celebrities. As Oleg Cassini wrote, explaining how he came to think about designing a dress for Jackie for an inaugural ball, "Suddenly, it came to me. this [*sic*] is like a film and you have the opportunity to dress the female star. This was not so different from my old job in Hollywood, designing for motion pictures."[48] In his gloss on what he calls the It-Effect, the performance studies scholar Joseph Roach emphasizes the celebrity's capacity to mobilize "an apparently singular nexus of personal quirks, irreducible to type, yet, paradoxically, the epitome of a type or prototype."[49] Roach's account of the eighteenth-century development of the It-Effect traces it as far back as Quintilian, identifying it with the concept of "*ethos*, the compellingly singular character of the great orator."[50] This is a convincing genealogy – and it can be useful to think of Camelot as the *ethos* of Kennedy's presidency – but we should not lose sight of the historical and technological specificity of Kennedy's particular manifestation of the It-Effect. To become a celebrity in the context of midcentury television culture, to embody the "contradictory qualities simultaneously" Roach identifies with "It," the president first had to become something like a lifestyle brand, fully integrated into the circuits of advertising and image culture.[51] Indeed, Blair Clark and Fred Friendly, two CBS executives, helped Kennedy make his inauguration more telegenic. Eisenhower had famously pioneered the use of television advertising during his 1952 campaign. Nonetheless, for all his innovation, Eisenhower was hardly successful as a locus of national affective investment. His personality did not promise, as Mailer might put it, to fuse the mainstream and the underground of American life. By contrast, Kennedy launched the American presidency into the age of cultural politics. In this sense, Camelot should not be regarded as merely the product of collective memory but as one name for the active political project of making and managing collective memory toward specific ends.

Kennedy, more than many prior presidents, understood the work of the imagination in shaping the power, meaning, and legacy of the presidency. He understood the figure of the president to be a manly, heroic model of agency and decision, and he linked this model to stylistic choices. In an age of electronic media, style became a new vehicle of presidential authority, enabling a new intimacy and celebrity for the figure of the president. A recent Gallup poll report suggests that Kennedy was successful in his efforts to secure his legacy. Nearly three-quarters of Americans rank Kennedy as an "outstanding or above-average president," higher than any of the eleven presidents who served since 1960, despite the fact that Kennedy "does not appear on most historians' lists of the nation's greatest presidents."[52] Kennedy became a template according to which future candidates, both Republican and Democrat, modeled themselves, as historians such as Thomas Brown, Paul R. Henggeler, and Larry J. Sabato have shown.[53] Henggeler writes:

> The rise of John Kennedy altered the stylistic standards by which succeeding presidents sometimes measured greatness, and by which they were measured . . . The goal was to emote the elusive Kennedy "charisma," an indefinable essence that entailed conflicting qualities of intelligence and courage, detachment and charm, glamour and a common touch, toughness and compassion, humor and seriousness, self-depreciation and confidence.[54]

After Kennedy, most presidential candidates have sought, in one way or another, to recreate Camelot.

Kennedy's self-conscious deployment of charisma was ultimately not an adjunct to the business of governing, but central to the effectiveness of the presidency in an age of the pseudo-event. Rule-by-celebrity president is the necessary counterpart of rule-by-expert, as was already understood at the time of Kennedy's election. One sees this dialectic at play in an anecdote Theodore White recounts in his memoir. When White visits Kennedy to interview him for his book *The Making of the President, 1960*, he finds the new president furious about Congress's unwillingness to pass a farm bill:

> I was aware that Kennedy knew as little as I did about feed-grains, corn, wheat, pigs, beef, or from which side of a cow you take the milk. But I was surprised by the intensity of his emotion and of his commitment to this feed-grain bill. I have no idea to this day whether that bill was good, bad, practical, or chimerical. The best agricultural mandarins had devised it; therefore as President he must move the bill by skill, stealth, seduction, or pressure through to a congressional majority.[55]

By this view, the president is an executive figure who – through "skill, stealth, seduction, or pressure" – streamlines the complexities of ruling a pluralistic and technocratic society whose policies are designed by "mandarins." This is politics for the age of the end of ideology.[56]

The presidency might, on this vision, solve the technical problem of organizing the imagination and sense of purpose of the nation. Indeed, the Camelot figure answered the call of the so-called National Purpose debate of 1960. In response to a series of crises at the end of his administration – such as the Soviet launch of Sputnik 1 in 1957 and Nikita Khrushchev's demoralizing 1959 U.S. tour, called a "second Sputnik" in the *Atlantic* – Dwight D. Eisenhower created his Commission on National Goals. Its aim was to "identify the great issues of our generation and describe our objectives in these various areas . . . to sound a call for greatness to a resolute people."[57] Henry Luce organized a five-part *Life* series on the question, since "the people of America are asking for a clear sense of National Purpose."[58] In the opening editorial note of the series, the National Purpose debate was called "the most crucial debate of our generation."[59] One might rightly doubt whether Americans were actually asking this question, but the so-called debate gives a helpful window on elite opinion circa 1960. John K. Jessup feared that "[a] U.S. without a purpose . . . may well be a U.S. in decline," and if the United States declines from lack of purpose "the leadership of Communism" will fill the gap.[60] In other words, increasingly affluent Americans might lose the nerve to fight the Cold War. One finds a similar narrative of crisis – and a solution – in Arthur Schlesinger's writing of the late 1950s and early 1960s. In "Liberalism in America: A Note for Europeans" (1956), Schlesinger writes, "Contemporary American liberalism . . . has no overpowering mystique. It lacks a rhapsodic sense. It has jettisoned many illusions."[61] The liberal tradition's lack of mystique increasingly came to seem like a problem to Schlesinger. In "The New Mood in Politics" (1960), Schlesinger fears that the close of the Eisenhower era betrays "dangerous tendencies toward satire and idealism, a mounting dissatisfaction with the official priorities, a deepening concern with our character and objectives as a nation."[62] The rise of the "Beat generation," satire, the religious revival led by Billy Graham, the popularity of books such as *The Affluent Society*, *The Lonely Crowd*, and *The Organization Man* were in Schlesinger's view symptoms of American spiritual stagnation and a desultory sense of mission.[63] "It is as if increasing numbers of Americans were waiting for a trumpet to sound," he wrote. "We are coming to realize that we need a new conviction of national purpose not only as a matter of taste but as a matter of desperate necessity."[64] Schlesinger, like other participants in the National Purpose debate, "looked to the president" and presidential power to revive the nation.[65]

The lack of national purpose was identified with a failure of executive leadership. Indeed, in "On Heroic Leadership," Schlesinger makes the case that "the American political system, though misconceived by some as made up of three co-ordinate branches of equal powers, has worked best as a presidential system. Only strong Presidents have been able to overcome the tendencies towards inertia inherent in a structure so cunningly composed of checks and balances."[66] This language strongly harmonizes with Kennedy's own description of heroic leadership, expressed as early as *Why England Slept* (1940) and again in his own contribution to the National Purpose debate. Kennedy's definition of the National Purpose was "the combined purposefulness of each of us when we are at our moral best: striving, risking, choosing, making decisions, engaging in a pursuit of happiness that is strenuous, heroic, exciting and exalted."[67] This portrait of the American citizen at his "moral best" evokes many of the same categories that Jackie used when describing her dead husband's vision of history. These are terms well suited to a fantasy of executive power. The age of television gave these fantasies a new effective reach. Discussing Kennedy's live press conferences, David Halberstam argues that television empowered the American presidency, "changing the institutional balance of the country and helping to create what would soon be called the Imperial Presidency."[68] Television corrected the deficit of charismatic leadership in a democracy, neutralizing the problem of print journalism. Print could be "too querulous, could include too much journalistic analyzing of motive, could filter out too much of the original message, could in sum spread too much doubt."[69] By contrast, television "was powerful and it was direct, and by and large it was the property of the chief executive."[70] In his essay on leadership, Schlesinger favorably cites Thomas Jefferson's claim that "that form of government is the best, which provides the most effectually for a pure selection of these natural *aristoi* into the offices of government."[71] By contrast, on Halberstam's account, "mastery of the press conference became a substitute for mastery of public affairs."[72] Jefferson's *aristoi* now lurked behind the scenes, finding themselves functionally differentiated from the celebrity leaders who occupied center stage. The American president's twin functions – as head of government and as head of state – are in this formulation pulled apart.

Given the cynicism of this view, it is easy to attack Camelot, and I would agree right to do so on political grounds. Deriding Theodore White's power-loving style of access journalism, Rick Perlstein writes, "If you hate the kind of writing Bob Woodward does now; if you hate *Politico* or, going back further, if you hate the kind of things Sally Quinn wrote on Monicagate . . . or the childish abuse and systematic distortions meted out to Al Gore in 2000 because he didn't fit into the Washington insiders' village, blame Camelot – or 'Camelot.' "[73] One might go further, arguing that Camelot not only empowers bad journalism but also enthrones an empirically unrealistic theory of government power. In an astute analysis that resonates well beyond the Kennedy administration, but uses Kennedy as a major touchstone, the political scientist and law professor Edward L. Rubin calls Camelot an "escapist fantasy from the initial development of the administrative state in Western European nations."[74] Rubin argues that modern theories of government rely on "social nostalgia for the pre-administrative state," a dangerous nostalgia that he names Camelot.[75] In Rubin's account, Jacqueline Kennedy's interview with White becomes just another example of this misguided view of power.

However, I will end by suggesting that Camelot-style nostalgia is not an alternative to a clear-sighted idea of government's functioning, but – in the era of public relations, celebrity culture, and the pseudo-event – an instrumental part of effective governing. There is thus something more than cynicism at work in the Camelot figure. As Joseph Roach has put it, "Celebrities . . . like kings, have two bodies, the body natural, which decays and dies, and the body cinematic, which does neither."[76] We ignore Kennedy's two bodies at our peril. In time, even the journalist Walter Lippmann – who supported Kennedy only reluctantly – came to appreciate Camelot and the president's undying cinematic body. This might be surprising, given the disdain Lippmann showed throughout his career for "the self-centered opinions that happen to be floating around in men's minds," and his Jeffersonian preference for expert rule (or rather, rule by political scientist).[77] But in 1967, Lippmann came to a different conclusion: "I, for one, have learned a new respect for the myth-making process . . . a passionate multitude all over the world . . . believes [Kennedy] to have been the herald of better things in a dangerous and difficult time . . . I am glad of the legend and I think it contains that part of the truth which is most worth having."[78] If we do not like this model of the presidency, our objective should be clear: we would first have to dismantle the institutions and power relations that make our escapist fantasies politically effective in the first place.

NOTES

1 Arthur M. Schlesinger Jr., *A Thousand Days: John F. Kennedy in the White House* (New York: Mariner Books, 2002), xi.
2 Ibid.
3 Theodore H. White, "For President Kennedy: An Epilogue," *Life*, December 9, 1963, 159.
4 Linda Czuba Brigance, "For One Brief Shining Moment: Choosing to Remember Camelot," *Studies in Popular Culture* 25, no. 3 (2003): 2.
5 Joyce Hoffman, *Theodore H. White and Journalism as Illusion* (Columbia: University of Missouri Press, 1995), 3.
6 Theodore H. White, *In Search of History: A Personal Adventure* (New York: Franklin Library, 1980), 518.
7 Jackie wrote the British prime minister Harold Macmillan that the Camelot metaphor had been "overly sentimental." Sally Bedell Smith, *Grace and Power: The Private World of the Kennedy White House* (New York: Random House, 2011), xix. She told John Kenneth Galbraith the metaphor had been "overdone." Schlesinger Jr., *A Thousand Days*, xi.

8 Schlesinger Jr., *A Thousand Days*, xi.

9 For attacks on the idea that the Kennedy years were a version of Camelot, see Henry Fairlie, *The Kennedy Promise* (New York: Dell, 1974); Garry Wills, *The Kennedy Imprisonment: A Meditation on Power* (New York: Mariner, 1982); Seymour M. Hersh, *The Dark Side of Camelot* (New York: Little, Brown, 1997); Noam Chomsky, *Rethinking Camelot: JFK, the Vietnam War, and U.S. Political Culture* (Cambridge, MA: South End Press, 1999).

10 Barry Schwartz, *George Washington: The Making of an American Symbol* (New York: Free Press, 1987); Paul K. Longmore, *The Invention of George Washington* (Charlottesville: University of Virginia Press, 1999); Gerald E. Kahler, *The Long Farewell: Americans Mourn the Death of George Washington* (Charlottesville: University of Virginia Press, 2008).

11 Sean McCann, *A Pinnacle of Feeling: American Literature and Presidential Government* (Princeton, NJ: Princeton University Press, 2008), x.

12 John F. Kennedy, "Inaugural Address," January 20, 1961. John F. Kennedy Presidential Library and Museum, http://www.jfklibrary.org/Asset-Viewer/BqXIEM9F4024ntFl7SVAjA.aspx, accessed December 12, 2014.

13 On the relationship of Kennedy to image culture, see Thomas Brown, *JFK: History of an Image* (Bloomington: Indiana University Press, 1988); John Hellmann, *The Kennedy Obsession: The American Myth of JFK* (New York: Columbia University Press, 1997); David M. Lubin, *Shooting Kennedy: JFK and the Culture of Images* (Berkeley: University of California Press, 2003); Mark White, *Kennedy: A Cultural History of an American Icon* (New York: Bloomsbury, 2013).

14 Robert Dallek, *An Unfinished Life: John F. Kennedy, 1917–1963* (New York: Back Bay Books, 2004), ix.

15 White, *Kennedy*, 14.

16 White, *In Search of History*, 515.

17 Ibid.

18 Ibid., 517.

19 Ibid., 516.

20 Daniel J. Boorstin, *The Image: A Guide to Pseudo-Events in America*, 50th anniversary ed., afterword Douglas Rushkoff (New York: Vintage, 2012), 11–12.

21 Diane Rubenstein, *This Is Not a President: Sense, Nonsense, and the American Political Imaginary* (New York: New York University Press, 2008). See also Richard Rose, *The Postmodern President* (Thousand Oaks, CA: CQ Press, 1991); Steven Schier, *Postmodern Presidency: Bill Clinton's Legacy in U.S. Politics* (Pittsburg, PA: University of Pittsburg Press, 2000); John F. Freie, *The Making of the Postmodern Presidency: From Ronald Reagan to Barack Obama* (Boulder, CO: Paradigm Publishers, 2011).

22 Caitlin Flanagan, "Jackie and the Girls," *Atlantic*, July–August 2012, http://www.theatlantic.com/magazine/archive/2012/07/Jackie-and-the-girls/309000/, accessed December 12, 2014.

23 On the Peacock Revolution, see Thomas Frank, *The Conquest of Cool: Business Culture, Counterculture, and the Rise of Hip Consumerism* (Chicago: University of Chicago Press, 1998).

24 Christian Chensvold, "Setting the President," *Arbiter*, February 2010, 50–53.

25 "JFK, Mad Men, and Vintage Americana," *Threads Count*, August 25, 2010, http://threadscount.blogspot.com/2010/08/jfk-mad-men-and-vintage-americana.html, accessed January 22, 2014.

26 This is, of course, a historically dubious claim. For an entertaining history of the decline of the hat, which takes Kennedy's distaste for hats as the occasion for a much more careful analysis of "complex range of social forces that doomed the hat," see Neal Steinberg, *Hatless Jack: The President, the Fedora, and the History of an American Style* (New York: Plume 2004), xiii.

27 Ibid., viii.

28 Thurston Clarke, *Ask Not: The Inauguration of John F. Kennedy and the Speech That Changed America* (New York: Penguin, 2011), 126.

29 Steinberg, *Hatless Jack*, 19.

30 Clarke, *Ask Not*, 126.

31 Ibid.

32 John L. Steele, "Well Suited for the White House," *Life*, October 13, 1961, 29.

33 Ibid.

34 Ibid.

35 Ibid.

36 Clarke, *Ask Not*, 126.

37 The full tour can be viewed at http://www.youtube.com/watch?v=CbFt4h3Dkkw, accessed December 12, 2014.

38 Carol B. Schwalbe, "Jacqueline Kennedy and Cold War Propaganda," *Journal of Broadcasting & Electronic Media* 49, no. 1 (2005): 116.

39 Ibid.

40 Ibid., 111.

41 Chensvold, "Setting the President," 53.

42 Norman Mailer, "Superman Comes to the Supermarket," *Esquire* (November 1960), http://www.esquire.com/features/superman-supermarket, accessed December 12, 2014.

43 Stephen E. Kercher, *Revel with a Cause: Liberal Satire in Postwar America* (Chicago: University of Chicago Press, 2006), 231.

44 Mailer, "Superman Comes to the Supermarket."

45 For an analysis of the Democratic Party's use of midcentury hip culture, see Michael Szalay, *Hip Figures: A Literary History of the Democratic Party* (Stanford, CA: Stanford University Press, 2012).

46 Steve Watts, *Mr. Playboy: Hugh Hefner and the American Dream* (New York: Wiley, 2009), 152.

47 Hugh Sidey, "The President's Voracious Reading Habits," *Life*, March 17, 1961, 59.

48 Oleg Cassini, *A Thousand Days of Magic: Dressing Jacqueline Kennedy for the White House* (New York: Rizzoli, 1995), 15.

49 Joseph Roach, *It* (Ann Arbor: University of Michigan Press, 2007), 6.

50 Ibid., 7. For a compelling analysis of the category of ethos, see Amanda Anderson, *The Way We Argue Now: A Study in the Cultures of Theory* (Princeton, NJ: Princeton University Press, 2005).

51 Roach, *It*, 8.

52 Andrew Dugan and Frank Newport, "Americans Rate JFK as Top Modern President," *Gallup*, November 15, 2013, http://www.gallup.com/poll/165902/americans-rate-jfk-top-modern-president.aspx, accessed December 12, 2014.

53 Thomas Brown, *JFK: History of an Image* (Bloomington: Indiana University Press, 1988); Paul R. Henggeler, *The Kennedy Persuasion: The Politics of Style since JFK* (Chicago: Ivan R. Dee, 1995); Thomas Brown, *JFK: History of an Image* (Bloomington: Indiana University Press, 1988); Larry J. Sabato, *The Kennedy Half-Century: The Presidency, Assassination, and Lasting Legacy of John F. Kennedy* (New York: Bloomsbury, 2013).

54 Henggeler, *The Kennedy Persuasion*, 8.

55 White, *In Search of History*, 494.

56 The phrase belongs, of course, to Daniel Bell, *The End of Ideology: On the Exhaustion of Political Ideas in the Fifties* (Cambridge, MA: Harvard University Press, 2000).

57 "Memorandum Concerning the Commission on National Goals," February 7, 1960, in Dwight D. Eisenhower, *Public Papers of the Presidents of the United States* (Washington, DC: Office of the Federal Register, 1960), 160.

58 Henry Luce, "Foreword," in *The National Purpose*, ed. John K. Jessup et al. (New York: Holt, Rinehart, and Winston, 1960), v.

59 "The National Purpose," *Life*, May 23, 1960, 23.

60 John K. Jessup, "A Noble Framework for a Great Debate," in Jessup et al., *The National Purpose*, 2.

61 Arthur M. Schlesinger Jr., *The Politics of Hope and the Bitter Heritage: American Liberalism in the 1960s*, foreword Sean Wilentz (Princeton, NJ: Princeton University Press, 2007), 92.

62 Ibid., 105.

63 Ibid. After the election of Kennedy, satire no longer seemed "dangerous" to Schlesinger. As he wrote in the introduction to *The Politics of Hope*, "Wit has become respectable; it has even become presidential now" (9).

64 Ibid., 108.

65 John W. Jeffries, "The 'Quest for National Purpose' of 1960," *American Quarterly* 30, no. 4 (1978): 458.

66 Schlesinger Jr., *The Politics of Hope*, 20.

67 John F. Kennedy, "We Must Climb to the Hilltop," *Life*, August 22, 1960, 70. Kennedy's and Nixon's contributions to the series were omitted from Jessup et al., *The National Purpose*.

68 David Halberstam, "Introduction," in *The Kennedy Presidential Press Conferences*, ed. George W. Johnson (New York: Earl M. Coleman Enterprises, 1978), iii.

69 Ibid., i.

70 Ibid.

71 Thomas Jefferson to John Adams, October 18, 1813, *The Founders' Constitution*, ed. Philip B. Kurland and Ralph Lerner, http://press-pubs.uchicago.edu/founders/print_documents/v1ch15s61.html, accessed December 12, 2014.

72 Halbertstam, "Introduction," iii.

73 Rick Perlstein, "Kennedy Week: The Myth of Camelot and the Dangers of Sycophantic Consensus Journalism," *Nation*, November 22, 1963, http://www.thenation.com/blog/177333/kennedy-week-myth-camelot-and-dangers-sycophantic-consensus-journalism#, accessed December 12, 2014.

74 Edward L. Rubin, *Beyond Camelot: Rethinking Politics and Law for the Modern State* (Princeton, NJ: Princeton University Press, 2007), 5.

75 Ibid., 6.

76 Roach, *It*, 36. Roach is, of course, alluding to the classic study, Ernst Kantorowicz, *The King's Two Bodies: A Study in Medieval Political Theory* (Princeton: Princeton University Press, 1957).

77 Walter Lippmann, *Public Opinion*, intro. Michael Curtis (New Brunswick, NJ: Transaction Publishers, 1998), 313.

78 Walter Lippmann, "John F. Kennedy," in *Public Persons*, ed. Gilbert A. Harrison (New York: Lightriver Publishing, 1976), 185.

11

PETER KNIGHT

The Kennedy Assassination and Postmodern Paranoia

The Kennedy assassination has haunted the American cultural imagination for the last half century. In *Flying in to Love*, for example, the novelist D. M. Thomas interweaves the known facts of the event with outlines of an alternative history in which Kennedy isn't assassinated, the latter expressing a collective wish fulfillment fantasy on the part of a nation in thrall to JFK's seductive image. The novel begins with a declaration from a Dallas psychologist that "ten thousand dreams a night . . . are dreamt about Kennedy's assassination."[1] And, in fact, the event has been the focus of thousands of books, magazine and newspaper articles, novels, films, paintings, and computer animations, its story told in genres including journalism, memoir, history, biography, government reports, sociological inquiries, popular conspiracy exposés, literary and pulp fiction, museums and monuments, Hollywood film, and avant-garde art.[2] These retellings evince a sharp divide between those who believe that Oswald acted alone (as the Warren Commission insisted), and those who are convinced that there was some kind of cover-up or conspiracy.

The assassination is now routinely viewed as the mother of all conspiracy theories, the defining event responsible for a widespread and ongoing sense of suspicion that the official version of things is a lie.[3] According to an annual opinion poll, three-quarters of Americans trusted their government in the early 1960s; by the early 1990s, three quarters of Americans *distrusted* their government. With respect to the assassination, the overwhelming majority of Americans now believe that it was not the work of a lone gunman but was part of a large conspiracy.[4]

In the immediate aftermath of the shooting, however, it was not obvious that a popular culture of paranoia would be the inevitable reaction to the event. Given the recent experience of the Cuban Missile Crisis in 1962, as well as decades of FBI director J. Edgar Hoover's anticommunist scaremongering, the majority of Americans suspected some form of communist conspiracy. We now know that behind the scenes Hoover was – ironically – keen

164

to downplay any suggestion that Oswald was part of a larger conspiracy, lest embarrassing details emerge about the FBI's failure to keep a close enough watch on a character who was indeed on their radar. Likewise the CIA, during the Warren Commission's investigations, dragged its heels on providing any information that might have shed light on the conspiratorial connections swirling around the shooting, such as the obviously crucial revelation that the Kennedy brothers had known about (and perhaps even urged) plots involving the Mafia to assassinate Castro in Cuba. In the immediate hours following the shooting, Lyndon Johnson was panicked lest the killing of Kennedy was the first part of a much wider enemy plot to overthrow the U.S. government. Although it quickly became apparent that this was not the case, the new president remained extremely concerned that any revelations about a Cuban or Soviet connection to the assassination would lead to public demand for retaliation, which could result in a nuclear war. Johnson used the paranoid specter of global destruction to strong-arm Chief Justice Earl Warren and other reluctant politicians into serving on the Warren Commission, and behind the scenes made it clear to all involved that the FBI's story of a lone misfit gunman was to be the end of the matter. There is reasonable evidence to suggest, however, that LBJ privately continued to believe that there had been some kind of conspiracy.[5]

The publication of the Warren Commission Report in 1964 indeed succeeded to some extent in quelling public fears. However, from the moment that Jack Ruby shot Oswald many Americans felt an increasing sense of disbelief that the president could have been killed by an insignificant loser like Oswald. As William Manchester, the historian initially endorsed by Jackie Kennedy to write an account of her husband's death, later commented:

if you put the murdered President of the United States on one side of a scale and that wretched waif Oswald on the other side, it doesn't balance. You want to add something weightier to Oswald. It would invest the President's death with meaning, endowing him with martyrdom. He would have died for *something*. A conspiracy would, of course, do the job nicely.[6]

The emergence from the mid-1960s onward of critical accounts that challenged the official version of events can in part be explained by the overwhelming mood of national grief, coupled with a sense of the metaphysical mismatch between the grandeur of Kennedy and the pettiness of Oswald. More important, however, was the increasingly realization among a growing network of amateur researchers that the Warren Commission Report had serious flaws. Although at first the "assassination buffs" were concerned with documenting the inconsistencies and contradictions in the official account, later in the 1960s they began to produce full-blown conspiracy theories, provoked in part by a suspicion that many of the traumatic events of the decade – most notably the assassinations not just of JFK but of Martin Luther King, Malcolm X, and Robert Kennedy – were all connected in a sinister way.

Obsessive interest in these events might in some cases have been the result of a worldview bordering on the clinically paranoid, but it is important to note that conspiracy-minded interpretations were a justifiable reaction to the secrets, lies, and cover-ups that marred the official account. Revelations about skullduggery on the part of the government, the military, and the intelligence agencies began to emerge in the late 1960s, with the publication, for example, of the Pentagon Papers. These revelations only quickened pace with the Watergate hearings and the Church Committee investigations into the CIA in the mid-1970s.[7] If the American government had been involved in madcap plots in collusion with the Mafia to assassinate Castro, the thinking went, then who knew what else they were capable of? Likewise when viewers saw the Zapruder footage for the first time on Geraldo Rivera's television show in 1975, many were convinced that the official version of events was a blatant lie that had been kept from them for more than a decade – in this case because they were able to see with their own eyes that Kennedy must have shot from in front rather than from Oswald's position in the Texas School Book Depository behind the president. At least, so it seemed to those convinced of the authority of their own perceptions.

Believing that the Kennedy assassination was part of a larger plot involving a secret government within the government thus came in the 1970s to seem like an entirely rational proposition to many Americans. Moreover, many ordinary citizens felt that it was their duty to investigate the assassination themselves, by keeping up with the rapidly growing library of critical accounts; by delving into the twenty-six volumes of testimony and exhibits that formed part of the Warren Commission Report; or even by undertaking their own detective work. Many of these amateur investigations slid into fanciful scenarios involving multiple shooters, forged autopsy reports, switched corpses, faked footage, and elaborate plots. Their real significance, however, is not the immediate light they shed on the specifics of the assassination, but the collective – albeit often contradictory – challenge they presented to the official version of events. In short, they raised the question of who has the moral authority to tell a nation's history, particularly if the government is regarded as illegitimate because of the abuses of trust it has committed. Conspiracy theorists of differing stripes pitted their versions against the detailed accounts of the events in Dallas produced by Kennedy aides, biographers, historians, newspaper and television journalists, and official government inquiries.

This produced a competition to provide the most accurate account, with claims to authority based on familiarity, objectivity, immediacy, comprehensiveness, and various other criteria.

As part of this jostling for cultural authority, American novelists and film-makers have repeatedly returned to the assassination of President Kennedy, sometimes directly but at other times obliquely, and most have tended to challenge the official version of events. Some of the most prominent post-war American novelists – Don DeLillo, Norman Mailer, James Ellroy, and Stephen King – have focused on the Kennedy assassination because it raises fundamental questions about the connection between conspiracy plot and narrative plot, and because it resonates thematically and emotionally with many of their existing concerns. They have all claimed in their own way that the novel is able to provide privileged insights into the event. Norman Mailer, for example, advocated a more radical, democratic approach to the inquiry: "One would propose one last new commission, one real commission – a literary commission supported by public subscription to spend a few years on the case . . . I would trust a commission headed by [literary critic] Edmund Wilson before I trusted another by Earl Warren. Wouldn't you?"[8] One of the problems that these writers have encountered, however, is the sense that the primary sources they are drawing on are already stranger and more unnerving than anything they could write. DeLillo and Mailer in particular acknowledged that the Warren Commission Report might well be the ultimate postmodern novel, dwarfing any of their own efforts. Mailer characterized it as "a prodigious work, compendious enough to bear comparison to the Encyclopedia Britannica (had the Britannica been devoted to only one subject)," a form of "Talmudic text begging for commentary and further elucidation," and "a Comstock Lode of novelistic material."[9] DeLillo memorably called the report "the megaton novel James Joyce would have written if he'd moved to Iowa City and lived to be a hundred."[10]

Although it might appear that the Kennedy assassination pushed American literature toward an aesthetic of paranoia, even before the event novelists including William S. Burroughs, Philip K. Dick, Joseph Heller, Ken Kesey, Thomas Pynchon, and Kurt Vonnegut had explored the idea of the embattled individual as a victim of a vast yet secret system of bureaucratic, medical, media, and even linguistic control.[11] The notion of a vast secret organization controlling an individual's body and even his or her mind continued to resonate through a wide range of American cultural and political expression both before and after the assassination. This widespread sense of agency panic (in Timothy Melley's evocative phrase) drew upon the deep well of possessive individualism, such that any erosion of a tightly policed boundary between self and society is viewed as if it were the result of a conspiracy of social control.[12]

In its most extreme versions the level of suspicion reaches epidemic proportions, as characters begin to distrust the very nature of reality, suspecting that it is in fact constructed by some mysterious, all-powerful enemy. These more metaphysical writings, which threaten to plunge characters and reader alike into a mise en abyme of doubt, suggest a close connection between paranoia and postmodernism. If, as some postmodern theory has suggested, there is no direct, unmediated access to an agreed-upon reality, then it follows that there is no way of distinguishing for certain between reality and what "They" are trying to make you think is the case – and thus no guaranteed way of telling the difference between a paranoid and a sane interpretation of events.

Kennedy's assassination gave focus to this preexisting anxiety about the individual's agency and his or her ability to correctly interpret the nature of reality, generating what many commentators saw as a widespread existential crisis. As Norman Mailer put it, "Since the assassination of John F. Kennedy we have been marooned in one of two equally intolerable spiritual states, apathy or paranoia."[13]

Richard Condon's novel *Winter Kills* (1974) explores these twin spiritual states of apathy and paranoia.[14] His novel projects the Kennedy assassination through the lens of mid-1970s cynicism, telling the story of the younger brother of a murdered president who belatedly tries to get to the bottom of his sibling's death fourteen years previously. Condon had already explored the idea of a presidential assassination in his 1959 novel *The Manchurian Candidate*, a tale of a soldier who becomes a mind-controlled assassin after being brainwashed by communists during the Korean War (and who, in an Oedipal twist very much in keeping with the paranoid sense of an imperiled masculinity, was being controlled by his own mother all along). *Winter Kills* amps up this atmosphere of conspiracy even further, setting up a seemingly endless chain of investigation in which Nick pursues various wild geese in the form of fake confessions, false leads, and double crosses. The novel provides a catalogue of the various theories about the Kennedy assassination that had fallen in and out of vogue by the mid-1970s, conjuring up the specter of a vast yet shadowy conspiracy so powerful and ruthless that it is able to set in motion a mind-boggling play of misdirection. Nick finds out that the man he thought was a police chief implicated in the plot had in fact died years ago, and that the chief's assistant was himself a fake, as indeed was the oil millionaire who had also offered up a seemingly sincere revelation. Like Thomas Pynchon's *The Crying of Lot 49* (which itself can be read as a parable of the Kennedy assassination), Condon's novel raises the alarming possibility that the final truth might never be found, and that the search for a conspiracy ultimately leads to perpetual paranoia rather than insight.[15] But the ever-accelerating free-fall plunge of paranoia is halted in the last few pages of the novel when we learn that, in fact, all the false clues have been deliberately fabricated and planted for Nick by an all-too-real conspiracy of the secret ruling elite led by his father – a superrich, supercorrupt Joseph P. Kennedy figure.

The idea that the Kennedy assassination produced a thoroughgoing crisis of knowledge underpins (albeit at times obliquely) a remarkable cluster of conspiracy thrillers made in the 1960s, 1970s, and 1980s, including *Blow-Up* (1966), *Klute* (1971), *The Parallax View* (1974), *The Conversation* (1974), *Three Days of the Condor* (1975), *All The President's Men* (1976), and *Blow Out* (1981). Michelangelo Antonioni's *Blow-Up* is one of the most interesting films inspired by the Kennedy assassination, even though it doesn't actually address the event itself. The story concerns a London fashion photographer (played by David Hemmings) who takes a picture of an unknown couple in a park. When he develops the print, the woman in the shot (in a subtle echo of the Kennedy case) seems to be looking toward a shadowy figure with a gun who is hidden behind a fence. When, like Kennedy assassination researchers, the photographer blows the image up further and further, he thinks he can spot in the blurry shapes a body hidden in the bushes. Like the Zapruder footage and other images that accidentally captured the moment of the Kennedy assassination, the photo in *Blow-Up* promises to yield the true narrative of a crime. Yet it also raises the possibility that the "murder" visible in the photo is entirely a product of the photographer's paranoid imagination, the "body" merely the grain of the film stock.

Alan J. Pakula's *The Conversation* and Brian De Palma's *Blow Out* both function as homages to Antonioni's New Wave film. The former stars Gene Hackman as an audio surveillance expert who thinks he has captured on tape evidence of a murder committed by the couple he is spying on. He begins, however, to doubt his own perceptions and even his own mind, by the end of the film frantically ripping apart his apartment in an attempt to discover the bugs that he is convinced must be there. *Blow Out*, meanwhile, tells the story of a sound effects technician played by John Travolta who accidentally records what turns out to be a Chappaquiddick-like incident involving a senator and a car crash off a bridge. In *The Parallax View*, a newspaper reporter played by Warren Beatty is an accidental witness to the assassination of a presidential candidate, in a story with strong echoes of the assassinations of both John and Robert Kennedy. Beatty's character uncovers clues to a vast conspiracy that reaches from the sinister Parallax Corporation into the heart of the U.S. government, but his life and his mind begin to unravel as he becomes obsessed with the case, and he is eventually killed by the shadowy organization that he thought he had penetrated. Each of these films balances subliminal glimpses into a colossal and potentially limitless conspiracy against the possibility that the conspiracy is all in the mind of the obsessive amateur detective haunted by the case in which he has become embroiled. Unlike the traditional detective novel or Hollywood thriller, these gritty exercises in paranoid cynicism offer no satisfying resolutions. Instead they suggest that the ultimate truth of an impossibly vast corporate and government conspiracy (which the amateur investigations into the Kennedy assassination seemed to bring to light) might always remain frustratingly just out of reach. This notion is coupled with the equally disturbing possibility that all the clues are not part of some meaningful if horrifyingly sinister plot but are simply random.

These films thus make clear the connection between the Kennedy assassination and the desire for and distrust of knowledge at the heart of postmodernism. As the narrator of Pynchon's *Gravity's Rainbow* puts it: "If there is something comforting – religious, if you want – about paranoia, there is still also anti-paranoia, where nothing is connected to anything, a condition not many of us can bear for long."[16] In the wake of the Kennedy assassination additional evidence led not to convergence but to further dispute, producing an infinite regress of suspicion that began to cast everything into doubt – even the fundamental ground rules of proof and evidence. The problem was not that there is too little evidence to solve the case, but too much.

In contrast to these conspiracy thrillers, Oliver Stone's *JFK* (1991) tries to weave its numerous strands of evidence into a single coherent plot. A residual faith in efficient agency and simple causality remains visible in the film's whirlwind presentation of just about every conspiracy theory surrounding the case. *JFK* suggests that every seeming discrepancy in the case (such as the shadows on Oswald's chin in the infamous backyard photos) is not the result of the inevitable messiness of actual historical events but the handiwork of an all-powerful conspiracy: we see unknown hands forging the photos with clinical precision. Stone's evocation of a vast yet vague "military-industrial complex" plotting to get rid of Kennedy at first resembles the shadowy plots depicted in the other films discussed above. But the conspiracy in Stone's film is not so much a loose network of intersecting interests as a tight-knit cabal – albeit an improbably far-reaching one that nevertheless operates with the coordination and determination of a ruthless individual or a traditional image of a small group of dedicated plotters.

Literary fiction took up these issues in its own way. Don DeLillo's *Libra* (1988) provides a fascinating meditation on the problems of agency, causality, and conspiracy in its account of the Kennedy assassination. DeLillo subsequently took issue with Stone's *JFK* because it offered not much more than a "particular type of nostalgia: the nostalgia for a master plan, the conspiracy which explains everything."[17] Yet establishment critics such as George Will had attacked *Libra* itself for dabbling in conspiracy theory, claiming that it was a work of a "literary vandal."[18] On his part, DeLillo argued that fiction might provide some comfort in the face of the crisis of knowledge that the assassination brought about. For DeLillo, "that day in Dallas changed the way we think about the world,"[19] producing what he calls in *Libra* an "aberration in the heartland of the real" (15). The event had become surrounded by such ambiguity that it had undermined "our trust in a coherent reality," leading us "to feel that what's been missing over these past twenty-five years is a sense of manageable reality."[20] With all the contradictory evidence, the "official documents lost, missing, altered, classified and destroyed" and the "flood of coincidence," it is no surprise that after the assassination "a culture of distrust and paranoia began to develop, a sense of the secret manipulation of history," a feeling that had only intensified since.[21] In the "Author's Note" at the end of *Libra*, DeLillo insists that "because this book makes no claim to literal truth, because it is only itself, apart and complete, readers may find refuge here – a way of thinking about the assassination without being constrained by half-facts or overwhelmed by possibilities, by the tide of speculation that widens with the years" (458).

One plot strand of *Libra* provides a self-conscious reflection on the way the case has overwhelmed people's ability to make sense of it. DeLillo focuses this problem through the fictional character Nicholas Branch, a historian who has been commissioned by the CIA to write the "secret history" of the case for the agency. Branch, a stand-in for both DeLillo and the reader, is in theory in the ideal position to write the definitive history of the assassination thanks to his unrestricted access to all documents. Instead, however, he is floored by the sheer mass of evidence. In the Warren Commission Report, that "Joycean book of America," Branch discovers that "everything is here": "Baptismal records, report cards, postcards, divorce petitions, canceled checks, daily timesheets, tax returns, property lists, postoperative x-rays, photos of knotted string, thousands of pages of testimony, of voices droning in hearing rooms in old courthouse buildings, an incredible haul of human utterance" (181). The problem for Branch is that he cannot be sure whether a particular piece of evidence is significant or trivial, and in what conceivable universe all these details could form part of a single plot (in both senses of the word). Branch speculates that the most obvious way to "regain our grip on things" is to "build theories that gleam like jade idols, intriguing systems of assumption, four-faced, graceful" (15) – in other words, to construct elaborate conspiracy theories. Yet he resolutely tries to avoid this temptation: "There is no need to invent the grand and masterful scheme, the plot that reaches flawlessly in all directions" (58). He reminds himself that he is "writing a history, not a study of the ways in which people succumb to paranoia" (57). But faced by the mountain of suggestive evidence, even he begins to succumb to the vertigo of paranoid interpretation that he had hoped to resist:

> The Oswald shadings, the multiple images, the split perceptions – eye color, weapons caliber – these seem a foreboding of what is to come. The endless fact-rubble of the investigations. How many shots, how many gunmen, how many directions? Powerful events breed their network of inconsistencies. The simple facts elude authentication. How many wounds on the President's body? What is the size and shape of the wounds? The multiple Oswald reappears. Isn't that *him* in a photograph of a crowd of people on the front steps of the Book Depository just before the shooting begins? A startling likeness, Branch concedes. He concedes everything. He questions everything, including the basic suppositions we make about our world of light and shadow, solid objects and ordinary sounds, and our ability to measure such things, to determine weight, mass and direction, to see things as they are, recall them clearly, be able to say what happened. (15)

Fifteen years into his task, Branch – faced with this embarrassment of riches – still has not been able to start writing.

For all its self-conscious reflection on the epistemological quicksand surrounding the case, *Libra* does seem to provide a form of "redemptive truth" and "a sense that we've arrived at a resolution."[22] The novel creates a psychologically plausible account of Oswald as a politically motivated yet ultimately misguided lone gunman, but it also provides an equally believable account of a conspiracy of renegade CIA operatives and Cuban exiles. It might therefore seem that DeLillo is hedging his bets by including both a lone gunman and a conspiracy theory, but the connections and tensions between the two plot lines makes the reader rethink what have come to seem logically and politically incompatible positions. The traditional view of a conspiracy is that it is tight-knit and coldhearted:

> If we are on the outside, we assume a conspiracy is the perfect working of a scheme. Silent nameless men with unadorned hearts. A conspiracy is everything that ordinary life is not. It's the inside game, cold, sure, undistracted, forever closed off to us. We are the ones, the innocents, trying to make some rough sense of the daily jostle. Conspirators have a logic and a daring beyond our reach. All conspiracies are the same taut story of men who find coherence in some criminal act. (440)

In *Libra*, however, the conspiracy is not a "perfect working of a scheme." Branch, for example, has "learned enough about the days and months preceding November 22 to reach a determination that the conspiracy against the President was a rambling affair that succeeded in the short term due mainly to chance" (441). The initial plan was to stage a spectacular attempt on the president's life, with a faked paper trail leading back to a fictional patsy with connections to Castro's Cuba, in order to get the idea of invading the island back on the public agenda after the 1961 Bay of Pigs fiasco. However, at a point that none of the conspirators can quite identify, the plan morphs into a full-blown plot to assassinate Kennedy, not least because Oswald turns up on the conspirators' doorstep exactly matching the "cardboard cut-out" (339) they had been constructing. At the heart of the conspiracy plot, then, lie a number of uncanny coincidences and happenstance events that undermine the notion that the conspirators are ruthlessly in control of every detail. Unlike Stone's scarily efficient conspiracy in *JFK*, the plot in *Libra* consists of a loose and seemingly uncoordinated network of low-level intelligence agents. A scene showing an intelligence operation being planned inverts the usual hierarchical pyramid of corporate decision making, since the doctrine of plausible deniability demands that those at the top of the tree have little idea what is happening at ground level. The conspiracy in *Libra*, then, emerges as much from its own inscrutable logic ("secrets build their own networks" [152]) and the complexity of a decentered network as from the intentions of the conspirators.

Lone gunman and conspiracy theories are usually seen as diametrically opposed, but *Libra* shows how both interpretations equally rely on a fantasy that history is the result of the clear-sighted intentions of ruthless individuals, whether alone or in conspiracy with other plotters. The novel reveals that both Oswald and the plotters are not in control of their own actions, as both sides get caught up in circumstances, coincidences, and forces beyond their control. Both the CIA conspirators and Oswald (who wants to think of himself as a lone wolf, albeit one who is in step with the onward march of history) suffer from the paranoid belief that their lives and their thoughts are controlled by external forces, be they the CIA, the media, fate, or the logic of history itself. In compensation they turn to violence to try to restore a sense of agency. The irony, however, is that both the CIA officers and Oswald have internalized images of heroic gunslinging action from Hollywood without entirely realizing it; their innermost desires are already constructed by the mass media.

For DeLillo the wider significance of the assassination is the effect that this postmodern process of mediated experience has had on American society at large, not least because of endless, numbing repetition in the media of the violent deaths of Kennedy and Oswald. With his attempt to turn himself into a celebrity hero by murdering the television idol president, Oswald becomes "the first of those soft white dreamy young men who plan the murder of a famous individual – a president, a presidential candidate, a rock star – as a way of organizing their loneliness and misery, making a network out of it, a web of connections." Ultimately "Oswald changed history not only through his involvement in the death of the president, but in prefiguring such moments of the American absurd," that morbid catalogue of celebrity assassinations, serial killings, and high school shootings over the last five decades.[23]

For DeLillo is it only in the light of subsequent events and a "condition of estrangement and helplessness, an undependable reality" that the real meaning of the Kennedy assassination becomes clear.[24] The assassination, it might be argued, has played a similar role in the career of DeLillo. It is an event that provides the subterranean motivation for much of his work, and which only belatedly comes to the surface:

> DECURTIS: The Kennedy assassination seems perfectly in line with the concerns of your fiction. Do you feel you could have invented it if it hadn't happened?
>
> DELILLO: Maybe it invented me ... As I was working on *Libra*, it occurred to me that a lot of tendencies in my first eight novels seemed to me to be collecting around the dark center of the assassination. So it's possible I wouldn't have become the kind of writer I am if it weren't for the assassination.[25]

The same could be said for many of the other artists, filmmakers, and writers who have tackled the Kennedy assassination. With his already evident fascination with violent death, mass culture and celebrity, it comes as little surprise that in the aftermath of the assassination Andy Warhol should churn out a whole series of silkscreen portraits of Jackie Kennedy – portraits that are not so much poignant depictions of the grief of the dead president's widow as flat reworkings of the saturation coverage in *LIFE* magazine, the tragedy now reduced to a commodity. With its argument that everything went wrong with America when Kennedy was killed because he threatened to pull out of Vietnam, Stone's *JFK* finally provided the logically and emotionally missing piece in a filmmaking career that up to then had concentrated on the idea that the Vietnam War had unmanned America in general and Oliver Stone in particular. Although Norman Mailer's massive nonfiction novel *Oswald's Tale* (1995) departs from his earlier view of the assassination as a conspiracy of reactionary forces against the existentialist glamour of the Kennedy White House, the novel is also a crystallization of many of the concerns that had been circling around Mailer's writing in the intervening years, including a fascination with state secrets in general and the CIA in particular, and an obsession with the romantic possibility of individual agency in the face of massive social forces. "Oswald," Mailer writes, "was a protagonist, a prime mover, a man who made things happen – in short, a figure larger than others would credit him for being."[26] James Ellroy's two assassination-related novels also provide an intensification of ideas that had been central to his earlier works. *American Tabloid* and *The Cold Six Thousand* continue chronologically from Ellroy's LA Trilogy, a pulp-fictional exploration of the seedy side of Los Angeles from the 1940s to the 1950s.[27] For Ellroy the assassination was not the product of pure and clear motives, but the inevitable consequence of an endemic condition of crime, corruption, and compromise in which the Kennedys were as much players as victims. In a similar fashion, Stephen King finally got around to completing his Kennedy assassination novel, *11/22/63*, nearly four decades after he had started writing it in the early 1970s. Like others of his generation, King starts from the emotional pull of wanting history to have taken a different path: "Save Kennedy, save his brother. Save Martin Luther King. Stop the race riots. Stop Vietnam, maybe . . . Get rid of one wretched waif, buddy, and you could save millions of lives." With the distance of time, however, King's time-travel alternative history provides him with the narrative structure for working through this fantasy in the light of a subsequently more cynical view of Kennedy.[28]

Alongside the shadow that the Kennedy assassination has cast over the individual careers of significant postwar American artists and writers, it has also come to play a key role in theoretical discussions of postmodernism and paranoia. The cultural critic Fredric Jameson, for example, argues that the Kennedy assassination is significant not because of the political changes it may have brought about, but because as the first global television event it offered a utopian glimpse of a new type of collective experience that emerged from within mainstream mass culture rather than in opposition to it. Jameson sees the assassination as the "inaugural event" of the 1960s and postmodernism, ushering in a world in which experience is never direct and unmediated but always channeled through media representations.[29] Jameson also argues that popular conspiracy thrillers such as *The Parallax View* are revelatory not because they challenge the orthodox version of events, but because, in their self-reflexive attention to technologies of connectivity, they provide an analogy for the totality of global capitalism that, Jameson contends, is impossible to apprehend directly. "Conspiracy theory," Jameson concludes, "is the poor person's cognitive mapping in the postmodern age."[30]

In a similar vein, the media theorist Jean Baudrillard views the Kennedy assassination as marking the beginning of a crisis of representation, the full import of which would only become clear later. In his account of the way that style has replaced substance in the political arena, Baudrillard suggests that the Kennedy assassination only comes to take on the role of the original moment of trauma with the discovery of its fake copies, those "puppet attempts" on later presidents that provide an "aura of artificial menace in order to conceal that they were nothing other than mannequins of power."[31] In effect it is only following the "vertigo of interpretations" surrounding Watergate that we can belatedly posit the Kennedy assassination as the real deal. And yet that sense of vertigo is itself partly an effect of a crisis of confidence that emerged from the Kennedy assassination.

The Kennedy assassination has thus come to function as a convenient fiction, an imagined origin for many of the profound changes in the way that Americans experience reality – changes that in other contexts go by the name of postmodernism. The event thus functions as the primal scene of postmodernism, a symbolically necessary but fantasized cause of the "society of the spectacle" – a period that, as William Burroughs noted, is also marked by the belief that the "paranoid is the person in possession of all the facts."[32]

NOTES

1 D. M. Thomas, *Flying in to Love* (London: Bloomsbury, 1992), 3.
2 For a survey of different ways in which the assassination has been represented, see Peter Knight, *The Kennedy Assassination* (Edinburgh: Edinburgh University Press, 2007).
3 See, for example, Thane Burnett, "JFK Assassination: The Mother of All Conspiracy Theories Turns 50," *Toronto Sun*, November 16, 2013, http://www.torontosun.com/2013/11/15/jfks-murder-the-mother-of-all-conspiracy-theories-turns-50, accessed December 10, 2013.
4 Craig DiLouie, "Opinion Polls about Conspiracy Theories," in *Conspiracy Theories in American History: An Encyclopedia*, ed. Peter Knight (Santa Barbara, CA: ABC-CLIO, 2003), 2:561–64.
5 For a detailed account of the wrangling behind the Warren Commission, see Kathryn E. Olmsted, *Real Enemies: Conspiracy Theories and American Democracy, World War I to 9/11* (Oxford: Oxford University Press, 2009), 111–48.
6 William Manchester, "No Evidence of a Conspiracy to Kill Kennedy," *New York Times*, February 5, 1992, A22.
7 See Olmsted, *Real Enemies*, 111–48.
8 Norman Mailer, "The Great American Mystery," *Book Week Washington Post*, August 28, 1966, 1, 11–13.
9 Norman Mailer, *Oswald's Tale: An American Mystery* (London: Little, Brown, 1995), 351.
10 Don DeLillo, *Libra* (New York: Viking, 1988), 181. Subsequent references to this edition are cited in parentheses in the text.

11 For an account of these and other writers, see Tony Tanner, *City of Words: American Fiction 1950–1970* (London: Jonathan Cape, 1971).

12 Timothy Melley, *Empire of Conspiracy: The Culture of Paranoia in Postwar America* (Ithaca, NY: Cornell University Press, 2000).

13 Norman Mailer, "Footfalls in the Crypt," *Vanity Fair*, February 1992, 29.

14 Richard Condon, *Winter Kills* (London: Weidenfeld and Nicolson, 1974).

15 On Pynchon and paranoia, see Peter Knight, *Conspiracy Culture: From the Kennedy Assassination to "The X-Files"* (London: Routledge, 2001), chap. 1.

16 Thomas Pynchon, *Gravity's Rainbow* (New York: Viking), 434.

17 Maria Nadotti, "An Interview with Don DeLillo," *Salmagundi* 100 (1993): 94.

18 Frank Lentricchia discusses the reception of *Libra* in "The American Writer as Bad Citizen," in *Introducing Don DeLillo*, ed. Frank Lentricchia (Durham, NC: Duke University Press, 1991), 1–6.

19 Don DeLillo, "Oswald: Myth, Mystery, and Meaning," PBS *Frontline* forum (with Edward J. Epstein and Gerald Posner), 2003, http://www.pbs.org/wgbh/pages/frontline/shows/oswald/forum, accessed December 21, 2014.

20 DeLillo, "Oswald"; Anthony DeCurtis, "'An Outsider in This Society': An Interview with Don DeLillo," in Lentricchia, *Introducing Don DeLillo*, 48.

21 DeLillo, "Oswald."

22 DeCurtis, "An Outsider," 56.

23 DeLillo, "Oswald."

24 Ibid.

25 DeCurtis, "An Outsider," 47–48.

26 Norman Mailer, *Oswald's Tale: An American Mystery* (London: Little, Brown, 1995), 605.

27 James Ellroy, *American Tabloid* (New York: Vintage, 1995), and *The Cold Six Thousand* (New York: Vintage, 2001).

28 Stephen King, *11/22/63* (New York: Scribner, 2011), 59.

29 Fredric Jameson, *Postmodernism; or, The Cultural Logic of Late Capitalism* (London: Verso, 1991), 354–55.

30 Fredric Jameson, "Cognitive Mapping," in *Marxism and the Interpretation of Culture*, ed. Cary Nelson and Lawrence Grossberg (Basingstoke: Macmillan, 1988), 356.

31 Jean Baudrillard, *Selected Writings*, ed. Mark Poster (Cambridge: Polity Press, 1988), 177.

32 Quoted in Eric Mottram, *William Burroughs: The Algebra of Need* (London: Calder and Boyars, 1977), 159.

12

J. D. CONNOR

An Eternal Flame: The Kennedy Assassination, National Grief, and National Nostalgia

Flying back to Washington on Friday afternoon, Jacqueline Kennedy had already begun to plan her dead husband's memorial service. In William Manchester's account, "She herself was a new Jackie, transformed by her vow that the full impact of the loss should be indelibly etched upon the national conscience."[1] She stayed with the coffin, and told Assistant Press Secretary Mac Kilduff to "go and tell them that I came back here and sat with Jack." He did. And as others on the plane began to importune her to change out of the lurid, blood-splattered pink suit, she refused them. "'No,'" she whispered fiercely. 'Let them see what they've done'" (348).

This tale is often told, in part because Jackie so successfully emerges as a figure of national resolution and in part because it carries the Kennedy administration's relentless orchestration of intimate display into a new era. But Manchester's account, as flattering as it aims to be, captures more than Jackie's new gravitas; like a seismograph, he registers the first tremors of a new sense of time, one that, however much it shares with a more general temporality of mourning and memorial, is particular to the Kennedy era and essential to the change in Jackie's character. And while this new temporality was not an exact version of the public's new experience, as we'll see, it traversed the spaces of memory in ways that seemed to chart a path forward from the assassination.

Still in Dallas, when the Johnsons broach the subject of the swearing in, Jackie continues to operate according to the usual protocols. "Yes. What's going to happen?" (317). What was going to happen was that Judge Sarah Hughes would arrive in an hour to administer the oath and Jackie would join the group. But in that hour Jackie's thoughts would be "elsewhere," according to Manchester. "She was thinking about time" (323). This "time" is a time of extended experience and unexpected interruptions: "It was such a long time," she thinks, only to be caught by surprise when Hughes arrives early. "It was unbelievable: *they* had been waiting for *her*" (323). After the oath, Jackie is gripped by a "refrain" "running through her mind: *I'm not going to be in here, I'm going back there"* (327). "Here" is with the "Johnson people"; "there" is by the coffin with the Kennedy loyalists. Sitting "back there" next to Ken O'Donnell, she cries, "Oh, it's happened ... Oh, Kenny ... what's going to happen ... ?" (327; last ellipsis original). This is at least the second time she has said that on the plane, and although the words are the same, the meaning has transformed. In the subsequent hours, these two modes of happening – one bureaucratic and ritual, subject to protocols, the other experiential and imbricated, where the past keeps on happening in such a way that the future seems unplannable – will be woven together. And atop them both there will be a steady reflection on the events and experiences as they occur. The appearance of a figure who could claim, with authority, that "she was thinking about time" would have been paradigmatic of the Kennedy era, when experiences and reflection on the nature of those experiences were drawn ever more tightly together in the hope that they might converge. Now that figure would be embedded in a new context . . .

The funerary apparatus was, as was typical for the Kennedy era, an assemblage of bureaucracy and family. Planning would ordinarily have fallen to the Military District of Washington (MDW), which comprised the necessary ceremonial units and could bring to bear the wide range of other resources the events required, from cartographers to construction troops to honor guards. Yet even on the flight back from Dallas, Jackie and Robert Kennedy had begun to coordinate with MDW officers. Kennedy cousin Sargent Shriver would serve as liaison from the outgoing administration. Jackie was not only central to the planning but was assiduously promoted as such. "General Wehle afterward declared that 'she held all the strings, and we marveled at her clear thinking and sense of command'" (482).

This proved too much even for Manchester, who details the limits of Jackie's ambit and the vast contributions made by others. Nonetheless, nearly all of the major decisions about the funeral were made by or routed through Jackie. She pushed for the echoes of Lincoln's funeral; she chose the old-fashioned mantilla; she insisted on walking the route to Saint Matthew's. Most important, she envisioned the eternal flame. The model was the French tomb of the unknowns, which she and Jack had visited in 1961. But where the original yoked national memory to an indeterminate group, this version would tie that memory to an individual. Such perpetual devotion seemed (to some) to be misplaced, but it was high Kennedy era in its insistence on the middle-aged president's youth.

Jackie's commitment to the eternal flame configured the commemoration of JFK as a set of oppositions. The first lay in the clash between the implicit temporal boundedness of the "four days in November" and the temporal

unboundedness implied by the flame itself. The second, between planning and spontaneity, disrupted the inveterate image management of the
Kennedy administration. Jackie's resolution – "Let them see what they've
done" – found its own opposition in the eruptions of spontaneity beginning
with the image of her on the back of the Lincoln and continuing through
the botched arrival at Andrews AFB. Two paired oppositions, a matrix of
possibilities, confronted the world and became the paradigm for Kennedy's
memory. At the still point where the oppositions cross we find the icon,
the spontaneous revelation of durable character, fixed as an image, lasting
through time.

After the assassination *Life* magazine famously ripped out its planned
November 29 cover story on Navy quarterback Roger Staubach. The magazine substituted thirty-five pages of Kennedy coverage, including four
pages of stills from the Zapruder film, in time for its deadline of Sunday,
November 24. The next week's issue included extensive coverage of the
memorial service along with Theodore H. White's "Epilogue" in which
Jackie (and White) christened the era Camelot. Less famously, *Life* rushed
a special "Memorial" issue into print that was a hybrid of the two – "All of
Life's Pictures and Text on the Most Shocking Event of Our Time." It featured the same cover image as the Nov. 29 issue; the same White epilogue
as Dec. 6. Where the regular issues were plump with Christmastime ads and
long general interest features – on the photography of Lartigue, on "The
Last Word in Operating Rooms" – the memorial issue had none. Its one
innovation was a four-page spread of Zapruder images in full color. The
broad kelly-green sward backstops Jackie's pink suit. The whole is doubly
bordered in black: the page itself is set on a black ground, and within the
images the big blue-black convertible drifts to the bottom of the frame,
underlining the saturated colors above it. The spread was a new shock for
readers who had only seen the day's events in black and white. The color
template of the assassination would be complete when the blood-spattered
pink suit was replaced by Jackie's mourning black and the sky-blue coats
of Caroline and John-John. That blue was essential because it bracketed
the event: in the Arthur Rickerby photo of Jack and Jackie at Love Field,
the sky nearly blends into the blue accents on Air Force One. In the can-
vass of emotions after the assassination, bystanders noted that when the
morning overcast rose "like an awning" it left behind "a translucent sky," a
"faultless blue."[2] That blue returns, condensed, in Fred Maro's photo of the
family waiting at the top of the White House stairs, where the color of the
children's matching coats is picked up by the marine sergeant's braid in the
foreground. Maro's photo ran on the back cover of the memorial edition
and the front of the December 6 issue.

If *Life*'s images provided the art direction for the weekend's memory, its text offered two other ways of thinking about the end of Kennedy's administration. The lead editorial by managing editor George P. Hunt, "The President's Empty Chair," emphasized Kennedy's "guts," portraying Jack toughing out his chronic back pain, strategizing his way through political conflicts, and, as always, "fascinated by the press," playing it "quite frankly to enhance himself and his Administration." The rocking chair had been a major part of the president's image, and *Life* had both encouraged and covered the country's fascination with it.[3] Rocking back and forth, taking in the debate among his advisers, Kennedy affected a canny, almost contemplative style. His self-conscious stylization would become the paradigm for *Esquire*'s "New Sentimentality," the polar opposite of Lyndon Johnson's physicality and directness.[4]

The alternative to the empty chair – to the image of the president as the good-naturedly canny competitor – was the mythmaking of Camelot. And it was Jackie who insisted to *Life*'s Theodore H. White that history-minded Jack regularly listened to the musical's soundtrack before he went to bed. "The lines he loved to hear were: *Don't let it be forgot, that once there was a spot, for one brief shining moment that was known as Camelot.*" She drove the point home, repeating the lines. White repeated them, as well, giving rise to the period's pop mythos. For all the drama that surrounded *Life*'s acquisition of the Zapruder film the weekend before, there was nearly as much wheedling surrounding White's piece for the magazine's next issue. As Joyce Hoffman has chronicled, on that rainy Saturday night, with the presses held, White served as Jackie's stenographer. David Maness, White's editor, felt the theme was too on the nose, but it stayed. Later, White felt that he had been used as a mouthpiece for the administration's final propaganda campaign; historian Arthur M. Schlesinger Jr., Secretary of State Dean Rusk, and other key members of the administration objected, as well.[5] For the men committed to the idea of "The President's Empty Chair," to Kennedy as the New Frontiersman-in-chief and the ultimate strategist, the doomed wistfulness of Broadway's King Arthur was utterly out of character.

No attempt to secure the legacy of the administration could avoid becoming mired in the metapolitics of image management. *Life*'s memorial edition could not maintain its commemorative integrity against the pull of the news, where "news" meant either the addition of a new level of commentary or a new sensory assault. It was the first instance of what would become an essential feature of Kennedy commemoration: the irresistible conjunction of memorial and news, of attention to "his enduring words" and the insistent return to "the most shocking event." For the next fifty years, every anniversary of his death, every attempt to commemorate his life, would be decisively inflected by the emergence of potentially new information.

Two documentary films produced in the wake of the assassination embody and advance the complexities of the Kennedy memorial temporality: *Four Days in November* (1964) and *Faces of November* (1964). Both reasserted cinema's primacy in the wake of television's newfound ascendancy. The Oscar-nominated *Four Days*, produced by David L. Wolper and directed by Mel Stuart, combines documentary footage with docudrama reenactments to carry viewers back through the events of the year before. Those four days were known as television's Black Weekend, when 96 percent of American households tuned in, and on average viewers watched thirty-two hours over the four days.[6] The film condensed the weekend and folded in the missing context. Both its form and narration echo the *Life* issues in many ways, concluding with a dissolve from the eternal flame to a montage of JFK and his family frolicking on Cape Cod, recalling America to a time "when its own youth had just begun and everything was possible." But *Four Days*'s version of "flaming youth" is forced to contend with two other temporalities. The first is cyclical. Instead of beginning with the Texas trip, the film opens with the funerary fifty-gun salute and eventually circles back around to it. The second is bureaucratic. The film ends with a dolly across the Oval Office, pushing in close on the nameplate affixed to the back of "the president's empty chair" (in this case not the famous rocker but an overstuffed leather wingback desk chair). The rhythms of political succession join the cycle of funerary ritual and the stilled promise of a life cut short. Formally dispersed, *Four Days* is not simply a comprehensive collection of documentary footage of the weekend's events but an anthology of attempts to give those events form. In its awkward multiple endings, it captures the four quadrants of the matrix, each of them closer to the gravitational center, the iconic JFK. Yet even here, *Four Days* follows *Life*'s lead, putting Jackie at the center of events: "Amid tolling bell and bagpipes' dirge, black-veiled like some ritual figure of classic myth, Jacqueline Kennedy follows her husband's coffin on foot, leading the greatest assemblage of world statesmen to pay homage in half a century." If the axes of the matrix cross at the point of maximum tension, then the substitution of one icon for another – of Jackie for Jack – allows the intense demand for social mourning to work itself out across time, in the unfolding of a new focal image.

Robert Drew Associates' *Faces of November* is the more rigorous complement to *Four Days*. Drew Associates had been the essential documentarians of the Kennedy era, all but inventing Direct Cinema along the way. Drew, D. A. Pennebaker, Ricky Leacock, and others captured the era's origins in *Primary* (1960), came close to serving as court filmmakers on *Adventures on the New Frontier* (1961), and gained access so intimate it was unclear whether the administration's political aims or Drew's aesthetic ideals were better served by *Crisis: Behind a Presidential Decision* (1963).

Kennedy's death, however, seemed to cut Drew Associates loose from its intellectual partnership with the administration. *Faces* opens with the same gunnery salute as *Four Days*, and it will cycle back to it. But cyclical endurance is the film's only temporality. The soundscape is resolutely nondiscursive: there is neither voice-over nor discernable dialogue; there is rain, the sound of flags snapping and halyards clanking against the flagpoles at the Washington Monument, and the clop of hooves. Unconcerned with capturing events, policy, or personality, the two-reel film concentrates on faces in a very particular way. Drew and his cameramen hold on individuals long enough to allow them to acquire an authority over their own reactions, and that authority is preserved in the editing. A quicker montage would turn these onlookers into reactors and would restore the events of the funeral to the center. By slowing the pace, the continuing series of faces shows us how particular emotions rise up, achieve visibility, and require response. The woman who opens the series *has* to hide her head behind the spectators in the row in front of her when the horses pass. The African American marine *has* to turn his eyes away from his destination. These are reactions not to an event, but to a feeling, recognitions of the yawning asymmetry of a relationship (to Kennedy, to power, to politics, to desire) now at an end (Figure 12.1).

The two films divide the funereal temporality between them, and each is ghosted by the other. *Four Days* relentlessly stipulates content and context; what does not have an explanation can be blamed on irony – intended or otherwise. In the wake of the shooting, we are told, "Streets go silent; without plan, businesses close, even a honky-tonk in Dallas." The lack of planning, here, is self-consciously ironically part of Ruby's eventual plan to kill Oswald; hushed streets are, self-consciously ironically, narrated by the film. What is true for sound is also true for time. Outside the White House, we hear, "The children's swings are still. For a moment, but a moment only, time pauses in this quiet room of presidents." Time, of course, does not pause in *Four Days*, not even to register the pause of the swings or the quiet in the Oval Office.

Faces, in contrast, can find no place for planning since its world is beyond discourse. Jackie appears but is not in charge. Forms and sounds are captured with precision, but there are no maps or agendas to guide us through. Clearly Drew Associates felt that the ticktock of the proceedings could be delegated to more reportorial media institutions. In broader terms, *Faces* liberates Kennedy-era reflection from eventfulness, casting it adrift toward

Figure 12.1 Private moments in public.
Faces of November (1964), Robert Drew Associates. Fair use (DVD stills).

the eternal. As strategy, politics, and the man (or woman) in the arena fade, Direct Cinema verges on mere impressionism. No longer does being in the world entail the generation of a self-extracting theory of being in the world. *Four Days* is consumed by eventfulness, even when that requires an almost neurotic demand that every occurrence be slotted into a schedule. Put another way, *Four Days* tries to dwell in Jackie's initial temporality: "What is going to happen?" where that means "What is supposed to happen *next*?" while *Faces* exists in Jackie's second temporality, where "what is going to happen" is more emotional and more intimate. What *Faces* fails to recognize is that it was Jackie, "thinking about time," who could maintain the equilibrium between these senses of time during that crucial weekend, refusing to allow the desperate question to overwhelm the bureaucratic one.

Andy Warhol's *Jackies* of 1964 combine the eventfulness of *Four Days* with the iconic insistence of *Faces*. Warhol's fascination with the assassination deserves longer treatment and has received it from others.[7] What I want to emphasize is that the almost frictionless way he was able to accommodate the events of the Black Weekend confirms his preternatural sense of timing during the 1960s. By 1964, Warhol had already been working through the limits of planning and spontaneity, the eternal and the occasional for several years. Procedurally, the photo-silkscreen process positioned his work within an economy that balanced impersonality and mass repetition against mediation and delay (first choosing images, then sending them out for screen preparation, then producing at intervals of his own choosing). What is more, his sense of the interplay of intention and time gave him a unique ability to manipulate the icons that animated the matrix of possibilities. With the assassination, Warhol's extensive series of celebrity portraits, on the one hand, and his depictions of more ordinary disasters, on the other, could now be joined.

Art historian David M. Lubin contends that among artists responding to the assassination, Warhol "most powerfully conveyed the piercing trauma of that November weekend." But Lubin has a harder time locating the source of the success of the *Jackies*. Was it due to Warhol's indifference, his empathy, his puckishness, his fascination with death, or his obsession with consumer culture? Lubin, like Art Simon, marshals quotations from Warhol's *POPism* and other biographies that provide widely varying accounts of the artist's reaction to the news of the assassination. Giving up on intent, Lubin finally suggests that the works' provocation stems from their combination of "icy classicism" and Warhol's "[keeping] faith with the media cult of celebrity" JFK "had so assiduously nurtured."[8] But it is, perhaps, a mistake to yoke the pictures too tightly to the events at their source. Warhol may not have "missed a stroke" when he heard, or he may have turned to his assistant Gerard Malanga and said "Let's go to work," or he may have spent part of the weekend crying on the couch with poet John Giorno. Regardless, over the succeeding months, he committed himself to making these particular pictures. Warhol's reaction might indeed be indicative of his *feelings*, but the *events* that need explanation are his decisions to make paintings of the Black Weekend, to make them of Jackie only, and to make them according to (but in important ways differently from) the protocols he had been developing that summer. We should attend to the paintings within the stream of Warhol's work before we follow the mythmaking surrounding it.

The *Jackies* continued the modularity of Warhol's portrait of Ethel Scull (*Ethel Scull 35 Times* [1963]), but relied on published source images drawn from *Life* and *Look*. A limited series of tondi followed the model of earlier *Marilyn* portraits: single images, black on gold. And like the *Marilyns*, the smiling picture of Jackie at Love Field neatly insisted on the gap between the captured moment (noon on the 22nd) and the impending tragedy. But when Warhol combined the frontal views of Jackie's ironic smiles with the shocked profiles from Johnson's swearing in, the deadened three-quarter views on the White House steps, and the resolute, nearly frontal images with and without the veil, he moved beyond portraiture into something closer to history painting. *The Week That Was . . . I* (CR 945) and *II* (CR 946) each comprise sixteen images in a four-by-four array; each of the source images is used twice, each flipped once.⁹ Unlike *Ethel Scull*, here each image is contiguous with its mirror. *The Week That Was . . . I* retains the gold of the tondi on thirteen of the sixteen canvases; two are white, one phthalo blue (Figure 12.2). The white canvases are the correctly oriented versions of the swearing-in profile and the most immediate registrations of shock. The blue canvas is the correctly oriented version of the picture of Jackie with JFK in the convertible on Main Street, and the most immediately ironic. *The Week That Was . . . II* is all blues, but the hue varies in ways that seem both decorative and solicitous of attention. In both versions, the blue leaps out, just as it does in the photos of the children's coats. In *I*, blue constitutes the coloristic shock to the celebrity image; in *II*, it amounts to the suffusion of the whole by reminiscence. Warhol's composite *Jackies* (including versions beyond these two) suggest not a multiplied portrait but a process; the irony of an individual tondo is now excavated, spread across the surface of multiple images. The temporal unfolding is so effective that even in those versions of "multiplied" Jackie where the image does not change (a triptych or a frieze version), the picture nevertheless feels ripped from a temporal flow rather than boiled down to irony or pathos.

As the catalogue raisonné notes, it was unusual for Warhol to give his paintings titles, but these two have been known as *The Week That Was . . .* since 1964. That title, whether bestowed by Warhol or someone at the Leo Castelli gallery, alludes to the *That Was the Week That Was*, the BBC faux-news program that anchored the early 1960s "satire boom" in the UK and then spawned an American version in the fall of 1963. Yet as Lubin notes, the Warhol paintings are not "in any discernible way satirical."¹⁰ So why the title? The week of the assassination, the BBC version famously suspended its usual humor in favor of an extended encomium to JFK. A recording of that episode was then flown to the United States and aired on NBC the evening of November 24.¹¹ *The Week That Was*, in reference to the Kennedy assassination, then, indicates not satire, but the suspension of satire. What is more, the episode featured such ultra-schmaltzy moments as Dame Sibyl Thorndike reciting Caryl Brahms's poem "To Jackie," ("Yesterday the sun was shot out of your sky, Jackie,") and Millicent Martin singing "In the Summer of His Years." Within the first week, then, critiques of commercialization and "good taste" had begun to dog the aftermath of the assassination. Calling the paintings *The Week That Was . . .* transforms the question of intent into a question of media response. In the *Jackies* Warhol is not taking the measure of his immediate reactions so much as measuring up to

Figure 12.2 The suspension of satire in Andy Warhol's *Jackie ... The Week That Was. . . I.*
Acrylic, spray paint, and silkscreen ink on linen, 80 x 64 inches.
© 2014 The Andy Warhol Foundation for the Visual Arts,
Inc./Artists Rights Society (ARS), New York.

her responses, and the image of her responses filtered through the screen of self-interrogation and self-congratulation launched by media industries.

Warhol's first public showings of the *Jackie*s occurred in November 1964, at the one-year anniversary of the assassination. The Warren Commission report had been released in September in the hope of forestalling the assassination as a central subject of the election. But volume after volume of hearings and exhibits in fact meant that the entire fall would be taken up with analysis. Indeed, for the first time in the wake of the assassination, there would be more publicly accessible information than analysis. The Black Weekend had inaugurated an era of televisual surplus – hour after hour rehearing the same bits of information, pleading for more, admitting that there was so much no one knew. But with the Warren Report, the information economy returned to normal. The report's overwhelming evidentiary backup all but demanded popular interpretive effort.

With the Warren Report, the interplay of temporality and intention also began to congeal into a simpler oscillation. With each anniversary – a year, then ten, twenty, twenty-five, forty, and fifty – a wave of reconsiderations arrived, reassessments pegged to the market for memory. But those waves always carried the double burden of analysis and reiteration. New documents, new versions of the Zapruder film, new interviews with aging players who no longer had anything to hide, new reports on the strange deaths of witnesses – they could all be slotted into television specials and magazine articles that would once again work through the chronology of the assassination. The scale of attention dilates and contracts, spreading backward to consider events of the summer of 1963 or forward through the investigation of the Warren Commission, but ultimately bearing down on the one-eighteenth of a second between Zapruder frames 312 and 313.

For historian Beverly Gage, the accumulation of unsavory material on Kennedy has had no effect on the commemorative mind. "Rather than revise their views of Kennedy or his presidency, Americans seem to have channeled the barrage of new information into an ever-growing willingness to believe in some sort of conspiracy *against* him."[12] Holding aside the inaccuracy of an "ever-growing willingness" – belief in conspiracy has been flat or declining since 1975, with Gallup recently noting that the percentage of Americans who "believe others besides . . . Oswald were involved" is "the lowest found in nearly fifty years"[13] – this seems almost precisely wrong. The conspiracies serve as repositories of political memory, social agents of moral blowback. For almost every particular complaint about Kennedy, there is a conspiracy that demonstrates how that failing led to his downfall. Promiscuity? Judith Exner → Giancana → Mafia hit. A bought or stolen election? Joseph P. Kennedy to the Mafia. Reliance on the secrecy state? Oswald striking out in defense of a beleaguered Castro. Callowness? Revenge of the betrayed anti-Castro forces. The conspiracies against Kennedy mirror the hidden (and sometimes imagined) operations of his administration.

While the cascade of viewpoints in the first year set the pattern for the economy of information that would come to define assassination studies, another pattern of commemoration was also taking shape. Across America, institutions were being renamed in honor of the dead president, rechristenings bound to the pattern of overreaching personalized bureaucracy that had first appeared at Arlington National Cemetery. In New York City, Idlewild was renamed John F. Kennedy Airport by the end of 1963, and it has remained happily so ever since.[14] Schools and streets, an aircraft carrier, and a stadium followed.[15] Less successfully, Kennedy replaced Benjamin Franklin on the half-dollar coin in 1964, and although his profile continues to be used in collectors' proof sets, the coin has not been minted in mass circulation quantities since 1976; the last year that any general circulation Kennedy coins were struck was 2001.[16] And while President Johnson renamed Cape Canaveral Cape Kennedy in what seemed to be an especially fitting tribute to the alliance between Kennedy and the Space Coast, the name only lasted a decade before being returned.[17]

The John F. Kennedy Center for the Performing Arts was a more successful arrogation. Initially projected under President Franklin Roosevelt as the National Cultural Center, authorizing legislation for the building was not passed until 1958. The design by Edward Durell Stone was a "box with a porch," typical of Kennedy era neoclassicism.[18] At the time of the assassination, the fund-raising for the project remained incomplete. The project struggled along, eventually opening in 1971. By then, the style had passed, Vietnam was at its height, and Anthony Lewis saw in the building a classic instance of bureaucratic self-aggrandizement, a "giant catastrophe" that had "ruined the river front."[19] The Kennedy Center Honors, begun in 1978, would become the center's flagship event, a celebration of American culture, matching awards with commemorative performances. By this point, historical research had made Kennedy's legacy far more complex and conspiracy theorizing was at its high-water mark, having been endorsed by the House Subcommittee on Assassinations. In the era of malaise, the honors amounted to exactly the wan "living legacy" that no one could really gainsay.

The most ambivalent of the institutional Kennedy commemorations, however, is surely Philip Johnson's cenotaph for the fallen president in Dallas. The great open box with its unadorned central slab quickly became something of a white elephant, largely unvisited, certainly unloved. The president's death did little to temper Dallas's conservative elites, who were far more interested in promoting the city than in commemorating the assassination. Stanley Marcus, of the Neiman Marcus department store, had been to Johnson's Glass House and asked him to design the memorial.[20] Johnson waived his fee, the county donated a block they wanted cleared anyway, and the Marcus-led commission raised the necessary funds. Johnson had initially suggested that passages of Kennedy speeches be carved into the memorial's walls, but he was, apparently, thwarted by members of the commission who opposed the president's politics. The constraint seems to have freed the architect, who made the cenotaph a monument to absence. He later explained, "Kennedy was such a remarkable man I didn't want to have a statue or hackneyed 'narrative,' but sought rather for something very humble and spartan."[21]

Spartan to be sure. Johnson authority Frank Welch ticks off the dimensions of the "50' x 50' x 30' roofless volume": its seventy-two "square, chamfered vertical concrete members are bound together with concealed steel cables forming rigid enclosing planes. The cable ends are capped with round concrete bosses" (Figure 12.3). The open box was something of a departure for the architect, who was working through his departure from Mies and the International Style by exploring variations on arches and colonnades. The loggia for the Amon Carter Museum, for example, featured four tapered columns with arches that seemed to continue from the arrises of the columns. Johnson continued building arches in commissions large (the New York State Theater at Lincoln Center, 1964) and small (Pavilion at Pond, New Canaan, Connecticut, 1962), reaching baroque overkill in the house for Mr. and Mrs. Henry C. Beck Jr. (Dallas, 1964). But for Kennedy, he opted not to build any sort of arch. Instead, as architecture critic David Dillon has noted, the monument draws on Mies van der Rohe's (unrealized) plans for a memorial to the Great War Dead in Germany. Just as the eternal flame in Washington made a monument to French unknowns a memorial to the most famous person in the world, so Johnson replaced Mies' monument to DIE TOTEN with one inscribed to JOHN FITZGERALD KENNEDY. Yet the Miesian severity of the box is illusory. Only eight of the columns reach the ground, making the whole thing seem to float, especially at night when lights shine down from the raised members. The hovering solidity makes the box, however unadorned, a signal instance of the creeping theatricality of Johnson's post–International Style work. Indeed, the memorial is an even purer example of minimalist theatricality than Tony Smith's *Die* (1962/1968). Michael Fried saw in Smith's six-foot cube "a kind of latent or hidden naturalism, even anthropomorphism."[22] Smith defended his choice of scale. Asked why he had not made *Die* larger, "so that it would loom over the spectator," Smith responded, "I wasn't making a monument." Johnson is; hence the looming. Yet the five-by-five central slab in Johnson's memorial produces the anthropomorphic effect. It seems less like an invocation of solidity and more like a vacated pedestal. Read this way, Johnson's memorial casts out narrative only to have it return as the narrative of absence.

Figure 12.3 Philip Johnson's Kennedy Memorial Plaza from Dallas County
Courthouse Roof. Bryan Cabin is in the distance.
© 1999 Paul Hester, from a project by Frank D. Welch, published as
Philip Johnson & Texas, University of Texas Press.

Yet despite Johnson's avowed hostility to narrative, the memorial takes
its place in context. His abandonment of columns stems in part, one sus-
pects, from the proliferation of memorial colonnades on Dealey Plaza. The
plaza entrance was flanked by matching peristyles and reflecting pools along
Houston Street, and matching pergolas along Elm and Commerce. Each of
the pergolas was named for a city founder; Abraham Zapruder was standing
on the concrete abutment to the northern pergola – the John Neely Bryan
pergola – when he filmed the motorcade. The tiny John Neely Bryan Cabin
stood even closer to the memorial. The cabin was, legend had it, built by
Dallas's founder on the banks of the Trinity River. Since its construction, it
had been moved, reassembled, moved again, likely destroyed, likely rebuilt,
and had, after the Texas Centennial, come to rest on the grounds of the Old
Red Courthouse near the corner of Houston and Commerce.[23] A downtown
landmark for generations of schoolchildren, it would stay on the courthouse
lawn until the late 1960s when it would be moved yet again to make way for
a parking garage entrance, at which point it would be located on the block
just north of the Kennedy memorial. Here, the cabin formed a micro version

of the Parisian *Axe historique* and was visible, in all its diminutive perpendicularity, through the slits in the Kennedy memorial until the Founders Plaza renovation of the early 2000s.[24] In this light, the Kennedy memorial is the anti–Bryan Cabin. Johnson replaces the Lincoln logs with Kennedy concrete, forgoes shingles for open sky, turns the horizontal bands vertically, and retains the "butt end" effect of cabin logs in the memorial's round bosses. Johnson had been cobbling together a new justification for historicism for some time, announcing in 1961, "We find ourselves now all wrapped up in reminiscence. We cannot today *not* know history."[25] Now, in the Kennedy memorial, he had found a way to stay true to his – our – emerging historicism by making the architecture – the architecture he was in the process of making – a comment on the contextualization of architectural memory.

Johnson called his memorial "a tacit interpretation of the memorial per se," but that interpretation was increasingly explicit.[26] By the time he was designing the Kennedy monument, he was prepared to declare that the main point of architecture was not space or mass, but "the organization of procession. Architecture exists only in *time*."[27] For both Johnson and Warhol, the assassination pushed art toward the opportunistic historicism that would characterize postmodernism in general. Johnson's open box traced the absence of the iconic JFK; Warhol's *Jackies* installed her in Jack's stead. Other, later institutions would find their places in this new economy of memory. The Kennedy Library in Boston, which opened in 1979, burnished the president's legacy and avoided the assassination while becoming a major research center. The Sixth Floor Museum in the Texas School Book Depository at Dealey Plaza, which finally opened in 1989, compensated for the library's diffidence by opening itself up to the exploration of various and sundry assassination scenarios (Figure 12.4).[28] As a result, and in contrast to Johnson's all but empty memorial, the Sixth Floor Museum became filled with both visitors and materials. Johnson's monument was the last attempt to enshrine the experience of the assassination, to make it endure by erasing any obvious specificity. As the organizer of the procession, Johnson more or less knew what was "going to happen" when visitors arrived – how they would approach, what they would see. In other words, his answer to Jackie's first question was comparatively simple. As for what would happen next, what visitors would experience once they'd entered the box, he had no idea. "It would be left to the viewers to find their own meaning."[29] In answer to Jackie's second question, then, Johnson all but threw up his hands. As he saw it, historicism opened up the past for interpretation, a chance for people to find their own meanings. The result, for him, was a "new feeling of freedom." That gesture was one origin of postmodernism and has long been understood as a triumph. But the gesture amounted to an abandonment

DEALEY PLAZA -- DALLAS, TEXAS

1. TEXAS SCHOOL BOOK DEPOSITORY
2. DAL-TEX BUILDING
3. DALLAS COUNTY RECORDS BUILDING
4. DALLAS COUNTY CRIMINAL COURTS BUILDING
5. OLD COURT HOUSE
6. NEELEY BRYAN HOUSE
7. DALLAS COUNTY GOVERNMENT CENTER (UNDER CONSTRUCTION)
8. UNITED STATES POST OFFICE BUILDING
9. PERGOLAS
10. PERISTYLES AND REFLECTING POOLS
11. RAILROAD OVERPASS (TRIPLE UNDERPASS)

COMMISSION EXHIBIT No. 876

33

Figure 12.4 A guide for the perplexed: Dealey Plaza in the Warren Commission Report. *Report of the President's Commission on the Assassination of President John F. Kennedy* (Washington, DC: U.S. Government Printing Office, 1964), 33.

of the Kennedy era's willed unification of national mission and personal style through the immediate application of reflection. As she flew back from Dallas, organizing that weekend's processions and thinking about time, Jackie had perpetuated all three aspects. Johnson – postmodernism – retained only the last.

193

NOTES

1 William Manchester, *The Death of a President, November 20–November 25, 1963* (New York: Harper and Row, 1967), 347. Further citations in the text.

2 Manchester, *The Death of a President*, 125, 160; the remark about the awning comes from Pamela Turnure.

3 "Presidential Chair Rocks the Country," *Life*, April 7, 1961, 20. http://books.google.com/books?id=-FEEAAAAMBAJ, accessed September 26, 2013.

4 David Newman and Robert Benton, "The New Sentimentality," *Esquire* (July 1964). For an account of the article's role in 1960s culture more broadly, see J. Hoberman, *The Dream Life* (New York: New Press, 2005).

5 Joyce Hoffman, *Theodore H. White and Journalism as Illusion* (Columbia: University of Missouri Press, 1995), 2–3.

6 For an account of audience responses to the broadcasts of the weekend, see Aniko Bodroghkozy, "Black Weekend: A Reception History of Network Television News and the Assassination of John F. Kennedy," *Television and New Media* 20, no. 10 (2012): 1–19. Bodroghkozy's research provides an important qualification to Philip Rosen's justly famous essay "Document and Documentary: On the Persistence of Historical Concepts," in his *Change Mummified: Cinema, Historicity, Theory* (Minneapolis: University of Minnesota Press, 2001), 225–63.

7 Important reflections on the *Jackies* include Art Simon, *Dangerous Knowledge: The JFK Assassination in Art and Film* (2006; repr., Philadelphia: Temple University Press 2013), 101–18; David M. Lubin, *Shooting Kennedy: JFK and the Culture of Images* (Berkeley: University of California Press, 2003), 256–61; Thomas Crow, "Saturday Disasters: Trace and Reference in Early Warhol," in his *Modern Art in the Common Culture* (New Haven, CT: Yale University Press, 1996), 49–65.

8 Lubin, *Shooting Kennedy*, 261.

9 Georg Frei and Neil Printz, eds., Sally King Nero, exec. ed., *The Andy Warhol Catalogue Raisonné, vol. 2A, Paintings and Sculptures 1964–1969* (New York: Phaidon, 2004).

10 Lubin, *Shooting Kennedy*, 260.

11 "A British Program Honoring Kennedy Shown Over NBC," *New York Times*, November 25, 1963.

12 Beverly Gage, "Who Didn't Kill JFK?" *The Nation*, December 17, 2013, http://www.thenation.com/article/177632/who-didnt-kill-jfk, accessed December 4, 2014.

13 See http://www.gallup.com/poll/165893/majority-believe-jfk-killed-conspiracy.aspx, accessed December 4, 2014.

14 Richard I. Ulman, "The 'New' Airport," *New York Times*, December 29, 1963.

15 Philip Benjamin, "Drives Under Way for Kennedy Memorials," *New York Times*, November 28, 1963, 22.

16 See http://coins.about.com/library/US-Coin-Specifications/US0050-Half-Dollars/bl-US0050I-1964-Date-Kennedy-Half-Dollar-Coin-Specs.htm, accessed December 4, 2014.

17 "Floridians Urge Cape Kennedy Be Renamed Cape Canaveral," *New York Times*, November 25, 1969, 33; "Name 'Cape Canaveral' Is Restored by Board," *New York Times*, October 10, 1973.

18 Philip Johnson quoted in Frank D. Welch, *Philip Johnson & Texas* (Austin: University of Texas Press, 2000), 93.

19 Anthony Lewis, "Notes from Overground," *New York Times*, April 12, 1971, 37.

20 My account here follows that of Welch, *Philip Johnson & Texas*, 122–31.

21 Ibid., 125, citing Johnson conversation in New York City, August 1997.

22 Michael Fried, *Art and Objecthood* (Chicago: University of Chicago Press, 1998), 157. The quote from Smith is on 156.

23 The career of Bryan Cabin is complex, and the first important doubts about its authenticity were only beginning to surface in the 1960s (as in the letter from Carl Beeman, "Interesting History of Log Cabin," *Dallas Morning News*, March 28, 1966, 2). For a roundup of its peregrinations, see Sam Acheson, "Bryan Cabin Makes Sixth Move," *Dallas Morning News*, March 11, 1968, 2.

24 See Welch, *Philip Johnson & Texas*, 126.

25 Philip Johnson, "The International Style – Death or Metamorphosis," in *Writings* (New York: Oxford University Press, 1979), 118–22, 122.

26 Welch, *Philip Johnson & Texas*, 124, citing Johnson conversation in New York City, August 1997.

27 Philip Johnson, "Whence and Whither: The Processional Element in Architecture," in *Writings* (New York: Oxford University Press, 1979), 150–55, 151.

28 For a comprehensive history, see Stephen Fagin, *Assassination and Commemoration: JFK, Dallas, and the Sixth Floor Museum at Dealey Plaza* (Norman: Oklahoma University Press, 2013).

29 Welch, *Philip Johnson & Texas*, 124, citing Johnson conversation in New York City, August 1997.

13

SALLY BACHNER

Free the World and Your Ass Will Follow: JFK and Revolutionary Freedom in 1960s Youth Culture

On the cover of *Mad Magazine*'s December 1970 issue, at the tail end of what has come to be known as the long 1960s, Alfred E. Newman stands grinning in a raccoon coat and saddle shoes, gripping a pennant that reads "Beat State." The always out-of-place mascot is oblivious to the frothing mob of filthy, angry young people who clamor behind him. A related gag appears in one panel of a five-page spread on "The Lighter side of ... The Revolutionary Movement": while most of the panels feature angry longhairs – jokes are made both on their behalf and at their expense – one features two wholesome college students who are being interviewed by a journalist. When the kids insist that "the Revolutionaries are only a very small minority," the journalist turns to his assistant and whispers, "Cut the mike, Bill! These are a bunch of likeable kids! They're not news!!"[1] Youth at any time, the magazine suggests, is never as monolithic as we imagine. From a much greater historical distance, Jane and Michael Stern's charming pop ethnography *Sixties People* counteracts such narrowing effects by offering a more diverse range of 1960s icons than the square and the militant longhair. They catalogue such figures as "Perky Girls" (Twiggy, Goldie Hawn on *Laugh-In*, Marlo Thomas's *That Girl*); "Young Vulgarians," who adopted the style of the working-class "hoodlum baroque" that persisted from the 1950s into the 1960s; and "Surfers, Twisters, and Party Animals," who "yearned to escape the status quo" and yet were more likely to "chug a keg of brew, blast 'Louie, Louie' on the stereo, [and] lie out in the sun until [their] hair turned blond" than to attend protests.[2]

Yet whatever the media magnification, the youth culture linking both student radicals and the counterculture is central to what we mean when we invoke that capacious term "the 1960s." *Mad*'s own relentless coverage of such figures from the mid-1960s onward constitutes just one archive chronicling the development of a distinct, oppositional youth culture. In this chapter, I will argue that this youth culture was influenced and inspired by the model of charismatic leadership, idealism, and personal authenticity that its members associated with John F. Kennedy, both during his presidency and in the aftermath of his assassination. My analysis focuses on two key sectors of this sprawling culture: the largely middle-class white college students who participated in a range of causes and movements and whose political consciousness was raised by their observation of and, sometimes, participation in the civil rights movement, and those young people – also often white and middle class – who identified with the extra-political ideals of the counterculture. I focus more narrowly on the men in these movements, men who identified with Kennedy and imagined themselves as charismatic leaders in their own right. In this sense, while concerned with the sometimes grandiose self-understanding of the young men in the student Left and the counterculture, I hope to articulate the role that the image of Kennedy played, as an icon of charismatic masculinity, in the marginalization of women in 1960s youth. In both cases, I develop my claims through a look at the rhetorical underpinnings of specific texts linked to representative figures and movements – respectively, the early Students for a Democratic Society (SDS) of *The Port Huron Statement*,[3] and the psychedelic movement as described by Timothy Leary in a 1968 account of a 1960 encounter with the poet Allen Ginsberg. I also draw at length on two important speeches by John F. Kennedy – his inaugural address of 1961 and his speech upon being nominated by the Democratic Party as their presidential candidate in 1960 – that were widely viewed as central to the shaping of his public persona.

The qualities of the Kennedy persona are not merely well known; they are clichés. Examining the cover of *Life* magazine from 1953 featuring the not yet married Jack and Jackie, David M. Lubin sums up JFK's early image as one of "Youth. Freshness. Teeth."[4] By the time he was president, "millions of people throughout the world felt as if they knew Jack Kennedy. He appeared frequently in their living rooms, brought there almost daily by newspapers, magazines, radio and television . . . Observers in America and beyond experienced a rapport with Kennedy, whose aura was that of someone remarkable yet reassuringly familiar."[5] Glamour, youth, charisma, vigor, and idealism are all terms that continue to dominate descriptions of Kennedy, no matter that their accuracy has been seriously called into question by accounts of his constant and debilitating illnesses, the corrupt deployment of his father's fortune, and his own practice of a political pragmatism that often shaded into cynicism. But if Kennedy's influence on youth culture seems as undeserved as his reputation as a man of youthful vigor, we might also add that his appeal to this group was often largely subterranean. He was not so much embraced as a hero as he was internalized as a model. This chapter thus addresses a paradox: that a pragmatic, hawkish U.S. president, one who drew the United States into conflict with Vietnam, became an iconic figure of the 1960s youth culture committed to freedom from oppression and bureaucracy.[6]

Nowhere was Kennedy's image as a charismatic man of revolutionary action and high principle more influential than among the white, predominantly male student activists who served as the public face of the emergent youth movement. This is not to say that Kennedy was universally or even widely admired among those who appear to have taken up his persona with such force. While he positioned himself as an inspiring alternative to Eisenhower era complacency, Kennedy was deeply pragmatic in his politics. His career in the Senate established him as a staunch anticommunist, albeit one with adequate liberal bona fides in domestic policy to eventually gather the support of Stevenson holdouts at the Democratic National Convention. But Kennedy's persona and, often, his rhetoric stood in contrast to his hawkishness on both budgets and communism. Not only was Kennedy the youngest president in living memory to occupy the White House; his assassination before the end of his first term suspended his image in the popular imagination as a figure of martyred youth and idealism. *Ramparts*, the leftist monthly, was among the first magazine to publish conspiracy theories about the assassination, which it did alongside writings from such luminaries of Third World revolution as Che Guevara and Eldridge Cleaver. Although the decades since have brought careful documentation of Kennedy's role in militarizing the nation's involvement in Vietnam, in the immediate years after his death it was Lyndon Johnson who emerged – and has remained – as the grim face of the unpopular conflict. Kennedy was in death granted the sincerity of his idealistic rhetoric, in a way that would likely not have survived a full term and the evaluative scrutiny that a full-blown reelection campaign would have brought.

Yet it was not merely Kennedy's relative youth that allowed him to function as an icon for the youth movements of the 1960s. His status as a charismatic Irish Catholic outsider to the narrowest definitions of the American ruling class; his image as a man of action who transcended the constraints of organizations and institutions (enhanced by his reputation as a war hero and by his writings about heroism); and his rhetorical yoking of the revolutionary spirit of the Third World to both the United States and, by extension, his person: all enabled an associative link between Kennedy and the newly independent peoples to whom he appealed. It is Kennedy's symbolic status as a kind of homegrown charismatic revolutionary leader that is at the heart of his otherwise perplexing appeal to the student Left. In linking Kennedy's lasting impact on student activists to the glamour and idealism of the Third World's struggle against imperialism, I am following the lead of Leerom Medovoi, who has suggested that "Kennedy, through his election in 1960 to the presidency, came to figure American freedom in a very particular fashion to the Cold War world. Kennedy's youth, his off-white ethnicity as an Irish Catholic, and his self-presentation as an independent leader resembled in noticeable ways the . . . 'young,' largely non-white, newly independent nations of the globe."[7]

Lest the thread connecting Kennedy's Irish American Catholicism to the people of the Third World seem too thin a strand to travel so far, it's worth recalling the frequency and force with which this racial logic of associative transvaluation came into play. Normal Mailer's "Superman Comes to the Supermarket," a profile that appeared in *Esquire* magazine (under the title "Superman Comes to the Supermart") just before the November election, refers in one section title to "The Hipster as Presidential Candidate." Mailer invokes Kennedy as the latest incarnation of the "White Negro" he celebrated in his infamous 1957 essay in *Dissent*. In Kennedy, Mailer senses a break with the WASP establishment. Michael Szalay's elegant parsing of the apparent contradiction of the term "white Negro" is helpful here: "while Mailer's hipsters look white, they are in the process of becoming something other than a group of 'whites.' But crucially, in becoming 'Negro,' they change that identity such that it describes neither external markers nor inherited traits, but instead a set of performable dispositions."[8] Mailer is, indeed, interested in such dispositions, although in Kennedy they are not wholly divorced from that which is inherited. In "Superman," Mailer praises Kennedy's political machine, likening it to "a crack Notre Dame football team . . . never dull, quick as a knife, full of the salt of hipper-dipper, a beautiful machine."[9] Kennedy, in other words, may have played football for WASP-dominated Harvard – albeit intermittently and unsuccessfully, given his many illnesses – but Mailer sees him as inextricably tied to the Irish Catholic Notre Dame. Kennedy's Irishness is capable not only of turning him into a Notre Dame man but, more miraculously, into a kind of white Negro. As Mailer has it, this conventional candidate with "his good, sound, conventional liberal record, has a patina of that other life, the second American life, the long electric night with the fires of neon leading down the highway to the murmur of jazz."[10] To return to Medovoi's argument linking JFK to the peoples of Asia and Africa, Kennedy's Irish Catholicism was, in being associated with American blackness, structurally aligned with aspirations for freedom across the decolonizing world: "Like youth, the 'Negro' became a potent ideological figure for the post-colonial character of a free United States. If youth figured America in its newness, as a young nation akin to those of the Third World, then blacks signified America as a space for the achievement of racial emancipation."[11]

Kennedy's legacy as an actual supporter of and ally to the civil rights movement is complex and contested.[12] Dr. King and other civil rights leaders saw
in him a fair-weather friend of limited moral courage, but he was nonetheless
widely perceived as an ally, a view that was solidified in the period immediately after his assassination. Cathy Wilkerson remembers that, during the
time when she was active in the Swarthmore Political Action Club (SWAC)
and the Committee for Freedom Now (CFCC) in an effort to improve the
conditions of a 95 percent black school in Chester, Pennsylvania, Kennedy
was "mythologized in many poor black households. His death was seen by
many, in the immediate aftermath, as the martyrdom of a white ally to the
civil rights movement. Within weeks, almost every household I entered in
Chester had a picture of Kennedy on display."[13] Kennedy's self-assessment
is adequately summed up in his comment, after being pressed by Eugene
Rostow, the dean of the Yale Law School, to offer more vigorous public
support for the movement in 1961, "Doesn't he know I've done more for
civil rights than any President in American history?"[14] But with civil rights
as with Third World anti-imperialism, a chasm remains between Kennedy's
actual political record and the valence of his persona and rhetoric as they
were taken up by the activist wing of the youth culture. Even among these
more politically attuned young people, Kennedy's charisma and apparent
authenticity, combined with his rhetoric on behalf of personal freedom and
responsibility, were seen as inspiring and influential.

To make sense of the power of JFK's emancipatory rhetoric upon youth
culture, we can start with the most enduring phrase of his short presidency.
In his 1961 inaugural address, Kennedy exhorted Americans to reconfig-
ure their citizenship in terms of service and sacrifice: "And so, my fellow
Americans: ask not what your country can do for you – ask what you can do
for your country."[15] This familiar chiasmus is followed by another, less well
remembered, that frames such patriotic service as part of an extra-national
effort in the name of freedom: "My fellow citizens of the world: ask not
what America will do for you, but what together we can do for the freedom
of man." This closing pivot to the newly independent and emerging nations
of the Third World invites Americans to think of themselves as in structural
solidarity with (noncommunist) mankind, and vice versa. In making this
comparison, Kennedy returns his audience to his description of Americans,
in the middle part of the speech, as "the heirs" of "the first revolution."
Kennedy's most memorable gesture at self-sacrifice on behalf of the nation
is thus only fully understood when placed in an international context, one
that frames the United States as an older sibling whose success in achieving
independence from the repressive European powers can be imitated by the
decolonizing world.

Not quite a year and a half later, SDS distributed *The Port Huron Statement*. SDS was in 1962 oriented toward an ecumenical socialism founded upon participatory democracy, and had yet – in these years before the Gulf of Tonkin resolution – to become focused on ending U.S. involvement in the conflict in Vietnam. The final document, drafted by Tom Hayden months earlier and then revised at the SDS National Convention in Port Huron, Michigan, was ambitious in its breadth. Nuclear weaponry and the defense industry, environmental degradation, U.S. imperialism, civil rights, economic justice, university curricula, culture, and administration: all are subject to an analysis that aims to be comprehensive and philosophically consistent. This complex agenda is bound together by an explicit articulation of the "values" of sacrifice and the commitment to emancipatory freedom that directly recalls Kennedy's inaugural address. In one of its central statements of principle, the statement asserts that the members of SDS "regard men as infinitely precious and possessed of unfulfilled capacities for reason, freedom, and love," as well as "unrealized potential for self-cultivation, self-direction, self-understanding, and creativity."[16] The passage builds to its own Kennedyesque chiasmus: "This kind of independence does not mean egoistic individualism – the object is not to have one's way so much as it is to have a way that is one's own."[17] This way leads inexorably, as does Kennedy's vision, to an ideal of action and sacrifice on behalf of a universalized mankind whose freedom is under threat.

Although SDS understood itself at this moment as filling a moral vacuum left vacant by the political establishment, the statement nonetheless positively contrasts political leadership in the United States with that abroad. Early in the statement the authors note that "unlike youth in other countries we are used to moral leadership being exercised and moral dimensions being clarified by our elders."[18] The apparent contradiction is clarified by SDS's analysis of an inadequately visionary political *culture*: "To be idealistic is to be considered apocalyptic, deluded. To have no serious aspirations, on the contrary, is to be 'toughminded' . . . All around us there is astute grasp of method, technique – the committee, the ad hoc group, the lobbyist, that hard and soft sell, the make, the projected image – but, if pressed critically, such expertise is incompetent to explain its implicit ideals."[19] If this seems to critique Kennedy's own political pragmatism, or the circle of technocrats in his administration, it also sounds a theme from Kennedy's self-presentation as an alternative to Eisenhower era complacency. Indeed, a major part of the appeal of Kennedy's rhetoric of service is that it presents an alternative image of the American. No longer the passive and emasculated suburban consumer, the American is enabled, in his commitment to global freedom and human betterment, to escape the institutions that would otherwise entrap him.

Indeed, as much as *The Port Huron Statement* is nominally organized around participatory democracy, its real leitmotif is the authentic, empowered, masculine individual. While we might expect it to emphasize interdependence, cooperation, and collaboration, *The Port Huron Statement* declares, "The goal of man and society should be human independence: a concern not with image or popularity but with finding a meaning in life that is personally authentic . . . one which openly faces problems which are troubling and unresolved: one with an intuitive awareness of possibilities, an active sense of curiosity, an ability and willingness to learn."[20] The centrality of the charismatic man of action to this vision was powerful enough to shape the first histories of the organization. James Miller, in the introduction to his indispensable history of SDS, explains, without seeming to be aware of the contradiction, "The form that I have chosen is biographical. By focusing narrowly on the experience of a few young radicals who ratified *the Port Huron Statement* and took its political vision to heart, I have hoped to recapture, from the inside, some of the excitement and sense of adventure that made the idea of participatory democracy come alive in the sixties."[21] Later scholars have sought to correct for this focus, insisting that "[It] is highly problematic to make age, whiteness, and student status the defining characteristics of the New Left; however unintended, the consequence is to put those white youth at the center of the narrative, with other movements at the margins . . . The typical local leader of the antiwar or Civil Rights movements was a middle-aged woman or a Protestant minister, not a college student."[22] The influence of the charismatic narrative is equally apparent in the repudiations of a predominantly white, male radicalism that began appearing near the decade's end. In the critiques from women who had worked behind the scenes in radical groups, it was the Kennedyesque man – now revealed for his sexual predations and hunger for power in the name of idealism – that came under scrutiny.

In a reflection on *The Port Huron Statement* published in the fiftieth anniversary issue of *Dissent*, Michael Kazin suggests that what the statement offered was not a contradiction, but a creative fusion of "two types of ideological advocacy that are often viewed as antagonists: first, the romantic desire for achieving an authentic self through crusading for individual rights and, second, the yearning for a democratic socialist order that would favor the collective good over freedom of the self."[23] This fusion, I would argue, was less stable than Kazin's analysis would suggest, as is well testified to in the complaints among female activists, black militants, and international allies. At the very least, Kazin's argument helpfully reminds us that Kennedy's influential presentation of himself as a charismatic man of action was hardly sui generis. It can be placed narrowly in the "romantic" American tradition

Kazin traces back to the abolitionist movement or, broadly, in the context of a patriarchal "Great Man" theory of history. Without gainsaying those contexts or others, what allows us to trace this thread in 1960s youth culture to Kennedy specifically is its insistent turn to the language of sacrifice in the name of an emancipatory freedom that is threatened not so much by direct tyranny as by the lure of complacency and prosperity. It is relief from this very particular postwar danger that Kennedy's charisma and emancipatory rhetoric promises.

In offering this reading of *The Port Huron Statement*, my point is not to enshrine either that document or SDS at the center of either the New Left or the youth culture. One might reasonably look at other movements or speeches – Mario Savio's famous speech at Berkeley about "the machine" comes to mind – for evidence of Kennedy's influence. Many later SDS-ers, such as the so-called Action Faction of future Weathermen, thought the statement tepid and specifically called it out as too steeped in American liberalism. Yet even these more radical groups bear the mark of Kennedy's influence. The Yippie Manifesto's call for "Every man a revolution!" is, on its face, a call for participatory revolution from the ground up, but it is counterbalanced by the ongoing centrality of Hoffman and Rubin as the charismatic faces of that revolution. In his 1988 documentary, *Growing Up in America*, Morley Markson returns to the figures who had earlier been at the center of his 1971 documentary, *Breathing Together: Revolution of the Electric Family*. Like Miller's seminal history of SDS, Markson's project is organized biographically, with each segment structured around footage devoted to the charismatic leaders in their prime. Hoffman, in particular, is shown at his magnetic best. With his masses of black curls, large, dark eyes, dimpled chin, and a regional accent just as marked as – although less idiosyncratic than –Kennedy's own distinctive intonation, Hoffman looks like a Kennedy for the counterculture. He stands at a blackboard and riffs, "We think, if you ask us, how is the government going to be brought down, or lost in the shuffle, as we tend to put it, our motto is 'Ask not what you can do for your country, but what your country can do for you.' "[24] Hoffman makes it clear that he doesn't approve of this anti-service philosophy – he calls it another version of the "gimme, gimmes" – just as his charismatic persona is not a repudiation of Kennedy but an appropriation of him.

The language of freedom was pervasive not just among the avowedly political student Left, but also among those sectors of the youth culture that sought a freedom they understood to transcend the merely political: it's no accident that "Free Love," a term that was once associated with radical critiques of marriage practices in the nineteenth century, has come to serve as an enduring shorthand for the ideals of the counterculture. Among these groups, the model of freedom inspired by Kennedy is inflected differently; he is important less as a figure who embodies the emancipatory vitality of the emerging Third World than as one marked by his symbolic transcendence of institutions and hierarchies. Kennedy nowhere more deliberately forged this aspect of his image than in his speech upon receiving the Democratic Party's nomination for president at its 1960 convention in Los Angeles.

This is the famous "New Frontier" speech, in which Kennedy uses his location at the westernmost edge of the continental United States to transvalue the imperial ideology of Manifest Destiny into a program of independent-minded exploration of new symbolic terrain: "I believe the times demand new invention, innovation, imagination, decision. I am asking each of you to be pioneers on that New Frontier."[25] Kennedy in this speech casts the New Frontier as a drama in which bold men cast off older modes of thinking and governmentality in order to revivify the nation. And in voting for him, Kennedy suggests, Americans could partake of this renewed pioneering spirit:

> That is the question of the New Frontier. That is the choice our nation must make – a choice that lies not merely between two men or two parties, but between the public interest and private comfort – between national greatness and national decline – between the fresh air of progress and the stale, dank atmosphere of "normalcy" – between determined dedication and creeping mediocrity.[26]

Kennedy here presents himself not just as a figure of youthful energy, but as a champion of resistance to a repressive political establishment. He figures not just himself but the Democratic Party as a whole as under attack from entrenched powers. Invoking Richard Nixon, Kennedy draws a sharp contrast between his approach and that of his likewise young opponent:

> The Republican nominee-to-be, of course, is also a young man. But his approach is as old as McKinley. His party is the party of the past. His speeches are generalities from Poor Richard's Almanac. Their platform, made up of left-over Democratic planks, has the courage of our old convictions. Their pledge is a pledge to the status quo – and today there can be no status quo.[27]

Kennedy also drew on this rhetoric of resistance in addressing his Roman Catholicism, answering those who feared that a Catholic President would be in thrall to Rome by insisting, "It is not relevant what pressures, if any, might conceivably be brought to bear on me. I am telling you now what you are entitled to know: that my decisions on any public policy will be my own – as an American, a Democrat and a free man."[28] Here Kennedy brilliantly recasts his Catholicism as a test of and testament to his ability to transcend the tyranny of entrenched and enervated institutions, turning a potential liability into another testament to his individualism.

The neoimperial language of the frontier, drawn in part from Kennedy's electoral rhetoric, was not just the province of foreign policy: it was also central to the psychedelic movement from the outset. Proponents of LSD and other hallucinogens believed that these drugs would enable the exploration of the "new frontiers" of human consciousness. But even more pervasive was the influence of Kennedy as a figure who resisted the status quo and the institutions that maintain it. Timothy Leary, the charismatic figurehead of the psychedelic movement, offers in his 1968 book, *High Priest*, an origin story of both the psychedelic movement and his own emergence as a leader capable of transcending obsolete hierarchies, conventions, and social structures. The chapter entitled "Turning on the World" details the events of a day in November 1960, a few months after Kennedy's "New Frontier" speech, when Allen Ginsberg came to Leary's home to take psilocybin capsules. The chapter offers twinned narratives of bold leadership and the casting off of repressive institutions via the actions of Leary and Ginsberg. It begins with a historical overview, one in which Leary looks back on himself as torn between multiple factions. At the time he recalls, Leary was a lecturer in psychology at Harvard, and he begins by noting, "By the fall of 1960 there was in existence an informal international network of scientists and scholars who had taken the psychedelic trip and who foresaw the powerful effect that the new alkaloids would have on human culture."[29]

Yet even among this innovative group of forward thinkers, Leary detects a divide between the truly visionary and those who want to play it safe. Among the "turned-on doctors," many preached cautious advances from within existing institutions and procedures:

> There were those who said work within the system. Society has assigned the administration of drugs to the medical profession. Any non-doctor who gives or takes drugs is a dope-fiend. Play ball with the system. Medicine must be the vanguard of the psychedelic movement. Any non-medical use of psychedelic drugs would create a new marijuana mess and set back research into the new utopia.[30]

These Nixonesque figures, who pretend to leadership but remain mired within the stultifying structures of the past, are crucial to Leary's narrative of his own journey from meek follower to bold leader. Leary describes the pressure he was under to maintain such respectability: "I had been visited by most of the psychedelic eminences by this time and was under steady pressure to make the psychedelic research a kosher-medically-approved project. Everyone was aware of the potency of Harvard's name. Timothy, you are the key figure, said Dr. Al Meyner . . . But the message was clear: Keep it respectable and medical."[31]

It is at this historical moment that Ginsberg makes a strategic appearance. Any chance that respectability will be maintained is shattered by the appearance of "the secretary-general of the world's poets, beatniks, anarchists, socialists, free-sex/love cultists." Ginsberg, in this description, is a kind of turned-on Kennedy: at once the wielder of institutional power – he is "secretary-general" – but one who does so in the name of a transformative challenge to the status quo. Although Leary portrays what follows as a kind of marvelous historical accident – the explosive product of Ginsberg's visionary insight and the power of psychedelics themselves – there's ample evidence that Leary invited Ginsberg to his home precisely in the hopes of harnessing this well-connected ally for his cause.[32] Soon after taking his capsule, Ginsberg, now high, is visited by Leary, his self-appointed spiritual adviser. Although snippets of the *I Ching* and Tolkien have already been interspersed through the chapter, after Ginsberg begins tripping his capitalized exclamations are added to the mix. The first of these come when Leary checks on Ginsberg for the first time:

> He was lying on top of the blanket. His glasses were off and his black eyes, pupils completely dilated, looked up at me. Looking down at them they seemed like two deep, black wet wells and you could look down them way through the man Ginsberg to something human beyond. The eye is such a defenseless, naïve, trusting thing. PROFESSOR LEARY CAME INTO MY ROOM, LOOKED INTO MY EYES, AND SAID I WAS A GREAT MAN. THAT DETERMINED ME TO MAKE AN EFFORT TO LIVE HERE AND NOW. – Allen Ginsberg.[33]

The capitalized section, like all that follow, appears to quote Ginsberg in the moment, although such a reading is complicated by the fact that later capitalized sections include quotes from "Howl" and "America." Only this initial capitalized section is explicitly attributed to the poet. In this first direct entrance of Ginsberg's voice into the chapter, the authority of his trip – and that of the well-connected and (in)famous poet himself – is rendered as something produced by Leary: he plays nominating convention to Ginsberg's Kennedy. The chapter builds to the moment when, having fully taken on the pioneering authority granted him by Leary in speech ("A GREAT MAN") and writing ("the secretary-general"), Ginsberg decides he must call "KHRUSHCHEV, KEROUAC, BURROUGHS, IKE, KENNEDY, MAO TSE-TUNG, MAILER, ETC.," so that they can come to Harvard for "A SPECTRAL CONFERENCE OVER THE FUTURE OF THE UNIVERSE."[34] After failing to get the operator to connect him to Khrushchev, he settles for calling Kerouac instead.

Despite the local failure of Ginsberg's vision – which even Leary presents as inspired farce – the incident is central to Leary's narrative of the movement's emerging authority and notoriety. Leary tells how Ginsberg develops the revolutionary plan that they had been unable to construct the night before: "And so Allen spun out the cosmic campaign. He was to line up influentials and each weekend I would come down to New York and we'd run mushroom sessions." On the one hand, Leary suggests that "this fit our Harvard research plans perfectly."[35] But he also describes it as part of something much bigger: "Allen's political plan was appealing too . . . The bigger and better men we got on our team the stronger our position."[36] By the end of the chapter, Leary has been propelled, by Ginsberg and by his own insufficient instincts for caution, into a leadership position in the psychedelic vanguard. By the time an anthropology grad student who had been present at the house during Ginsberg's trip spreads rumors of what he saw and unleashes institutional disapprobation against Leary, the researcher has all but left Harvard behind. He decides that "from this evening on my energies were offered to the ancient, underground society of alchemists, artists, mystics, alienated visionaries, drop-outs and the disenchanted young, the sons arising."[37]

By 1968, the image of the "sons arising" looks backward at both President Kennedy and Allen Ginsberg. But it also gestures toward the legions of young people who heard Ginsberg chant and Leary intone his famous slogan – "Turn on, tune in, drop out" – at the 1967 "Human Be-In" in Golden Gate Park. As one attendee described it, the Be-In "presented a new world," one that was "new and clean and pastoral."[38] While the recollections of less-starry-eyed participants in the scene belie the vision of utopia realized, such rhetoric suggests the way in which Kennedy's language of the new frontier, and the charismatic leadership that was at its center, proved both useful and inspiring to the counterculture.

Only a few years later, of course, the scene was dead. George Clinton's psychedelic funk band, aptly named Funkadelic, titled their 1970 album with a witty phrase – "Free Your Mind . . . And your Ass Will Follow" – that presciently anticipated the shift of the frontier of freedom to the bedroom and the dance floor. But if the youth movements that had come to define "the 1960s" were in deep decline, Kennedy's influence was not. Insofar as Kennedy's appeal lay in his promotion of a charismatic personal authenticity at odds with the constraints of organizations and institutions, he also, ironically, became an important figure to the right in the decades following Watergate. Kennedy's presidency and its aftermath gives birth to a structure of feeling that would allow the liberal Kennedy and the conservative Reagan to emerge as the most popular presidents of the twentieth century.

In an interview from *Growing Up in America*, Jerry Rubin conjures the sudden collapse of the movement in the early to mid-1970s: "I mean, there was just a day in 1973 or '74 when my phone book just became outdated. Everybody, everybody's phone was disconnected. Everybody had moved to the country, or had cut off their hair and joined their father's business, or gone back to school; it was just, like, unbelievable."[39] Rubin, like Ginsberg with *his* address book after he fails to reach Khrushchev, pulls himself together. After a stint on Wall Street, Rubin pursues a Kennedyesque course to the very place Funkadelic looked toward: the dance floor. His *New York Times* obituary – Rubin was fatally struck by a car in 1994 – fills us in on his last years of success, before he was reduced to marketing a powdered drink mix called Wow!: "By 1985, Mr. Rubin's soirees at the Palladium on East 14th Street were bringing together thousands of networkers. 'I don't like to use the word, but every Yuppie in New York comes,' he told an interviewer."[40]

NOTES

1   *Mad Magazine*, ed. Albert B. Feldstein, December 1970, 19.
2   Jane and Michael Stern, *Sixties People* (New York: Knopf, 1990), 79.
3   Students for a Democratic Society, *The Port Huron Statement* (Chicago: Charles H. Kerr, 1990).
4   David M. Lubin, *Shooting Kennedy: JFK and the Culture of Images* (Berkeley: University of California Press, 2003), 39.
5   Ibid., ix.
6   Leerom Medovoi, "Cold War American Culture as the Age of Three Worlds," *Minnesota Review* 55–57 (2002): 167–86, 167.
7   Ibid., 168.
8   Michael Szalay, *Hip Figures* (Stanford, CA: Stanford University Press, 2012), 18.
9   Mailer, "Superman Comes to the Supermarket," *Smiling Through the Apocalypse: Esquire's History of the Sixties*, ed. Harold Hayes (New York: Crown Books, 1987), 6.
10 Ibid.
11 Medovoi, "Cold War American Culture as the Age of Three Worlds," 179.
12 See Douglas Field's chapter in this volume.
13 Cathy Wilkerson, *Flying Close to the Sun: My Life and Times as a Weatherman* (New York: Seven Stories Press, 2007), 57.
14 Robert Dallek, *An Unfinished Life: John Kennedy 1917–1963* (New York: Back Bay Books, 2003), 387.
15 Stephen R. Goldzwig and George N. Dionisopoulos, "In a Perilous Hour": The Public Address of John F. Kennedy (Westport, CT: Greenwood, 1995), 157.
16 Students for a Democratic Society, *The Port Huron Statement*, 11.
17 Ibid., 12.
18 Ibid., 10.
19 Ibid.
20 Ibid., 11–12.

21 James Miller, *Democracy Is in the Streets: From Port Huron to the Siege of Chicago* (Cambridge, MA: Harvard University Press, 1994), 17.
22 Van Gosse, *Rethinking the New Left: An Interpretive History* (Gordonsville, VA: Palgrave Macmillan, 2005), 5.
23 Michael Kazin, "The Port Huron Statement at Fifty," *Dissent* (Spring 2012), http://www.dissentmagazine.org/article/the-port-huron-statement-at-fifty, accessed February 22, 2014.
24 *Growing Up in America* (Dir. Morley Markson, Cinephile, 1988).
25 John F. Kennedy, "1960 Democratic Convention, 15 July 1960." John F. Kennedy Museum and Library, http://www.jfklibrary.org/Asset-Viewer/AS08q50YzoSFUZg9uOi4iw.aspx, accessed January 24, 2014.
26 Ibid.
27 Ibid.
28 Ibid.
29 Harold Hayes, ed., *Smiling through the Apocalypse: Esquire's History of the Sixties* (New York: Crown, 1987), 328.
30 Ibid., 329.
31 Ibid., 330.
32 Peter Conners, *White Hand Society: The Psychedelic Partnership of Timothy Leary and Allen Ginsberg* (San Francisco: City Lights, 2010).
33 Hayes, *Smiling through the Apocalypse*, 333.
34 Ibid. 334.
35 Ibid., 337.
36 Ibid.
37 Ibid. 338.
38 Alexander Bloom and Wini Breines, *"Takin' It to the Streets": A Sixties Reader* (New York: Oxford University Press, 1995), 33–34.
39 *Growing Up in America.*
40 Ibid.

14

MICHAEL TRASK

The Kennedy Family Romance

The ambiguous role of the Kennedy family in the history of modern liberalism is inseparable from the ambiguous role of the family as an institution in American culture. It is only a slight exaggeration to say that the family has become the ideal U.S. citizen in the last half century. And while that achievement has been due largely to the late arrival of Evangelicals onto the political stage, it would be a mistake to imagine that defenders of secular and liberal values have not done their part in advancing the family as a rights-bearing subject. At the risk of confounding the issue beyond interpretive headway, we might even say that the hallmark of modern liberalism itself is its equivocal position between advancing social justice within institutional frameworks and advancing the business as usual of those frameworks as such. And we might add that the Kennedy family, with its bottomless coffers and sense of mission, a commitment scarcely distinct from paternalism, has embodied just this conflicted status in the post-1945 world. That the Kennedy name, now synonymous with liberalism, once signified a red-baiting jingoism and a lukewarm approach to civil rights testifies as much to the leftward shift of the Kennedy compound as to the rightward shift of American culture. It is a tribute to its by now largely symbolic stature that the Kennedys have succeeded in recasting liberalism in their own name and image – which is to say, a liberalism of image, and perhaps in name only.

Given the truism that governance is the business of compromise, it is fitting that the First Family of American politics has proved such a shrewd handler of its own frequently compromised identity. The Kennedy family is a novel blend of private sanctum and publicly traded company, both a bourgeois haven in a heartless world and a royal house. If the Kennedy family has become the most recognizable brand in modern politics, it is safe to say that John F. Kennedy, more so than his kingmaker paterfamilias, was that brand's creator. For JFK not only surrounded himself with family members, in a manner unprecedented in presidential history, but also fused those ties with the media campaigns he brilliantly exploited. The Kennedys had long been "something of a clan,"[1] to borrow F. Scott Fitzgerald's line about the Carraways, but it was JFK who made family values pay by making his own unimpeachably cozy nuclear unit appear seamless with what Protestant America saw as the never quite couth prolificacy of the Catholic household from which he arose. JFK's canny awareness that the family could cover a multitude of sins was not incidental to the fact that his own family contained multitudes. Among American Catholics with any pretensions to public life, their faith's demurral from family planning calls for the most gingerly public relations, lest it devolve into the spectacle of a fecundity that verges on class and even erotic impermissibility.

Later in this chapter, I shall consider the possibilities of appropriating the Kennedy family to a subversive or "queer" end, at least when its presumed excesses appear to threaten the abidingly puritanical norms of American life (a threat already implicit in the title of Alastair Cooke's 1963 cover story in *Show* magazine: "Too Many Kennedys?"). Any such recruitment would have to account for the virtuosity with which JFK in particular managed to fashion the family as an alibi for the most outré behaviors in and out of the domestic pale. So enduring is the mystique of the Kennedy brand that one is unsurprised when the scions of its cadet branches demonstrate a credulous faith in the immunity conferred by the family arms. In the 2002 trial of Michael Skakel, accused of killing Martha Moxley, Gregory Coleman testified that Skakel bragged to him, "I'm a Kennedy. I'm going to get away with murder."[2] While Skakel's faith in the Kennedy exemption was disproved by his actual conviction of the crime, and while the testimony of the unstable Coleman was perhaps less than sound, there is still some justification for the view that being a Kennedy grants a license, if not a get-out-of-jail-free card, for all manner of indiscretions. However much scandal accrues to individual Kennedys, after all, surprisingly little has attached to the *family name* itself, which circulates in the public imagination as the repository of tragic sympathy. We speak of the Kennedy curse but rarely of the Kennedy disgrace. Even its convicted murderers and accused rapists, to say nothing of its vigorous philanderers, seem incapable of tarnishing the brand beyond a surface blemish.

A large part of this seeming invulnerability is owing to the early association of the family business with power – or, more precisely, to the fortuitous and remarkably successful effort to launder the acquisition and wielding of power into its most idealized form: "public service." Such renovations had long been incumbent on the Kennedy patriarch, whose move from Boston to New York coincided with the recasting of his family from Boston Irish to "semi-English," to use Garry Wills's term, and of the family fortune from bootlegging to finance.[3] Yet the ability to harness power to the family brand has a special place among Joseph Kennedy's makeovers if only because, unlike the Anglicization (which would always retain the mark of the striver), the family's triumphant identification with American power placed it above the fray of the competitiveness (or simply bullying) for which, according to every observer of the family dynamic, the Kennedys were most known. In this respect, the coronation of JFK as president licensed the assumption, until very recently unquestioned, that a Kennedy who ran for office was simply going through the motions required of him before swearing his oath. Ted Kennedy's 1980 takeover bid of the Carter nomination represents the *reductio ad absurdum* of the family hubris: "Edward rented a private 'Air Force One,' " Wills writes, "and campaigned as an incumbent."[4]

However ruthless the rivalry on the lawn at Hyannis Port, the family's united front sought to impress upon the world at large that, in the realm of politics, Kennedys favored a policy of succession. "They were all intensely competitive and at home vied with each other," according to Kennedy speechwriter and hagiographer Ted Sorensen. "But when it came to competing with the rest of the world, the warmth of their solidarity strengthened Jack and awed his adversaries."[5] Such fortitude in turn grounded the attitude of both Kennedys and their admirers ("the network of honorary Kennedys," to cite Victor Navasky[6]) that election to office followed the rules of primogeniture rather than those of constitutional democracy. "Just as I went into politics when Joe died," Sorensen cites JFK telling an interviewer, "if anything happened to me tomorrow my brother Bobby would run for my seat."[7] That blithe approach toward inherited privilege was echoed with somewhat more eagerness in a 1957 puff piece by Harold Martin in the *Saturday Evening Post*, which "confidently" – and accurately – predicted "the day when Jack will be in the White House, Bobby will serve in the Cabinet as Attorney General and Teddy will be the Senator from Massachusetts."[8]

Americans are supposed to frown on dynasts, of course, a fact that explains why JFK worked diligently to mute the image of an executive branch staffed with courtiers by drawing attention to the even more charmed circle occupied by his own wife and children. It was above all through the softening lens of the nuclear family that JFK was able to orchestrate his signature political gesture – the wearing of power as though it were a varsity sweater draped across his shoulders. The canonical accounts of JFK teem with references to his legendary "unpoliticianlike style,"[9] as Kenny O'Donnell and Dave Powers put it in their memoir. Here is Ted Sorensen on the soon-to-be First Couple: "They lived in a fashionable but unpretentious house and avoided the Washington cocktail circuit to an unusual degree. Both strongly preferred small groups of friends to large crowds."[10] Here is Arthur Schlesinger on JFK's "charm and grace": "His 'coolness' was itself a new frontier. . . .

It promised the deliverance of American idealism."[11] That this style was in fact deeply self-conscious – "he not only could objectively measure his own performance," Sorensen notes, "but also cared deeply about how that performance would be measured by future historians"[12] – makes all the more brilliant its pretense of what O'Donnell and Powers call "unpretentious restraint."[13] "Even his faking," Schlesinger observes in a revealing sentence, "had to stay within character."[14]

If "there is nothing easy about effortlessness,"[15] as the sociologist David Riesman noted in 1952, there is nonetheless a significant reward for those equal to the rigors of projecting casualness in any situation, as JFK did. The "careless and purposeful" manner with which he wore his clothes and parsed his diction, the leisurely esprit with which he escorted his wife and played with his children, spoke to the ease with which he took the assumption of nearly absolute power for granted.[16] This is only to point out one of the more frequent refrains in Kennedy lore: JFK was the first celebrity president, embodying what Theodore White called "a 'star quality' reserved only for television and movie idols."[17] The implications of this persona were neither faddish nor innocuous, for it is arguable that JFK's Hollywood-flavored charisma inaugurated the conversion of the national press into a publicity department of the executive branch. "His style, finally, began to capture even the newsmen who had heard all he had to say long before," White writes of JFK on the campaign trail, "but continued to listen, as one continues to return to a favorite movie."[18] White might just as well be describing the press conferences of Ronald Reagan or Barack Obama.

Like any superstar, JFK perfected his own fame because he was himself a true believer in celebrity, or rather in the virtues of what Philip Fisher calls the "high visibility" bestowed on luminaries by the value-added technologies of consumer culture.[19] The regime of high visibility, according to Fisher, divides the world into cynosures and spectators, somebodies and nobodies, with the catch that the somebodies must continually perform their exalted function – whether the mastery of folksiness (as with Mark Twain) or the mastery of statesmanship (as with JFK) – in an ongoing "process of mutual conferring of reality" between viewer and viewed.[20] There is the added complication that, in an officially egalitarian society, the celebrity must also act as though he is in essence, but for the blessing of the limelight, a nobody. Celebrities: they are just like us, only *better*. Nothing captures the presidential couple's tightrope act of distinction and accessibility quite so vividly as the effort to make the grand-touring socialite Jacqueline Bouvier, at home among that transatlantic elite for which Wharton and James served as ethnographers, into the all-American housewife: Camelot by way of *Leave It to Beaver*.

In managing this improbable rehabilitation, it helped that Jackie herself was not immune to the lures of fandom. If "the ethereal Jacqueline," as Wills notes, "was more than half in love with Hollywood,"[21] this starstruck quality served her in good stead as she pursued what Schlesinger calls "her perfection of style,"[22] an impression management delicately poised between divinity and approachability. Though she "found the Kennedys 'terribly bourgeois,'" to cite W. J. Rorabaugh, she nonetheless recognized that bourgeois sold well in a social order whose regnant ideology maintains the universality of middle-class identity. What Rorabaugh calls "the desire many women had to be like Jackie" issued in part from the First Lady's astute application to her own life of the signature middle-class dynamic of emulation:[23] "Within six weeks of the inauguration, the 'Jackie look' had swept the country. Department store advertising featured drawings of women who looked remarkably like Jackie."[24] Such mirror effects go a long way toward explaining the First Family's paradoxical appeal. The chain of analogies through which the Kennedy presidency forged its enduring embrace of the body politic begins with the uncanny doubling of the given name itself. Jack and Jackie, reciprocating each other, cinch the family circle in the image ideal of companionate marriage. That both Jack and Jackie are diminutives further mitigates the highborn status of their possessors. The Francophile Jacqueline, with her decidedly un-American appanage, is spared the charge of hauteur by a handle that transforms her into the girl next door. "Honorary Kennedys" are in fact unimaginable without nicknamed Kennedys. The Schlesingers and Sorensens require the Jackies and Bobbies and Teds (not to mention John-Johns) lest the whole enterprise degrade into vassalage – in other words, lest it appear that there is anything more than *informal* about the family's prerogative to knight outsiders and compel their fealty. It is of the essence that Kennedy diminutives ring with none of the recherché onomastics favored by the preppy elite; you will find no Scooters or Otters or Muffies in the Kennedy family album. Jack, Bob, and Ted are derivative – and, to that extent, populist – nicknames, even when they belong to individuals who are anything but ordinary.

Although Jackie's resemblance to a suburban homemaker always seemed a stretch, we need only remind ourselves that televised housewives circa 1960, from June Cleaver to Samantha Stevens, were given to accessorizing their impeccably tailored housecoats with pearls and diamonds. If the aprons they wore over their finery bespoke their domestic rounds, such toil was nevertheless surprisingly hard to pin down as drudgery. For the imaginary family of network television, as for the slightly less imaginary family that occupied the Kennedy White House, meals come already prepped to the table, rooms are immaculately neat and clean, and the only women's work that is never done is shopping for the home. "The only way that the young housewife was supposed to express herself, and not feel guilty about it," Betty Friedan writes in *The Feminine Mystique*, "was in buying products for the home-and-family."[25] Contrary to the conventional wisdom, the nuclear family of post–World War II America scarcely embodied a return to traditional values. It was a radically new formation that, while absorbing the customary roles of male breadwinners and female homemakers, advanced a powerful "progressive" ideal. "Faith in a mass consumption postwar economy," Lizabeth Cohen argues, "stood for an elaborate, integrated ideal of economic abundance and democratic political freedom, both equitably distributed."[26] "Department stores," according to Friedan, thus aspired "not only to 'sell' the housewife but . . . to satisfy the yearning she has, alone in her house, to feel herself a part of the changing world."[27] While Jackie Kennedy "lacked dishpan hands," as Rorabaugh observes, it is not the case that "nobody really believed" that she was a "housewife."[28] For she became the standard-bearer of Cohen's "Consumers' Republic,"[29] whose home economics consisted precisely in choosing and acquiring things for the house rather than homemaking as such.

Thus while she might have found the Kennedys a rather déclassé crew, Jackie had in common with them an unimpeachable taste – an eye for the right cut of suit, an ear for the right music (Stravinsky and Casals both played après-dinner concerts at the White House). Like the Catholic Kennedys, the Catholic Jackie launched a stealth assault on the Protestant ascendancy by way of connoisseurship. She was just cultured and cosmopolitan enough to permit identification across class divides while radiating an ecumenical cultural sensibility that, measured against the cramped exclusivity of the WASP establishment, looked positively demotic. This is why the charge that JFK bought the presidency, like the charge that his father bought Pulitzers, ambassadorships, or SEC chairs, ultimately has little force: there is nothing un-American about purchasing power. Indeed, to the degree that JFK was an educated consumer, he duplicated rather than differed from his smart shopper of a wife. For just as female labor was all but invisible in the postwar programming of domestic sitcoms, so the male labor that allowed televised households to be so nicely provisioned was always off camera. In performing the high visibility of the Oval Office, JFK performed a version of leisure-class retirement – the presidential term as permanent weekend, or at the very least a position that entitled its holder, like his spouse, to work from home.

This is only to say that what Elaine Tyler May calls the "restructuring" of the family as "a liberating arena of fulfillment through professionalized homemaking" applied as much to men as to women, including the First

Family.[30] The freedom that the family promised, and for which the Kennedy White House served as a kind of aspirational model home, was precisely the autonomy of the professional class, those brainworkers who stand above and apart from partisan ideologies in the pursuit of self-justifying and rewarding intellectual labor. No less remarkable than Jackie's transition from blue-blooded equestrienne to middle-class homemaker was JFK's own shift from playboy of the Western world to the father who knows best. Perhaps the oldest chestnut regarding JFK's 1960 victory over Nixon is the presumption that he won the televised debates "by addressing himself to the audience that was the nation,"[31] as Theodore White puts it, rather than to his opponent. Yet it might be more accurate to say that JFK's highly telegenic presence proved winning because it hewed so closely to those of the sitcom fathers preapproved by home audiences. He was both orchestrator and beneficiary of a feedback loop between the small screen and the national stage. To quote the political scientist Larry Sabato, "The World War II generation came of age with television and a made-for-TV family named the Kennedys."[32] In keeping with the gift for conventional wisdom that has made him a cable news fixture, Sabato's phrasing implies that serendipity rather than adroit calculation was at the root of the First Family's televisual appeal.

May observes that JFK "seemed to embody the American domestic ideal par excellence: the tough cold warrior who was also a warm family man," yet that his "rhetoric, emphasizing vigor and the promise of change, encouraged Americans to embrace political activism and risk."[33] To the extent that it treats JFK's family idyll as somehow at odds with his exhortations to social engagement, this characterization ignores the degree to which JFK's charismatic authority radiated outward, not least in the direction of an attention-getting "youth message," from the basis of his infallible fatherhood. The "warm family man," manifesting the soft power JFK used to impel intellectuals and other "honorary Kennedys" into the orbit of his governance, did not compete with either the Cold Warrior or the proto-1960s figurehead. He was, rather, their progenitor. If the Kennedy White House was a technocrat's paradise, it was also an extended family, with JFK as its easygoing yet never less than imperious head. The relaxed and jaunty style was the outer lining of his imposing command.

That JFK could rescue his undemocratic pedigree by fixing on a patriarchal appeal shot through with "candor and humor,"[34] "wit and resolve,"[35] speaks to the Kennedy administration's frequently lauded rhetorical deftness. If the sacral myth of JFK after his assassination was all but assured by the presence of many gifted and devoted writers in his inner circle (Sorensen and Schlesinger above all), it was no less the case that those same handlers, as keenly attuned to midcult cues as Jackie was to high-brow ones, positioned JFK as the consummation of the "culture of daddy-hood," Ralph LaRossa's term for the "modernization of fatherhood" that proceeded apace in the decades on either side of World War II.[36] In contrast with the distant patriarchs of American myth (like JFK's own father, "absenting himself much of the time"[37]), dads prided themselves on quality time with the kids. Whereas Herbert Parmet notes that "Jack and the other children were raised largely by their mother and hired help,"[38] JFK himself embodied what LaRossa calls "fatherhood with a happy face."[39] "It was in the White House . . . that the President truly discovered his children," Sorensen observes. "How best to rear children . . . suddenly became one of his favorite topics of discussion."[40] JFK's updating of old-school roles like fatherhood is of a piece with his oxymoronic messaging, his monotonous reference to novelty despite his unshakeable commitment to the inertial frameworks of the American establishment. The instrument for getting across this mixed message was the same television set that disseminated "New Fatherhood" as a way of life.[41] The White House in which JFK learned to love parenting, Sorensen notes, "also became the focal point of numerous television . . . presentations which took the public behind the scenes."[42]

To say, with David Halberstam, that Kennedy "was the first of a new kind of media candidate flashed daily into our consciousness by television during the campaign" is to risk redundancy, for television itself entails the eternal return of newness. Halberstam understands Kennedy's media savvy as coming "at a price"; television affords JFK a connection to the public, but it can only be temporary, since the gap between how television works and how the real world works is so wide that not even the most dashing politician can surmount it. If television's "unbelievable velocity," capable of "exciting desires and appetites" and "changing mores almost overnight," is out of sync with "the slowness of traditional government institutions," the candidate whose victory was a tribute to television was bound to renege on the optimistic rhetoric of his campaign.[43] But this is to underestimate both television's co-optive powers and those of JFK himself, whose speechwriters (the very "new men to cope with new problems and new opportunities" he invoked in his acceptance speech at the 1960 Democratic Convention[44]) seemed more than up to the task of writing his presidency as a serial drama starring a preternaturally youthful leading man. We might register this modulation by noting the regularity with which JFK's flacks invoked the word "fresh" when describing his tenure (as when Pierre Salinger describes his former boss as "a fresh voice in American politics"[45]). Freshness is television's preferred state. The medium might trumpet newness, but it never really flouts tradition. It is by now certain that the revolution will never be televised.

The reformist impulses that have long been the hallmark of broadcast television mirror the reformist impulses of the Kennedy White House, which was neither so radical nor so reactionary as later political minorities of different leanings would make it out to be. ("On . . . television," as the medium's great critic John Leonard once put it, "the Enlightenment is far from dead."[46]) One need not deny the Kennedys' obvious and far-reaching appeal to recognize that the Kennedy mystique succeeded in part by generating the appearance of broad acclaim in the absence of unanimity. Far more than its anodyne politics, what JFK's presidency had in common with the fare of network television was the latter's inbuilt mechanism for inundating the culture with what Daniel Boorstin, in his 1962 book, *The Image*, called "the rising tide of pseudo-events,"[47] those public rituals that, though they exist merely to be reported on, are simultaneously capable of quickening the most "extravagant expectations."[48] Boorstin clearly wrote his book with the thirty-fifth president in mind; JFK's outsize political stardom made him the exemplary "human pseudo-event."[49] At the same time, Kennedy had a gift for recognizing the powerful fantasy that television effected: the possibility that even nobodies could be inflated into somebodies. "Reporters . . . in the 1960 Presidential campaign," Boorstin writes, "noted how many of the 'supporters' in large crowds that were being televised had come out because they wanted to be seen on the television cameras." If "television reporting allows us all to be the actors we really are,"[50] part of JFK's genius was to open the extended family to an indefinite number of walk-on roles: even a viewer like you can become an "honorary Kennedy" simply by showing up at a televised rally.

This is perhaps too cynical a take on the sense of purpose that Kennedy-as-father inspired, particularly in the young. "For many years," Stanley Meisler reminds us, volunteers for the Peace Corps (spearheaded, of course, by JFK's brother-in-law Sargent Shriver) "were known in some Latin American countries as *los hijos de Kennedy* – the children of Kennedy."[51] Such a tantalizing patrimony, in which JFK could serve as everyone's dad, was arguably incompatible with the tightly guarded stronghold that was the reality of the Kennedy White House. As Parmet observes, JFK favored the view that in their heart of hearts his fellow citizens wanted nothing more than to be managed. "Democracy," Parmet says, "was something Kennedy had to put up with."[52] Then, too, even apart from the "revelations" about JFK's prodigious adultery, the simulacrum of conjugal bliss projected by the Kennedy White House was bound to be a brittle formation in any event. For the shift in the ensuing decade away from the family structure, subject to permanent critique by the whole panoply of New Left causes, did not arise as a rash assault on the harmonious rewards of domesticity; it proceeded from the discovery that such rewards were *nonexistent*, or bore at most a tenuous relation to many people's lived experience. We do not need the muckraking of *The Feminine Mystique* to confirm what numerous Americans understood at the time. Far from enforcing a monolithic stay-at-home role, according to Joanne Meyerowitz, the print media of the early 1960s teemed with "articles [that] subverted the notion that women belonged at home, presented a wide variety of options open to women, and praised the women who had chosen to assert themselves as public figures."[53] Using sources cognate with those of *The Feminine Mystique*, Meyerowitz sets out to debunk the partiality of Friedan's own pop-cultural archive and concludes: "Her forceful protest against a restrictive domestic ideal neglected the extent to which that ideal was already undermined."[54]

One could argue that the Kennedys similarly neglected the erosion of the domestic ideal when they transformed the family romance into the groundwork of a new American idealism in general. Yet this conclusion may be shortsighted. And given JFK's success in making only partially welcome ideas appear like universal values, it may also be irrelevant. It is a common move among scholars of queer theory to look at institutions like the family as containing within themselves, in a more or less dormant state, the very means of their own undoing. In the case of JFK, we would not have to look far for such contradictions. What Seymour Hersh somewhat primly calls Kennedy's "incessant womanizing" during his residency in the Oval Office was the great open secret of his presidency, indeed one that it ironically fell to an embarrassed Secret Service to manage.[55] Given the ceaseless parade of "hookers" and "bimbos" shunted in and out of the White House, not to mention the copious off-site affairs in which JFK indulged, often with his own aides' wives, virtually every member of his staff assumed that a "public scandal . . . was inevitable."[56]

There is a temptation in the face of such raucous sexual exploits to see past the obvious equation between male power and female objectification to the ludic surplus of JFK's erotic appetite, whose disruptions must then be checked by quite dubious norms of decency. We might push this thinking slightly further and say that the threat of a public scandal reflects worse on the public itself than on its target, given that any liberal society worthy of the name would surely have to include freedom of sexual expression among its ideals. As Lauren Berlant and Lisa Duggan argue in their introduction to an anthology of essays on the Clinton-Lewinsky affair, "scandal" is a problematic concept when it comes to such basic constitutional protections as the separation of powers, not to say church and state. "Scandal enabled long-term political differences to be played out as distinctions of moral hier-archy," they note in rehashing the forty-second president's famous indis-cretion. "It became plausible to think that moral disgust was a politically serious enough response to warrant the president's impeachment."⁵⁷ From Berlant and Duggan's point of view, which rejects the "conservative notions of sexual normalcy and propriety taken for granted in the public sphere,"⁵⁸ JFK might appear not so much a lecher as a harbinger of an affirmatively deviant *jouissance*. This louche and Dionysian Kennedy is no doubt prefer-able to the tormented sex addict who slinks through the reproachful pages of Hersh's *Dark Side of Camelot*.

Whereas JFK may now be ripe for a revisionist sex-positivity, Jackie has long proved to be a cherished object of camp affection, sex-positivity's boon companion. For the camp aficionado, Jackie's homemaking is a transparent charade, "a role whose hollowness and constriction," according to Wayne Koestenbaum, "she could not deny."⁵⁹ Left cold by the myth of her wifely decorum ("Jackie's wife persona was," if anything, an exercise in "*defamil-iarization*" [110]), Koestenbaum instead commemorates "a perverse Jackie" (14), a "spy on a dangerous mission" (24), "Jackie-as-dandy" (182). *Jackie under My Skin* records Koestenbaum's fathomless transference onto the late First Lady and his discovery in her of an equally oceanic reservoir of chal-lenges to the status quo. One the one hand, "she can function as a subversive figure (an instrument of longings we can't name)," and, on the other hand, "by refusing to behave like an ordinary 1950s political wife, she subtly broadcasts shifts in female protocol and possibility" (17). The gnomic poli-tesse with which she telegraphed such cues is a testament as much to Jackie's sphinxlike reticence as to the more or less *closeted* affinity she had with those venturesome women and gay men over whom she "continues to hold sway" (18). Those groups feel especially hailed by her because, equipped with the subaltern's X-ray vision – the heightened alertness demanded by a world that does not guarantee their safety – they can unfold the subtext beneath the surface of her glittering life. "Jackie was a show," Koestenbaum writes, "but its plot was buried" (19). Her "palpably ungenuine" persona (52), he suggests, not only "awoke longing for a different life" (19) but also lighted the way for her "constituency" (60). If we embrace artifice with "her superior sense of irony" (54), her refusal to be "held accountable to one identity" can be ours, too (24).

The problem with these sorts of readings is that – even as they pay heed to a politically desirable alterity, a more commodious libidinal economy, or a radical performativity – their authors rely in the final reckoning on an ideal of *relatability*, an ideal that ranks the acknowledgment of personal identity among the chief ends of social justice. Where the half-ironic title of Berlant and Duggan's book insists on the political urgency of identification (*Our Monica, Ourselves*), Koestenbaum's title, *Jackie under My Skin*, is a cheeky reclamation of the old canard about male homosexuals as women trapped in men's bodies. These are very knowing forms of identity politics, but their sophistication should not blind us to their devout commitment to the politics of recognition as such. It is not news that this is the default politics of our culture, the shape that liberalism has taken since approximately 1960. That JFK "gave public expression to the private thoughts of millions,"[60] as Rorabaugh puts it, is the go-to cliché in virtually every account of his presidency. His gift for relatability, for forcing recognition to the front lines of consciousness, was inseparable from the fact that he presented himself as a kind of universal *relative*. "It makes perfect sense that most Americans told pollsters in the wake of November 22," Sabato writes, "that they were grieving as though they had lost a member of their own family."[61] If one of the lasting bequests of the Cold War consensus was the "effort to create a home that would fulfill virtually all its members' personal needs through an energized and expressive personal life,"[62] as Elaine Tyler May puts it, we might locate the epicenter of this project in the Kennedy White House. And while the nuclear family has obviously gone in and out of ideological fashion since the early 1960s, the political value accorded to an "expressive personal life," or of giving "public expression to private thoughts," has remained remarkably stable.

To the extent that it means to trivialize its accomplishments, then, the frequently bruited charge that the Kennedy administration represented "the triumph of style over substance" neglects how profoundly motivating the Kennedy style turned out to be.[63] Out of the reach of millions (precisely because it was funded by the family millions), JFK's style nonetheless found countless aspirants in the "new generation" to which he passed the torch in his celebrated inaugural address. For the New Left practitioners of what Douglas Rossinow calls "the politics of authenticity," after all, style was the cornerstone of a politically substantive program. "The 'problem of ourselves,'" according to one student activist, "was the problem of what perspective, vision, effort, and courage we can call forth to embody competence and authentic style."[64] This mission statement could easily have been scripted by Ted Sorensen or Arthur Schlesinger Jr., both of whom understood – long before it became a motto of the women's movement – that the personal is political.

In the wake of second wave feminism's decisive critique of patriarchy, the family might seem the last place one might expect to find oneself. But as May argues, far from repressing subjectivity, the midcentury family offered up self-expression as a live possibility. That the family confined persons (particularly women) in predefined roles is not in doubt; but the discontent to which such confinement led was a consequence of the family's double-binding insistence that personal identity should be fulfilling. This point was hardly lost on *los hijos de Kennedy*, who rejected the suburban lifestyle of their parents not because it was antithetical to expressive authenticity but because it was an insufficient guarantor of it. In his brilliantly jaundiced account of JFK and his brothers, Garry Wills depicts the Kennedy family as a scene of "imprisonment" (it features in the title of his book). Yet this description is one-sided. For it is hardly the case that JFK sought to escape either his family of origin or the family of his own making. Indeed, far from confining him, the family afforded the thirty-fifth president almost boundless opportunities for personal discovery (writer, statesman, sexual Olympian). The form of life we inhabit by contrast, infused with the Kennedy family's still captivating example, is one in which self-expression has become a mandatory life sentence.

NOTES

1   F. Scott Fitzgerald, *The Great Gatsby* (New York: Scribner, 1925), 3.
2   Cited in Leonard Levitt, *Conviction: Solving the Moxley Murder: A Reporter and Detective's Twenty-Year Search for Justice* (New York: William Morrow, 2013), 238.
3   Garry Wills, *The Kennedy Imprisonment: A Meditation on Power* (1981; repr., New York: Mariner, 2002), 73.
4   Ibid., 295.
5   Ted Sorensen, *Kennedy* (1965; repr., New York: HarperCollins, 2009), 36.
6   Victor Navasky, *Kennedy Justice* (New York: Harper and Row, 1971), 391.
7   Sorensen, *Kennedy*, 35.
8   Harold Martin, "The Amazing Kennedys," *Saturday Evening Post*, September 7, 1957, 44–50, 50.
9   Kenny O'Donnell and Dave Powers, *"Johnny We Hardly Knew Ye": Memories of John Fitzgerald Kennedy* (Boston: Little, Brown, 1972), 72.
10 Sorensen, *Kennedy*, 20.
11 Arthur M. Schlesinger Jr., *A Thousand Days: John F. Kennedy in the White House* (1965, repr., Boston: Houghton Mifflin, 2002), 115.
12 Sorensen, *Kennedy*, 4.
13 O'Donnell and Powers, *"Johnny We Hardly Knew Ye,"* 59.
14 Schlesinger Jr., *A Thousand Days*, 115.
15 David Riesman, "Some Observations on Changes in Leisure Attitudes," *Antioch Review* 12, no. 4 (1952): 418.
16 Schlesinger Jr., *A Thousand Days*, 91.
17 Theodore White, *The Making of the President 1960* (1961; repr., New York: HarperCollins, 2009), 291.
18 Ibid., 326.
19 Philip Fisher, *Still the New World: American Literature in a Culture of Creative Destruction* (Cambridge, MA: Harvard University Press, 1999), 121.

20 Ibid., 132.
21 Wills, *The Kennedy Imprisonment*, 295, 48.
22 Schlesinger Jr., *A Thousand Days*, 352.
23 W. J. Rorabaugh, *Kennedy and the Promise of the Sixties* (Cambridge: Cambridge University Press, 2002), 130.
24 Ibid., 129.
25 Betty Friedan, *The Feminine Mystique* (1963; repr., New York: W. W. Norton, 2001), 222.
26 Lizabeth Cohen, *A Consumers' Republic: The Politics of Mass Consumption in Postwar America* (New York: Vintage, 2003), 127.
27 Friedan, *The Feminine Mystique*, 223.
28 Rorabaugh, *Kennedy and the Promise of the Sixties*, 132.
29 Cohen, *A Consumers' Republic*, 127.
30 Elaine Tyler May, *Homeward Bound: American Families in the Cold War Era* (New York: Basic Books, 1988), 16.
31 White, *The Making of the President 1960*, 288.
32 Larry J. Sabato, *The Kennedy Half-Century: The Presidency, Assassination, and Lasting Legacy of John F. Kennedy* (New York: Bloomsbury, 2013), 254.
33 May, *Homeward Bound*, 195.
34 Sorensen, *Kennedy*, 383.
35 Schlesinger Jr., *A Thousand Days*, 74.
36 Ralph LaRossa, *The Modernization of Fatherhood: A Social and Political History* (Chicago: University of Chicago Press, 1997), 198.
37 Herbert Parmet, *Jack: The Struggles of John F. Kennedy* (New York: Dial P, 1980), 13.
38 Ibid., 15.
39 LaRossa, *The Modernization of Fatherhood*, 198.
40 Sorensen, *Kennedy*, 397.
41 LaRossa, *The Modernization of Fatherhood*, 200.
42 Sorensen, *Kennedy*, 328.
43 David Halberstam, *The Best and the Brightest* (1972; repr., New York: Modern Library, 2002), 64.
44 Cited in Schlesinger Jr., *A Thousand Days*, 60.
45 Pierre Salinger, *With Kennedy* (Garden City: Doubleday, 1966), 31.
46 John Leonard, *Smoke and Mirrors: Violence, Television, and Other American Cultures* (New York: New Press, 1997), 16.
47 Daniel Boorstin, *The Image: A Guide to Pseudo-Events in America* (1962; repr., New York: Vintage, 2012), 23.
48 Ibid., 3.
49 Ibid., 45.
50 Ibid., 28.
51 Stanley Meisler, *When the World Calls: The Inside Story of the Peace Corps and Its First Fifty Years* (Boston: Beacon Press, 2011), 11.
52 Parmet, *Jack*, xvi.
53 Joanne Meyerowitz, "Beyond the Feminine Mystique: A Reassessment of Postwar Mass Culture, 1946–1958," in *Not June Cleaver: Women and Gender in Postwar America 1945–1960*, ed. Joanne Meyerowitz (Philadelphia: Temple University Press, 1994), 237.

54 Ibid., 250.
55 Seymour Hersh, *The Dark Side of Camelot* (New York: Little, Brown, 1997), 240.
56 Ibid.
57 Lauren Berlant and Lisa Duggan, eds., *Our Monica, Ourselves: The Clinton Affair and the National Interest* (New York: New York University Press, 2001), 2.
58 Ibid.
59 Wayne Koestenbaum, *Jackie under My Skin: Interpreting an Icon* (New York: Farrar, Straus, and Giroux, 1995), 110. Subsequent references to this edition are cited in parentheses in the text.
60 Rorabaugh, *Kennedy and the Promise of the Sixties*, 215.
61 Sabato, *The Kennedy Half-Century*, 254.
62 May, *Homeward Bound*, xvii.
63 Schlesinger Jr., *A Thousand Days*, x.
64 Cited in Douglas Rossinow, *The Politics of Authenticity: Liberalism, Christianity, and the New Left in America* (New York: Columbia University Press, 1998), 68.

15

ROBERT MASON

Kennedy and the Conservatives

Ronald Reagan watched the 1960 Democratic National Convention with alarm. The idealistic liberalism of John F. Kennedy's acceptance speech struck the actor as not only wrongheaded but dangerously corrosive of American political values. "Under the tousled boyish haircut it is still old Karl Marx – first launched a century ago," he wrote to Richard Nixon, Kennedy's Republican opponent for the White House. "There is nothing new in the idea of a government being Big Brother to us all." Against this programmatic activism, Reagan insisted to Nixon, an emphasis on conservatism was an electoral winner. He told the vice president of widespread enthusiasm for the economically conservative ideas that he promoted in traveling the country as a spokesperson for General Electric.[1] This conservative commitment aligned Reagan with a significant political trend of the Kennedy era. Often understood as a golden age for American liberalism, the Kennedy administration was also a moment of revitalization on the right. Writing in 1972, William Rusher, publisher of *National Review* and a leading figure in the effort to draft Barry Goldwater as Republican presidential candidate during those years, observed, "In the administration of John Kennedy, the American conservative movement grew from the fancy of a coterie to a national force."[2]

And yet in the 1980s Reagan would align his political vision with that of Kennedy on economics and on foreign policy, and he advanced the argument that his presidency pursued Kennedy's political principles more faithfully than did contemporary Democrats. Kennedy's enduring and outstanding popularity encouraged conservative politicians to join liberals in claiming his legacy. To do so made a comment on the political flux that the United States experienced in the post-Kennedy years, which had sowed division among Democrats, boosted the electoral popularity of Republicans and conservatism, and – by the late 1980s – rendered the once-winning tag of liberalism a political epithet (the "'L' word"). Writing in 2007, James Piereson of the Manhattan Institute even posited a direct connection between Kennedy's assassination and the transformation of American liberalism, arguing that Kennedy's death fostered pessimism in place of optimism among liberals, encouraging an angry radicalism that left them at odds with majority opinion.[3]

Reagan's characterization of Kennedy as a dangerous radical in 1960 was not one that many shared. Other contemporaries saw him as offering a break from the Eisenhower years that was more rhetorical than real. Many saw his agenda in the 1960 campaign as differing in detail but not in broad approach from that of Richard Nixon on the Republican side; in the mid-1970s Godfrey Hodgson wrote of "the ideology of the liberal consensus" that involved much common ground across the political spectrum, a consensus that would break down during the Johnson years.[4] The narrowness of Kennedy's victory over Nixon, moreover, sapped his administration's capacity to pursue a liberal agenda, because the president lacked a strong mandate and because the "conservative coalition" of southern Democrats and Republicans on Capitol Hill remained powerful. Rusher watched with approval, noting that "while Kennedy's pace toward perdition may be 10% faster than Nixon's would have been, the opposition (thanks to the conservative coalition in this much-improved new Congress) will be about 100% more effective."[5] Kennedy's own political outlook, finally, was complex, which "enabled others to find in him what qualities they wanted," as Arthur Schlesinger observed in *A Thousand Days*. "They could choose one side of him or the other and claim him, according to taste, as a conservative, because of his sober sense of the frailty of man, the power of institutions and the frustrations of history, or as a progressive, because of his vigorous confidence in reason, action and the future."[6]

The conservative revitalization that took place during the early 1960s was responsive to the Kennedy agenda only in part; it was also the product of conservatism's internal dynamics. In particular, the narrowness of Nixon's loss to Kennedy ignited soul-searching inquiry within the Republican Party, an institution by then frustratingly consigned to minority status in two-party competition against the Democrats for the three decades since the arrival of the Great Depression; the failure of the Eisenhower administration to boost the party's fortunes had deepened these divisive frustrations.[7] The Republican National Committee's analysis of the Nixon defeat pinpointed electoral weakness in the cities and suburbs as critical.[8] The result was an official investigation into the party's big-city problem, which – seeking to avoid factional conflict – adopted an ideologically neutral position in emphasizing the Republicans' lack of organizational capacity. The party, according to Ray Bliss, who chaired the investigation, was "out-manned, out-organized, out-spent and out-worked" in most urban areas.[9] For Connecticut activist

L. Patrick Gray, this situation was so acute that, absent any revival, "JFK stands a good chance of presiding over the demise of the two party system."[10] Some in the party, supporters of a moderate or progressive path, insisted that Kennedy liberalism increased the need for a Republican version of activist government. Kennedy was successful in identifying problems for government to tackle, they argued, but his remedies were unsuccessful – creating an opportunity for GOP progress at the polls. Kennedy's approach to government "does increase federal power," stated *Advance*, a journal of moderate Republicans, in fall 1963. "But it does little else except dole out money under the auspices of the Democratic administration."[11]

More powerful than the moderate Republican response to Kennedy was the conservative resurgence in which both Reagan and Rusher took part. The focus of an unsuccessful draft movement in opposition to Nixon for the 1960 nomination, the movement's standard-bearer, Senator Barry Goldwater of Arizona, soon found himself the beneficiary of a new effort to capture the Republican nomination for the conservative cause. In early 1961, at a Young Americans for Freedom rally, Goldwater boldly confronted the long-standing characterization of conservatism as purely negative and oppositional, charging Kennedy liberalism instead with being obsolete: "America can ill-afford government by men who live in the political past – who would apply the out-moded and discredited programs of the 1930's to the problems of the 1960's."[12] Goldwater had on his side not only activist enthusiasms and a commitment to conservative principle but also an argument about electoral strategy. While Republican moderates insisted that effective opposition to Kennedy depended on support for many of his goals but criticism of the administration's ineffectiveness in achieving them, conservatives argued that only a more fundamental attack on the Democrats' agenda promised victory. Outlining such a view in *National Review* in early 1963, Rusher argued that Kennedy was vulnerable in the South, where a conservative appeal could gain new support for the GOP. "The Republican Party, like it or not, has a rendezvous with a brand new idea," wrote Rusher.[13] Controversy surrounded this new idea of a "southern strategy" for Republican revitalization, because it seemed to reach out to segregationists among southern Democrats. Its advocates denied the connection with race, but opposition to Kennedy on civil rights seemed crucial to discontent toward the Democratic Party among southern whites.[14]

Goldwater looked forward to the prospect of a contest against Kennedy, with whom he was on friendly terms; it was a prospect also welcomed by Kennedy, sure that reelection was likely over a challenger who emphasized conservatism.[15] "I won't even have to leave the Oval Office," he joked to strategists.[16] Some on the conservative side would continue to question the president's prospects against a Goldwater challenge – suspecting that the assassination and Kennedy's replacement by Johnson crucially undermined their candidate's chances, consigning him to defeat by overwhelming landslide. For Goldwater, Americans had no appetite to contemplate a further change at the White House.[17] And he anticipated that Kennedy would have engaged in direct debate, which Johnson sidestepped – a debate that would have permitted him to mobilize new support for conservatism. "I felt that I had a fair to middling change of defeating him," he said in 1965. "I wouldn't have bet a lot of money on it."[18]

The Kennedy years not only helped to mobilize a new brand of conservatism within the Republican Party but also witnessed the zenith of extra-party organization in favor of a more extreme brand of conservatism that contemporaries tagged "the radical right" – a movement encompassing a variety of individuals and groups, most famously Robert Welch's John Birch Society. Summarizing this "radical right" as "[viewing] the Nation as imperiled on every front by a pro-Communist conspiracy" – a perspective that saw Kennedy as an inadequate adversary against that peril – aide Myer Feldman advised the president in the summer of 1963 that these organizations "[constitute] a formidable force in American life today." They claimed the support of several thousand Americans, and in some areas connections existed between the John Birch Society and local Republicans.[19] Alongside concern at the White House about the phenomenon of extreme conservatism in American society, however, existed the perception of electoral opportunity – the belief that the prospects for Kennedy liberalism were stronger if its opponents were tainted by connections with extremism.[20] Such was the conclusion of Wyoming Senator Gale McGee, who advised, "The right-wing problem may well turn out to be a/or the winning issue for 1964."[21]

During the Kennedy years, Goldwater saw the administration as wrongheaded, inept, and even perilous. The new enthusiasm for conservatism that he observed among young people, he noted in his diary, reflected "an awareness of the dangers of the New Frontier and uneasiness over JFK's very apparent inability to lead."[22] But the passage of time, and of political change, amended his judgment. In his 1988 memoirs, Goldwater defined Kennedy as a pragmatist rather than a Democrat, as a politician cynical about the liberalism that he promoted – indeed, as a conservative by personal conviction.[23]

Goldwater was by no means alone among Reagan era conservatives in claiming Kennedy as one of their own. Most prominently, Ronald Reagan's reelection bid in 1984 put forward the claim that the Republican Party now represented Kennedy's political ideas more faithfully than did the Democrats. Building on this claim, George Gilder – famous for his promotion of "supply-side economics" – even called for a Reagan victory against his opponent Walter Mondale as a way to achieve Kennedy's unrealized promise as president. Reagan's first-term achievements in the White House, Gilder wrote, "comprise in large part the belated fulfillment of the legacy of the young Democrat whom Reagan bitterly opposed," representing the renewal of "the Kennedy promise of rapid investment-led growth, replete with new technologies, declining energy prices, low inflation and an upsurge of entrepreneurship."[24]

It took time for conservatives to embrace Kennedy as a political inspiration in this way. In a 1971 speech to the Young Americans for Freedom convention, for example, Reagan characterized the Kennedy administration as a failure in both economic and foreign policy.[25] For President Richard Nixon, the memory of his erstwhile rival was important; he saw Kennedy's record as a yardstick by which he could measure his own success, but usually in ways that involved style rather than substance. "Nixon's standard as a modern President, conscious or not, was John F. Kennedy," wrote William Safire, a Nixon aide.[26] Nixon's was a perspective shaped by envy, because he saw himself as the victim of hostile press coverage sharply different from media treatment of Kennedy.[27] He told aides that JFK "did nothing but appeared great; LBJ did everything and appeared terrible," his chief of staff H. R. Haldeman noted.[28] For Nixon, a president anyway obsessed by PR, the example of the Kennedy administration acted as a spur to devote greater attention to image and the press; he did not dwell on potential parallels between his policies and Kennedy's.[29] Kennedy "was colder, more ruthless, etc., than [Nixon] is, but look at his PR," Nixon observed, according to Haldeman's diary. "He came through as the warm, human guy, sponsoring the arts, loving his family, and all that kind of stuff."[30] In early 1973, preparing for his second term, Nixon read with interest journalist Henry Fairlie's *The Kennedy Promise*, which supported his interpretation of Kennedy as weak in achievement but strong on image.[31] Soon afterward, Nixon read with fascination Malcolm Smith's 1968 self-published book, *Kennedy's 13 Great Mistakes in the White House*, which had been withdrawn from sale after Robert F. Kennedy's assassination. Nixon observed, in Haldeman's words, "that Kennedy blew practically everything and still got the credit for it."[32]

The presence in national politics of Senator Edward M. Kennedy of Massachusetts – popular and ambitious, feared by Nixon as a potential rival for the presidency – also complicated any Republican or conservative embrace of JFK's political legacy. Nixon, moreover, identified JFK with a hostile liberal establishment; he defined his political goals as a challenge to and an attack on that elite.[33] Yet it was during the Nixon administration that Republicans began the effort to assert connections between their agenda and that of Kennedy – though usually in the more general context of Democrats' record in the White House. Electoral politics provided the motivation. The travails of liberalism by the end of the 1960s, and divisions within the Democratic Party, created new opportunities for the Republican Party, most famously projected by political analyst Kevin P. Phillips as "the emerging Republican majority."[34] As president, Nixon undertook serious efforts in pursuit of these opportunities. In 1972 he sought the support of a "new American majority" that included disaffected Democrats, making the claim that he represented their party's traditional principles more faithfully than did George McGovern, his opponent for the White House. The key element of this claim involved foreign policy. Nixon criticized McGovern on the Vietnam War, and he defended his own policy as situated within a Cold War mainstream.[35] Nixon's acceptance speech discussed a bipartisan commitment to a strong defense and against isolationism, as demonstrated by presidents from Franklin Roosevelt to Lyndon Johnson, and he called on Democrats to "come home" to the "great principles we Americans believe in together."[36] The subsequent campaign developed the theme of a contrast, especially on foreign policy, between McGovern and the Democratic tradition.[37] Most explicitly, and most forcefully, John Connally – who had served both Kennedy, as secretary of the navy, and Nixon, as secretary of the treasury, and was then leading "Democrats for Nixon" – declared that Kennedy "never for a moment advocated retreat, surrender or a weakened America."[38]

Soon after McGovern's landslide defeat, some of his intraparty opponents launched the Coalition for a Democratic Majority (CDM), branding that defeat "a clear signal to the Democratic Party to return to the real tradition through which it had come to represent the wishes and hopes of a majority of the American people – the tradition of Franklin D. Roosevelt, Harry S Truman, Adlai Stevenson, John F. Kennedy, Lyndon B. Johnson, and Hubert H. Humphrey."[39] This disaffection with "New Politics" Democrats informed a strand of neoconservatism critical of contemporary liberalism.[40] For many neoconservatives of this kind, Kennedy provided a particularly important model, a comparator for intraparty change. According to Norman Podhoretz, *Commentary*'s longtime editor in chief, by 1976 "[Senator Edward M. Kennedy's] policies both on the cold war and on the economy deviated by 180 degrees from those that had been pushed by his older brother John F. Kennedy fifteen years earlier."[41] Edward Kennedy's political presence was at this point starting to inform the conservative embrace of JFK, rather than complicating it. Most neoconservatives of this early generation had started as liberal anticommunists in the mold of Kennedy; as their liberalism died away, their anticommunism remained intense.[42] In many cases, so did their admiration for Kennedy, whom Ben J. Wattenberg – a CDM founder and a former aide to Lyndon Johnson, Hubert Humphrey, and Henry "Scoop" Jackson – defined as "an anti-Communist hawk with some neo-con tendencies."[43] Influentially defining American foreign policy in terms of values rather than power, in the 1980s Charles Krauthammer exemplified this trend by quoting Kennedy's statement of America's main goal as not just security but also "the success of liberty."[44]

On foreign policy, Kennedy's Cold War record was symbolic of a bipartisan tradition that now faced challenges within the Democratic Party; during the late 1970s his economic record – especially the tax cut that he proposed and Johnson implemented – became a key argument in support of "supply-side economics," which emerged as an important conservative and Republican response to the decade's economic travails and what conservatives described as the redundant ideas of Keynesianism. Kennedy was no supply-sider. Indeed, his proposal rested on a Keynesian belief about the economic stimulus of a deficit in creating demand, whereas 1970s conservatives advocated tax reduction to spur investment. Often supply-siders – Jude Wanniski, for example, in *The Way the World Works* – acknowledged that he was not one of them, even as they construed his tax cut's impact as a powerful argument for their case.[45] Other conservatives, however, more directly asserted that Kennedy's approach to the economy was friendly to business investment and fiscally cautious, and therefore closer to that of contemporary Republicans than that of Democrats.[46] And in practice the parallels encouraged the perception that the thinking behind Kennedy's policies and those of the supply-siders was essentially the same.[47] Conservatives of the "New Right" memorably quoted Kennedy's statement that "a rising tide lifts all boats" (an expression of his confidence in economic growth to tackle inequality and deprivation) to align their rationale for tax reduction with his.[48] In 1980, for example, Representative Jack Kemp (New York) used the quotation to posit agreement between Kennedy and Reagan.[49]

As presidential aspirant and then as president, Reagan deployed this parallel in support of his agenda. In November 1978, he devoted a piece of radio commentary to the Kemp-Roth plan for supply-side tax reduction, supporting the plan by arguing that the Kennedy tax cut had created "the longest, sustained, economic expansion in the history of our country."[50] During the 1980 primaries, the Reagan campaign ran a television commercial asserting the connection between Reagan and Kennedy; Frank Donatelli, who ran the Wisconsin campaign, credited the ad with victory in his state.[51] As president, Reagan drew a parallel between his tax-reduction project and the Kennedy tax cut; he also used a comparison with the Kennedy budget in support of his administration's levels of defense spending.[52]

In analyzing the political memory of the 1960s, historian Bernard von Bothmer argues that Republicans from Reagan to George W. Bush enjoyed success in encouraging a popular distinction between the "good" 1960s, associated with Kennedy and such achievements as progress on civil rights, and the "bad" 1960s – the years of political division, of social tumult and cultural upheaval, that increasingly characterized that decade after Kennedy.[53] This distinction partly rested on the popularization of the assertion that Kennedy's economic and foreign policies aligned him with the Republican cause, rather than that of contemporary Democrats. According to Paul Weyrich – who played a leading role in helping to build conservatism in the 1970s and beyond via organizations such as the Heritage Foundation and the Moral Majority – Kennedy was both "a supply-sider" and "a rabid anticommunist."[54] And Michael Deaver, a close aide to Reagan, asserted that "Kennedy was much more a Republican than he was a Democrat."[55] This affiliation with Kennedy possessed electoral promise because of the outstanding popularity, revealed by opinion polls, that he continued to enjoy among Americans, including those who identified with the Republican Party.[56] There was real admiration, too, for Kennedy within the Reagan White House – especially among younger aides who saw his idealism and commitment to public service as a formative inspiration.[57] Although these Kennedy-conservatism parallels were politically powerful, their advocates were not confined to the arena of practical politics. For example, in his study of Ronald Reagan, intellectual historian John Patrick Diggins writes of similarities between Reagan and Kennedy on foreign policy and on economic policy, although in proposing these similarities Diggins does not assert that Kennedy was a neoconservative supply-sider.[58]

Throughout his political career, Reagan – earlier in his life a Democrat and a supporter of the New Deal – had attacked his pre-1962 party for its liberalizing direction. "I didn't leave the Democratic Party," he liked to say. "The Democratic Party left me."[59] Before 1981, Franklin Roosevelt was Reagan's favored Democrat; as president, Reagan – who chose JFK's old desk for the Oval Office – quoted Kennedy more than any other president.[60] Reagan discussed Kennedy most extensively at a fund-raising event hosted by the Kennedy family for the John F. Kennedy Library Foundation in June 1985, dwelling glowingly on the personal strengths that made Kennedy a successful leader.[61] It had been during the previous year, however, when Reagan was seeking reelection, that Republican forces deployed Kennedy's memory most frequently, and Reagan's own references to JFK reached a peak. The goal was outreach to "Reagan Democrats," via assertions that leftward change left the Democratic Party unresponsive to traditional constituencies. In her keynote at the national convention, Katherine Davalos Ortega spoke of "two Democratic parties": on the one hand, "Democrats of the mainstream . . . in the tradition of Harry Truman and John F. Kennedy"; on the other, "the party of special interests, the party of doomsayers, the party of demagogues who look to America's future with fear, not hope." Because the latter group now dominated the Democratic leadership, the former group formed a potential constituency for Reagan, Ortega argued.[62] As Ortega's comments suggest, the case made by Republicans in search of support among Reagan Democrats by no means rested solely on the appropriation of Kennedy's legacy.[63] "They're claiming the names of all Democrats – but they have to be dead," Walter Mondale said.[64] Yet Kennedy possessed special power among the younger and independent voters targeted by Republicans. For younger Americans, Kennedy was "an historic figure" and "almost a myth," Reagan campaign manager Edward J. Rollins said. "His tax cuts and strong defense echo the Reagan program."[65]

It was at the height of the 1984 campaign, during which Ronald Reagan was drawing parallels between his agenda and the Kennedy record, that his 1960 letter to Richard Nixon was released following its discovery by a researcher at the National Archives. That letter drew parallels not only between Kennedy and Karl Marx, but also between JFK and Adolf Hitler (as another proponent of a "Big Brother" approach to government, "who called his 'State Socialism'"). In his defense, Reagan's spokesperson said that Reagan had been "pleasantly surprised to find the difference between Kennedy the candidate and Kennedy the President."[66] And Reagan himself noted that the letter was an effort to explain his small-government philosophy. On the attack, Mondale said that it revealed his true opinion, "which is when government helps people, it moves us inevitably on the road to dictatorship."[67] For a while, Reagan omitted references to Kennedy in campaign appearances, but he returned to the theme forcefully in his final swing.[68] Citing Kennedy's tax cuts as sources of economic growth and prosperity, Reagan's election-eve address attacked the Mondale-Ferraro ticket as "not in the tradition of President Kennedy and his predecessors, Truman and Roosevelt. Their policies never sent out an S.O.S. They proudly proclaimed U.S.A.!"[69]

By no means all conservatives joined the embrace of Kennedy as a lost brother-in-arms. Describing "a conservative cult of Jack Kennedy" that had developed by the 1980s, *National Review* remained unimpressed by the politician whose presidency had helped to incite an upsurge of conservative activism: "True enough, the liberalism of JFK was a lot better than the liberalism of [Michael] Dukakis, or Jesse Jackson. That's not saying much. The 25-year-old variety was bad enough."[70] A decade later, rating the presidents for the same magazine, historian Walter A. McDougall classified Kennedy as "Below Average," offering some praise for his tax cut but characterizing his foreign policy as "awful." "He was mostly show, not substance," McDougall wrote, "and what substance there was either failed (civil-rights bill) or did harm ('Pay any price, bear any burden . . .')."[71] And by no means did Democrats give up Kennedy as an icon of political inspiration. At the end of the Reagan years, in 1988, most Democratic contenders for the presidential nomination positioned themselves in Kennedy's shadow.[72] Most notably, in the 1990s Bill Clinton reasserted Democratic ownership of the Kennedy legacy. No president tried to walk in JFK's shadow more enthusiastically than Clinton; Clinton sought to forge a connection with Kennedy's idealism both to revitalize his own party and to wrest political momentum from the Republicans.[73]

Despite the Clinton project, however, conservative identification with JFK was strong enough to survive. When the Republican agenda again involved tax reductions, and when interparty argument returned to notions of a strong defense, once more Republicans made use of Kennedy to advance their case. Advocates of George W. Bush's proposals to cut taxes deployed Kennedy in their support. Television ads featured footage of Kennedy speaking in favor of his tax-reduction proposal. The tactic ignited opposition among the Kennedy family; Edward Kennedy and Caroline Kennedy denied the parallel on the grounds that the Bush proposal was unfair and irresponsible – tilted to benefit the rich and likely to feed the deficit.[74] Yet tax reduction barely informed the conclusion of columnist Andrew Sullivan in 2004 that Bush was "a Kennedy-style Democrat." The boldness of the military interventions in Iraq and Afghanistan was one factor within Sullivan's analysis, but another was rooted in domestic policy – agricultural subsidies, protectionist tariffs, the expansion of Medicare.[75] Bush's first-term record led computer scientist David Gelernter toward a not dissimilar view. He argued that "in terms of policy and worldview, John F. Kennedy and George W. Bush are practically identical, as close to equivalent as two presidents can be across a forty-year span." The domestic parallel involved not only tax cuts but also an expanded role for the federal government in education and welfare, though both "don't want to spend too much money on it (or say they don't)." According to Gelernter, what united them most of all was "an activist foreign policy, the goal of which is to protect the United States and fight totalitarian tyranny; to speak up, stand up, and fight for American ideals all over the world."[76] In positing similarities between Kennedy's approach to the Cold War and Bush's approach to the "War on Terror," conservatives sometimes mentioned religion – a new parallel to support and inform their identification with JFK. "The real JFK," wrote Noemie Emery of the *Weekly Standard*, "was an American exceptionalist, who sometimes invoked God in discussing the national mission, and who saw American power as a beneficent force."[77]

Fifty years after the assassination of John F. Kennedy, the extent of his liberalism remained the subject of lively discussion. Among the flurry of new books on Kennedy published in 2013 was journalist Ira Stoll's *JFK, Conservative*. Stoll's work offers perhaps the fullest account of Kennedy's career through the conservatism paradigm, underscoring the importance of religion in informing his political agenda.[78] The book's publication ensured that on the anniversary that paradigm achieved widespread comment.[79] On radio, some of the most strident, controversy-seeking voices against liberalism joined in. Rush Limbaugh said that Kennedy "was not in any way a liberal as you know liberals today," while Glenn Beck argued that "he wouldn't be accepted by the Republican Party because he would be a Tea Party radical."[80] Barack Obama sometimes connected his political agenda with the legacy of JFK (if more loosely than Bill Clinton had done); securing the endorsement of Ted Kennedy and Caroline Kennedy Schlossberg in early 2008, he said, "I think my own sense of what's possible in this country comes in part from what [my grandparents and mother] said America was like in the days of John and Robert Kennedy."[81] Yet conservatives remained skeptical about such parallels, sometimes using Obama's record on economic policy and foreign policy instead to reassert the claim that contemporary Democrats followed a path that little resembled Kennedy's.[82]

Opposition to Kennedy as president, then, helped to inspire the modern conservative movement. Paradoxically, when that movement achieved power via the Republican Party, leading conservatives claimed JFK as a positive exemplar of their political concerns. Republican electoral efforts looked to support from former Democratic loyalists, and the political memory of no leading Democrat was as powerful as Kennedy's; his enduring appeal extended across the political spectrum. Especially when the conservative agenda edged toward controversy – on tax cuts for the wealthy, on increases in defense spending, on the "War on Terror" – the Kennedy parallel was irresistible. But for many conservatives the parallel was politically real as well as attractive, and they found evidence in the Kennedy record to advance their case.

NOTES

1 Letter, Ronald Reagan to Richard Nixon, July 15, 1960, in Kiron K. Skinner, Annelise Anderson, and Martin Anderson, eds., *Reagan: A Life in Letters* (New York: Free Press, 2003), 704.
2 William A. Rusher, *The Rise of the Right* (New York: William Morrow, 1984), 249.
3 James Piereson, *Camelot and the Cultural Revolution: How the Assassination of John F. Kennedy Shattered American Liberalism* (New York: Encounter, 2007).
4 Godfrey Hodgson, *America in Our Time* (Garden City, NY: Doubleday, 1976).
5 Letter, William A. Rusher to Christopher T. Bayley, November 21, 1960, folder 9, box 10, William A. Rusher Papers, Manuscript Division, Library of Congress, Washington, DC.
6 Arthur M. Schlesinger Jr., *A Thousand Days: John F. Kennedy in the White House* (Boston: Houghton Mifflin, 1965), 112.
7 Robert Mason, *The Republican Party and American Politics from Hoover to Reagan* (New York: Cambridge University Press, 2012), 148–83.
8 RNC Research Division, "Preliminary Analysis of the 1960 Presidential Vote," November 23, 1960, "Progressive Republicans, 1960" folder, box 36, subseries 2, series 5, Jacob K. Javits Collection, Special Collections and University Archives, Stony Brook University Libraries, Stony Brook, New York.
9 Transcript, "Oklahoma City Presentation of Big City Politics Report," January 12, 1962, "Moderate Republicans" folder, box 36, subseries 2, series 5, Javits Collection.
10 Letter, L. Patrick Gray III to Richard Nixon, April 8, 1962, "Gray, Louis P. III" folder, box 301, series 320, Richard M. Nixon Pre-Presidential Papers, Richard Nixon Presidential Library and Museum, Yorba Linda, California.
11 "Kennedy Can Lose," *Advance* 2:5 (Fall 1963): 4–8.
12 Barry Goldwater, speech, March 3, 1961, "Barry Goldwater 1964" folder, box 38, subseries 2, series 5, Javits Collection.
13 William A. Rusher, "Crossroads for the GOP," *National Review*, February 12, 1963, 110.
14 Mason, *Republican Party*, 188–89.
15 John W. Dean and Barry M. Goldwater Jr., *Pure Goldwater* (New York: Palgrave Macmillan, 2008), 135; Robert Alan Goldberg, *Barry Goldwater* (New Haven, CT: Yale University Press, 1995), 177–78.
16 Sean J. Savage, *JFK, LBJ, and the Democratic Party* (Albany: State University of New York Press, 2004), 205.
17 Barry M. Goldwater with Jack Casserley, *Goldwater* (New York: Doubleday, 1988), 150.
18 Barry M. Goldwater oral history interview, January 24, 1965, John F. Kennedy Oral History Collection, John F. Kennedy Presidential Library and Museum, 22, http://www.jfklibrary.org/Asset-Viewer/Archives/JFKOH-BMG-01.aspx, accessed December 18, 2013.
19 Memo, Myer Feldman to the president, August 15, 1963, "Right-wing movement" folder, series 8, President's Office Files, Presidential Papers, Papers of John F. Kennedy, John F. Kennedy Presidential Library and Museum.
20 Jonathan M. Schoenwald, *A Time for Choosing: The Rise of Modern American Conservatism* (New York: Oxford University Press, 2001), 57–64, 96–97.

21 Memo, Gale McGee to Mike Feldman, August 14, 1963, "Right-wing move-
    ment" folder, series 8, President's Office Files, Presidential Papers, Papers of John
    F. Kennedy, John F. Kennedy Presidential Library and Museum.

22 Dean and Goldwater, *Pure Goldwater*, 131.

23 Goldwater with Casserley, *Goldwater*, 139.

24 George Gilder, "Reagan Can Finish What JFK Started," *Washington Post*,
    October 28, 1984, C1.

25 Kiron K. Skinner, Annelise Anderson, and Martin Anderson, eds., *Reagan, in
    His Own Hand: The Writings of Ronald Reagan That Reveal His Revolutionary
    Vision for America* (New York: Free Press, 2001), 450–52.

26 William Safire, *Before the Fall: An Inside View of the Pre-Watergate White
    House* (Garden City, NY: Doubleday, 1975), 152.

27 See, for example, H. R. Haldeman, *The Haldeman Diaries: Inside the Nixon
    White House*, complete multimedia ed. (Santa Monica, CA: Sony Electronic
    Publishing, 1994), May 18, 1969; March 17, 1971.

28 Ibid., February 2, 1970.

29 See, for example, Ibid., May 18, 1969; February 2, 1970; April 14, 1971; June
    9, 1971.

30 Ibid., May 16, 1971.

31 Henry Fairlie, *The Kennedy Promise: The Politics of Expectation* (Garden
    City, NY: Doubleday, 1973); Haldeman, *Haldeman Diaries*, January 13, 1973;
    January 16, 1973; January 27, 1973; and February 9, 1973.

32 Malcolm E. Smith Jr., *Kennedy's 13 Great Mistakes in the White House*
    (New York: National Forum of America, 1968); Haldeman, *Haldeman Diaries*,
    February 28, 1973; March 9, 1973.

33 Haldeman, *Haldeman Diaries*, May 1, 1969; June 23, 1971.

34 Kevin P. Phillips, *The Emerging Republican Majority* (New Rochelle,
    NY: Arlington House, 1969).

35 Robert Mason, *Richard Nixon and the Quest for a New Majority* (Chapel
    Hill: University of North Carolina Press, 2004).

36 Max Frankel, "Nixon Asks for Support for a New Majority after Agnew is
    Renamed as Running Mate," *New York Times*, August 24, 1972, 46.

37 Warren Weaver Jr., "GOP Begins a Drive on TV to Counter Democrats,"
    New York Times, September 22, 1972, 30; Lou Cannon, "Agnew Charges
    McGovern Vow Dishonors U.S.," *Washington Post*, October 10, 1972, A6.

38 Ben A. Franklin, "Rustling the Strays from the Big D Ranch," *New York Times
    Magazine*, October 1, 1972, 14.

39 Jacob Heilbrunn, *They Knew They Were Right: The Rise of the Neocons*
    (New York: Doubleday, 2008), 114.

40 Justin Vaïsse, *Neoconservatism: The Biography of a Movement*, trans. Arthur
    Goldhammer (Cambridge, MA: Belknap, 2010), 8.

41 Norman Podhoretz, *Ex-Friends: Falling Out with Allen Ginsberg, Lionel
    and Diana Trilling, Lillian Hellman, Hannah Arendt, and Norman Mailer*
    (New York: Free Press, 1999), 9.

42 David Farber, *The Rise and Fall of Modern American Conservatism: A Short
    History* (Princeton, NJ: Princeton University Press, 2010), 201.

43 Ben J. Wattenberg, *Fighting Words: A Tale of How Liberals Created
    Neo-Conservatism* (New York: Thomas Dunne, 2008), 216.

44 Heilbrunn, *They Knew They Were Right*, 8.
45 Jude Wanniski, *The Way the World Works: How Economies Fail – and Succeed* (New York: Basic, 1978).
46 See, for example, Warren T. Brookes, "JFK Tax Cut: Recipe for Prosperity?" *Human Events*, May 7, 1977, 8–9.
47 Steven R. Weisman, "What Is a Conservative?" *New York Times Magazine*, August 31, 1980, 32.
48 Mickey Edwards, *Reclaiming Conservatism: How a Great American Political Movement Got Lost – and How It Can Find Its Way Back* (New York: Oxford University Press, 2008), 36.
49 Jack Kemp, "Republicans: A 'Radical' Vision," *Washington Post*, September 23, 1980, A15.
50 Skinner et al., *Reagan, in His Own Hand*, 280.
51 Rowland Evans and Robert Novak, "Reagan, JFK and Taxes," *Washington Post*, April 7, 1980, A25.
52 Skinner et al., *Reagan*, 407, 594, 624.
53 Bernard von Bothmer, *Framing the Sixties: The Use and Abuse of a Decade from Ronald Reagan to George W. Bush* (Amherst: University of Massachusetts Press, 2010).
54 Ibid., 50, 51.
55 Ibid., 48.
56 George Goodwin Rising, "Stuck in the Sixties: Conservatives and the Legacies of the 1960s" (PhD diss., University of Arizona, 2003), 285.
57 Donnie Radcliffe, "One Writer behind Reagan," *Washington Post*, June 26, 1985, F4.
58 John Patrick Diggins, *Ronald Reagan: Fate, Freedom, and the Making of History* (New York: W. W. Norton, 2007), 12, 109, 177–78.
59 Murray Friedman, *The Neoconservative Revolution: Jewish Intellectuals and the Shaping of Public Policy* (Cambridge: Cambridge University Press, 2005), 151.
60 Peggy Noonan, *When Character Was King: A Story of Ronald Reagan* (New York: Penguin, 2002), 162; van Bothmer, *Framing the Sixties*, 47, 52.
61 Ronald Reagan, "Remarks at a Fundraising Reception for the John F. Kennedy Library Foundation," June 24, 1985, *The Public Papers of President Ronald W. Reagan*, Ronald Reagan Presidential Library, http://www.reagan.utexas .edu/archives/speeches/1985/62485d.htm, accessed December 30, 2013; Donnie Radcliffe, "In Tribute to JFK," *Washington Post*, June 25, 1985, C1, C6.
62 "Text of Keynote Speech by Ortega to Delegates," *New York Times*, August 21, 1984, A20.
63 Haynes Johnson, "GOP Adopts Democrats' Themes, If Only to Sway Some Votes," *Washington Post*, August 23, 1984, A8; Meg Greenfield, "Dallas: Forgiving and Forgetting," *Washington Post*, August 27, 1984, A13.
64 Bernard Weinraub, "Reporter's Notebook: On the Hustings as Mondale Fights Back," *New York Times*, September 27, 1984, D23.
65 Hedrick Smith, "Invoking Democratic Heroes: GOP Lures Wavering Voters," *New York Times*, October 27, 1984, 31.
66 Bernard Weinraub, "Mondale Says Reagan Note Compared Kennedy to Marx," *New York Times*, October 24, 1984, A24.

67 Fay S. Joyce, "Mondale Campaign Adopts Some Tactics from Reagan," *New York Times*, October 26, 1984, A17.
68 Steven R. Weisman, "Reagan, on a Final Swing, Urges His Backers to Vote," *New York Times*, November 2, 1984, B6.
69 Ronald Reagan, "Address to the Nation on the Eve of the Presidential Election," November 5, 1984, *The Public Papers of President Ronald W. Reagan*, Ronald Reagan Presidential Library, http://www.reagan.utexas.edu/archives/speeches/1984/110584e.htm, accessed December 30, 2013.
70 "Dallas, November 22, 1963," *National Review*, December 9, 1988, 13.
71 Walter A. McDougall, "Rating the Presidents," *National Review*, October 27, 1997, 36.
72 Rising, "Stuck in the Sixties," 237.
73 Larry J. Sabato, *The Kennedy Half-Century: The Presidency, Assassination, and Lasting Legacy of John F. Kennedy* (New York: Bloomsbury, 2013), 370–89; Steven M. Gillon, *The Pact: Bill Clinton, Newt Gingrich, and the Rivalry That Defined a Generation* (New York: Oxford University Press, 2008), 13, 78, 207, 270.
74 Matthew Robinson, "Senator, You're No Jack Kennedy," *Human Events*, March 19, 2001, 1, 8; Bruce Bartlett, "JFK's Tax Cut Was a 'Tax Cut for the Rich,'" *Human Events*, March 26, 2001, 15; Stephen Moore, "Remembering the Real Economic Legacy of JFK," *Human Events*, May 19, 2003, 7.
75 Andrew Sullivan, "Why the Old Labels Don't Stick," *Time*, November 1, 2004.
76 David Gelernter, "What 'Republican' Should Mean," *National Review*, March 8, 2004, 38.
77 Noemie Emery, "Two JFKs, Divisible," *National Review*, September 13, 2004, 21.
78 Ira Stoll, *JFK, Conservative* (New York: Houghton Mifflin Harcourt, 2013).
79 Jeff Jacoby, "Would Democrats Embrace JFK Now?," *Boston Globe*, October 20, 2013, K7; L. Gordon Crovitz, "Exposing the Myth of JFK's Politics," *Wall Street Journal*, online, November 17, 2013; George F. Will, "JFK, the Conservative," *Washington Post*, November 21, 2013, A19; Paul E. Gottfried, "JFK: Neocon ahead of His Time," *Intelligencer Journal–Lancaster New Era*, November 20, 2013, A11; Amity Shlaes, "Kennedy Strikes Back," *Forbes*, December 2, 2013, 30.
80 Oliver Willis, "Stealing Kennedy: Conservatives Try to Hijack the JFK Legacy," Media Matters for America blog, November 22, 2013, http://mediamatters.org/blog/2013/11/22/stealing-kennedy-conservatives-try-to-hijack-th/197020, accessed January 2, 2014.
81 Sabato, *The Kennedy Half-Century*, 397.
82 Peter Ferrara, "Obama Democrats versus Kennedy Democrats," *Forbes*, March 10, 2014, http://www.forbes.com/sites/peterferrara/2014/03/10/obama-democrats-versus-kennedy-democrats/, accessed April 4, 2014.

16

LOREN GLASS

The Kennedy Legacy: From Hagiography to Exposé and Back Again

In the 1969 afterword to his classic 1960 study, *Presidential Power and Modern Presidents*, political scientist and Kennedy adviser Richard Neustadt claimed that John F. Kennedy had had too little time in office to establish a solid political legacy, but "he left a myth: the vibrant, youthful leader cut down senselessly before his time."[1] In this chapter, I will briefly trace the arc of this "myth" over the last fifty years. Unlike traditional myths, which emerge authorless out of the depths of prehistory, this was a modern myth, consciously crafted by contemporary intellectuals with definite ideas about what myths mean and how they function in history, especially American history. Originally in collaboration with the Kennedy family, and then increasingly in opposition to it, American public intellectuals forged the figure of a glamorous, youthful hero, deified him in the wake of his assassination, and then proceeded to expose and dismantle him as a false god whose image concealed a craven, cowardly, and sickly man. Yet the myth of the hero persists, continuously reborn and refashioned to fulfill the needs of the present day. As the outpouring of books and articles attendant upon the fiftieth anniversary of Kennedy's assassination attests, Americans are not through mythologizing the president who stays forever young.

John Kennedy, in cooperation with his staff and family, had been exploiting his youthful glamour and style as a political asset since his first congressional campaign, but it was Norman Mailer who began the process of rhetorically reshaping this image into a heroic myth in his article "Superman Comes to the Supermarket." The piece originally appeared in *Esquire* (under the title "Superman Comes to the Supermart," which was not Mailer's) only weeks before the election, and Mailer liked to think that it afforded Kennedy the slim margin of victory he managed to eke out in those final days. In the essay, Mailer announced that "this candidate for all his record, his good, sound, conventional liberal record has a patina of that other life, the second American life, the long electric night with the fires of neon leading down the highway to the murmur of jazz."[2] For Mailer, Kennedy promised to unite two strands of American culture, the underground and the mainstream, which had heretofore remained separate, and he took a highly prophetic tone in anticipating what such an event might mean for the United States. According to Mailer, the country didn't just need a new president; rather, "it was a hero that America needed, a hero central to his time, a man whose personality might suggest contradictions and mysteries which could reach into the alienated circuits of the underground, because only a hero can capture the secret imagination of a people, and so be good for the vitality of the nation" (*PP* 41–42). Kennedy, Mailer predicted, would be the first hipster president, and his election would therefore constitute an existential event.

The 1960 Democratic Convention was held in Los Angeles, a city that, according to Mailer, looked as though "it was built by television sets giving orders to men" (*PP* 33). This location enabled Mailer to situate Kennedy's heroism in terms of the glamour of Hollywood. As he affirms, "the Democrats were going to nominate a man who, no matter how serious his political dedication might be, was indisputably and willy-nilly going to be seen as a great box office actor, and the consequences of that were staggering" (*PP* 38). Mailer knew that Kennedy's image and style trumped his politics and policies, which were, in any case, not that terribly different from those of his Republican opponent.

Shortly after the assassination, Mailer reprinted his essay in *The Presidential Papers of Norman Mailer*, boasting in a postscript that it had "had more effect than any single work of mine" (*PP* 60). During Kennedy's tragically truncated presidency, Mailer had made a series of journalistic forays into contemporary politics, writing, he claims in his preface, as "a court wit, an amateur advisor" (*PP* 1). Indeed, he affirms, "The Presidential Papers were written while Jack Kennedy was alive, and so the book was put together with the idea that the President might come to read it" (*PP* v). The expectation was not entirely unrealistic. As Harvard historian Arthur Schlesinger notes in *A Thousand Days*, his encyclopedic memoir of his time in the White House as a special assistant to Kennedy, presidential aide Richard Goodwin had shown "Superman Comes to the Supermarket" to Kennedy, who had reportedly responded, "It really runs on, doesn't it."[3]

Mailer in fact plays a bit part in *A Thousand Days*. Mailer and Schlesinger had met by chance at the Kennedy compound in August 1960, when Mailer was there to interview the young nominee for his *Esquire* piece. Specifically invoking Mailer's article, Schlesinger celebrates Kennedy as a new type of "contemporary man," one who charts "a way of life, a way of autonomy, between past and present, the organization man and the anarchist, the square and the beat." Clearly troping on Mailer's idiosyncratic existentialism, Schlesinger claims that Kennedy "had wrought an individuality which carried him beyond the definitions of class and race, region and religion. He was a free man, not just in the sense of the cold-war cliché, but in the sense that he was, as much as a man can be, self-determined and not the servant of forces outside him." For Schlesinger, "this sense of wholeness and freedom gave [Kennedy] an extraordinary appeal not only to his own generation but even more to those who came after, the children of the turbulence."[4]

Mailer had proclaimed that the existential hero "is the one kind of man who *never* develops by accident, that a hero is a consecutive set of brave and witty self-creations" (*PP* 6). And Schlesinger agreed, affirming that Kennedy's "charm and grace were not an uncovenanted gift. The Kennedy style was the triumph, hard-bought and well-earned, of a gallant and collected human being over the anguish of life." He concludes, "His 'coolness' was itself a new frontier."[5] Schlesinger puts "coolness" in quotes, conceding that in 1965 it was still something of an outsider term, and indeed a few lines later he acknowledges that it was precisely this subcultural style that Mailer caught on to. Kennedy's presidency may not have achieved the existential transformation Mailer hoped for, but Kennedy did create a new image to which future Democratic presidents could aspire. As the first hipster president, he took the scare quotes off "coolness," bringing underground currents into the mainstream.

A Thousand Days was only one of a slew of memoirs and memorials that perpetuated the modern myth of Kennedy as a fallen hero in the wake of his assassination. In quick succession, Kennedy's special counsel and personal adviser Theodore Sorenson came out with *Kennedy* (1965), presidential press secretary Pierre Salinger published *With Kennedy* (1966), old friend and army buddy Paul B. Fay followed with *The Pleasure of His Company* (1966), and a few years later Kennedy aides Kenneth O'Donnell and David Powers collaborated on *"Johnny, We Hardly Knew Ye"* (1970). All of these books were highly hagiographic, extolling the fallen president's virtues and concealing or nuancing his many personal and political liabilities; all were best sellers, widely reviewed and widely read.

Kennedy was not the only protagonist in the myth that emerged from his administration. The image of the youthful hero that these memoirs perpetuated was part of a larger myth that came to be called "Camelot," and it would not have been complete without the lady who named it. Mailer took a stab at Jackie Kennedy as an "Existential Heroine" in a controversial follow-up article for *Esquire*, but he had already soured on the president after the Bay of Pigs fiasco, and the First Lady had, not surprisingly, refused to agree to an interview. His clumsy critique of her televised tour of the

White House does no justice to the feminine icon she had already become, complementing John Kennedy's glamour with her own feminine cool, a stylish sophistication that would captivate the world. On their European tour, Kennedy only half-jokingly referred to himself as the man who accompanied Jackie Kennedy to Paris, affirming not only her iconic popularity but also her high-profile association with French haute couture. Jackie not only brought style to the White House; she set style trends throughout the world.

Mailer was particularly disappointed by Jackie Kennedy's voice, which, he claimed in his essay "The Existential Heroine," seemed "like a quiet parody of the sort of voice one hears on the radio late at night, dropped softly into the ear by girls who sell soft mattresses, depilatories, or creams to brighten the skin" (PP 93). Unlike the president, whose aristocratic New England accent was ubiquitously familiar and eminently imitable, the First Lady's voice was rarely heard in public. As Wayne Koestenbaum affirms in *Jackie under My Skin* (1995), "Jackie's silence was profound, proverbial, virtually unbroken."[6] If Jack was televisual, and therefore an amalgam of image and voice, Jackie was photographic, pure image, and her almost sublimely silent iconicity was captured by Andy Warhol's endless iterations of her image throughout the late 1960s.

Like John Kennedy, Jackie Kennedy was mythologized in the wake of the assassination, but his death and her remarriage five years later caused her public image to migrate, as Koestenbaum affirms, "from her proper sphere (First Lady) to an improper sphere (profligate actress, Queen of Wish)."[7] This volatile transformation from grieving widow Jacqueline Kennedy to fashion queen Jackie O was endlessly re-created in Warhol's silkscreen series, making her image both proto-feminist and quasi-queer. Warhol both affirmed and reframed Jackie's iconicity. If, on one hand, all the images from the day of the assassination and the funeral served as a perpetual reminder of her widowhood, then, on the other hand, the incorporation of these images (and others less associated with the assassination) into Warhol's proliferating oeuvre gave her a more transgressive edge.

As Koestenbaum's account of Jackie's rapid fall from grace illustrates, the backlash against the Camelot myth was not long in coming, and it began, appropriately enough, in an article by Kennedy family relative and new journalistic gadfly Gore Vidal in *Esquire* magazine. Provocatively titled "The Holy Family," the article affirms that "most of the recent books about the late president are not so much political as religious."[8] Bluntly stating that "Kennedy dead has infinitely more force than Kennedy living," Vidal establishes at the outset that the ensuing "legend is the deliberate creation of the Kennedy family and its clients" (99). Vidal quite explicitly explains how this "legend" can be understood as an exercise in modern mythmaking:

> As an Osiris-Adonis-Christ figure, JFK is already the subject of a cult that may persist, through the machinery of publicity, long after all memory of his administration has been absorbed by the golden myth now being created in a thousand books to the single end of maintaining in power our extraordinary holy family. (100)

Throughout this lengthy article, Vidal seems unsure whether to endorse or debunk this myth. On the one hand, he is eager to expose the venality of the Kennedys and their coterie, asserting that the real trinity is "money, image making, family" (100). On the other hand, he himself is in awe of the myth, and ultimately concedes that its persistence must be attributed to something beyond the power of the trinity he's just named. Thus he concludes, "The death of a young leader necessarily strikes an atavistic chord. For thousands of years the man-god was sacrificed to insure with blood the harvest, and there is always an element of ecstasy as well as awe in our collective grief." And then he adds, "Jack Kennedy was a television star, more seen by most people than their friends or relatives. His death in public was all the more stunning because he was not an abstraction called the President, but a man people thought they knew" (203–4). On the one hand, a man-god; on the other hand, a television celebrity. This syncretic formation became the post-humous fate of the existential superhero Mailer first named. Vidal gently reminds us that the real Jack Kennedy "did not much resemble the hero of the books under review here," but his article, in the end, does more to perpetuate the myth than to unmask it (203). Breathlessly juggling the discordant terminologies of ancient ritual and contemporary publicity in the service of a prophetic register, Vidal's article bespeaks its own powerlessness to reverse the hagiographic process he works to expose.

In the ensuing decades, writers worked more assiduously to expose the man behind the myth. Starting with Joan and Clay Blair's *The Search for JFK* (1976), achieving a certain comprehensiveness in Garry Wills's *The Kennedy Imprisonment* (1982), and then reaching a devastating finality with Nigel Hamilton's *JFK: Reckless Youth* (1993) and Seymour Hersh's *The Dark Side of Camelot* (1997), the facts about Jack Kennedy's compulsive womanizing, frail health, and overall political and personal venality have been fully fleshed out in the fifty years following his assassination.

Early hagiographers like Sorenson and Schlesinger Jr. had noted Kennedy's Addison's disease and related health problems, but they had framed them as obstacles overcome through toughness and vigor, and therefore were able to accommodate Kennedy's poor health to his heroic character. Thus

Sorenson claims, "Pain was always with him . . . but Kennedy accepted it with grace."[9] Schlesinger goes further, attributing Kennedy's courage and energy to his lifelong struggles with his health, which "seemed to give his life its peculiar intensity, its determination to savor everything, its urgent sense that there was no time to waste."[10] Framed in this way, Kennedy's poor health enhances Mailer's classification of him as an existential hero insofar as it compelled him to face death. Hersh reveals the truth to have been far more sinister, affirming not only that "Kennedy had lied about his health throughout his political career, repeatedly denying that he suffered from Addison's disease," but also that "Kennedy was . . . a heavy user of what were euphemistically known as 'feel-good' shots – consisting of high dosages of amphetamines – while in the White House."[11] As far as Hersh is concerned, Kennedy was not fit, literally, to be president, and his lying about his ailments made him vulnerable to blackmail.

If the truth about Kennedy's health tarnished his reputation, the revelations about his compulsive womanizing did far more damage. Sorenson had coyly noted that Kennedy "enjoyed in his bachelor days carefree parties and companions on both sides of the Atlantic,"[12] but none of the hagiographies written in the wake of the assassination said a thing about what every author knew well: that, as Hersh claims, during his presidency "Kennedy was consumed with almost daily sexual liaisons and libertine partying" (10) Hersh details these dalliances meticulously, identifying Kennedy aide Dave Powers as the procurer who would regularly and reliably obtain women for Kennedy both in the White House and abroad while the Secret Service nervously turned a blind eye. Hersh also claims that Kennedy early on contracted chlamydia, and that he "was being repeatedly reinfected – and, presumably, infecting his partners" (231) throughout his presidency. And Hersh corroborates and confirms the names of a number of the president's more prominent paramours, including Judith Exner, who was also having an affair with Chicago mobster Sam Giancana; Ellen Rometsch, an East German with ties to the Communist Party; and Marilyn Monroe, who Hersh claims had been sleeping with Kennedy both before and after his election to the presidency.

The Dark Side of Camelot was explicitly written to destroy the vestiges of the myth invoked by its title, and Hersh pulls no punches in exposing the venality of the entire Kennedy family. He states up front that the "1960 presidential election was stolen" (4) through Joe Kennedy's mob connections in Chicago, and he is as devastating on Kennedy's politics and policies as he is on his private life. He confirms Kennedy's obsession with assassinating Fidel Castro, as well as his administration's involvement in the assassinations of Patrice Lumumba, Rafael Trujillo, and Ngô Đình Diệm. He details the back channel Bobby and Jack Kennedy kept open with the Russians during the Cuban Missile Crisis, allowing them to "talk tough in public and compromise in private" (256). And he concludes that "John Kennedy's enduring legacy as the thirty-fifth president of the United States was not the myth of Camelot or the tragic image of an attractive young leader struck down at the peak of his career. It was the war in Vietnam" (412).

Hersh also concludes, somewhat astonishingly, that Lee Harvey Oswald "acted alone" (451); it is fair to say that many, if not most, Americans would disagree. The myth of Kennedy quickly generated a parallel narrative in the mystery of Oswald, whose peculiar story and contradictory character have attracted as much attention as Kennedy's glamour and style. Indeed, for American novelists Oswald has offered a fascination exceeding the appeal of the president he purportedly killed. It should come as no surprise that Norman Mailer again figures prominently in the pursuit of the man whose insignificance seemed to offer an unacceptable affront to the world-historical importance of the fallen man-god.

In the wake of the fall of the Soviet Union, Mailer, with the help of his longtime associate Larry Schiller, traveled to Russia to interview the people who knew Lee Harvey Oswald during his brief sojourn there. Mailer also conducted numerous interviews and extensive research in the United States in order to produce his eight-hundred-page study, *Oswald's Tale: An American Mystery* (1995). About one half of the way through the first part, which meticulously re-creates Oswald's life in Minsk, Mailer accounts for his late-career turn from the myth of Kennedy to the mystery of Oswald:

> It is virtually not assimilable to our reason that a small lonely man felled a giant in the midst of his limousines, his legions, his throng, and his security. If such a non-entity destroyed the leader of the most powerful nation on earth, then a world of disproportion engulfs us, and we live in a universe that is absurd.[13]

Eager to save us from this existential fate, Mailer attempts to create an antihero, positioning Oswald as "a protagonist, a prime mover, a man who made things happen" (*OT* 605). As far as Mailer is concerned, the creation of this countermyth is a more noble objective than the revelation of the truth, "for if Oswald remains intact as an important if dark protagonist, one has served a purpose: The burden of a prodigious American obsession has been lessened, and the air cleared of an historic scourge – absurdity" (*OT* 606). Solving the mystery of Lee Harvey Oswald is less a fact-finding mission than an existential errand; Mailer's objective is to sublimate, by a kind of existential alchemy, absurdity into tragedy since, as he confidently proclaims, "tragedy is vastly preferable to absurdity" (*OT* 607).

246

This effort to create a redemptive counternarrative to the unacceptable absurdity of the lone gunman theory put forth by the Warren Report has been the motivation behind many of the high-profile re-creations of the events leading up to the assassination of President Kennedy, from Don DeLillo's *Libra* (1988) to Oliver Stone's *JFK* (1991; based partly on DeLillo's novel) to Stephen King's recent *11/22/63* (2012), an 850-page counterfactual time-travel story sporting as an epigraph Mailer's refusal to accept an absurd universe in which "a small lonely man felled a giant." By Mailer's logic, the endless proliferation of conspiracy theories that continue to balloon in the wake of the assassination are, in effect, attempts at existential group therapy; they are efforts to replace the angst of absurdity with the catharsis of tragedy.

Ironically, the fascination with Oswald is also a symptom of the culture of contemporary celebrity that Jack and Jackie Kennedy helped inaugurate. The "nobody" constantly haunting Kennedy's "somebody," Oswald is almost invariably represented as obsessed with fame and desirous of notoriety, and this obsession crucially promises to solve the mystery of his motives in assassinating the president. As most accounts agree, there is no evidence that Oswald had any particular animus against Kennedy, and some evidence that he actually admired the president. But Kennedy was famous and Oswald was obscure, and by killing the president, Oswald, so this argument goes, would in turn become famous. Lee Harvey Oswald thus comes to signify the criminal underbelly of contemporary celebrity, affirming that fame can be achieved simply by killing the famous. The dialectical couplet of Kennedy and Oswald inaugurates what one might call the assassination era in celebrity culture, anticipating figures like John W. Hinckley Jr. and Mark David Chapman, who commit assassinations more for psychological than political reasons.

But myths cannot be killed, and in the new millennium we are witnessing an oddly seamless accommodation of the realities of John Kennedy's character to the fantasies of his youthful cool. Thus Robert Dallek's recent biography, *An Unfinished Life*, which aims "to penetrate the veneer of glamour and charm to reconstruct the real man" concedes all the revelations about Kennedy's health and philandering, but nevertheless concludes that "Kennedy courageously surmounted his physical suffering" and that his "dalliances were no impediment to his being an effective president."[14] While not a hagiography, Dallek's biography leaves much of the myth intact; Kennedy still exhibits glamour and grace under pressure, regardless of his failings. Indeed, it is not too much to say that the ill health and the womanizing have now become incorporated into the myth. As we have already seen, the struggles with illness and pain are easily assimilable into the stoic ethic of the existential hero, while the philandering can be seen as an indication of, rather than a liability for, Kennedy's charismatic cool.

In "The Elusive President," one example of the torrent of recent articles reviewing the deluge of books about Kennedy being released in recognition (and exploitation) of the fiftieth anniversary of his assassination, Jill Abrahamson claims that "an estimated 40,000" books have been written about JFK since his death.[15] And yet, as the title of her article affirms, Kennedy himself remains "elusive," seemingly buried under the morass of material – from hagiography to exposé and back again in an endless cycle of appraisal and reappraisal – that continues to proliferate in the wake of his assassination. It seems revelatory that Mailer all those years ago used similar language in describing Kennedy, observing that "there was an elusive detachment in everything he did."[16] Coolness is elusive, which is part of what makes it so alluring and so susceptible to fantasy and projection. And this basic uncertainty, not only about character but also about political commitment, is, in our contemporary political world, an asset rather than a liability. Like Bill Clinton and Barack Obama today, Kennedy was basically a liberal pragmatist, but his image and style allowed him to embody the ideals of the generation that he came to represent, and his assassination fixed that image of youthful idealism in the minds of the generation that followed.

John Kennedy's legacy is possibility itself, as both paranoid fantasy and idealistic aspiration. On the one hand, there is doubt. We will never know what really happened in the days and months leading up to November 22, 1963, and this uncertainty has become a veritable vortex for conspiracy theories. On the other hand, there is hope. Kennedy was assassinated at the age of forty-six. He had been and remains the youngest man to have been elected president, and his youthful image has become a renewable resource of hope for anyone invested in the promise of America. Thus we continue to see articles and books that imagine what a great president he would have become had he lived. There is no way of knowing this, but the very fact that we feel continuously compelled to speculate confirms that Kennedy's legacy is more about promise than politics.

NOTES

1 Richard Neustadt, *Presidential Power and Modern Presidents: The Politics of Leadership from Roosevelt to Reagan* (New York: Free Press, 1990), 177.
2 Norman Mailer, *The Presidential Papers of Norman Mailer* (New York: Bantam, 1964), 31. Subsequent references to this edition are cited in parentheses in the text as *PP*.
3 Arthur Schlesinger Jr., *A Thousand Days: John F. Kennedy in the White House* (New York: Fawcett, 1965), 114n3.

4   Ibid., 112.

5   Ibid., 113.

6   Wayne Koestenbaum, *Jackie under My Skin: Interpreting an Icon* (New York: Farrar, Straus, and Giroux, 1995), 42.

7   Ibid., 66.

8   Gore Vidal, "The Holy Family," *Esquire* (April 1967): 200. Subsequent references to this article are cited in parentheses in the text.

9   Theodore C. Sorenson, *Kennedy* (New York: Harper and Row, 1965), 42.

10 Schlesinger Jr., *A Thousand Days*, 95.

11 Seymour M. Hersh, *The Dark Side of Camelot* (New York: Little, Brown, 1997), 5. Subsequent references to this edition are cited in parentheses in the text.

12 Sorensen, *Kennedy*, 27.

13 Norman Mailer, *Oswald's Tale: An American Mystery* (New York: Random House, 1995), 198. Subsequent references to this edition are cited in parentheses in the text as *OT*.

14 Robert Dallek, *An Unfinished Life: John F. Kennedy, 1917–1963* (New York: Back Bay Books, 2003), ix, 705, 707.

15 Jill Abramson, "The Elusive President," *New York Times Book Review*, October 27, 2013, 1.

16 Ibid., 45.

GUIDE TO FURTHER READING AND VIEWING

Works by John F. Kennedy, Speeches, Diaries, and Collections

Kennedy, John F. "Address on Civil Rights, June 11, 1963." http://millercenter.org/president/speeches/detail/3375.

"Inaugural Address, 20 January 1961." *John F. Kennedy Presidential Library and Museum.* http://www.jfklibrary.org/AssetViewer/BqXIEM9F4024ntFl7SVAjA .aspx.

John F. Kennedy in Quotations: A Topical Dictionary with Sources. Ed. David B. Frost. Jefferson, NC: McFarland and Company, 2013.

The Letters of John F. Kennedy. Ed. Martin W. Sandler. London: Bloomsbury Press, 2013.

A Nation of Immigrants. 1964. New York: Harper Perennial, 2008.

Prelude to Leadership: The European Diary of John F. Kennedy: Summer 1945. Ed. John Fitzgerald Kennedy. Washington, DC: Regnery Publishing, 1997.

Profiles in Courage. 1956. New York: HarperCollins, 2011.

The Strategy of Peace. Ed. Allan Nevins. New York: Harper & Bros., 1960.

"We Must Climb to the Hilltop." *Life*, August 22, 1960, 70, 72, 75–77.

Why England Slept. Santa Barbara, CA: Praeger, 1981.

Biography, History, and Criticism

Bernstein, Irving. *Promises Kept: John F. Kennedy's New Frontier.* New York: Oxford University Press, 1991.

Beschloss, Michael R. *The Crisis Years: Kennedy and Khrushchev, 1960–1963.* New York: HarperCollins, 1991.

Blight, James G., Janet M. Lang, and David A. Welch. *Virtual JFK: Vietnam If Kennedy Had Lived.* Lanham, MD: Rowman and Littlefield, 2009.

Borstelmann, Thomas. "'Hedging Bets and Buying Time': John Kennedy and Racial Revolutions in the American South and Southern Africa." *Diplomatic History* 24, no. 3 (Summer 2002): 435–63.

Branch, Taylor. *Parting the Waters: America in the King years, 1954–63.* New York: Simon and Schuster, 1988.

Brauer, Carl M. *John F. Kennedy and the Second Reconstruction.* New York: Columbia University Press, 1977.

Brinkley, Alan. *John F. Kennedy.* New York: Henry Holt and Co., 2012.

Brogan, Hugh. *Kennedy*. New York: Longman, 1996.

Brown, Thomas. *JFK: History of an Image*. Bloomington: Indiana University Press, 1988.

Brugioni, Dino A. *Eyeball to Eyeball: The Inside Story of the Cuban Missile Crisis*. New York: Random House, 1991.

Bryant, Nick. *The Bystander: John F. Kennedy and the Struggle for Black Equality*. New York: Basic Books, 2006.

Burner, David. *John F. Kennedy and a New Generation*. Library of American Biography. Series ed. Mark C. Carnes. New York: Pearson, 1988.

Burns, James MacGregor. *John Kennedy: A Political Profile*. New York: Harcourt, 1960.

Carter, James M. *Inventing Vietnam: The United States and State Building, 1954–1968*. New York: Cambridge University Press, 2008.

Carty, Thomas. *A Catholic in the White House?: Religion, Politics, and John F. Kennedy's Presidential Campaign*. New York: Palgrave Macmillan, 2004.

"The Catholic Question: The 1960 Democratic Presidential Nomination." *Historian* 63, no. 3 (2001): 582.

"Religion and the Presidency of John F. Kennedy." In *Religion and the American Presidency: George Washington to George W. Bush with Commentary and Primary Sources*. Ed. Gastón Espinosa. New York: Columbia University Press, 2009, 283–320.

Casey, Shaun. *The Making of a Catholic President: Kennedy vs. Nixon 1960*. Oxford: Oxford University Press, 2009.

Chomsky, Noam. *Rethinking Camelot: JFK, the Vietnam War, and U.S. Political Culture*. Cambridge, MA: South End Press, 1999.

Clarke, Thurston. *Ask Not: The Inauguration of John F. Kennedy and the Speech That Changed America*. New York: Penguin, 2011.

JFK's Last Hundred Days: The Transformation of a Man and the Emergence of a Great Presidency. New York: Penguin, 2013.

Cobbs Hoffman, Elizabeth. *All You Need Is Love: The Peace Corps and the Spirit of the 1960s*. Cambridge, MA: Harvard University Press, 1998.

Daalder, Ivo H., and I. M. Destler. *In the Shadow of the Oval Office: Profiles of the National Security Advisers and the Presidents They Served – From JFK to George W. Bush*. New York: Simon & Schuster, 2009.

Dallek, Robert. *Camelot's Court: Inside the Kennedy White House*. New York: HarperCollins, 2013.

John F. Kennedy. Oxford: Oxford University Press, 2011.

An Unfinished Life: John F. Kennedy, 1917–1963. New York: Back Bay Books, 2004.

Daum, Andreas W. *Kennedy in Berlin*. New York: Cambridge University Press, 2008.

Dean, Robert D. "Masculinity as Ideology: John F. Kennedy and the Domestic Politics of Foreign Policy." *Diplomatic History* 22, no. 1 (Winter 1998): 38–39.

Dobbs, Michael. *One Minute to Midnight: Kennedy, Khrushchev, and Castro on the Brink of Nuclear War*. New York: Alfred A. Knopf, 2008.

Durks, Herbert. *John F. Kennedy and Israel*. Westport, CT: Praeger Security International, 2005.

Emery, Noemie. "Two JFKs, Divisible." *National Review*, September 13, 2004, 20–21.

Evans, Rowland, and Robert Novak. "Reagan, JFK and Taxes." *Washington Post*, April 7, 1980, A25.

Fairlie, Henry. *The Kennedy Promise: The Politics of Expectation*. Garden City, NY: Doubleday, 1973.

Freedman, Lawrence. *Kennedy's Wars: Berlin, Cuba, Laos, and Vietnam*. Oxford: Oxford University Press, 2000.

The Pleasure of His Company. New York: Harper and Row, 1966.

Friedberg, Aaron L. *In the Shadow of the Garrison State: America's Anti-Statism and Its Cold War Grand Strategy*. Princeton, NJ: Princeton University Press, 2000.

Fuchs, Lawrence H. *John F. Kennedy and American Catholicism*. New York: Meredith Press, 1967.

Fursenko, Aleksandr, and Timothy Naftali. *"One Hell of a Gamble": The Secret History of the Cuban Missile Crisis*. New York: W. W. Norton, 1998.

Gaddis, John Lewis. *We Now Know: Rethinking Cold War History*. New York: Oxford University Press, 1997.

Galbraith, John Kenneth. *The Affluent Society*. Boston: Houghton Mifflin, 1958.

Giglio, James N. *John F. Kennedy: A Bibliography*. Westport, CT: Greenwood Press, 1995.

Gilman, Nils. *Mandarins of the Future: Modernization Theory in Cold War America*. Baltimore, MD: Johns Hopkins University Press, 2007.

Goduti, Philip A., Jr. *Robert F. Kennedy and the Shaping of Civil Rights, 1960–1964*. Jefferson, NC: McFarland and Company, 2013.

Goldzwig, Steven, and George N. Dionisopoulos. *"In a Perilous Hour": The Public Address of John F. Kennedy*. Westport, CT: Greenwood Press, 1995.

Gottfried, Paul E. "JFK: Neocon ahead of His Time." *Intelligencer Journal–Lancaster New Era*, November 20, 2013.

Halberstam, David. *The Best and the Brightest*. 1972. New York: Modern Library, 2002.

"Introduction." In *The Kennedy Presidential Press Conferences*. Ed. George W. Johnson. New York: Earl M. Coleman Enterprises, 1978, i–iv.

Hamilton, Nigel. *JFK: Reckless Youth*. New York: Random House, 1992.

Hellmann, John. *The Kennedy Obsession: The American Myth of JFK*. New York: Columbia University Press, 1997.

Henggeler, Paul R. *The Kennedy Persuasion: The Politics of Style since JFK*. Chicago: Ivan R. Dee, 1995.

Herring, George C. *America's Longest War: The United States and Vietnam, 1950–1975*. 4th ed. New York: McGraw-Hill, 2002.

Hersey, John. "Survival: From a PT Base in the Solomons Comes This Nightmare Epic of the Will-to-Live." *Reader's Digest* 45 (1944): 75–80.

Hersh, Seymour M. *The Dark Side of Camelot*. New York: Little, Brown, 1997.

Hershberg, James G. "The Crisis Years, 1958–1963." In *Reviewing the Cold War: Approaches, Interpretations, Theory*. Ed. Odd Arne Westad. London: Frank Cass, 2000, 319–20.

Jones, Howard. *Death of a Generation: How the Assassinations of Diem and JFK Prolonged the Vietnam War*. New York: Oxford University Press, 2004.

Kaiser, David. *American Tragedy: Kennedy, Johnson, and the Origins of the Vietnam War*. Cambridge, MA: Belknap Press, 2002.

The Road to Dallas: The Assassination of John F. Kennedy. Cambridge, MA: Belknap Press of Harvard University Press, 2008.

Kennedy, Jacqueline. *Jacqueline Kennedy: Historic Conversations on Life with John F. Kennedy.* New York: Hyperion, 2011.

Knight, Peter. *Conspiracy Culture: From the Kennedy Assassination to "The X-Files."* London: Routledge, 2001.

The Kennedy Assassination. Edinburgh: Edinburgh University Press, 2007.

Kunz, Diane B. *Butter and Guns: America's Cold War Economic Diplomacy.* New York: Free Press, 1997.

Jones, Howard. *The Bay of Pigs.* New York: Oxford University Press, 2008.

Joseph, Peniel E. "Kennedy's Finest Hour." *New York Times,* June 10, 2013. http://www.nytimes.com/2013/06/11/opinion/kennedys-civil-rights-triumph.html?_r=0.

Latham, Michael E. *Modernization as Ideology: American Social Science and "Nation Building" in the Kennedy Era.* Chapel Hill: University of North Carolina Press, 2000.

The Right Kind of Revolution: Modernization, Development, and U.S. Foreign Policy from the Cold War to the Present. Ithaca, NY: Cornell University Press, 2010.

Lawson, Steven F. "Freedom Then, Freedom Now: The Historiography of the Civil Rights Movement." *American Historical Review* 96, no. 2 (1991): 456.

Lefebvre, Jeffrey A. "Kennedy's Algerian Dilemma: Containment, Alliance Politics and the 'Rebel Dialogue.'" *Middle Eastern Studies* 35, no. 2 (April 1999): 62.

Leuchtenburg, William E. *In the Shadow of FDR: From Harry Truman to Barack Obama.* Ithaca, NY: Cornell University Press, 2009.

Lippmann, Walter. "John F. Kennedy." In *Public Persons.* Ed. Gilbert A. Harrison. New York: Liveright Publishing, 1976, 185–186.

Logevall, Fredrik. "Vietnam and the Question of What Might Have Been." In *Kennedy: The New Frontier Revisited.* Ed. Mark J. White. New York: New York University Press, 1998, 19–62.

Logsdon, John M. *John F. Kennedy and the Race to the Moon.* New York: Palgrave Macmillan, 2010.

Longford, Lord. *Kennedy.* London: Weidenfeld and Nicolson, 1976.

Lubin, David M. *Shooting Kennedy: JFK and the Culture of Images.* Berkeley: University of California Press, 2003.

Manchester, William. *The Death of a President: November 20-November 25, 1963.* New York: Harper & Row, 1967.

Massa, Mark S., SJ. *Anti-Catholicism in America: The Last Acceptable Prejudice.* New York: Crossroad, 2003.

Matusow, Allen J. "John F. Kennedy and the Intellectuals." *Wilson Quarterly* 7, no. 4 (Autumn 1983): 140–53.

May, Ernest R., and Philip D. Zelikow, eds. *The Kennedy Tapes: Inside the White House during the Cuban Missile Crisis.* Cambridge, MA: Harvard University Press, 2009.

McCann, Sean. *A Pinnacle of Feeling: American Literature and Presidential Government.* Princeton, NJ: Princeton University Press, 2008.

McCormick, Thomas J. *America's Half-Century: United States Foreign Policy in the Cold War and After.* 2nd ed. 1989. Baltimore, MD: Johns Hopkins University Press, 1995.

Medovoi, Leerom. "Cold War American Culture as the Age of Three Worlds." *Minnesota Review* 55–57 (2002): 167–86.

Rebels: Youth and the Cold War Origins of Identity. Durham, NC: Duke University Press, 2005.

Meisler, Stanley. *When the World Calls: The Inside Story of the Peace Corps and Its First Fifty Years*. Boston: Beacon Press, 2011.

Melley, Timothy. *Empire of Conspiracy: The Culture of Paranoia in Postwar America*. Ithaca, NY: Cornell University Press, 2000.

Meriwether, James H. "'Worth a Lot of Negro Votes': Black Voters, Africa, and the 1960 Presidential Campaign." *Journal of American History* 95, no. 3 (December 2008): 737–63.

Miller, Edward. *Misalliance: Ngo Dinh Diem, the United States, and the Fate of South Vietnam*. Cambridge, MA: Harvard University Press, 2013.

Miroff, Bruce. *Pragmatic Illusions: The Presidential Politics of John F. Kennedy*. New York: David McKay, 1976.

Moore, Stephen. "Remembering the Real Economic Legacy of JFK." *Human Events* 59, no. 17 (May 19, 2003): 7.

Muehlenbeck, Philip E. *Betting on the Africans: John F. Kennedy's Courting of African Nationalist Leaders*. Oxford: Oxford University Press, 2012.

Nasaw, David. *The Patriarch: The Remarkable Life and Turbulent Times of Joseph P. Kennedy*. New York: Penguin Press, 2012.

Navasky, Victor. *Kennedy Justice*. New York: Harper and Row, 1971.

Newcomb, Joan I. *John F. Kennedy: An Annotated Bibliography*. Metuchen, NJ: Scarecrow Press, 1977.

Noer, Thomas J. *Cold War and Black Liberation: The United States and White Rule in Africa, 1948–1968*. Columbia: University of Missouri Press, 1985.

O'Brien, Michael. *John F. Kennedy: A Biography*. New York: Thomas Dunne Books/St. Martin's Press, 2005.

Owen, Dean R. *November 22. 1963: Reflections on the Life, Assassination, and Legacy of John F. Kennedy*. New York: Skyhorse Publishing, 2013.

Parmet, Herbert S. *Jack: The Struggles of John F. Kennedy*. New York: Dial Press, 1980.

JFK: The Presidency of John F. Kennedy. New York: Dial Press, 1983.

Pauley, Garth E. *The Modern Presidency and Civil Rights: Rhetoric on Race from Roosevelt to Nixon*. College Station: Texas A&M University Press, 2001.

Pearce, Kimber Charles. *Rostow, Kennedy, and the Rhetoric of Foreign Aid*. East Lansing: Michigan State University Press, 2001.

Piereson, James. *Camelot and the Cultural Revolution: How the Assassination of John F. Kennedy Shattered American Liberalism*. New York: Encounter, 2007.

Porter, Gareth. *Perils of Dominance: Imbalance of Power and the Road to War in Vietnam*. Berkeley: University of California Press, 2005.

Preston, Andrew. *The War Council: McGeorge Bundy, the NSC, and Vietnam*. Cambridge, MA: Harvard University Press, 2010.

"John F. Kennedy and Lyndon B. Johnson." *Mental Maps in the Early Cold War Era*. Ed. Steven Casey and Jonathan Wright. New York: Palgrave Macmillan, 2011, 261–80.

Rabe, Stephen G. *The Killing Zone: The United States Wages Cold War in Latin America*. New York: Oxford University Press, 2011.

The Most Dangerous Area in the World: John F. Kennedy Confronts Communist Revolution in Latin America. Chapel Hill: University of North Carolina Press, 1999.

Rakove, Robert B. *Kennedy, Johnson, and the Nonaligned World.* Cambridge: Cambridge University Press, 2013.

Reeves, Richard. *President Kennedy: Profile of Power.* New York: Simon & Schuster, 1993.

Rorabaugh, W. J. *Kennedy and the Promise of the Sixties.* Cambridge: Cambridge University Press, 2002.

Rosenberg, Bruce A. "Kennedy in Camelot: The Arthurian Legend in America." *Western Folklore* 35, no. 1 (1976): 52–59.

Rostow, W. W. *Eisenhower, Kennedy, and Foreign Aid.* Austin: University of Texas Press, 1985.

Rubin, Edward L. *Beyond Camelot: Rethinking Politics and Law for the Modern State.* Princeton, NJ: Princeton University Press, 2007.

Rust, William J. *Kennedy in Vietnam.* New York: Scribner, 1985.

Sabato, Larry J. *The Kennedy Half-Century: The Presidency, Assassination, and Lasting Legacy of John F. Kennedy.* New York: Bloomsbury, 2013.

Sachs, Jeffrey D. *To Move the World: JFK's Quest for Peace.* New York: Random House, 2013.

Salinger, Pierre. *With Kennedy.* Garden City: Doubleday, 1966.

Savage, Sean J. *JFK, LBJ, and the Democratic Party.* Albany: State University of New York Press, 2004.

Schlesinger, Arthur M., Jr. *The Letters of Arthur Schlesinger, Jr.* Ed. Andrew Schlesinger and Stephen Schlesinger. New York: Random House, 2013.

—— *A Life in the Twentieth Century: Innocent Beginnings, 1917–1950.* Boston: Houghton Mifflin, 2000.

—— *The Politics of Hope.* Boston: Houghton Mifflin, 1962.

—— *The Politics of Hope and the Bitter Heritage: American Liberalism in the 1960s.* Foreword Sean Wilentz. Princeton, NJ: Princeton University Press, 2007.

—— *A Thousand Days: John F. Kennedy in the White House.* 1965. Boston: Houghton Mifflin, 2002.

Schwalbe, Carol B. "Jacqueline Kennedy and Cold War Propaganda." *Journal of Broadcasting & Electronic Media* 49, no. 1 (2005): 111–27.

See, Jennifer W. "An Uneasy Truce: John F. Kennedy and Soviet-American Détente, 1963." *Cold War History* 2 (January 2002): 161–94.

Shapley, Deborah. *Promise and Power: The Life and Times of Robert McNamara.* New York: Simon & Schuster, 1993.

Shaw, John T. *JFK in the Senate: Pathway to the Presidency.* New York: Palgrave Macmillan, 2013.

Smith, Malcolm E. *John F. Kennedy's 13 Great Mistakes in the White House.* New York: Suffolk House, 1980.

Smith, Sally Bedell. *Grace and Power: The Private World of the Kennedy White House.* New York: Random House, 2011.

Sorensen, Ted. *Counselor: A Life at the Edge of History.* New York: Harper, 2008.

—— *Kennedy.* 1965. New York: HarperCollins, 2009.

—— *The Kennedy Legacy.* New York: MacMillan, 1969.

—— *"Let the Word Go Forth": The Speeches, Statements, and Writings of John F. Kennedy, 1947–1963.* New York: Delacorte Press, 1988.

Steinberg, Neal. *Hatless Jack: The President, the Fedora, and the History of an American Style*. New York: Plume, 2004.

Stephanson, Anders. "Cold War Degree Zero." In *Uncertain Empire: American History and the Idea of the Cold War*. Ed. Joel Isaac and Duncan Bell. New York: Oxford University Press, 2012, 19–49.

Stern, Jane, and Michael Stern. *Sixties People*. New York: Knopf, 1990.

Stern, Sheldon M. "John F. Kennedy and the Politics of Race and Civil Rights." *Review in American History* 35, no. 1 (March 2007): 118–19.

Stoll, Ira. *JFK, Conservative*. New York: Houghton Mifflin Harcourt, 2013.

Szalay, Michael. *Hip Figures: A Literary History of the Democratic Party*. Palo Alto, CA: Stanford University Press, 2012.

Taylor, Maxwell D. *The Uncertain Trumpet*. New York: Harper, 1960.

Trachtenberg, Marc. *A Constructed Peace: The Making of the European Settlement, 1945–1963*. Princeton, NJ: Princeton University Press, 1999.

Vidal, Gore. "The Holy Family." *Esquire* 67 no. 4 (April 1967): 99–103.

Watson, Mary Ann. *Defining Visions: Television and the American Experience in the 20th Century*. Boston: Blackwell Publishing, 2008.

The Expanding Vista: American Television in the Kennedy Years. New York: Oxford University Press, 1990.

"How Kennedy Invented Political Television." *Television Quarterly* 25, no. 2 (1991): 61–71.

"Kennedy Live: John F. Kennedy and Robert Kennedy vs. Gov. George Wallace: The Story Behind the Most Intimate Documentary of Leaders in Crisis Ever Filmed." *Washington Journalism Review* 12, no. 8 (October 1990): 52–56.

"The Kennedy-Television Alliance." In *John F. Kennedy: Person, Policy, Presidency*. Ed. J. Richard Snyder. Wilmington: Scholarly Resources Books, 1988, 45–54.

"The New Frontier and the Vast Wasteland." In *John F. Kennedy: The Promise Revisited*. Ed. Paul Harper and Joan P. Krieg. New York: Greenwood Press, 1988, 261–72.

"Television and the Presidency: Eisenhower and Kennedy." In *The Columbia History of American Television*. Ed. Gary Edgerton. New York: Columbia University Press, 2007. 205–33.

"A Tour of the White House: Mystique and Tradition." *Presidential Studies Quarterly* 18, no. 1 (Winter 1988): 91–99.

"'Vast Wasteland': Newton Minow Looks Back." *Television Quarterly* 22, no. 3 (1986): 57–64.

Webster, David. "Regimes in Motion: The Kennedy Administration and Indonesia's New Frontier, 1960–1962." *Diplomatic History* 33, no. 1 (January 2009): 95–123.

Weinraub, Bernard. "Mondale Says Reagan Note Compared Kennedy to Marx." *New York Times*, October 24, 1984.

Wheeler, Mark. *Celebrity Politics*. Cambridge: Polity, 2013.

White, Mark. *Kennedy: A Cultural History of an American Icon*. New York: Bloomsbury, 2013.

White, Theodore. "The Action Intellectuals." *Life*, June 9, 1967, 43–76.

"For President Kennedy: An Epilogue." *Life*, December 9, 1963, 158–59.

In Search of History: A Personal Adventure. New York: Franklin Library, 1980.

The Making of the President 1960. 1961. New York: HarperCollins, 2009.

Willis, Oliver. "Stealing Kennedy: Conservatives Try to Hijack the JFK Legacy." Media Matters for America blog, November 22, 2013. http://mediamatters.org/blog/2013/11/22/stealing-kennedy-conservatives-try-to-hijack-th/197020.

Wills, Garry. *The Kennedy Imprisonment: A Meditation on Power.* 1981. New York: Mariner, 2002.

Windt, Theodore Otto, Jr. *Presidents and Protesters: Political Rhetoric in the 1960s.* Tuscaloosa: University of Alabama Press, 1990.

Wofford, Harris. *Of Kennedys and Kings: Making Sense of the Sixties.* New York: Farrar, Straus, and Giroux, 1980.

Wolfe, James S. "The Religion of and about John F. Kennedy." In *John F. Kennedy: The Promise Revisited.* Ed. Paul Harper and Joann P. Krieg. New York: Greenwood Press, 1988, 287–99.

Literary Works of Interest

Baldwin, James. *Another Country.* 1962. New York: Vintage, 1993.
  Collected Essays. Ed. Toni Morrison. New York: Library of America, 1998.
  "From Nationalism, Colonialism, and the United States: One Minute to Twelve – A Forum." In *The Cross of Redemption: Uncollected Essays.* Ed. Randall Kenan. New York: Pantheon Books, 2010, 10–18.

Ballard, J. G. *The Atrocity Exhibition.* New York: Flamingo Modern Classics, 1970.

Condon, Richard. *Winter Kills.* London: Weidenfeld and Nicolson, 1974.

DeLillo, Don. *Libra.* 1988. New York: Penguin, 2011.
  Underworld. New York: Scribner, 1997.

Didion, Joan. *Democracy.* New York: Vintage, 1984.
  Slouching toward Bethlehem. New York: Farrar, Straus, and Giroux, 1968.

Ellison, Ralph. *Three Days Before the Shooting.* New York: Modern Library, 2010.

Ellroy, James. *American Tabloid.* New York: Vintage, 1995.
  The Cold Six Thousand. New York: Vintage, 2001.

Ginsberg, Allan. *Deliberate Prose: Selected Essays, 1952–1995.* New York: HarperCollins, 2000.

King, Stephen. *11/22/63.* New York: Gallery Books, 2012.

Lawson, Mark. *Idlewild.* New York: Picador, 1995.

Llosa, Mario Vargas. *The Feast of the Goat: A Novel.* New York: Picador, 2001.

Mailer, Norman. *Advertisements for Myself.* 1959. Cambridge, MA: Harvard University Press, 1992.
  "Footfalls in the Crypt." *Vanity Fair* (February 1992): 124–29, 171.
  "The Great American Mystery." *Book Week Washington Post,* August 28, 1966, 1–13.
  "1958–1967: Rounding Camelot." In *A Century of Arts and Letters: The History of the National Institute of Arts and Letters and the American Academy of Arts and Letters as Told, Decade by Decade, by Eleven Members.* Ed. John Updike. New York: Columbia University Press, 1998, 156–97.
  Oswald's Tale: An American Mystery. London: Little, Brown, 1995.
  The Presidential Papers. New York: G. P. Putnam's Sons, 1963, 1970.
  "Superman Comes to the Supermart." *Esquire* 54 no. 5 (November 1960): 119–27; reprinted as "Superman Comes to the Supermarket" in *The Presidential Papers,* 25–61.

The Time of Our Time. New York: Modern Library, 1998.
"The White Negro: Superficial Reflections on the Hipster." In *Advertisements for Myself.* 1959. Cambridge, MA: Harvard University Press, 1992, 337–58.
McCarry, Charles. *The Tears of Autumn.* New York: Overlook Press, 1974.
Pynchon, Thomas. *Gravity's Rainbow.* New York: Viking Press, 1973.
Styron, William. *Havanas in Camelot: Personal Essays.* New York: Random House, 2008.
Thomas, D. M. *Flying in to Love.* London: Bloomsbury, 1992.
Updike, John. *Couples.* 1968. New York: Random House, 2012.
  Rabbit, Redux. 1971. New York: Random House, 2012.
  Rabbit, Run. 1960. New York: Random House, 2012.
Vidal, Gore. *United States: Essays 1952–1992.* New York: Random House, 1993.
Woolf, Tobias. *Old School.* New York: Vintage, 2004.

Actors Who Have Portrayed John F. Kennedy On-Screen

Andrew Robinson, "Profile in Silver" (*Kraft Theater* episode, May 16, 1956).
Cliff Robertson, *PT-109* (Dir. Leslie H. Martinson, 1963).
William Devane, *The Missiles of October* (Dir. Anthony Page, 1974).
Sam Chew Jr., *Young Joe, the Forgotten Kennedy* (Dir. Richard T. Heffron, 1977).
Joe Piscopo, *Saturday Night Live* (1980–84).
James Franciscus, *Jacqueline Bouvier Kennedy* (Dir. Steve Gethers, 1981).
Martin Sheen, *Kennedy* (Dir. Jim Goddard, 1983).
Sam Groom, *Blood Feud* (Dir. Mike Newell, 1983).
Mike Farrell, *JFK: A One-Man Show* (Dir. Frank Perry, 1984).
Cliff De Young, *Robert Kennedy & His Times* (Dir. Marvin J. Chomsky, 1985).
Charles Frank, *LBJ: The Early Years* (Dir. Peter Werner, 1987).
Hart Hindle, *J. Edgar Hoover* (Dir. Robert L. Collins, 1987).
Robert Pine, *Hoover vs. the Kennedys: The Second Civil War* (Dir. Michael O'Herlihy, 1987).
Steven Weber, *The Kennedys of Massachusetts* (Dir. Lamont Johnson, 1990).
Stephen Collins, *A Woman Named Jackie* (Dir. Lawrence Peerce, 1991).
James F. Kelly, *Sinatra* (Dir. James Steven Sadwith, 1992).
Patrick Dempsey, *JFK: Reckless Youth* (Dir. Harry Winer, 1993).
Michael J. Shannon, "Tikka to Ride" (*Red Dwarf* episode, January 17, 1997).
Michael Murphy, *The Island* (Dir. Cyrus Nowrasteh, 1998).
William Peterson, *The Rat Pack* (Dir. Rob Cohen, 1998).
Bruce Greenwood, *Thirteen Days* (Roger Donaldson, 2000).
Tim Matheson, *Jacqueline Bouvier Kennedy Onassis* (Dir. David Burton Morris, 2000).
Daniel Hugh Kelly, *Jackie, Ethel, & Joan: The Women of Camelot* (Dir. Larry Shaw, 2001).
Martin Donovan, *RFK* (Dir. Robert Dornhelm, 2002).
Ossie Davis, *Bubba Ho-Tep* (Dir. Don Coscarelli, 2002).
Brett Stimely, *Watchmen* (Dir. Zack Snyder, 2009); *Transformers: Dark of the Moon* (Dir. Michael Bay, 2011); *Kill the Dictator* (Dir. Felix Limardo, 2013); and *Parkland* (Dir. Peter Landesman, 2013).
Greg Kinnear, *The Kennedys* (Dir. John Cassar, 2011).

Stephen Culp, "Shadow" (*Perception* episode, September 10, 2012).
James Marsden, *Lee Daniels' The Butler* (Dir. Lee Daniels, 2013).

Additional Films and Television Shows of Interest

Primary (Dir. Robert Drew, 1960).
The John Glenn Story (Dir. Michael R. Lawrence, 1962).
The Manchurian Candidate (Dir. John Frankenheimer, 1962).
Crisis: Behind a Presidential Commitment (Dir. Robert Drew, 1963).
The Trial of Lee Harvey Oswald (Dir. Larry Buchanan, 1964).
Topaz (Dir. Alfred Hitchcock, 1969).
Executive Action (Dir. David Miller, 1973).
Hearts and Minds (Dir. Peter Davis, 1974).
Parallax View (Dir. Alan J. Pakula, 1974).
Winter Kills (Dir. William Richert, 1979).
The Right Stuff (Dir. Philip Kaufman, 1983).
Volunteers (Dir. Nicholas Meyer, 1985).
JFK (Dir. Oliver Stone, 1991).
"The Boyfriend: Part I" (*Seinfeld* episode, dir. Tom Cherones, February 12, 1992).
Citizen Cohn (Dir. Frank Pierson, 1992).
Love Field (Dir. Jonathan Kaplan, 1992).
Malcolm X (Dir. Spike Lee, 1992).
Ruby (Dir. John Mackenzie, 1992).
In the Line of Fire (Dir. Wolfgang Peterson, 1993).
Matinee (Dir. Joe Dante, 1993).
Forrest Gump (Dir. Robert Zemeckis, 1994).
Ghosts of Mississippi (Dir. Rob Reiner, 1996).
The House of Yes (Dir. Mark Waters, 1997).
Blast from the Past (Dir. Hugh Wilson, 1999).
The Dish (Dir. Rob Sitch, 2000).
The Fog of War: Eleven Lessons from the Life of Robert S. McNamara (Dir. Errol Morris, 2003).
The Good Shepherd (Dir. Robert De Niro, 2006).
Call of Duty: Black Ops (video game set during and after the Cuban Missile Crisis, 2010).
The Rum Diary (Dir. Bruce Robinson, 2011).
X-Men: First Class (Dir. Matthew Vaughn, 2011).
Killing Kennedy (Dir. Nelson McCormick, 2013).

INDEX

Abramson, Jill, 85, 248
action intellectuals, 106, 108
Advisory Council on the Arts, 145
Africa, 82
Alford, Mimi, 14
Algerian independence movement, 121–125
  See also "Kennedy, John Fitzgerald,
  1957 speech in support of Algerian
  independence movement"
Alliance for Progress, 98, 109–110, 112, 128
Anderson, Carol, 123–124
anticolonial movements, 11–12, 118–131,
  199–200
Antonioni, Michelangelo, 12
  Blow-Up, 169
apartheid (South Africa), 119–120

Baldwin, James, 10, 75–78, 84, 124
  Another Country, 64–65
  Fire Next Time, The, 67, 76, 85
  "Letter from a Region in My
  Mind," 75–76
Ball, George, 91
Barkaoui, Miloud, 125
Barnett, Ross, 40
Baudrillard, Jean, 151, 175–176
Beatty, Warren, 169
Beck, Glenn, 235
Belafonte, Harry, 76, 81
Bell, Nelson, 35
Bella, Ben, 123
Berlant, Lauren, and Lisa Duggan, *Our
  Monica, Ourselves*, 219–221
Berlin, 2, 11, 90, 92, 94–95
  Berlin Wall, 2, 95
Bernstein, Irving, 7
Bevel, Reverend James, 75
Biden, Joe, 42

Birmingham church bombing, 85
Bishop, Elizabeth, 145
Black Panthers, 123
Blair, Joan and Clay, 244
Blanshard, Paul, 35–36, 42
Bloom, Alexander, 139
Bond, James, 8, 97, 154
Boorstin, Daniel, 151, 218
Boston, 9, 18–21
  and Irish Americans, 18–19, 27–29
Boston Latin School, 19
Bourdieu, Pierre, 22
Branch, Taylor, 80, 82
Brauer, Carl, 78
Brennan, William, 33
Bretton Woods system, 92
Brinkley, Alan, 5, 14
Brown, Robert McAfee, 37
Brown, Thomas, 156
Brown v. Board of Education, 80
Bryan, C. D. B., 154
Bryant, Nick, 79–80, 85
Brzezinski, Zbigniew, 91
Buckley, William F., 38
Bunche, Ralph, 124
Bundy, McGeorge, 91, 94, 105
Burdick, Eugene and William Lederer, *The
  Ugly American*, 104–105, 110
bureaucracy, 7, 11, 60–64, 67–68, 91, 179,
  182–184, 189, 197
Burke, Edmund, 64
Burns, James McGregor, 62
Burroughs, William, 167, 176, 206
Bush, George W., 13, 41, 232, 234–235

Camelot myth, 149–159, 213, 246
  Jacqueline Kennedy's role in creating, 5,
  12, 149, 181, 242

Jacobs, Jane, *The Death and Life of Great American Cities*, 66
James, Henry, 213
Jameson, Fredric, 175
Jefferson, Thomas, 5, 158–159
Jessup, John K., 157
John Birch Society, 228
  Welch, Robert, 228
John F. Kennedy Airport, 189
John F. Kennedy Center for the Performing Arts, 189
John Neely Bryan Cabin, 191
Johns, Jasper, 63
Johnson, James Weldon, 124
Johnson, Philip
  Glass House (New Canaan, Connecticut), 189
  Kennedy Memorial (Dallas), 189–193
Johnson, Lyndon B., 1–2, 53, 60, 78, 92, 99, 165, 181, 198, 226, 228–231
  renames Cape Canaveral Cape Kennedy, 189
  sworn in as JFK's successor, 3, 185
Jones, Clarence 76
Joseph, Peniel A., 78
Jumonville, Neil, 139

Kahn, Herman, 96
Kaprow, Alan, 63
Karabel, Jerome, 24
Katz, Elihu, 49
Kazin, Alfred, 137, 145
Kazin, Michael, 202–203
Keating, Kenneth, 96
Kelley, Richard W., 26
Kemp, Jack, 231
Kennedy, Caroline, 56, 180, 234–235
Kennedy Center Honors, 189
Kennedy, Edward, 56, 212, 229–231, 234–235
Kennedy, Jacqueline Bouvier, 2, 37, 134, 137, 144, 151, 158–159, 165, 213–215, 217, 242–243, 247
  as queer icon, 13, 220–221
  influence on JFK's fashion sense, 152–153
  reaction to JFK's assassination, 178–180, 182–184, 192
  televised tour of the White House, 53–56, 153–154
  see also "Camelot Myth, Jacqueline Kennedy's role in creating"
  see also "Warhol, Andy, *Jackies*"
Kennedy, John Fitzgerald

1957 speech in support of Algerian independence movement, 121–122, 124
1960 speech declaring his independence from the Catholic Church, 17
1960 speech at Democratic Convention in Los Angeles, 4, 46, 92, 197, 204–206, 217
1961 inaugural address, 90, 197, 200
1962 speech announcing manned mission to the moon, 2
1963 speech declaring his support for civil rights movement, 40–41, 51, 68–69, 77–78, 85, 126
assassination of, 3, 12–13, 78, 99, 164–176, 178–193, 198, 248
conservative embrace of, 6, 13, 225–235
dislike of hats, 12, 152
first president born in the twentieth century, 1
interest in foreign policy, 11, 13, 39, 82, 92
Nation of Immigrants, A, 33
naval career of, 1–2, 7, 26–27
poor health of, 1, 5, 13, 28, 197, 244–245
posthumous revelations of affairs, 13, 219–220, 245
Profiles in Courage, 2, 5, 12, 14, 45, 61, 134–144, 146
relationships with intellectuals, 12, 134–146
reputation for favoring style over substance, 5, 82, 85, 96, 156, 159, 200, 229
"Rocking Chair Chat" 51–52
self-image as modernizer, 91–92
state visit to Ireland, 29, 32, 39–40
Strategy of Peace, The, 61
support for tax cuts, 7, 13, 231–233
terms in Congress, 2, 3, 121–122
Why England Slept, 1, 5, 26, 61, 157
youngest person ever elected to the presidency, 1
Kennedy, John F., Jr., 180
Kennedy, Joseph P., Jr., 1, 2, 83
Kennedy, Joseph P., Sr., 1, 3–4, 9, 18–21, 23–29, 31–32, 56–57, 212
Kennedy-Nixon debates, 10, 47–49, 151, 216
Kennedy, Robert F., 37, 40, 46, 48, 56, 75, 78, 81, 83–84, 124, 126, 127, 169, 179, 212, 235, 246
  assassination of, 166, 229
Kennedy, Robert F., Jr., 6